PROVIDENCE
1630-1800

WOMEN ARE PART OF ITS HISTORY

Barbara Mills

HERITAGE BOOKS
2009

HERITAGE BOOKS
AN IMPRINT OF HERITAGE BOOKS, INC.

Books, CDs, and more—Worldwide

For our listing of thousands of titles see our website at
www.HeritageBooks.com

Published 2009 by
HERITAGE BOOKS, INC.
Publishing Division
100 Railroad Ave. #104
Westminster, Maryland 21157

Copyright © 2002 Barbara Mills

Other books by the author:
"Got My Mind Set On Freedom"
Maryland's Story of Black and White Activism, 1663-2000
Justice, Peace and God: A Minister's Personal Odyssey

All rights reserved. No part of this book may be reproduced or transmitted in any form or by any means, electronic or mechanical, including photocopying, recording or by any information storage and retrieval system without written permission from the author, except for the inclusion of brief quotations in a review.

International Standard Book Numbers
Paperbound: 978-0-7884-2078-8
Clothbound: 978-0-7884-8136-9

Permission for use of quotes from materials under copyright, graciously given, as follows:

Bartlett, Irving H., *From Slave to Citizen: The Story of the Negro in Rhode Island*, Urban League of RI, Providence, ©1954.

Conley, Patrick T., *An Album of Rhode Island History, 1636-1986*, Rhode Island Publications Society, ©1986.

Conley, Patrick T., *First in War, Last in Peace*, RI Publications Society, ©1987.

Conley, Patrick T., *Liberty and Justice: A History of Law and Lawyers in Rhode Island, 1636-1998*, Rhode Island Publications Society ©1998.

Conley, Patrick T., *The State Houses of Rhode Island*, RI Publications Society 1988.

Coughtry, Jay, *The Notorious Triangle: Rhode Island and the African Slave Trade, 1700-1807*, Temple University Press, ©1981.

DePauw, Linda Grant & Conover Hunt, *"Remember the Ladies": 1750-1815*, ©1976 by The Pilgrim Society. Used by permission of Viking Penguin, a division of Penguin Putnam, Inc.

Earle, Alice Morse, *Home Life In Colonial Days*, (NY Macmillan, 1948) Reprinted with permission of Scribner, a Division of Simon & Schuster, Inc.

Haley, John William, *"Old Stone Bank" History of Rhode Island*, Providence Institution for Savings, Vols. I-IV, 1929, 1931, 1939, 1944 & Old Stone Bank, "R.I. Portrait in Sound," a script written by Florence Markoff for his radio program, 1975.

Hawes, Alexander Boyd, *Off Soundings: Aspects of the Maritime History of Rhode Island*, Posterity Press, MD, ©1999.

James, Sydney V., *Colonial Rhode Island: a History*, Charles Scribner's Sons, ©1975.[© held by author's widow]

Lancaster, Jane, "An ornament and honor to their sex", ©1994.

McLoughlin William G., *Rhode Island: A Bicentennial History*, W.W. Norton & Co., Inc, NY, ©1978.

Melish, Joanne Pope, *Disowning Slavery: Gradual Emancipation and "Race" in New England, 1780-1860*, ©1998 by Cornell University. Permission by publisher Cornell University Press.

Miner, Lilian Burleigh, *Our State of Rhode Island*, Oxford Press, ©1925.

Miner, Ward L., *William Goddard, Newspaperman*, ©1962, Duke University Press. All rights reserved, Reprinted with permission.

Plimpton, Ruth Talbot, *Mary Dyer: Biography of a Rebel Quaker*, Branden Publishing Co, ©1994.

R.I. Short Story Club (written by member of), *Revolutionary Portraits: People, Places and Events from RI's Historic Past*, RI Bicentennial Foundation, ©1976. (© held by Patrick T. Conley who granted permission)

Simister, Florence Parker, *The Fire's Center: RI in the Revolutionary Era, 1763-1790*, RI Bicentennial Foundation ©1979 (© held by Patrick T. Conley who granted permission)

Ulrich, Laurel Thatcher, *Good Wives: Image and Reality in the Lives of Women in Northern New England, 1650-1750*, © 1980,1982 by Laurel Thatcher Ulrich. Used by permission of Alfred A. Knopf, a division of Random House, Inc.

Woodward, Carl R., *Plantation in Yankeeland*, The Pequot Press, Inc., 1971. (© held by & permission given by Cocumscussoc Association, Smith's Castle)

Permission for use of quotes from the following Rhode Island Historical Society (RIHS) Publications from Marta Martinez, Dir. of Publications, Aldrich House, 110 Benevolent Street, Providence, RI 02906

Cady, John Hutchins, *Rhode Island History*, a quarterly, RIHS, Vol. VIII, 1/19/1949, #1, "Weybosset Bridge".

Levin, Linda Lotridge (ed.) *Providence: from Provincial Village to Prosperous Port, 1750-1790*, RIHS, ©1978

RIHS publication, *Rhode Island History*, May 1999, "Henry Marchant's Journal, 1771-1772."

Permission for use of materials from the following Diaries /Letters / Miscellaneous at the Rhode Island Historical Society (RIHS) given by Rick Stattler, RIHS Library, 121 Hope Street, Providence, R.I. 02906

Baker, Betsy Metcalf (1798-1804) Papers. Extracts from Memoir: mss 9001-B and letter dated 1858, in *Miscellaneous Manuscripts Collection.*

"Brown Family Paper Project," first draft," RIHS.

Brown, Henry A.L. Deposit, two letters by Anna and Elisa Bowen to Abigail Goddard, on deposit at RIHS, located in subgroup 6, folder 3 (Permission to use granted by Henry A.L. Brown, © owner.)

Brown, James (1698-1739) Papers. Letter to his wife, Hope Brown, August 23, 1737.

Carpenter, Alice, Furniture inventory, March 1796, Rhode Island Manuscripts, Vol. 1, p. 131

Carter Jenckes, Rebecca (Diary, 1794: mss336, Copybook, 1791 & an array of miscellaneous undated notes). Also her sister, Huldah Carter's, Arithmetic Book in the *Carter-Danforth Papers*.

Chace, Henry R. (1859-1916), Several notes/essays he wrote after retirement, on Olney's Tavern, Liberty Tree, Doctors, Peddlers, Dances, Old Providence. In *Chace Papers*, Box 2, Folder 12, MSS 338.

Dexter, Alice, Marriage Agreement to Jos. Jenckes, January 27, 1726/7, *Misc. MSS Collection*, D-523.

Duncan, Susanna Lear, June-August, 1788 (Diary: *Misc. MSS Collection* 9001-L)

Fenner, Arthur Memorial, 2/2/1788, Deed to Howlong 1690, & Accot. of his death, *RIHS Manuscripts*, Vol. XIV, p. 105.

Herreshoff, Sarah (Sally) Brown, Diary April-June, 1796 (: mss487S2) and correspondence with her father and brother, *Herreshoff-Lewis Family Papers*.

Martin, Julia Bowen, Diary, April-July, 1799, *Martin Family Papers*, mss 999) Also see, *A Guide to Women's Diaries* in the Manuscript Collection of the RIHS by Rick Stattler (unpublished typescript)

Olney, Rachel, , Death Inquest, June 1760 in the *Miscellaneous Manuscripts Collection*.

Tillinghast, Lydia, Letters to Capt. Robert Gray, dated 3/18/1807 (v.4, p.226) and an undated letter to her son, Jonathan (v. 4, p. 234), *Tillinghast Papers*.

Whipple, Lydia, Letter from Duncan Miacum (Macomb), 4/18/1700, *RIHS Manuscripts*, v.1, p. 85.

Whipple, Rebecca, Letters to John Whipple, 1692, *RIHS Manuscripts*, v.1, pp. 69-70.

CONTENTS

Brief Introduction	1
1. The Beginning	3
2. Beyond Providence	42
3. Early Families	52
4. Antinomians & Quakers	76
5. Cocumscussoc & R I's Second Charter	108
6. King Philip & Queen Weetamo	121
7. Mary, Roger & their Children	135
8. Prosperity & Commerce	148
9. Slaves	176
10. The Brown Family	194
11. Religion & Slavery's End	226
12. Newspapers: Goddards, Franklins & Carters	237
13. Women, War & Independence	262
14. Schools	304
15. Women & the Law	320
16. Doctors & Epidemics	355
17. Travel & Tourists	370
Appendix: Selected Family Trees	380

"Resources" (complete citations for footnotes)

ILLUSTRATIONS

1.	Indian Broiling Fish	16
2.	HomeLot Locations	24
3.	Providence Cove, 1636	28
4.	Blackstone on his Tame Bull	48
5.	Dexter-Jencks: Pre-Marriage Contract: 1726	54
6.	Arthur Fenner Will: About 1703	64
7.	Rachel Olney Inquest: 1760	75
8.	Whipping Quakers in the Street	96
9.	Mary Dyer, Quaker, Before the Judges	103
10.	Coastline, 1690	118
11.	Death of King Philip	132
12.	Alice Carpenter Inventory, 1796	151
13.	Weybosset Bridges	160
14.	The "Notorious Triangle"	176
15.	Slaving Voyages: Percent by Port	179
16.	Voyages/# of Slaves by Year: 1709-1807	181
17.	Slave Ship: Men, Women, Boys, & Girls	183
18.	Blacks Working at Wharf	207
19.	*Gaspee* Newspaper Articles	267/8
20.	Fort and Beacon	273
21.	The "Black Regiment"	275
22.	British Rob Women	277
23.	Population Table: 1776	290
24.	Brown University: Revolutionary War	294
25.	Mansion House/Golden Ball Inn	301
26.	Sarah Brown Herreschoff	315
27.	Madam "Betsy" Jumel	345
28.	Providence Street Map 1750	352
29.	Map of Providence, 1823	379

PROVIDENCE: 1630-1800
Women are part of its History

PROVIDENCE: 1630-1800
Women are Part of Its History

What follows is not a typical "women's history" devoted to home, food, dress, child-rearing and such; nor is it a recounting of the lives of individual women told one by one as though they existed in a vacuum, not affected by the mostly-men's world of war, politics and business. This *History* includes the women alongside the men— white women colonists, Native American women from whom the colonists learned and then displaced (from their land), apprentices and indentured servants made to serve for a given number of months or years, and slaves forced into permanent servitude unless freed by their owners.

These women, neglected as they are in most histories, were the *enablers* of the men—the servants, the companions, the keepers of their homes; the mothers of their children; the wives, daughters and sisters who supported them on the homefront in times of war; the women who delivered their children, tended their ills; the women who took over farms and businesses in the absence of husbands, brothers and sons; the women who taught schools and started their own businesses. Acknowledgement of all these women and others is necessary to make whole the unfolding of Rhode Island's history.

Rhode Island's pioneer white women in the 17th century, even in the 18th, had to be "a combination hunter, trapper, farmer, fire fighter, weight lifter, and woodchopper,"[1] just to put food on the table.

The women's role was so crucial from the beginning that it might be fair to say there would never have been a Providence if the men had not brought their wives and children with them when they came to this new land. Holliday in her book on women in colonial days summed it up thus:

> Perhaps we should conclude that the achievements of those famous founders of [our city and state] were due as much to their wives as to their own native powers.... [The women] lived ...heroic lives with ...unconscious patience and valor...They courted, married, and laughed and sorrowed.[2]

A true history of Providence cannot be written without acknowledging that women and men *together* carved this new city out of the wilderness, shaped it, and gave it a permanence of which to be proud.

---

[1] Booth, *Hung, Strung*, p. xi.
[2] Holliday, pp. 135-136.

1. The Beginning

Rhode Island's story begins in London, England at a time when wilderness had long since given way to the homes, institutions, schools, colleges and businesses of a thriving urban center. Fishing and hunting, clearing land of trees, building one's own home, furniture, and roads were no longer required for survival. So it's not surprising that the women and men who crossed the Atlantic and founded a new town in Rhode Island were ill-prepared. Yet, somehow, Roger and Mary Barnard Williams, credited by most historians as the first to arrive in what is now Providence, not only survived, but with the help of many others tamed the wilderness that surrounded them and laid the foundation for a new city that would itself become a thriving urban center.

✯✯✯

Alice Pemberton, Roger Williams' mother, was "a well-to-do lady who owned an inn known as the 'Harrow' located directly opposite the Williams' home on Cow Lane."[3] When she died in 1634, she left significant amounts of money to each of her four children and to her grandchildren. Baptized on February 18, 1564/5, Alice was the eighth child born to Katherine Stokes and Robert Pemberton, both of "ancient and notable families."[4]

Alice was only fourteen or fifteen when her father died in 1578; too soon to see her marry James Williams in 1597. Almost certainly he would have

---

[3] Haley, *Old Stone Bank*, Vol. IV, p. 5
[4] More information about the Pembertons and Williamses before Roger came to America can be found in *Genealogies*, V. 1, pp. 645-665 and in *Roger Williams Family Association*, #26, 3/1955.

been pleased that Alice had chosen a clothier like himself—a "Citizen and Merchant Taylor of London." James operated his profitable business from the front portion of their home, a practice which also became common in Providence's early days. The couple had two children, Catherine and Sydrach, before Roger was born about 1603, the same year that James I of England ascended the throne. He was named after his mother's older brother, Roger, also a clothier, who, according to his will left £10 to his Godson, Roger. Alice had one more child, Robert, who was the only other of her children to emigrate to America.

By the time Roger's mother died in 1634, requesting that she be buried in St. Sepulchres church, Roger was already in America. Her will named her mother, Katherine Stokes Pemberton, as executrix, suggesting Katherine was still alive, hence had outlived both her husband and her daughter.

★★★

Roger Williams might well have become a clothier or merchant, like his brothers, father and uncle, if Sir Edward Coke had not entered his life. Most boys "in the class of society to which the Williams family belonged became apprentices and learned a trade."[5] But, most likely through his mother's influential family, Sir Edward, an eminent attorney and overseer at the newly founded and exclusive Charterhouse School, became Roger's patron. He saw to it that on June 25, 1621 Roger was elected a scholar at Charterhouse, and three years after that a "pensioner" at Pembroke College Cambridge. In 1629, after having earned his Bachelor of Arts degree, Roger became domestic chaplain on the estate of Sir William Masham in Essex.

---

[5] Haley, Old Stone Bank, Vol. IV, p. 9

1. The Beginning

While there, Roger had occasion to visit the Barrington estate where he met Lady Barrington's niece, Jane Whalley—and, thereafter, found excuses to visit the estate quite often. The Mashams approved when Jane and Roger fell in love, but Lady Barrington, an aunt of Oliver Cromwell, disapproved, and forced Roger to stop calling. However, he did not go quietly, but pled his case for marrying her in writing—"a masterpiece of flowery compliment and eloquent courtesy." He frankly admitted that "his financial outlook was not particularly promising. He did, however, mention the fact that he had received offers for his services from New England, and that his prospects for success in life were good." Two other letters followed, but Lady Barrington remained unmoved. She deemed him "too poor and of a lower social class."[6] "In complete despair, [Roger] wrote to the obdurate lady on May 2, 1629: 'We hope to live together in the heavens though ye Lord Have denied that union on earth'" [7]

Roger didn't feel that way then, but the experience no doubt strengthened his belief in "equity among all men." Further, if Roger had married Jane Whalley, he might have met the same fate as the man Jane did marry. After Roger left the picture, she had been promptly married off to William Hooke, and after a brief stay in Taunton, Massachusetts, they returned to England in 1654 where Hooke became the private chaplain of Oliver Cromwell, Lord Protector of England and Jane's cousin.

Meanwhile, Roger was "sick at heart over his shattered romance" and "soon fell prey to bodily illness." Mary Barnard, also part of the Masham household, was the companion, or lady's maid, to

---

[6] Haley, Old Stone Bank, Vol. IV, p.13
[7] Richman, pp. 14-15.

Lady Masham's daughter by a previous marriage, Joan (Jug) Altham. During Roger's long lingering days of recovery, Mary helped nurse him back to health. She brought him books, talked with him at length, and did other "little courtesies." Mary clearly was attracted to him, and before long, Roger, too, realized he loved this charming and intelligent, young and pretty, woman very deeply. They were married the following December (1629).[8] Mary was the daughter of the "noted Puritan divine, the Rev. Richard Barnard, parson at Worksop and later at Batcombe, County Somerset." She was "baptized at Worksop, Co[unty] Nottt[inghamshire] in 1609." [9]

Today, many would expect a pairing such as that of Mary and Roger to bode problems; the one illiterate, signing her name with "her mark;" the other a university graduate, reading and writing Hebrew, Greek, Latin, French and Dutch. However, such pairings were commonplace at the time; most women were denied the education offered men, and even Roger's education, as noted, was unusual amongst his class. Undoubtedly in their talks while Roger was ill, they had discovered many interests and beliefs they had in common. There is no reason to share one author's concern that Roger might have intimidated Mary.[10] In fact, what evidence we have shows quite the contrary: she unhesitatingly countered Roger's wishes, as we'll soon see, when he renounced their church in Salem. In general, Mary "proved to be a faithful companion and loyal wife, and a woman of intelligence, courage, and practical foresight. Luckily, it was Mary and not Jane who became Mrs. Roger Williams" or there might never have been a Providence,

---

[8] Information and quotes are from Roger Williams Family Assoc. #26, March 1955. Also, Haley, Old Stone Bank, Vol. IV, pp. 13-14.
[9] *Genealogies*, V. 1, pp. 657-658.
[10] Plimpton, pp. 107-108

1. The Beginning

Rhode Island.[11]

★★★

At the time that Mary and Roger married on December 15, 1629, England was awash with conflict; on the one hand, between the established Anglican church and the Puritans and the Catholics; and, on the other, between the King's claim of divine rights and the rule of parliament. Roger's mentor, Sir Edward, an outspoken member of parliament, led the popular party opposing both James I and Charles I. Sir Edward believed strongly in individual liberty, advocated for people's rights, and opposed the Kings' claims of Divine rights. No doubt influenced by his mentor, Roger argued for these same positions while at Cambridge, then a hot-bed of liberalism and raging debates. With this background, it is not surprising that his preaching was radical enough to get him in trouble in England even before it did in America.

Early in 1629, the exodus of mostly Puritans (but Catholics, too), from England to America started as a trickle. It grew apace as Archbishop Laud, with the King's blessing, increasingly pressured all churches to follow the prescribed Anglican ritual. He attempted, in particular, to eliminate Puritans, a group he especially disdained, from any church position. Mary and Roger had not been married a whole year when Roger discovered that the King's Council intended to try him for his radical preaching. And so it was on December 1, 1630 that he and Mary hastily embarked from Bristol for New England on the ship *Lyon*.

The twenty passengers and crew reached the Boston harbor on February 9, 1631 after sixty-five grueling days on a wintry sea. But despite the hardships of their voyage, those on other ships must

---

[11] Quote from Haley, Old Stone Bank, V. IV, p. 14.

have suffered even more. One account tells of a ship (unnamed) departing from London full of men, women and children that spent twenty-six weeks at sea...

> their beer all spent and leaked out a month before their arrival, so as they were forced to stinking water (and that very little) mixt with sack or vinegar, and their other provisions very short and bad. Yet, through the great Providence of the Lord, they came all safe on shore, and most of them sound, and well liking.[12]

We can only wonder how Mary felt during those seemingly endless days at sea, wondering if she would ever set foot on land again, wondering what awaited her when she finally did. And unlike Roger, Mary apparently never again saw England. *Did Mary anticipate this when she climbed aboard the Lyon? Was she homesick? Did she know that her brother, Maraschell, followed her to America four years after her own trip? Did she have an opportunity to visit with him?* Maraschell's arrival was the same year as Roger's banishment from the Bay Colony, but we do not know if it was before or after. Other than the fact he settled in Weymouth, Massachusetts, histories tell us nothing of Maraschell, the only member of Mary's family known to come to America.

✯✯✯

The Puritans left England because of the persecution they suffered for attacking the corrupt practices (as they saw it) of the Church of England. But, in America, they did not become "apostles of freedom" as they are often portrayed. In fact, they had no fault with England's denial of the separation of church and state and hence established in the Bay

---

[12] Savage, James, *History of New England*, p. 3 (quoting Winthrop).

1. The Beginning

Colony what has been called a "Puritan theocracy." They tolerated no religious views except their own—and these were ruthlessly enforced. Roger Williams quickly found himself at odds with many of the beliefs and practices of these self-appointed authorities.

At first the Williamses settled in Plymouth and Roger worked primarily as a farmer and trader, occasionally preaching at the church, but more often carrying on missionary work among the Indians. He was largely tolerated in the colony and made a number of friends despite his reputation as an independent thinker. But, for some reason, in August 1633, the same month that their daughter, Mary, was born, Roger accepted an invitation by Salem to serve as their pastor. Even though they believed him "devout and sincere in his quest for the absolute truth of God's word," they quickly came into conflict with him when he insisted on openly proclaiming his belief in freedom of religion and separation of church and state. They also objected to his preaching to the "heathen Indians" and felt it was treason to support the Indian claim that "the source of all the land titles in New England originated with the Indians and not with the king."[13]

Further, Roger's "soul-searching led him to conclude that civil magistrates did not have the right to compel adherence to the first four of the Ten Commandments." He believed

> only God's spiritual power could enforce spiritual commands over men's consciences. To compel people to honor the Sabbath was 'forced worship.' Williams declared that 'Forced worship stinks in God's nostrils.' God wants only voluntary allegiance. He also argued that it was 'false swearing' to force an unconverted person to take an oath in God's name, a position that created difficulty in

---

[13] Haley, Old Stone Bank, Vol. IV, p. 16.

compelling honest testimony or obtaining oaths of allegiance. These views were deemed dangerous to the peace and good order of the bible Commonwealth."[14]

When ordered to recant Williams refused and instead took the position that the Salem church (and the Puritans generally) should repudiate the Church of England rather than holding on to the hope they could transform it.

Things came to a head in 1635 after the Colony's General Court denied the town of Salem a land claim they desired *because* Salem had chosen Williams to head their church. Williams reacted by requesting that their church break with all the other churches in the Bay Colony. When the town refused, Williams independently withdrew from the church. When Mary, exhibiting that streak of independence previously alluded to, refused to join him and continued to attend church services with their children, Roger called them "unregenerate" and "unfit to communicate with God." He refused to pray with Mary or even allow her and the children to be at the table when he blessed their food—though, apparently, he did not object to eating the food she had prepared!

In fact, here as elsewhere, there is compelling evidence that Williams believed women were inferior to men and should be subservient to them. What could be more revealing than his statement, "The Lord hath given a covering of longer hair to women as a sign or teacher of Covering, Modesty, and Bashfulness, Silence and Retardedness, and therefore women are not fitted for many actions and employments." [15] He regarded Queen Elizabeth as the exception to God's intent that a woman's place was in the home.

---

[14] McLoughton, p. 7
[15] Williams' quote found in Plimpton, p. 108

1. The Beginning

Despite Roger's general view that women were destined to be subservient to men, Mary's defiance of him in Salem apparently had no permanent impact on their relationship. The fact she did not initially accompany Roger when he left Salem, after his being banished, is unrelated; it was usual for men to seek out a suitable spot for a homestead in the untrammeled forests before women and children joined them. *We do wonder, however, what provision the men made for those families left behind. Did they, as a consequence of the men's departure, suffer undue hardships? How did they deal with the fears for their safety, their concern about ever seeing the men again? Were they left to cope alone with children?* In Mary's case there were two small daughters: Mary, a toddler, born in August 1633, and Freeborn, born October 4, 1635.

Freeborn was only five days old when the General Court sentenced Williams "to depart out of our jurisdiction within six weeks." However, in light of Williams' present illness and Freeborn's recent birth the court amended the sentence to allow him to wait until Spring before his departure. But because Williams learned that some in the colony were conspiring to have him returned to England, he quickly departed in January 1636, in the midst of a snowy winter, presumably making it even less likely that he made adequate provisions for the family he was leaving behind. Williams had chosen "exile in an Indian wilderness rather than be deported to his native land in disgrace." The colony wished to be rid of Roger entirely, fearing repercussions from meetings he was still holding in his home, and fearing that the establishment of any new settlement nearby would become a "fountain of sedition." Williams, for his part, sought to find a refuge away from the restraints of the Puritans; he had no thought at the time of founding a new town.[16]

Most historians agree that Thomas Angell, a minor, came to America with the Williamses. They more often disagree as to whether he accompanied Roger when he left Salem. That he did seems quite likely, since Thomas was Roger's cousin through his Uncle Roger, and had been indentured to him before they left England. Of course, he may also have left him behind to help Mary and the children.

Roger would probably been somewhat familiar with the surrounding woods since he had regularly been preaching to the Indians, but now, with or without Thomas, he would have been penetrating much further into forest, heading toward Narragansett Bay. Though there is not existing account of his exact route or the length of time he spent on his trek through the woods, his own records never suggest he felt in danger, and almost certainly he found succor with Indians along the way. Of his experience, Roger once wrote:

> I was unmercifully driven from my chamber to a winter's flight, exposed to the mercies, poverties, necessities, wants, debts, hardships of sea and land in a banished condition...I was sorely tossed for one fourteen weeks in a bitter winter season, not knowing what bread and bed did mean.

Even though the Indians Roger encountered along the way were friendly, his stay in their wigwams would not have been very restful, and as he continued wending his way through the woods, he almost certainly carried some provisions as well as one of the day's heavy, long and cumbersome flint-lock or matchlock firearms. The Indian trails he sought to follow must often have been covered with snow, and there would have been treacherous swamps and streams

---

[16] Quotes from Bicknell, V. 1, p. 146

1. The Beginning

that he had to cross.[17]

In the Spring of 1636, after Massasoit, chief of the Wampanoags, had given Roger a piece of land along the east bank of the Seekonk River for a settlement, others from Salem joined him—William Harris, whose family had come to America on the same boat with the Williamses; John Smith, a miller who also was banished; Francis Wickes (or Weeks), "a poor young fellow" known to Smith; and Joshua Verin, a roper, referred to as "a lad of Richard Waterman's." According to Bicknell, these men were not well-educated, and most, if not all, signed their names with "their mark".[18] Several of them, like Williams, left families behind.

The group proceeded to build themselves crude shelters, perhaps just wigwams, and undertook the planting of food crops. It must have been distressing when, soon after, they received a letter from Plymouth's Governor Winthrop, Roger Williams' friend, warning them to move on; that the area they had already put so much effort into was still within the bounds of the Bay Colony. The Governor feared the General Court's wrath would descend on him if they remained. So, dismayed at having lost their crops that year, they wearily left in their small canoe, taking little with them other than an axe, a mattock, and a spade. The group of six men continued along the Moshassuc [or Seekonk] River till they rounded Fox Point, landing on the West side at a point near where a fresh water stream emptied into the salt water. Now they were in the land of the Narragansetts.

Once again the six men built crude housing, probably little more than shacks, and planted new

---

[17] The quote from Roger Williams and this description care from Haley, Old Stone Bank, Vol. IV, p. 18.
[18] Bicknell, V. 1, pp. 109, 145 & 147.

crops, anticipating the arrival of their families early that summer of 1636. *Just how the women and children managed the trip to join them has never even been the subject of speculation by historians as far as this writer can determine.*

There was no longer snow on the ground to contend with, but the trails were no less rugged and at least some of these women had children to contend with as they undertook the still treacherous trip to join the men; Mary had two young daughters, three-year-old Mary and six-month old Freeborn. And unlike Roger, who had already trekked deep into the forests when initiating friendly contacts with the Indians while still in Salem, the women most probably had never been any further than the fringes where they gathered berries. It's unlikely they could speak the language should they encounter Indians, though Mary may have learned a few words and phrases from Roger. *One wonders if they had a guide for this difficult journey; perhaps Thomas Angell came back to show them the way; to help carry what-ever meager belongings they might be bringing with them; to help forage for food. Did they have a canoe to get across the river to the opposite bank as Williams and the other men had?* Whatever the answer to these questions, there can be no doubt that these wives and mothers displayed great courage, despite, surely, also being frightened—not only of the journey itself, but of what they might face even after they joined their husbands.

☆☆☆

At the time Williams' small group arrived in 1636, some estimate that as many as 30,000 Indians (others estimate, as few as 5,000) already lived in an area extending about twenty-five miles around the Narragansett Bay. The

1. The Beginning

Narragansetts had cleared this land for farming, and as a means of eliminating hiding spots for unfriendly Indian tribes, such as the Pequots, and even the Wampanoags.

Tradition has it that the men were warmly greeted and lavishly fed by the Narragansetts on landing at their chosen spot in 1636, a not unlikely proposition, since Williams had made a point of befriending the Indians from the beginning. He had learned their language, bestowed them with gifts, and even as the settlements grew, continued to recompense them for the land he sought for the white settlers. In return, the Narragansetts taught these new arrivals, occupiers of their land, much they needed to know for survival.

They taught them about growing tobacco (most all the men were heavy smokers); about fishing, clamming and such in the bay and rivers; about gathering berries and maple syrup in the woods; and about killing rattlesnakes, birds, rabbits, deer and other wild game in the surrounding woods. At the time, rabbits and squirrels were so plentiful they were pests, and salmon so plentiful in Rhode Island's rivers "that a certain apprentice contracted that his master should not feed him on it more than twice a week."[19] Most of the cows, sheep, and goats the settlers initially brought with them had died at sea or soon after had been killed by wolves. Only later did they build fences or use a safe island to better protect the cattle which fed on the "wholesome salt marshes of Weybosset" or "the juicy grass of the islands of Aquidneck and Conanicut."[20]

The Indian women introduced the pioneer wives to the cultivation and cooking of corn, squash, and beans, foods that became the colonists' mainstay. "Sukquttahhas", described as "corn seethed like beans"

---

[19] Miner, Lilian, p. 70.
[20] Miner, Lilian, p. 69.

is the source of our succotash—lima beans and corn. Wives soon could be seen roasting corn and grinding it into meal for the to-become-famous Rhode Island Johnny Cakes, and making it into dumplings, porridge, hasty pudding and "nookick." For those famous Johnny

Cakes the corn had to be finely ground to make a "flat" rather than "round" meal. "The meal was then made into dough and spread on the middle board of a red oak barrel head. Only walnut coals were worthy, and the

Broiling fish over an open fire (engraving from John White's painting done in 1585)

crust as it browned should be basted with cream."[21] As for the nookick, a powder made from parched Indian corn, Mary must have prepared it often, for Roger Williams regularly carried it when traveling, claiming that it made many a good meal. When mixed with water.[22]

Corn also provided an occasion for the new colony to celebrate, even more so than Christmas or Thanksgiving which many fewer celebrated than now. "Cornhuskings were attended by most members of the community with a special treat going to the man who found a red ear of corn. He was entitled to a kiss from

---

[21] Weedon, p. 285
[22] See Earle, *Home Life*, p. 134-136

1. The Beginning

the girl of his choice because of his good luck." [23]

The Indian women also taught the white women how to use animal skins for clothing and blankets. Their preparation was much easier than the time-consuming task of spinning, weaving, sewing, knitting and quilting which was pleasurable only when it gave the women an excuse to gather together in "bees" and socialize.

In his frequent meetings with the Indians, Roger learned many things about their language and culture which he eventually offered to the world in a small book, *Key into the Language of America,* written in 1643 en route back to England. What Roger observed about the Indian women is of especial interest, for they, like the white women, influenced the culture of this new settlement in a new land. At the same time, one should keep in mind that the observations were made from the male point of view, leaving us to wonder how different they might have been if made by a woman. Regarding women's work, Roger wrote:

> The [Indian] women set or plant, weede, and hill, and gather and barne all the corne, and Fruites of the field: Yet sometimes the man himselfe, (either out of love to his Wife, or care for his Children, or being an old man) will help the Women which (by the custome of the Countrey) they are not bound to.[24]

This sounds remarkably similar to Booth's

---

[23] Booth, *Hung, Strung*, p. 46 & 48. Christmas was generally ignored by the Puritans and was not celebrated in New England until well into the 18th Century when it again became a time for presents, family gatherings, lavish meals, mistletoe, visiting and festivities generally that could last for days; followed by another round of merri-making at New Years. For more on the holiday, see Haley, Old Stone Bank, V. II, pp. 76-78.
[24] Woodward, p. 3

assertion in her book on Colonial eating that white pioneer women needed to be "a combination hunter, trapper, farmer, fire fighter, weight lifter, and woodchopper."[25]

In *Key...*, Roger went on to describe the Indian women's role further:

> Their women constantly beat all their corn with hand," in a stone utensil, or in a rounded hole in a rock, with a stone pestle: "they plant, dress, gather, burn, and beat it; and take as much pains as any people in the world, which labour is questionless, one cause of their extraordinary care in childbirth....It is almost incredible what burthens the poor women carry of corn, fish, beans, or mats, and a child besides.[26]

How similar were the "burthens" of the white pioneer women who, according to Ulrich in *Good Wives*, had to understand "the rhythms of the seasons, the technology of fire-building, the persistence of the daily demands of cooking, the complexity of home production, and the dexterity demanded from the often conflicting roles of housekeeper, mother, and wife"?[27]

In another observation, Williams compares the ease of the Indian women in giving birth compared to that of European women.

> It hath pleased God in a wonderful manner to moderate that curse, the sorrows of child-bearing, so that ordinarily they have a more speedy, and easy travail, and delivery, than the women of Europe; not that I think God is more gracious to them above other women, but that it follows first from the hardness of their constitutions...I have often known, in one quarter of an hour, a woman, merry in the house and delivered, and merry again, and within two days abroad, and after four, or five days, at work.

---

[25] Booth, *Hung, Strung*, p. xi.
[26] Rider, pp. 9-10.
[27] Ulrich, p. 33.

1. The Beginning

In comparing birthing in the two cultures, Roger may have remembered observing Mary having difficulty during at least one of their children's births. Or perhaps he had stood outside with other husbands, as men were wont to do in earlier centuries; listened to the loud cries of pain let forth by Mary in giving birth, not allowed inside until it was all over. Of course, Roger was not even in the country when Mary gave birth to their last child, Joseph.

The importance of marriage to the Indians is obvious as expounded by Williams in *Key...*; the helpfulness of the tribe in providing the dowry when a member was poor; the community aspect of solemnizing the marriage.

> "When an Indian sought a young woman in marriage it was customary for him to give a dowry to her parents," the amount depending on the woman's status, and if he was poor, "his friends and neighbors made up the necessary amount by contributions of wampum." No form of service was stated but the marriage was "solemnized after consent of the parent, and by publique approbation, publiquely, by the contracting parties, not unlike the manner of the Society of Friends in later years." The husband was then obligated to provide a home for them, "usually round, having a diameter on the ground, of, from ten to fifteen feet, and tapering upward." "The ties of consanguinity were extremely strong..."

Regarding the Indian children, Williams wrote: "The extreme affection for their children makes their children saucy, bold, and undutiful." *Is Williams really thinking of over-indulgence; or alluding to a hands-on kind of affection which then was rare between father and child?* On a more positive note, Williams wrote: "There were no beggars among them, no fatherless children unprovided for."[28] *Can you see Mary and Roger sitting before the fire in the evening comparing these Indian customs with their own manner of bringing up their children and the results? What were their children like? How much, indeed, did Roger tell Mary, in general, about his contacts with the Indians that kept him from home for long periods at a time?*

★★★

Williams and the Indians were sufficiently friendly and trusting of each other that it is quite probable that his first agreement with them for land was verbal and did not bother to detail specific boundaries. The first preserved written deed we have, dated March 24, 1638, states there was a sale *two years earlier*. It is believed that at that time in 1636, Canonicus, the chief, and his son, Miantinomi, sold Williams "the lands and meadowes upon the two fresh Rivers called Mowshausuck and Wanasquatuckut." [29] This land was four square miles outside the bounds of the Bay colony.

The written deed became necessary in 1638 when the number of settlers grew to thirteen and arguments began about boundaries. This deed confirmed the earlier boundaries "of those lands from the Rivers & Fields of Pautuckett, The great hill of Notaquonuckanet on the norwest and the towne of Maushappog on the West....[and also] all that land from those Rivers Reaching to Pautuxett Rivers, as also the Grasse & meadowes upon Pautuxett River," *but it still specified no boundaries, leaving unresolved the problem this had previously created.*

---

[28] Rider, pp. 13, 17-18.
[29] The information and quotes in this section are from Arnold, Samuel G., V. 1, pp. 99-100 and Bicknell, V. 1, p. 160

1. The Beginning

Canonicus and Miantinomi made this extended grant, like the earlier one, to Roger Williams personally "in Consideration of the many Kindnesses and Services he hath continually done for us." The instrument is marked with their X. In a memorandum appended the following year, Miantinomi reconfirmed this 1638 grant and stated that "up the streame of Pawtuckett and Pawtuxett without limits wee might have for our use of Cattell."

This Moshassuck (Providence) grant of approximately twenty square miles was not fertile land but well located at the juncture of three rivers and directly on the "Pequot Path" that had been well-traversed by the Indians. This location gave the settlers both a water route and a ready land route for commerce with the Dutch colony in what is now New York. This was especially important at the time since Massachusetts still banned any trade with them. Typically, a sloop would leave Providence carrying wool, potatoes and cheese, taking as much as a week to reach the Dutch port, then another two weeks to negotiate the sale or exchange, and yet another to return home—all travel difficult and time-consuming through wilderness and in small craft.

★★★

In the two years prior to the written March 24, 1638 deed, the first thirteen settlers, including Roger Williams, built "in such places as were most convenient, and planted their corn on the old Indian fields as they could agree among themselves."[30] The two-year delay by Roger in formally dividing up the land is easily explained by his preoccupation, along with the others, in felling and hewing logs to build a

---

[30] Hopkins, p. 3

home; making needed chests, tables, settees, bedsteads, and other furniture; clearing paths, planting crops, digging clams, catching fish, hunting and all the other undertakings required to provide for their families. These tasks were all the more difficult because, as Williams commented in 1643, "there is not a sorry Hoe, Hatchet, Knife, nor a rag of cloth in all America but what comes over the dreadful Atlantic Ocean."[31] With both tools and skilled workmen lacking for this major undertaking, quite probably the women and children, after their arrival, pitched in, too, right alongside the men.

Under these conditions, the settlers' first cabins were necessarily crude one-room affairs, "roofed with logs or poles as rafters, covered with bark of trees" or thatch gathered from the surrounding forests. A chimney, if the rustic, dirt-floored cabin had one, was either built of logs or stones and plastered with mud or clay to fill cracks. "In the summer, cooking was done out of doors, under the trees, and the food was eaten from the vessels in which it was cooked, the family sitting around on logs or on the ground....It was not an uncommon thing for ten or more persons, men, women and children, with a dog or two and a sprinkling of cats and maybe a pig, sleeping in the one room of a log cabin, on a cold winter's night."[32]

By 1638, when Williams received the written deed from the Indians, the original families were ready for more permanence in their settlement. As a first step, the men cut "a road of about two miles long through the wilderness along the water; it followed the east side of the Moshassuck River, the Great Salt Cove and the Great Salt River." They had chosen the "east shore on

---

[31] Miner, Lilian, p. 68
[32] Bicknell, V. 1, pp. 148-149

1. The Beginning

which to build their homes because the land there was firm and easy of access, while across the river, it was flat, marshy and scarcely habitable because of the lack of fresh water." With only this road, which they named Towne Street [now North and South Main Street], separating them from the water's edge, each settler received "a long, narrow home lot" that extended for some distance back [probably to today's Hope Street]. In addition, each was given a six-acre lot for planting, and, on land west of the Moshassuck, "common lots" for their cattle. These included "meadow and salt marsh or bog, whereon was cut the winter fodder for the cattle and the wood land." [33]

Each historian describes these allocations a little differently. They all agree the home lots had narrow fronts, but Weedon says they were five-acre lots with an "area stretching up the hillside and eastward, each settler persist[ing] until he got his quota...A narrow strip of green separated the dwelling from passing traffic." He then adds: "the homesteads crept up the sloping side and unyielding grades of the ridge, which made the peninsular conformation of the early plantation. Barns sheltered the cattle for a generation and orchards soon gave plenty of fruit for the clustering families. Above and often in the orchard preserves, burial grounds soon attached the planter yet more closely to his homestead."[34]

Bicknell states that the home lot frontage on Towne Street was about 107 to 125 feet, the lots separated by lanes of about twelve feet for "passageway for cattle, teams and truckage to the rear ends of the lots."

---

[33] Information and quotes for this paragraph are from Uroff, p. 7, Hopkins, p. 14 & Haley, Old Stone Bank, Vol. 4, p. 24.
[34] Weedon, p. 35.

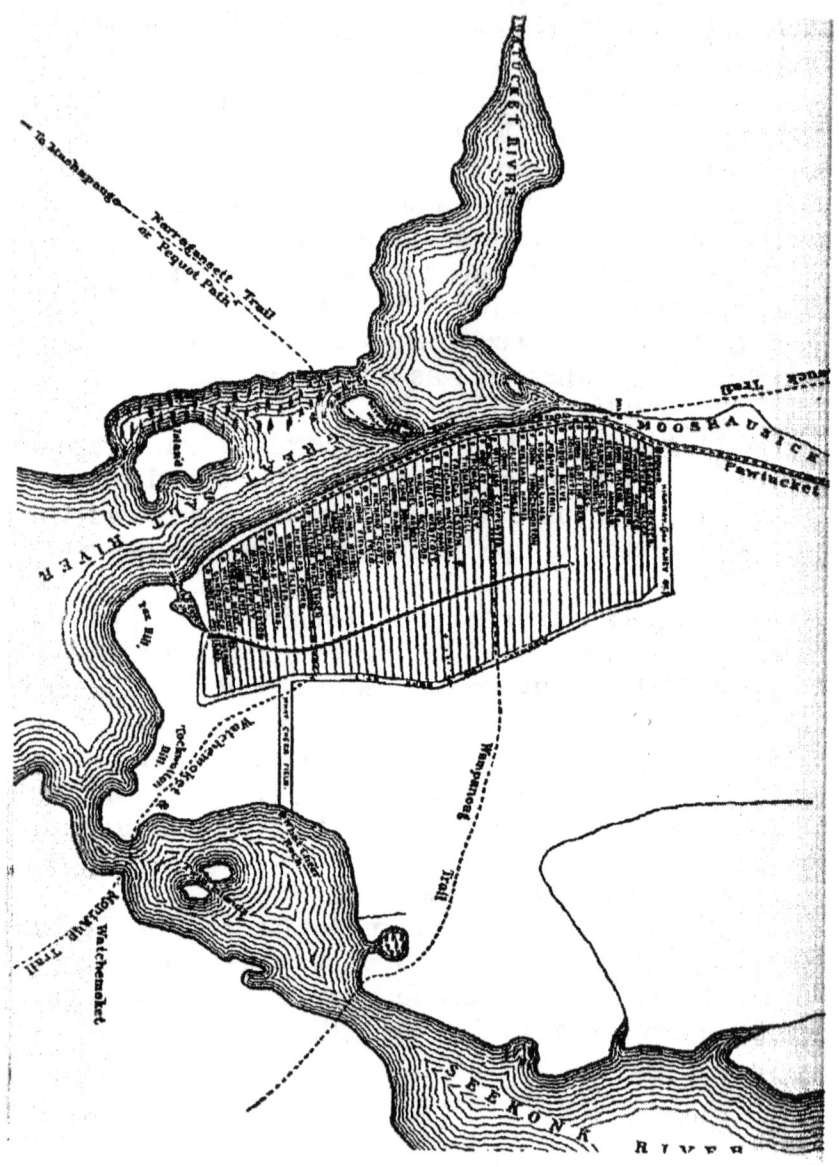

1. The Beginning 25

He adds that there was also "one hundred acres of timberland in some other section." In addition to the Providence allocations, there was a Pawtuxet section where each settler "received about 400 acres for a consideration of less than ten dollars."[35]

Bicknell in his history is more critical than admiring of Williams in his description of how he set up the new town—critical both of Williams' six-months delay in making land allocations even after receiving the written deed, and of his establishment of a landed oligarchical proprietary rather than a representative democratic government.

Regarding the delay: It was October 7, 1638 when Williams first divided the land into "The Grand Purchase of Providence" and "The Pawtuxet Purchase."

He then made allocations to Stukeley Westcott, William Arnold, Thomas James, Robert Cole, John Greene, Sr., John Throckmorton, William Harris, William Carpenter, Thomas Olney, Sr., Francis Weston, Richard Waterman, Ezekiel Holzman, and, of course, himself. *It's not clear just why these thirteen and only these; Joseph Verin, Thomas Angell and Francis Wickes all came to Providence with Williams, and others had arrived prior to the allocations. No real explanation for this has been offered.*

Regarding the oligarchical proprietary: "This body of thirteen men, at first owning and controlling all of the affairs temporal at Providence, decided on the admission of inhabitants, their qualifications, on the possession of franchise, the civil policy, the magistracy, civil and criminal courts, taxes, etc. It was known by several titles as 'the town,' 'the town fellowship,' 'Proprietors,' 'Masters of Families.' *This body of men and their later associates constituted the town of Providence* [writer's italics] until its

---

[35] Bicknell, V. 1, pp. 163 & 171-173

incorporation by the General Assembly in 1649."[36]

For the most part, women had no rights in the new town, yet, interestingly, only *married* men of this "body of men" could vote. *Does this mean that the settlers felt that only if a man had a woman at his side would he have the maturity and judgement needed to govern a town?*

Bicknell goes further and asserts that since Williams did not impose any conditions for government and made no mention of either civil or religious affairs in distributing these original land allotments, he should not be regarded as the founder of Providence, let alone of Rhode Island. Bicknell claims that "the creations of theorists and idealists of a later day have invested hard facts of ancient Providence history with a dress and a halo absolutely out of harmony with their real character and the motives that inspired it;...not law or liberty—it was land, property, wealth, individual, corporeal."[37] However, Williams was not quite as callous as to the future as this suggests. He had not distributed all the land the Indians granted him so there would be some available for future settlers; and he was concerned about civil order even if he had not then set up an actual governmental arrangement.

It did seem, at times, that by originally allowing each man total independence, unrestrained by a formal governmental or legal structure, near-anarchy reigned. Whatever Williams' intent, after these initial allocations, self interest seemed to rule amongst the settlers, and he, as often as not, found himself in the minority in decisions made by his friends and neighbors. The oligarchy Williams had established became an "aristocracy of poor men"—both elements

---

[36] Bicknell, V. 1, p. 194
[37] Bicknell, V. 1, p. 213.

1. The Beginning

hostile to democracy.

Despite this, more families did come to the new town; most were either forced to leave the Bay Colony, as Williams had been, or left of their own volition seeking a refuge from its harsh rule. Sometime before 1642, with its numbers increasing (lost records making it impossible to determine the exact date), the home lots on Towne Street were again divided. By agreement of the original thirteen, the then fifty-two settlers deemed worthy were granted lots.

For reasons unknown, four women were included in this allocation—Alice Daniels (who afterwards married John Green, Sr. and sold her lot to Valentin Whitman), and the widows Reeve, Jane Sears (or Sayer, who later sold her lot to William's son, Daniel), and Joane Tiler (or Tilar, who later married Nathaniel Dickens and sold her lot in 1640 to Nicholas Power). Reeves' allocation can best be explained by the fact that Williams had known the Reeves when they both attended the same Salem church before his banishment. Williams probably felt that now that her husband was deceased, she should have a home lot. At least a part of her lot later went to Richard Scott; the western part came to be occupied by "King's Church [later St. Johns]."[38] We do not know if any of the other women receiving lots had a prior connection with Williams.

Somewhat later, also without explanation, records indicate that a Mary Sweete received a grant of land, but the actual year is not mentioned.[39] It would certainly be interesting to know more about these women and why they were given lots. What we do know is that even though land ownership was a pre-condition to the right to vote, this right did not extend to the women even if they owned land.

---

[38] Hopkins, p. 27.
[39] Staples, *Annals*, p. 22.

Providence: 1630-1800

These imaginary sketches from *Angel's Lane*, by G.L. Miner

A VIEW OF THE COVE IN 1636

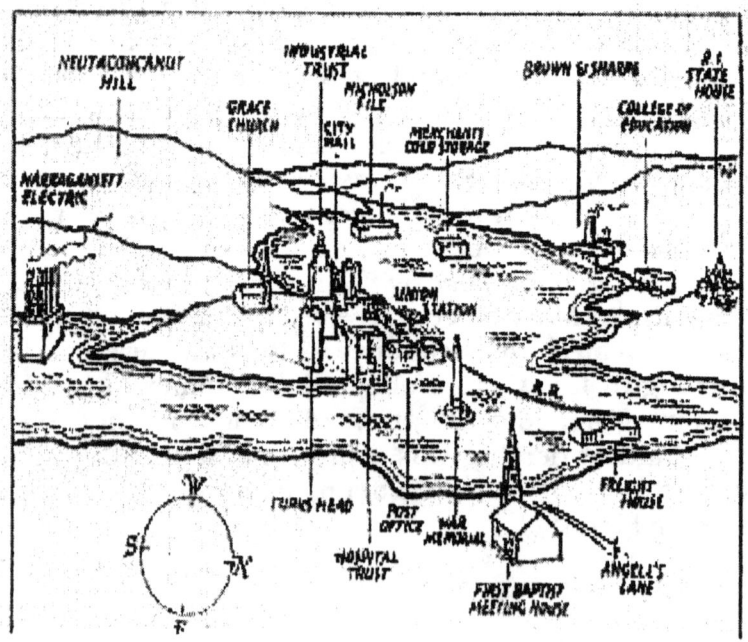

A key to the view as of 1948.

1. The Beginning

Women did have some rights. In a memorandum attached to a deed, dated October 22, 1666, Mary Williams assented to the disbursement of land given Roger. He had to have her agreement, since, in essence, he was giving away her dowry rights; a right all women then had when their husbands died—a lifetime tenure on family property, or until such time as the widow married again. Mary signed this deed with her mark.

The last allocation by this process occurred in 1718. A drawing took place to determine the allocation of home lots to the one hundred and one families then in Providence. The lots for warehouses and wharfs on the opposite side of the river from Towne Street, also included in the drawing, went, for the most part, to those with home lots on Towne Street.[40]

Despite its drawbacks, the "Proprietary" Williams established in 1638, objected to by Bicknell, lived on "for nearly two centuries, exercising its functions in various ways, civil and economic, as a separative, disjunctive, individual, selfish factor in the body politic." [41]

★★★

Initially, the settlers all built their homes close together along the length of Towne Streete, making friendships and support amongst the women easy and welcome.

> Women would visit each other with a clean checked apron, a striped loose gown, a handkerchief over the shoulders, and a sun bonnet; then pleasantly sit down and divert themselves over a dish of bohea tea[42] and a piece of

---

[40] Bicknell, V. 1, pp. 174-175 & 213.
[41] Bicknell, V. 1, p. 171.
[42] The name of hills in China where this black tea is grown.

> bread and butter. [It was only later that a] few who considered themselves somewhat superior, would wear [or even have to wear] a silk or calico gown, with long ruffled cuffs, a lawn apron, a little roll over the head, resembling a crupper to a saddle, with the hair smoothly combed over it, a flat chip hat, with a crown about one inch deep, ...some black, some white, others red, green, &, &.[43]

On the less attractive side, the physical closeness and small numbers in the community may have "undermined privacy, nurtured gossip, and reinforced the patriarchal authority of public institutions."[44] Even so, it had another not-so-obvious advantage for the women. The town's "primitive looking, unshaven men" [there were no razors for some time] took turns gathering in one of their homes to discuss the days' issues. This gave the wife in whose home they were, after bedding the children down for the night, the opportunity to join them in their serious and heated discussions of such as

> the knotty problems of theology, Gortonism or anti-Gortonism, the evils of pedo-baptism, the policy of Williams against that of Massachusetts Bay, the latest news from England then several months old, while the pewter flagon is passed around and the fiery beverage is generously quaffed.
>
> Neighbors were few and duly appreciated, communication with the other colonies was neither frequent nor rapid, nor was it regarded as particularly desirable. The colonies at Providence and on Rhode Island were earnestly engaged in making their own history and in carrying out their own liberal policy, and were anxious for non-interference while they laid the foundations of freedom in both church and state.[45]

---

[43] Staples, p. 603
[44] Ulrich, p. 66.
[45] *Genealogies*, V. 2, pp. 414-415

1. The Beginning

Of course, even as a wife sat with the men before their roaring fire, listening, possibly offering an occasional opinion, she was probably also shelling peas or snapping beans, readying them for the next day's meal, or mending clothes, or sitting at her spinning wheel. For, as relaxing and enjoyable as such evenings must have been, she knew that in the morning she would be spending a considerable amount of time in front of that same fireplace cooking meals for her family—while also tending to her children and all the other duties which filled most of the women's days.

☆☆☆

The same year, 1638, that Roger Williams obtained the colony's first written deed from the Indians, Mary bore their first son. Thought to be the first son born in Providence, they named him Providence. Two years later, on July 15, 1640, Mary had their third daughter, Mercy. And so they had four children when Bicknell, in his history, invites us to visit with the Williams in their home on " 'Ye Towne Streete,' at the corner of Howland Lane." [46]

> It is near twelve o'clock noon, the old-time dinner hour. As we open the door, our nostrils are greeted and delighted with the fragrance of boiling clams. Mrs. Williams holds her baby, Mercy, on her left arm and is lifting the iron pot of boiled clams from the iron crane over the fire and placing it on the stone hearth. Mr. Williams is sitting on the long settee, with his two-year old boy, Providence, sitting on his lap, while Mary and Freeborn are playing at cats-cradles in the chimney corner.
>
> Mr. Williams welcomes us with a "God bless you,..." as we enter, and Mrs. Williams has her cordial word of greeting, asking us to take a seat on a three-legged stool

---

[46] Bicknell, V. 1, pp. 150-151

near the blazing fire. " providential hour," says Mr. Willliams, "God, in His great mercy, has granted us wonderful blessings in this new land of religious freedom, in a bountiful supple of clams and fishes. Let us thank Him before we dine." Standing before the kettle of clams, Mr. Williams asked the Heavenly Father's blessing on the rich provision of His bounty in the wilderness, and then, lifting the pot of clams placed it on a long oak bench in the middle of the "fire room," and drew the settee in front of it for Mrs. Williams, himself and the children, while his guest sat opposite, astride the stool. On removing the cover, a luscious repast of clams, mussels, oysters and scallops, taken that morning by Mr. Willliams from the cove banks at the mouth of the Moshassuck river.

There is not a knife or fork in the house, and only a few wooden plates, on which the shell-fish are placed, when scooped from the pot by a long wooden spoon. The first course is clam broth, and all drink from the same source, using large clam shells for spoons. The clams now gratify and satisfy our appetites, each adult preparing his own dish, with a large loaf of Indian corn bread, from which each breaks the portion he desires. There is no butter, for there is not a cow or a goat in Providence Plantations. There is no tea or coffee, only the pure spring water from the great town spring, at the foot of the hill, and all drink to quench nature's normal thirst. Clams and bread and water,—our table an oak bench, our dishes only wooden plates, our hands and fingers, the tools of our appetites—a full, delightful meal and a grateful heart, followed by health and sleep, "of light digestion bred." This was a sample dinner at the home of the Founder of Providence.

Before we say "Good bye" and "Thanks" for our dinner, let us note that there were no chairs in the room, no bedstead, no desk, no books, except a Bible, no tools, except an axe, a gun and a spade; ...no carpet on the floor, but in its stead, sand from the river band; no horse, no cart, and what was worse, no money to buy any or all of these things. Such was the home condition of Roger Williams and most of his band for a number of years after coming to Providence.

1. The Beginning

☆☆☆

By the time of this visit houses had greatly improved over the original rustic one-room cabins, but they still were far from spacious, especially considering that most families included numerous children. And there were no modern conveniences such as we now take for granted—no electricity, no indoor plumbing, no running water, hot or cold, no washing machine—no wonder the men did not shave, that baths were less frequent, clothes washed less often. There was not even a convenient stove for cooking and heating water—the first American cookstove was not cast until 1765. And there was neither refrigerator nor ice box, nor even ice—yet a supply of food had to be preserved to last through the cold, snowy months, which meant drying, preserving, salting. Every family who could afford it "had a 'powdering tub,' in which meat was 'powdered,' that is salted and pickled. Many families had a smoke-house, in which beef, ham, and bacon were smoked." [47]

The wills left by the early settlers make clear that, as time passed, there were marked differences between the homes and furnishings of the rich and poor, and those headed by men in different occupations—laborers, merchants, farmers, seafarers, etc. Even so, for some time the similarities remained as striking as the differences—all still surrounded by vast forests and meadows.

The women, especially, must have been pleased when those first one-room, rough-hewn log homes, described earlier, gave way to frame houses, even though they, too, were rustic by today's standards, most not painted inside or out. There would be a single large room with a ladder or crude stairs leading

---

[47] Earle, *Home Life*, p. 153.

to a loft where the children had their beds, with straw mattresses (certainly not a bed for each), along with a chamber pot and possibly a chest or trunk their father had made for clothes and bedding. At first there may have been animal skins for covering, prepared as they had learned from the Indians.

The large "lower roome" had the parent's bed and a chest at one end; a cradle for the latest addition near-by; or possibly at the other end by the fireplace; a table and settees were in between. "Chairs were a luxury, and few families had more than one or two for more than fifty years from the founding." [48] For some time the house had only one or two small windows for light and air. There was no glass for windows until after the town's ports were built in the 1700s, and its sea commerce was sufficiently developed for the colonists to have something worthwhile to trade with England for the glass, paper, books, cloth, tea, spices and ammunition they wanted and needed. Instead, the windows were covered with paper made translucent (but not transparent) by saturation with linseed oil; protected by wooden shutters that were closed during bad weather—meaning there was seldom sunlight to brighten a room—most light coming from the open fireplace.

The living-bed space was rarely partitioned off from the kitchen, the whole heated (barely) by a wood-burning fireplace. Some of these fireplaces were large enough to accommodate four foot long logs (plentiful from the close-by woods), and large enough to walk in, look up and see daylight. Initially they were at one end of the house; less of a fire hazard than those later built in the center as houses grew larger. Most of the early fireplaces, some with small built-in seats at the corners for the children, were of "field stones, held

---

[48] Bicknell, V. 1, p. 151.

1. The Beginning

together by mud or a rude oyster shell mortar," and had a wide hearth that extended several feet into the room. This was useful for warming and "to prevent sparks and hot grease from landing on the wooden floor or rag rugs."[49]

It did not, of course, protect the women with their long skirts from "catching a spark" and getting burned as they leaned over the fire to reach pots, etc. Further, mothers must have been constantly concerned that their children would get burned as they played about. Regarding the women, Holliday writes in *Woman's Life in Colonial Days*:

> Over those great fire-places of colonial times many a wife presented herself as a burnt offering to her lord and master, the goodman of the house. The pots and kettles that ornamented the kitchen wall were implements for pre-historic giants rather than for frail women. The brass or copper kettles often holding fifteen gallons, and the huge iron pots weighing forty pounds, were lugged hither and thither by women whose every ounce of strength was needed for the too frequent pangs of child-birth. The colonists boasted of the number of generations a kettle would outlast; but perhaps the generations were too short—thanks to the size of the kettle.[50]

All cooking was done at open hearths; baking in the oven built into the chimney wall. A lug-pole or back bar was installed inside the fireplace from which chains or pot-hooks of varying lengths were hung to accommodate the iron pots; the shorter hooks, farther from the fire, for the slow simmering needed for soup, stew or ragout; lower hooks were placed nearer the fire for boiling and such. In the larger fireplaces, more than one fire might be built to accomplish the same purpose. A rotating spit held the game caught in the

---

[49] Booth, *Hung, Strung,* pp. 11 & 13.
[50] Holliday, p. 108

nearby woods while it cooked; or a chicken from those raised in the back yard. Turning the spit was one of the tasks often assigned the children, each child having an assigned household responsibility beginning at an early age.

Meal-preparation was time-consuming and difficult; accompanied year round, day and night, by "fire-tending" which itself required real skill to keep "a few brands smoldering ready to stir into flame as needed."[51]

These early kitchen areas held the women's herbs and spices, grain storage bins (sometimes in sacks hung from the rafters to keep them from rodents which were always a problem), barrels, and, if she could afford them, pottery or stoneware crocks for liquids. Sometimes the loft also served as a place for storing food. In addition to the heavy kettles, frying pans and pots referred to, for serving there would be some pewter and wooden dishes, porringers (shallow dishes with a handle mostly used by the children), wooden drinking tankards, called noggins (a sort of mug with a handle), and often only wooden spoons for eating—knives and other utensils a rarity. Even spoons were so precious that company would be asked to bring their own.

> Many women used their few cooking utensils to serve many functions. A paddle used to stir porridge in the morning could be used to make soap in the evening. Molds were handy not only for making puddings, but for breads, butter, and cheeses. Rolling pins were used not only for rolling pastry dough, but also for beating the toughness out of freshly killed game.[52]

The lack of utensils resulted in soups, ragouts, hashes and stews being the favored foods and their

---

[51] Ulrich, p. 20
[52] Booth, *Hung, Strung,* p. 22

1. The Beginning

slow-cooking allowed the busy housewife a chance simultaneously to pursue the many other chores that fell to her—tending the garden in back of most homes; killing and plucking chickens, as well as wild birds shot in the nearby woods. The children probably had the responsibility of feeding the family's chickens and collecting their eggs, maybe even helping with milking cows, and goats, too, if they had them. Some probably also had pigs.

As for meal-planning, women could not quickly turn to a favored recipe. There were no American recipe books until 1796 when Amelia Simmons "who described herself as an American orphan,"[53] wrote one titled *American Cookery*. The recipes wives had brought with them from England were, in general, useless, or, minimally, needed major adjustments to fit the foods available. Consequently, in addition to what they had learned from the Indians, the women became quite inventive and shared what they learned with each other; some sounding quite delicious— "stuffed partridge, baked duck or roasted pheasant;... pickled mushrooms; ...white soup from a knuckle of veal, ragout a buttock of beef, souse a pike, fricassee a hare;... cowslip wine;... potted fish."[54] And in more detail from the same source (and not sounding at all appetizing):

> [Take] a cow's udder and first boil it well, then stick it thick all over with cloves; then when it is cold, spit it, and lay it on the fire, and apply it well with basting of sweet butter, and when it is sufficiently roasted and brown, then dredge, and draw it from the fire, take vinegar and butter, and put it on a chafing dish and coals, and boil it with white bread crumbs, till it be thick; then put to it good store of sugar and cinnamon, and putting it into a clean

---

[53] Booth, *Hung, Strung*, p. 51.
[54] Haley, Old Stone Bank, Vol. IV, p. 36.

dish, lay the cows udder therein, and trim the sides of the dish with sugar and so serve it up.

Whatever the reader may think of this dish, imagine how long a wife had to spend in front of the open fireplace preparing it!

As commerce increased and the settlers became richer, both their houses and their food became more elaborate; they became less dependent on themselves and increasingly able to purchase what they wanted. But the majority of the populous continued for many years to depend on themselves and the surrounding woods, meadows, river and sea for their food. Hence, typically, a colonial wife needed to know "how to manage the ticklish chemical processes which changed milk into cheese, meal into bread, malt into beer, and flesh into bacon"—without any of today's conveniences.[55] No wonder so many men quickly remarried after a wife died; that widows had no trouble finding a new husband.

Just a few of the early recipes from Booth's, *Hung, Strung, & Potted*, have been selected, rather at random, to give the reader another brief look at other dishes a venturesome early colonial wife might have prepared for her family:

> <u>To Make Eel Broth</u>: Very nourishing for the sick. ...boil them in a small quantity of water, with a good deal of parsley, which should be served with them and the liquor... stew two hours, and add an onion and peppercorns; salt to taste. *The American Domestic Cookery, 1822*
>
> <u>To Stew a Hare</u>: Beat it well with a rolling pin in its own blood. Cut it into little bits and fry them. Then put the hare into a stew pan with a quart of strong gravy, pepper and salt according to the palate, and let it stew till

---

[55] Ulrich, p. 23

1. The Beginning

tender. Thicken it with butter and flour. Serve it up in its gravy with sippets in the dish and lemon sliced for garnish. *The Frugal Housewife, 1772*

Goose to Dry: Take a fair fat goose, powder it about a month, then hang it up in a chimney as you do bacon; and when it is thoroughly dry, boil it well and serve it to the table, with some mustard and sugar; garnish your dish with bay-leaves. Hogs cheeks are very good dried thus. *The Family Dictionary, 1705*

To Keep Green Peas Till Christmas: Take young peas, shell them, put them in a colander to drain, then lay a cloth four or five times double on a table. Then spread them on, dry them very well, and have your bottles ready. Fill them, cover them with mutton suet fat when it is a little soft; fill the necks almost to the top, cork them, tie a bladder and a leather over them and set them to a dry cool place. *American Cookery, 1796*

To Make Indian Slapjacks: One quart of milk, one pint of Indian meal, four eggs, four spoons of flour, little fat, beat together, bake on griddles or fry in dry pan, or bake in a pan which has been rubbed with suet, lard or butter. *American Cookery, 1796*

To Make A Boiled Rice Pudding: Take a quarter of a pound of rice, and a half a pound of raisins stoned. Tie them in a cloth so as to give the rice room to swell. Boil it two hours. And serve it up with melted butter, sugar, and grated nutmeg thrown over it. *The Frugal Housewife, 1772*

To Make Wine of Blackberries: Take and bruise the blackberries a little, then let them ferment for twenty-four hours, then put them into a barrel with a little tartar and a few ripe grapes, let the water just boil and stand till it be luke warm, and then put it to the blackberries. *The Family Dictionary, 1705*

In addition to the on-going need for meal preparations, the wife had numerous other tasks. She had to make sure the household had a sufficient supply of soap (the making of which required "constant care of the wood ashes and hunks of fat and lumps of grease") and of candles (which required "lugging about immense kettles, [and suffering] the smell of tallow, deer suet, bear's grease, and stale port-liquor." Initially "wax candles were a luxury, possessed only by the wealthy... 'Dips,' [were] made of odds and ends of grease, rescued from pot liquor or any form of cooking, fat of all kinds, and perhaps [sweet-smelling] bayberry tallow, provided the first candles for the average settlers, but even these were scarce at first." Another smoky source of light for many were "pitch-pine knots made into crude candle-like shapes" Whale oil and tallow, at a premium because cattle and sheep were not raised to any extent, had to be imported from England into Massachusetts, and it was a long time before those in Providence could afford such a luxury.[56]

Another laborious task left to the women was washing and ironing. All water (even for drinking) had to be carried from the springs along Towne Street, one in front of the Williams' home lot. Even after wells were later dug in front of every second or third house, it still had to be carried into house in heavy buckets. For laundry, the water had first to be boiled in huge pots hung in the fireplace; the clothes then scrubbed on a wash board, often leaving a woman's hands and knuckles red, even raw.

Ironing required heating heavy irons in the fireplace. It is unlikely that clothes were washed as often as today, simple and durable as they were, but surely not altogether avoidable. To be washed were men's wash-leather breeches and leather aprons; women's one or two gowns, handkerchiefs worn over the shoulder, shifts and aprons; children's long dresses, babies' diapers, whatever they might be made of; the belly bands of newborns. And there were the women's "rags" to keep

---

[56] Holliday, p. 113 and Haley, Old Stone Bank, V. IV, pp. 55-56 and V. II, pp. 46-47

1. The Beginning

clean, often torn from old petticoats, used during the "curse" as it was so often called. They may have felt that their avoidance of menstrual periods was at least one blessing that came of their frequent pregnancies and long-time breast feeding—sometimes lasting until the next child came along.

2. Beyond Providence

Soon after the Williams family settled in on Towne Street, Roger had started looking for an appropriate spot outside the new town to open a trading post. He sought both a way to supplement his meager income from the farming he initially undertook, and to escape what he called "the distressed bedlam of discontents." He increasingly felt alienated from his "loving neighbors" who, in his words, had become "malcontents,... wanting in organizing ability, disputatious and contentious in spirit."[57]

As for his income, Roger had little left over from his farming for bartering, the general method of trade in those early days, and he received nothing for his preaching during the few months he spent as the new colony's preacher—preaching then believed to be a privilege without need of compensation. And when they had been forced to leave Salem, they would have had to leave behind even the few treasured possessions they had brought from England.

[Noting the brevity of Roger Williams' tenure as a Baptist preacher, it is interesting that historians should credit him with founding Providence's first Baptist church. To add to this irony, he probably never preached in a church edifice since Baptists continued to hold their services in various settler's homes well into the 18th century. Further, it is not even clear that Roger regarded himself as a Baptist, preferring his independence and preaching to the Indians.]

For the opening of his trading post, Roger chose Cocumscussoc, the Indian name for the area bordering on Wickford harbor, twenty miles south of Providence, near his Indian friend, Canonicus. "There

---

[57] Bicknell, V. 1, p. 357.

2. Beyond Providence 43

were beaver dams nearby; deer, bears, wolves and smaller game [that] roamed the wilderness which stretched unbroken on every side. Nearby was an untroubled harbor, now the upper end of the Wickford north cove."[58] This would allow easy transport of the furs he anticipated trading and also enable him to use his canoe for traveling to and from his home on Towne Street—not always without incident. "On one of his business trips, his canoe was overturned, his goods lost and he narrowly escaped with his life."[59]

> He was cordially welcomed [at the spot chosen for his post] by the friendly chief [Canonicus], who 'with his own hand' laid out ground for a temporary trading post on the bank of the cove, close by the Indian trail known as the Pequot Path. And the Squaw Queen, not to be outdone, gave him the tiny island opposite the post for the pasturage of his goats, whence the island appears on old maps as Queen's Island, and has also been known variously as Goat Island and Rabbit Island.[60]

When Chief Canonicus died in 1647, he was much missed by all the colonists. Roger Williams, who regarded him as a true friend, wrote:[61]

> 'He was not to be stirred with money to sell his Lands to let in foreigners. Tis true he recd presents and gratuities many of me, but it was not Thousand not Ten thousands of money could have bought of him an English Entrance into the Bay,' adding, he never traded with me, but had freely what he desired, goods, money...to the last of that mans breath, who dying sent for me and desired to be buried in my cloth of free gift and so he was.'

★★★

---

[58] Clauson, p. 116
[59] Haley, Old Stone Bank, Vol. IV, p. 31.
[60] Woodward, p. 10.
[61] Quoted in Woodward, p. 18

From the beginning Roger had often been away from home preaching to the Indians; with his opening of the post at Cocumscussoc, he was away even more. He had become, perhaps, New England's first commuter, probably not daily, since the trip from post to home required either a twenty mile trek through the woods or canoeing a like distance. From necessity, Mary had learned to cope without her husband, to depend on her own resourcefulness in managing house and children—even before talk began in 1643 of Roger's returning to England to obtain a charter from the King that would validate Rhode Island as a state and unite its then existing settlements in Portsmouth, Newport and Providence into a single colony. A good thing since Roger would be gone more than a year, perhaps a third of that time spent at sea, en route and returning.

With only the deed from the Indians granting them the land, those in Rhode Island were still regarded as "squatters" by England and by the neighboring colonies. Without a royal charter, those families which had been designated as proprietors when Williams divided up the land had no valid recorded deeds. It was generally agreed that Williams was the logical person to make this trip and the town promised to pay him £100 for his expenses. However, perhaps not surprisingly since the town did not yet have an established way to collect revenue, there is no evidence he ever received it.

Fortunately, Roger had "turned a profit of about $3000 a year in Indian trade"[62] from Cocumscussoc so he was able to leave Mary what he hoped would be enough to provide for her and the children during his absence in England. Whether they discussed this before his departure is a mute question, as is the

---

[62] Clauson, p. 116.

2. Beyond Providence 45

possibility they discussed how much easier things might have been for them had he started receiving, in 1634 (just before they were thrown out of Salem), the annual stipend his mother, Alice, had accorded him in her will that year. They may also have discussed Roger's intent, while in London, to try to collect the money due him. And so it was that in London, on August 15, 1644, he and his brother, Sydrach, filed a suit in chancery court against Walter Chauncy and others for "conspiring to defraud them out of their legacies." [63]

Along with varying amounts for her other children and grandchildren, Alice had left Sydrach £100 and stipulated that Roger, "now beyond the seas" should receive "£10 yearly to be paid by my executor for and during the term and space of 20 years after my decease" (which was in 1634). It was "to be paid by the assignment of the lease or leases of my dwelling house and other tenements standing and being on that side of the way wherein my dwelling house is situated." [His mother apparently owned not only her home, but also an unusually large number of adjoining properties that included several tenements.] The will also stated that should Roger die, the monies were to go to Roger's wife and daughter [suggesting that only Mary was then born]. Though no definitive information was discovered, the fact that historians, in general, make no reference to Roger's ever receiving a stipend suggests that Alice's children, or at least Sydrach and Roger, never received their monies.

☆☆☆

When Williams departed for England via New York

---

[63] The quotes and information about the will are from *Genealogies*, V. 1, pp. 646 and following.

(for he still was not allowed in Massachusetts) in early summer 1643, it was his first return since leaving in 1630. He was leaving Mary with four young children to care for; Daniel, their second son and fourth child, having been born a year and a half after Mercy. Mary also was pregnant; their third son and final child, Joseph, arriving on December 12, 1643, six months after Roger left. *We cannot help but wonder if Mary tried to persuade Roger not to go; asked him if there were not others just as capable who could go instead. Or was Mary encouraging, feeling her husband had a special duty to see that the Providence settlement was secure? Did Roger even discuss the trip with Mary, giving her a say, before deciding?*

However Mary may have felt about Roger's leaving, at least she could console herself with the fact that he was successful in achieving the mission that took him to England. In March 1644, he received a charter that granted Rhode Island "full power and authority to govern themselves," though the Crown retained power to revise the charter. [If both dates are correct, this means the chancery suit was filed five months after this. Had Roger remained in England for this or had he left the filing and follow-through to his brother?]

The charter officially designated the colony as "Providence Plantation in Narragansett Bay in New England"—a name some historians have called ironic since Providence still had no government and only about one hundred people "scattered in the wilderness", while Newport and Portsmouth numbered closer to one thousand and had a well-functioning duly elected civil government, courts, etc. It was not until May 1647 that representatives from the then-existing towns of Providence, Portsmouth, Newport and Warwick (added in 1642, settled by Samuel Gorton) could reach an

2. Beyond Providence 47

agreement on forming a General Assembly that joined their towns in, even then, only a loose federation.

★★★

After Williams' return from this trip to England, he built a sturdier, though still modest, trading-house combination at Cocumscussoc. The family then moved in and remained there until 1651 when Roger sold it to help finance a second trip to England. It was during their time there that they met and became friends with William Blackstone. Blackstone had arrived in Boston in 1623, even before the Puritans, but left in 1635,[64] not because he was banished but because he did not want to join with them. He sold his property,

> invested his capital in cattle, and dressed in his 'canonicall Coate' and carrying his beloved books, set out through the wilderness with but one companion, a servant, named Abbot, from whom Abbot's Run in Cumberland takes its name. He finally came to a place which the Indians called Wawepoonseag. Here he settled in a territory which was without a white inhabitant. In what was then a part of Rehoboth but is now Cumberland, near Lonsdale, he built a home.[65]

Though his arrival preceded the Williams' by a year or so, there are several reasons he is not generally regarded as the settler of Rhode Island: as noted, his home was in an area that only later became a part of Rhode Island, and he was regarded as an eccentric hermit who wanted nothing except to be left alone. And alone he must have been for years, visited only by an occasional Indian in the area hunting or fishing.

In later years, after meeting and becoming friends

---

[64] Except as noted, the information and quotes that follow are from the Blackstone's *Lineage and History*, pp. 46-93.
[65] Haley, Old Stone Bank, Vol. II, p. 17

with Roger Williams, Blackstone resumed some preaching and monthly could be seen riding along the Pequot Path on the back of his large white bull. Often he had stop to visit with the Williamses at Cocumscussoc on his way to Providence to buy more books for his collection, as well as other necessities not available at his retreat—which were, incidentally, many and varied. They included milk and meat from his herds, fish from the river, game from the forest, and grain, fruit and vegetables from his garden, orchards and fields.

WM. BLACKSTONE AND HIS TAME BULL.

2. Beyond Providence

Seeing that big bull approaching, the Williams' children must have rushed out to greet Blackstone; the youngest, perhaps, hiding in her mother's skirts, the older ones begging for a ride. "He was beloved by children to whom he used to bring sweet apples, the first they had ever seen, from his orchard at Study Hill."[66] More than likely Mary Williams asked him to share a meal with the family, even to stay overnight.

Blackstone was sixty-four years old on July 4, 1659 when Governor John Endicott, as he had requested, united him in marriage to Sarah, the widow of John Stephenson. "What soft persuasions he whispered in her ear" to induce her "to forsake the society of relatives and friends in Boston to become the constant companion of the 'Sage of the Wilderness,' history has not revealed." They came from the same district in England and possibly knew each other there. Sarah already had three sons: Ouesimus (born in 1643), John (born in 1645), and James (born in 1653). We know nothing of two of them, but the middle son, John, came to live with William and Sarah. "Humors of Utopia," found in the Massachusetts Historical Collection, tells a fanciful story of another child, a supposed-daughter of Blackstone's—"a child of the forest and field, a flower of the wilderness"—whom he educated and who married John Stevenson. But in his book, a descendant, John Wilford Blackstone, denies the truth of this. He writes:[67]

> In this matter of fact world the 'mere frost work of fancy' must often be dissolved by the sunshine of truth. She had no existence except in imagination.

A year after their marriage, William and Sarah had

---

[66] Haley, Old Stone Bank, Vol. II, p. 18
[67] Blackstone, p. 68.

a son they also named John. He grew to early adolescence under a father who was described as "a man of culture, of independent spirit and kind and benevolent heart." His mother, Sarah, was said to be "a loving guide and counselor to the boy who was her latest born, and the only fruit of her marriage with an educated and eminent man." William and Sarah lived together with the two Johns in their isolated retreat for fourteen years, Sarah dying in June 1673. Blackstone was eighty years old when he died on May 26, 1675, two years after Sarah.

Blackstone's death, only a few weeks before the beginning of King Philip's War, spared him seeing much of his "fair domain" destroyed by the Indians with whom he had always been friendly—houses, barns, books, furniture, all became "a prey to devouring flames." The inventory prior to this showed that he had left to his only son considerable property, Blackstone's title to the property recognized because of his long occupancy. Amongst other land, it included 60 acres and two shares of meadow in Providence, the meadow called Blackstone's Meadow, 200 acres of land about the house and orchard. His personal property included books valued at £56.3.6. The Plymouth records note: "this Estate—the moveables—was destroyed and carried away by the natives." On October 27, 1675, the same records note that the courts appointed Nathaniel Paine and Daniel Smith as guardians of John Blackstone. Since he was then apprenticed to Whipple in Providence as shoemaker, it must have been their doing—and quite a change from the loving home he'd had with his parents.

In *Lineage and History of William Blackstone*, one of his descendants, John Wilfred Blackstone asks why the guardians did not rebuild the home, and renovate the fields, thus providing sufficient income for the support and education of their ward. He suggests that those made guardians of John Blackstone were

2. Beyond Providence 51

friends of the step-son, John Stevenson, and hence alleviated him of any fear of his step-brother, John, or of his indifferent guardians. This allowed John Stevenson to claim his step-father's lands for himself, and enabled him to live there until he died.

In 1692, David Whipple, then of advanced age bought Study Hill and passed it on to his descendents. *Was this not, most likely, the Whipple to whom the property's rightful owner, John Blackstone, was apprenticed?*

Tradition has it that about 1700, John Blackstone and his wife, Catherine, "came in their own ship from Rhode Island and bought land in Branford, Connecticut and the place is called Blackstoneville to this day. He sailed the seas and added to his holdings; most likely he died at sea (in 1785). He once went back to his former home to look after interests in lands that he had in Rhode Island or Attleborough." Weedon says that in September 1722, John apprenticed his son to R. Wickes "to be learned to Reade and the art of husbandry," but it is not clear which John he is referring to.[68]

---

[68] Quotes in this paragraph from Weedon, p. 214.

3. Early Families

The frequency of marriage, well into the 19th Century, between the various members of the various families of the early white settlers is striking. We know less about the liaisons between Indians, slaves and indentured servants, but there must have been considerable intermarriage amongst them, too, resulting in many mixed-race children. This frequency of intermarriage is not surprising since choices of mates for all of them were necessarily limited; the small early settlements were connected only by narrow paths winding through thick forests covered with centuries-old underbrush, tangled vines and thorny bushes. Without horses, which only became available later, one either tackled these paths on foot or went by canoe. In either case, to venture too far from a settlement, meant to risk an encounter with unfriendly Indians.

Even after the first thirteen horses arrived in New England in 1629, it was some time before any but the wealthiest could afford to own them. Further, an item appearing in Richard Browns' account book as late as 1713 (by which time the colonies had sufficient numbers of horses to be exporting them) suggests that outings still were not quick and easy:[69]

> Oct. the 25, 1737, Mary Tillinghast Dr. For the use of my mare, the three days past, a journey to East Greenwich, and carrying double on said mare, £0.12.0.

In contrast to the historical stereotype, at least of the Puritans, Smith claims in her women's history, *Daughters of the Promised Land*, that "premarital lovemaking" was a generally accepted practice. [70] If

---

[69] Staples, *Annals*, pp. 611-612.
[70] Smith, pp. 50 & 56.

3. Early Families

she is correct, it would help explain the obvious "vitality, virility and fertility" of both the men and women founders of Rhode Island, despite all the demanding circumstances of the day.

Smith asserts that although fornication "outside of a precontract" might be punished if discovered, for the most part it was accepted as a "practical utility." Precontracts of marriage were regarded as legitimizing the "folk custom of bundling,"[71] and a "permissive attitude," in general, was accorded "sexual irregularities, provided they did not imperil good order in the community." Thus, "for a couple *destined to get married* to encounter each other in a direct physical way seems to have resulted in marriages in which the sensual aspect was of considerable if not primary importance. In consequence, there was about Puritan society, and perhaps especially in Rhode Island, a directness, a practicality, a lack of hypocrisy and subterfuge, an absence of prudery in matters that affected sexual relations and the functions of the body that is unique, certainly, in American history. Much could be tolerated as long as the *social nature* of marriage was generally acknowledged."[72]

Another kind of pre-marital contract, that regarding disposition of property, is just as surprising, and this writer suspects as *not* typical (See following). The law did then require a husband to provide for his wife in his will, but no other such contract as that reproduced following, between Joseph Jencks and Alice Dexter, has been found. Since two Dexters signed the agreement as witnesses, one might conclude the contract was forced upon Joseph as a condition of their agreeing to the marriage. What is so unusual is that both parties retain

---

[71] Bundling was the practice of a couple sharing the same bed, but without removing their clothes.
[72] Smith, pp. 50-56.

all rights to their respective properties after marriage; each able to do as they wish with them.

3. Early Families 55

✯✯✯

One family writ large in Rhode Island history is that of William Arnold and his wife, Christian Peake. In fact, Bicknell suggested in his history that the Arnolds rather than the Williams should be cited as Rhode Island's founders. The claim is based on the fact that soon after the Arnolds arrived in New England on June 24, 1635, they moved on to Rhode Island—in April 1636, two months before the Williams arrived that June. Bicknell gives no rationale for why he is not so credited, but it could well be because it was Roger Williams who negotiated with the Indians for the white man's right to the land.

Christian and William Arnold came to this country accompanied by their oldest daughter, Elizabeth, and her husband, William Carpenter, their daughter Joane (named after William's sister), their sons, Benedict and Stephen, and the children of William's sister, Joane, then deceased. The latter's children were Thomas Hopkins, nineteen at the time, Frances Hopkins, twenty-one, and Elizabeth Hopkins. There is no evidence that their father, William Hopkins, was also with the family.[73] Arnold had taken over much of the responsibility of raising Joane's children after she suddenly died in 1622. They had been very close, Joane having practically raised her brother after their mother died while he was still an infant.

According to Bicknell, the April after their arrival the whole Arnolds family

> crossed the wilderness country between Massachusetts Bay and the Narragansett, explored the lands at Moshassuck and settled at the mouth of the Pawtuxet River, on the north bank, now in the town of

---

[73] Arnold, Elisha S., p. 43. One can only assume that this is the same William Hopkins who appears later in Rhode Island's story.

Cranston....The Arnolds built their cabins and were the first squatter sovereigns on the lands later called Providence....They came and stayed and were the first to evidence the work of town building,: clearing the forests, building cabins and fences, platting land, and making the acquaintance of their neighbors the Showaments....Here one sees the practical founders of a town,—men and women who came as freemen, not under banishment...[74]

Following soon after were "Zachariah Rhodes...,William Harris, William Field and Stukeley Westcott." Just when Stukeley and Presilla Westcott married is not stated but she bore at least three sons and two daughters. Little is known of them, but their daughter, Freelove, married a Turner (no other name was found); and Damaris, who married Benedict Arnold, learned to speak the Indian language.

To return to the Arnolds: records suggest that William Arnold outlived his wife, Christian. He died at age 88 during King Philip's War, by then old and feeble. Arnold had gone to his son Stephen's "garrison," actually his Mansion house, "which covered nearly all the land west of Broad Street to the Pawtuxet river."[75] Christian and William were buried side by side on their homestead lot in Pawtuxet.

On September 7, 1685, when William Carpenter, the husband of the Arnold's oldest daughter, Elizabeth, died, the last of the original Thirteen Proprietors of Providence had come to an end. Their daughter Joane, had already lost her husband, Zachariah Rhodes of Rehoboth, Massachusetts, when he drowned "off Pawtuxett Shore" in 1666. Joane seems to have been no better off after her second

---

[74] This and quote in following paragraph are from Bicknell, V. 1, pp. 143-144.
[75] *Genealogies*, V.1, p. 42.

3. Early Families 57

marriage to Samuel Reape. A court entry dated October 26, 1681 suggests that Reape either abandoned her, or died without providing her with sufficient funds to live on. The entry states:

> On petition of Joanna [Joane] Reape, wife of Samuel Reape of Pawtuxet, the Assembly considering the deplorable estate of said Joanna, being left destitute by her said husband, Samuel Reape, orders that all estate of Samuel Reape be sequestered for us of Joanna for her life, and appointed her son-in-law, Daniel Williams [her daughter Rebecca first had married Nicholas Power, Jr., then Daniel Williams], and son John Rhodes trustees to take possession in her behalf and receive rents for her use. [76]

Their son Benedict's will contained an interesting bequest; he left "a three-year-old gray horse, to be kept for twenty years, for 'the use of the women of the public ministry of the Quakers' who desired to visit New England, New York, or Philadelphia."

Christian and William Arnold's children had married into the Rhodes, Williams, Carpenter and Smith families, among others, who gave them thirty-five grandchildren and one hundred and twenty-one great-grandchildren. Credited as founders of Rhode Island or not, theirs was an illustrious family whose members held many of the state's offices. They include Jonathan Arnold, author of the Rhode Island Declaration of Independence and Samuel Arnold, whose history of Rhode Island is oft-quoted by this writer.

☆☆☆

Thomas Angell,[77] Roger Williams' cousin who came

---

[76] This and quote in subsequent paragraph are from Dexter, pp. 146 & 148. See Appendix for partial Family Tree.
[77] Information on the Angells comes from Holman and from Miner, *Angell's Lane*; exceptions noted.

to Providence with the Williamses as an indentured servant, was born in England in 1618 and died in September 1694 at age seventy-six. He was only eleven when he left England and had had no schooling, but this did not stop him from acquiring considerable property and much prestige during his long life. His wife, Alice Ashton, who died only three months after Thomas, came to Providence with her older brother, James Ashton, from Hertfordshire, England and prior to her marriage lived just down the street from Thomas. She was almost certainly the sister of Marie Ashton who married Thomas Olney. Alice and Thomas Angell were married sometime in the 1640s. Miner in his history of the Angells speculates on what his ancestors wore at their wedding.

> Thomas, we surmise, had hung up for the day his leather working-breeches to appear in a handsome new suit of local homespun—wool doublet and hose,—rather warm and baggy not doubt, but set off with a starched ruff and wrist bands. As for Alice, she had perhaps been torn between her new woolen petticoat and the old flowered tiffany gown she had brought from Hertfordshire in her sea-chest. We hope she had a new silk bonnet and scarf—the Boston ladies were wearing them until the court in 1651 tabooed them as worth of 'utter detestation.'[78]

Alice reveled in the freedom she found in Rhode Island to perform certain simple acts that would have subjected her to possible arrest and a fine in Massachusetts—things like kissing her children, all eight of them, cooking, making beds, sweeping and cutting hair, even on the Sabbath. But sadness entered her household when her son, Hope, mentioned in her will, "died young."

All too often in accounts of the colonial years,

---

[78] This quote (p.12) and subsequent quote and information are from Miner, *Angell's Lane*.

3. Early Families 59

historians and genealogists write of children who "died young," or "died in infancy," but such phrases do little to convey the pain and heart-break mothers felt in losing a child they carried for nine months—in watching a little one fade away, probably not knowing the cause, certainly not able to prevent it. The fact that there were usually numerous other living children, as in Alice's case, did little to mitigate the loss.

Aside from mentioning her child who died young, Alice's will conveys something of what she treasured in her household, probably typical of many Colonial women. Dated 1694, it begins thus:[79]

> Be it known unto all People by these presents that I Alice Angell of the Town of Providence in the Narragansett Bay in New England (widow) being now very weake of body but (through mercy) of sound & Perfect memory do make this to be my last will & Testament. I do give & bequeath unto my foure daughters...all my wearing Apparreill both Woollen & linnen Equally to be devided amongst them, & more over to my Daughter Deborah Sabbeer I give one Chamber Pott & two wooden Trayes which formerly belonged to my son Hope, & also I give unto my daughter Alice Whipple [wife of Eleazer] one Trunke & a Deske which my mother gave to me;...
>
> And farthr my will is, that Each of my foure daughters shall have so much of my Pewter as may be for a Remembrance of me.

The will goes on to give certain items and cash to her sons, and, after naming its Executor, is signed with her mark (as was that of her husband).

Miner adds to our picture of this family by describing the Providence he envisions Alice and Thomas's daughters and sons seeing as they gathered on the hillside for their parents' funerals, one so soon after the other:

---

[79] Holman, pp. 13-14

A town primitive in resources, with barter of farm produce, with no manufactures [except for pit saw mills, John Smith's grist mill and Olney's tannery], with home weaving, spinning, shoe making and blacksmithing, with no schools, no books to speak of, no streets except the muddy paths of the settlers [paving did not come to the town streets until 1785], and no communication even with neighboring towns except dilatory news brought on horseback or by the occasional sailing vessel that came up Narragansett Bay.[80]

However, by this time, there was a growing number of houses along Towne Street, some bringing "a little more comfort," and there were prosperous surrounding farms, some with "mansions." "Their home life was comfortable and wholesome [simple, cozy and hardy]; the plague of the Indians had passed, and the routine of Town Meetings and the Court and the Colony Assemblies had come through many bickerings and quarrels and had proved staunch."[81]

★★★

Another of the Williams' companions when they left Salem was John Smith, a miller from Dorchester, England, born in 1595. He was banished by the Bay Colony on September 3, 1635— "[he] shall be sent within this six weeks out of this jurisdiccion for dyvers dangerous opinions, wch hee holdeth, & hath dyvulged." Providence was fortunate to have a miller and almost immediately granted him land for a mill (where he undoubtedly also lived) on the west bank of the Moshassuc, at the falls—his primitive machinery used to break up grain in a manner similar to a pile driver. "The miller was to build and repair the mill at his own cost, and the town promised to erect or to permit no other.

---

[80] Miner, *Angell's Lane*, p. 33 & 35.
[81] Miner, *Angell's Lane*, p. 33 & 36-37.

3. Early Families

The corn was to be ground "every second and fifth day of the week." [82]

Smith, the miller (so-called to distinguish him from the other Smiths), was married to Alice (maiden name not found) who bore two children: John, Jr. and Elizabeth, who married Shadrach Manton, a cooper. They found Shadrach dead on the road in 1714, but the town declared it of natural causes. Thirteen grandchildren and sixty-five great-grandchildren descended from Alice and John's two children.

In his will John Smith left his mill to his son John, but it was his widow, Alice, who, after her husband's death in 1648, made an agreement with the town to continue his business, becoming, perhaps, the Colony's first businesswoman. They granted her and her son the "exclusive right to maintain a mill as long as they provided satisfactory service in grinding corn for the townspeople."[83] It was only after Alice had been operating it for two years that her son, John, Jr., took over the grist mill, soon after adding a saw mill. He operated both for the next thirty-five years.

John, Jr. married Sarah Whipple and on his death in 1682, he left her "halfe the mill with ye halfe of ye land neere...during her life, ye other halfe to my son John Smith" consisting of three hundred acres of land. Their two daughters, Sarah and Alice, each got forty acres and the third and youngest of his ten children, ten shillings. His seven boys got the remainder. John 3rd was the last of the family to bear the title miller.[84]

You may note that the Smiths named a daughter

---

[82] Quotes in this paragraph are from Farnman, p. 4. He added that "During one hundred and eighty years the Town Mill fulfilled its office, and was one of the last memorials of primitive times. It was destroyed at last by the Blackstone canal."
[83] *Genealogies*, V. 2, p. 2
[84] *Genealogies*, V. 2, pp. 6-11.

after her mother, just as they named a son after his father. This common practice suggests that these early Colonial women felt as strongly as the men about perpetuating their names, hence their identity. Though not legally allowed to keep their last names, at least this way they could pass on their first, but, regrettably, the women did not also suffix the 1st, 2nd, 3rd, etc., as usually *happened with the sons.* From the historians' and genealogists' point of view, this repeated use of the same first names within and between families, along with so many intermarriages amongst these early families, compounds the difficulty of tracing family members through the generations—and of ascertaining relationships.

✯✯✯

Richard Waterman was another of those who received a home lot in the initial allocations. The fact he had only come to Providence that year raises the question: *Why him and not others who had come earlier?* Perhaps he had "political pull" since he preceded Roger Williams to America, probably coming in 1629, having been sent for by the Governor and Company as an expert hunter.[85] Additionally, Williams would have been attracted to Waterman's openly expressing sympathy with his religious beliefs. His desire for greater liberty in worship had caused Waterman to become an object of suspicion in Salem—and thus had prompted his move to Providence in 1638. He was originally baptized a Baptist by Williams, but later became a Quaker, perhaps after serious controversies and fighting arose over property rights in the area of Warwick. Waterman was known as a man of "great force of character and more than ordinary ability." He died on October 26, 1673 "at an old age."

---

[85] *Genealogies*, V. 2, p. 334

3. Early Families 63

We do not know just when Richard married Bethia or what her religion may have been, but she did outlive her husband, not dying until 1680.

Bethia and Richard Waterman had two daughters and two sons.[86] Their oldest son, Nathaniel was one of the few who "stayed and went not away" from Providence during King Philip's War. Afterwards, at a meeting "before Thomas Field's house under a tree by the water side,"[87] he was voted a whole share of the Indian captives. He had inherited the lot next to the First Baptist Church where he and his wife, Susanna Carder, lived.

☆☆☆

One of the Waterman daughters, Mehitabel, married Arthur Fenner,[88] who came to Providence from Salem around 1638. Mehitabel and Arthur were said to have experienced "narrow accommodation, plain diet with little variety, [and] continuous toil [which] were the common domestic experiences." Their girls were said to "sing in unison with the whirr of resolutions" as they turned the spinning wheel; to spread the table "with the homely feast in the wooden trenchers, or upon the pewter plates, drawing up the wooden settle, and all within contented and happy."[89]

The exact date of Mehitabel's death is unknown, probably in 1682/3, but it was December 16, 1686

---

[86] See Jacobus and Waterman. The marriages of the children in this family result in multiple relationships with other early families.
[87] *Genealogies*, V. 2, p. 551.
[88] Though technically Arthur Jr., he is not so-called in history since his father and grandfather were never in America. However, Arthur did have two sisters and four brothers who also immigrated, still living in Connecticut with the exception of William who lived in Newport. See Family Trees in Appendix for Fenner, Waterman and Harris families.
[89] Quotes are from *Genealogies*, V. 1, pp. 315-316.

that Arthur Fenner married Howlong Harris.

Howlong's first marriage plans to Mr. Pococke were thwarted when her mother refused her blessing while her father was away on one of his trips back to England. Since her father never returned from this trip (of which we will soon hear more), this marriage never took place. Howlong perhaps feared becoming an old maid by the time Fenner proposed, so she readily accepted, undaunted by the thought of mothering his brood of six young children by his first wife. *But therein may lie the explanation as to why she and Arthur had no children.*

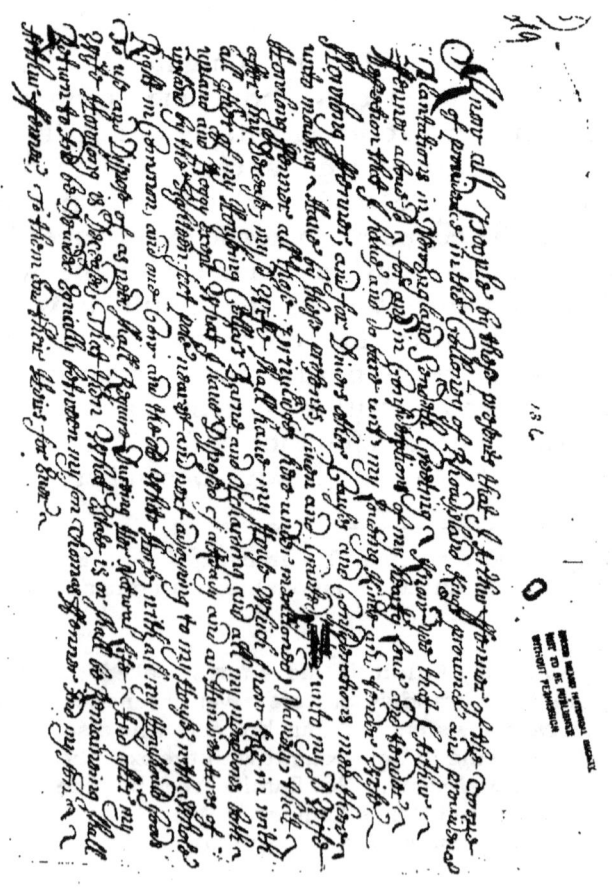

3. Early Families 65

Arthur was eighty-one years old when he died on October 10, 1703 after a prolonged illness. His will was unusually generous in its provision for his wife; perhaps an acknowledgement of the considerable property, left her by her father, Howlong had brought to the marriage. (A copy of the original above.)

The will leaves Howlong, "during her natural life," their house, with all its furnishings, his "barn and orchard and all my meadows both upland and boggy except what I have disposed of already and a hundred acres of upland," etc. He permits her to do with it as she wishes, and only after her death "what is remaining" is to be "divided equally between my son Thomas ffenner and my son Arthur ffener to them and their heirs forever." Another source indicates that "the inventory of Arthur's personal estate amounted to £166.8.0, and showed him to be a well-to-do farmer." [90]

After Howlong died on November 19, 1708, five years after her husband, the homestead went to Arthur, Jr. who lived there with his wife, Mary Smith, and their children until his own death on April 24, 1725. Arthur Jr. is described as "a yeoman, [who] followed agricultural pursuits, and seems to have attained no celebrity." When he died, the inventory of his estate amounted to £411.19.0.

The Fenner house, situated on a grassy knoll some distance from Providence, had a brook running through the property. Constructed of heavy oak timbers with a stone chimney, elaborately adorned with mouldings and pilasters, it was regarded as "one of the most prominent and picturesque" houses of the time. The house remained in the Fenner family until the death of Polly Fenner in 1861. After that, no longer occupied, it gradually began to "crumble and fall

---

[90] This and following quotes from *Genealogies*, V. 1, pp. 317 & 329.

apart...From lack of care, the winter storms and summer suns... wrack[ed] sad havoc. It afforded shelter for the beasts of the field and the fowls of the air, however, for it was many years before it became useless as a shelter, testifying to the good work of its early builders." [91]

As suggested in the above-quoted will, prior to the elder Arthur Fenner's death, he had already given a part of his property to his eldest son, Thomas. In 1677 Thomas built there a house for himself and his bride, Alice Ralph, the daughter of Thomas and Mary Ralph. From this homestead, Thomas ran both a tavern and store; a combination that was common, making it easier for a wife and daughters to become involved in a business than it otherwise would have been given their many additional house and family duties. Thomas and Alice had only one child, William, who "died young." We do not know what happened to Alice (perhaps she died in childbirth), but on July 2, 1682, Thomas married again—Dinah Borden, daughter of Thomas and Mary Harris Borden [another of William Harris's daughters].

During King Philip's War in 1676, Thomas Fenner gained the title of Major and was another of those in Providence who "staid and went not away." Before his death on February 27, 1718 at age sixty-six, he had become "possessed of considerable property besides that inherited from his father's estate....Major Fenner was a valuable citizen, a faithful public officer, and exerted a wide influence in the Providence plantations being also very active in colonial affairs."[92]

In his will, Thomas provided that his "beloved wife Dinah ffener" was to have the "olde parte of my dwelling house during her life." This house, too,

---

[91] Field, V. 3, pp. 603-606.
[92] *Genealogies*, V. 1, pp. 325-327.

3. Early Families

stayed in the family through the generations.[93] It also provided for his "poor helpless child Eleazar,'" and bestowed "£5 apiece on his three daughters, Freelove Westcott, Mehitabel Starkweather, and Mary Abbott, and divided his remaining property between his five other sons Thomas, Richard, Joseph, Arthur and John. (They also had a daughter, Sarah, not mentioned, perhaps deceased.) Thomas's inventory of personal property amounted to £433.19.09."

Dinah was ninety-eight years old when she died on December 18, 1761. She and her son, Eleazer, were buried side-by-side in the "old Fenner graveyard, near the ruins of Capt. Arthur's 'castle,' not far from the Pochasset River." The obituary on her gravestone reads:[94]

> During the course of a long life she praecuised all
> the relative Duties
> and died a
> SINCERE CHRISTIAN

We do not have similar records for her other four sons, but this seems to have been a family whose members lived to an old age. Thomas and Dinah's son, Arthur, lived till he was eighty-nine, dying on January 18, 1787. His funeral was held on Friday, February 1, 1788 at his "Mansion House," followed by his burial in the "North burying place." He was described as a merchant of eminence, and long-time member of the Baptist Church; "in all dealings an honest man, and a worthy and respectable member of society."

★★★

In 1631 Susannah and William Harris (Howlong Harris Fenner's parents), came to Boston with William's

---
[93] Field, V. 3, pp. 615-618
[94] Quotes from *Genealogies*, V. 1, pp. 327-328

brother, Thomas, on the same ship, the *Lyon*, as had Mary and Roger Williams. As you may recall, Harris was one of those who left their wives behind to follow Roger after he was forced to leave Salem. But it was not long after the original home lot allocations that the Harrises left Providence and located their home on the Pawtuxet in the "rich meadows and planting lands of the Pocasset Valley." This was near where the Arnolds had settled at Pawtuxet Falls, and where the Harris and Arnold men formed a business alliance.[95]

The Harrises move to this area no doubt accounts for the passionate antagonism that soon developed between William Harris and Roger Williams over the Pawtuxet boundaries. At one point Roger even charged Harris with treason and he was briefly held before the charges were dismissed. Their dispute, which had started long before King Philip's War (of which we will hear much more later) and continued long afterwards, became such an obsession with Harris, that he made four separate trips to England in an effort to resolve it.

Harris was seventy years old when he left Boston on yet another such trip in December 1679 on the ship *Unity*; this time representing Connecticut in its claims to a part of the disputed area.[96]

A month later, Barbary pirates captured the ship and took Harris and a number of other prisoners to Algiers. On April 6, 1680, Harris wrote his wife, Susanna, from Algiers telling her "his captors had sold him as a slave on the 23rd or 24th of February and then he had been put into solitary confinement till March 31st to make him amenable." He goes on to tell her of other ransoms paid and that he, "under duress, had promised to pay a ransom of 1,191 dollars, and he had until March 31st of the next year to come up

---

[95] Bicknell, V. 1, p. 148.
[96] Details can be found in James, *History*. Also in Hawes, pp. 5 & 8.

3. Early Families

with the sum."[97] *Providence's Early Records*, July 27, 1680, contain Susanna's response:

> Whereas my husband is by a providence now a Captive in Turkey & hath by a letter from himselfe late come to my hand signified that he will make over all his Estate that he hath to mr ffrances Brinley in order to procure his redemption: And ye said mr. Brinley having sent to me to meete him by my Atturney, or Agent in Boston for yt purpose. These are therefore to signifie that I Susanna Harris wife of ye sayd William Harris of Pautuxett in Providence in ye Collony of Rhode Island & Providence plantations in New England. Doe hereby Ordaine Constitute & Appoynt John Whipple of Providence (junr) my true & Lawfull Atturny on my behalfe to act doe & performe as to the prmises. And I doe by these presents fully wholy & Asolutely Juvest ye said John Whipple with as full power as myselfe, in my name, & for me to act & doe all things which may be for ye procureing of my said husband his Redemption, And what my sd Atturny shall performe as to ye prmises shall be as Authentick in Law to all intents & purposes as if I myselfe had done it in my owne person, as wittnesse my hand and Seale the fourteenth day of October in ye yeare one Thousand Six hundred & Eighty. [signed Susan Harris LS]

Apparently despite this order from Susannah, there was delay and wrangling over the amount of ransom that should be paid, and it was the state of Connecticut that finally came through (though later repaid by his relatives). Whatever the circumstances, Harris's release did not come until more than a year after his capture, by which time he was in very poor condition. En route home, Harris traveled through Spain and France to reach London, only to die three days later. His wife, Susannah, died a year after that, in 1682.

The fight over the Pawtuxet Purchase did not end

---

[97] Hawes, p. 5

with Harris' death and was not finally settled until May 1712. An old stained manuscript in Howlong's handwriting, found hidden among other papers, indicates Howlong's interest at least in 1708, when she had written a petition addressed to the "Honoured Cort Sitting at New Port on Rhod Ile land the fourth day of May 1708." Her father and husband were both dead by then and she would be just six months later. The petition suggests Howlong's concern with what was to happen to both her father's and her husband's lands. Like many of the writings of the time, it indicates how fluid spelling was—but also that Howlong was sufficiently schooled to be able to read and write.

> I am Prest in my spirit to lay before your Considerations the many Strang and Strong undermining Trancacttions acted & done by those men Called Pavtuxet men. I haue Seueral times heerd my honoured father giue a Relation of the settlement of the plantation of the Town of Prouidence I heerd my father say that himself with the other twelue agreed among themselves to lay out to every man a Share of meddow and then to cast a Lorts and so they that set to my father by lot did and they that see cause to set theire houses by their meddows and my father did setttel by his meddow Old mr William Arnold laid out my fathers meddow Old mr William Carpenter built the house for my father by my fathers meddow and my father settled down by his meddow.[98]

Harris had made a will before his last trip to England, calling himself sixty-eight at the time, and remarking upon the "great sickness and mortality that is among our neighbors (not far off), many being sick of small pox [sic] and fevers, and many being dying thereby." He also expressed his intent "if God please, to sail over the great and wide sea to England." He left his

---

[98] Information and quotes of Howlong are from Field, V. 3, p. 583.

3. Early Families 71

wife, Susanna, half of all lands, goods and cattle for life, and a third of farm, etc. of 750 acres, and a third of meadow "therto adjoining," the said third at her decease going to son Andrew. In addition, he left Andrew, immediately, another third; the remaining third to go to his daughter Howlong. There were other instructions that included fifty acres he had obtained from Thomas Borden to go to his daughter, Mary Borden.

The items listed in the inventory of William Harris's estate, appraised at £145.0.8, are interesting: a bay mare, 3 cows, 4 steers, 2 two years, 3 calves, 2 barrels summer cider, 2 barrels winter cider, firelock musket, 2 pistols, pinchers, nippers, two bibles and other books. We can only ask why the will does not mention the widow of his son, Toleration, and their one child (at least). (Toleration, himself, was killed in 1676 during the King Philip's War.) It also did not mention his daughter, Susanna, who married Ephraim Carpenter.[99]

An explanation for the absence of Susanna's name *could*, as unlikely as it seems, lie in a story told by Field that this writer has been unable to find any evidence for and Field says nothing of his source. Field tells of a Thomas Roberts who was taken into the home of Roger Williams and tenderly nursed and cared for by Mrs. Willliams after he came to Providence from Massachusetts "sick and destitute, being wounded during the Pequot war [1637]." Field goes on to say that "after his recovery he took up residence in the town *and married the daughter of William Harris* [writer's italics]." There seems a slight possibility that this was a second marriage of Susanna, which, if true (not noted in the genealogy), the connection with Roger Williams might sufficiently have angered Harris to have caused him to exclude her from his will. "Roberts died in Newport in 1676, to

---

[99] See Austin, p. 126.

which place he had fled for safety during Indian hostilities,"[100] and early Providence records indicate he died intestate. The record then mentions a brother, but no wife.[101] It cannot be ruled out that Susanna was not mentioned in her father's will because she had died by then. The Harris genealogies also record no other Harris daughter marrying a Thomas Roberts.

Howlong's unusually generous bequest in her father's will of a third of his land suggests she may always have shown an interest in his fight with Roger Williams over the Pawtuxet boundaries which would have greatly pleased him. As Ulrich puts it, the general custom was "land for sons, movables for daughters, and for widows a carefully defined dependency."[102] Wives often discovered their husband's "worth" only after his death when all their property was itemized and valued, and all their debts listed and paid off.[103]

The Harrises had five children—Andrew, Mary, Susannah, Howlong and Toleration—who eventually gave their parents, Susanna and William Harris, sixteen grandchildren and about fifty great-grandchildren.

★★★

The Olneys were another of Providence's early families. In 1635, Marie (Mary) Ashton[104] and Thomas Olney, Sr., originally from Hertfordshire, England, came on the ship *Planter* to Boston, Massachusetts. They had with them two young children: Thomas, Jr., three, and Epenetus. Before moving on to Providence in 1638, Mary and Thomas had another child who "died

---

[100] Field, V. 3, p. 590
[101] Early Records, V. 6, p. 7.
[102] Ulrich, p. 148.
[103] Norton, *Liberty's Daughters*, p. 6.
[104] Many of the histories name his wife as Mary Small but the Olney genealogies have it corrected to Marie Ashton.

3. Early Families

young." After their move, Mary bore three more sons: Nebadiah (who also "died young"), Stephen, who never married and James who had no children. Their two daughters were Mary, who married John Whipple, Jr., son of Capt. John Whipple; and Lydia, who married Joseph Williams, son of Roger and Mary Williams.

The fact that the family had belonged to the same Salem church as Roger Williams probably accounts for the family being amongst the original thirteen who received land grants, as well as the fact that Thomas quickly became one of a small group that established the Baptist Church. Thomas Olney, skilled as a shoemaker, tanner and surveyor of some experience, quickly proved his value to the new town. He died about 1682, at age eighty-two; the date of Mary Olney's death is not stated. In addition to the Williamses and Whipples, future generations saw marriages to the Browns, Watermans, Winsors and Angells, among others.

In 1659 Thomas established his son, Epenetus and his daughter-in-law, Mary Whipple, the daughter of an innkeeper, in a house adjoining his and next door to that of Gregory Dexter, Pastor of the Baptist Society of Providence. There they established the Olney Tavern that would soon become intertwined with Providence's history; a place where religious and political influences would happily converge. The tavern's traditions were continued by their son, James and his wife Hallelujah Brown, and then by *their* son, Joseph (1706-1777) under whom it became the site of the many festivities that made it famous. (More will be said of this tavern later.)

Earlier, during her youth, Joseph's sister, Mary (1704-1756), had frequently helped out her mother, Hallelujah, in running the tavern and was regarded as "a very attractive feature in the life about the tavern"—

and, especially so to the young Arthur Fenner (the 3rd), son of Major Thomas Fenner. He liked to recall his trips in from Cranston, where he lived, to court her prior to their marriage on June 21, 1723. Though Arthur lived to an old age, he proved to be sickly for many years and unable to do business. So while raising their six daughters and six sons, Mary not only ran his business but also continued her involvement with the Olney Inn. She was consistently regarded by her peers as "one of the smart and active women of her time. She was a merchant and owned more navigation than any other person then in town. [She] acquired the estate, kept a store and maintained the family in affluence".[105]

Given her achievements, it is hard to understand how she could have been ignored by so many historians in recounting Providence's turn from farm to sea. The primary reference to any Fenner seems to be to the Arthur Fenner, not Mary's husband, as being amongst those early-on granted permits for a wharf.

✯✯✯

The untimely death in June 1760 of another of the Olney women, Rachel,[106] is responsible for leaving us with an interesting coroner's report (an enlarged copy of the original attached). Signed by twelve of Providence's leading citizens, it concludes that her death was a accident; that she was "riding in a cart and by an accident sliped out of the cart and the whele run over her body which was the cause of her death."

---

[105] See Chace notes (RIHS manuscripts) & Olney Genealogy, p.20.
[106] Writer could not locate Rachel in any of the Olney genealogies at the Historical Society, so her relationship to the other Olneys could not be determined. Document is an RIHS manuscript.

3. Early Families

we the subscribers being Empanaled as a Jurey to
make Inquirey how and by what means Rachel
Olney late of providence widow came by her Death
whose body now lies
Dead before us this 24th. Day of June AD 1760
and having Enspected into the premises are
of Oppinion that she the S'd Rachel was in this
present Day Riding in a Cart and by an actident
Sliped out of S'd Cart and the wheele Run over
her body which was the Cause of her Death

John Jencks
Dan'l Mowry jun'r
Stephen Sly
David Whipple
[illegible]
Jeremiah Angel
Cap't Spalding
Jeremiah Arnold jun'r
Amos Arnold
John Dexter
Benj'a Slocum
Benjamin Arnold

4. Antinomians & Quakers

Returning to another of Providence's early settlers: Catharine Marbury and her husband, Richard Scott, a shoemaker. They came to Providence early in 1637 after encountering the same sort of religious conflicts with the Puritans that had brought Roger Williams and so many others there. It is curious, therefore, that they were not included in the original allocation of home lots, receiving theirs only after Williams made fifty-four additional allocations in December 1661. The Scotts also drew a lot in February 1665 when the common lands east of the seven mile line were divided.

Their exclusion from the original allocation is especially hard to understand since the Scotts and Williamses clearly were friends initially; Richard Scott exclaiming, "I walked with [Roger] in the Baptist Way about three or four months." Catharine Scott, for her part, persuaded him to join the Antinomians (meaning "against the law") and be rebaptized. A rebaptism was thought necessary to formally sever one's ties to the Bay Colony church since all who came from there were, technically, still members. Roger, like Catharine, was attracted to the tenets of the faith—separation of church and state, and opposition to the taking of oaths and the bearing of arms—and began holding frequent religious services in his home.

As we shall see in the following, this riled Joshua Verin after his wife, Mary, joined the Antinomians; he felt she was too much away from home. And, at least by some accounts, the result was America's first reprimand of a husband for wife abuse.

☆☆☆

Based on an account, after the fact, by Governor Winthrop who corresponded regularly with Roger

4. Antinomians & Quakers 77

Williams, on May 21, 1637 Joshua Verin was censured by formal vote of his townsmen for "endangering his wife" Mary by virtue of denying her the right to attend religious services with the frequency required (some say only by Roger Williams). At the spirited court hearing, William Arnold pointed out that Williams had declared that in Rhode Island no man would be molested for his conscience, but added that this did not apply to wives and children because this would be a breach of God's law that subjected them to the will of their husbands/fathers (a commonly held belief at the time).

Mr. Greene, seemingly more enlightened on the subject of women's rights, declared that if they should so restrain wives, "all the women in the country would cry out of them." Others in attendance were of the opinion that "if Verin would not suffer his wife to have her libertie, the church should dispose her to some other man, who would use her better." Arnold concluded that whatever Verin did, he did out of conscience and no man should be censured for his conscience. In the end, it was decided that Joshua Verin had breached a covenant for restraining "the libertie of conscience," and consequently should "be withheld from the libertie of voting till he shall declare the contrarie."[107]

At the time, Verin owned property next door to Williams on Towne Street (the site of the present Church Street), one hundred acres of land in total, and was a voting member of the Towne. Some continued to claim that Verin's "right to conscience" was being breached just because Verin did not want himself or his wife to attend religious services. On May 22nd, just after the censure vote, Roger Williams wrote to Governor Winthrop suggesting that he felt the issue was abuse, not religion.

---

[107] *Records of the Colony,* Bartlett, pp. 16-17

Sir, we have bene long afflicted by a young man, boysterous & desperate, Philip Verin's sonn of Salem, who, as he hath refused to heare the word with us this twelve month, so because he could not draw his wife, a gracious and modest woman, to the same ungodliness with him, he hath troden her under foote tyranically & brutishly; wch she and we long bearing, though with his furious blows she went in danger of life, at the last the major vote of us discard him from our civil freedom, or disfranchize, &c.; he will have justice (as he clamours) at other courts; I wish he might, for a foule & slanderous & brutish carriage, wch God hath delivered hm up unto; he will hale his wife with ropes to Salem, where she must needes be troubled & troublesome as differences yet stand. She is willing to stay & live with him or elsewhere, where she may not offend &c. I shall humbly request that this item be accepted & he no way countenanced until (if need be) I further trouble you.

One can only wonder what Mary was experiencing during this time and during the changes of faith of her husband. Did she remain a Baptist through all of Roger's conversions? Was she ever rebaptized as he was? Did Roger expect Mary to attend church more frequently than she may have wished; potentially as abusive as Verin's denial of attendance by his wife? Did Roger want Mary to stop attending Baptist services after he stopped? Judging by Mary's defiance of Roger's wishes regarding their religious observances while they were still in Salem, she probably, again, made up her own mind when these issues arose.

As for Verin, whatever the explanation of his appearance before the town and their reprimand, rather than comply with the terms of his censure, shortly after the court's verdict, "clamoring for justice," he left Providence and returned to Salem where his father and brother had remained and were now

4. Antinomians & Quakers

counted among it leading citizens. In 1650, Verin wrote the town [Providence] demanding compensation for the home lot and other property that was his, but there is no indication he ever collected. The records give no indication that he ever returned to present his case in person, as the town said he must do to make a valid claim.[108]

As for Verin's wife, she went with him when he left Providence, either because she felt she had no choice or because she had not found her husband's behavior sufficiently reprehensible to merit leaving him. Nonetheless, it must have been disturbing for her when her husband tried to keep her from church. Church was the one place where, despite not being allowed any say in its governance, wives could earn membership, whatever their social status, and hear sermons supporting "their guardianship of sexual mores, elevating charity over commerce and neighborliness over trade."[109] It was also a place where they could meet and socialize with their neighbors.

Even after settlements spread to Bristol, Rehoboth, Attleboro, Smithfield and Pawtuxet, the farmers and their wives would come in to Sunday services and town meetings. This Sunday ride or walk to and from the meetings was the one way both the men and women had, with their farms scattered one and two miles apart, to become better acquainted with each other and to keep up their fund of information about their neighbors.

Further, town meeting days also became shopping days. "Crafty traders" would circulate handbills "making a bid for the handiwork of the housewife and adroitly calling their attention to those goods that

---

[108] From Kimball, pp. 26-27, Conley, *Liberty...*, p. 60 & Bicknell, V.1, pp. 201-202.
[109] Ulrich, p. 216

would excite the curiosity of the farmer's wives as to the condition of their wardrobe."

> The traders took it for granted the farmers themselves would take a holiday from farm work, and accompany the women folks to see if they could not obtain some hardware for the farm or a new gun or wig for themselves.
>
> The merchants on these occasions engaged one or more rooms at the tavern and while tea was served in the room, a bowl of punch was in the other and there was trading outside of the house as well as inside. The merchants had a variety of goods wanted by the farmer's wives, from a bottle of snuff to a warming pan, and they would take anything from the farm in exchange. [110]

✯✯✯

For their part, both Catharine Scott and Roger Williams soon left the Antinomians, he becoming a Seeker, not wanting to be constricted by *any* creed's limitations; the Scotts becoming Providence's first Quakers. This undoubtedly marked the end of their friendship since Roger regarded the Quaker religion an abomination and heresy. This might at first seem out of character since Williams was a radical when it came to religious freedom, but when it came to civil government he was a conservative traditionalist and quite authoritarian. He firmly believed in the separation of church and state.

Williams feared the Quakers' "independence and antagonism toward rules and regulations, accepted willingly by the general public," would lead them to become subversive of all civil authority. This had become increasingly important as the town of Providence grew, since it did not have a single unifying religion to bind its inhabitants as did its neighboring

---

[110] From Chace notes regarding the farmers and their wives (RIHS manuscripts).

4. Antinomians & Quakers

colonies.

> Williams began tackling [this] problem in 1638 by means rather like a social contract. He set aside some land for the original settlers, the Pawtuxet reservation, in order to lessen [the original settlers] reluctance to admit later refugees from persecution. After that the town required newcomers, whether married men or single, to promise obedience to town rules before they could take up residence, vote, or obtain a share of the community's remaining land. In 1640 the system was refined into the Combination, a compact to be signed by all who wanted a voice in town meeting. (*A couple of women signed, but it is unlikely that they got the vote.*)[111]

Despite Williams' dislike and distrust of the Quakers, they were never persecuted in Rhode Island; quite the contrary. In 1657, when the Commissioners of the United Colonies wrote to Rhode Island asking that they banish the Quakers, the General Assembly immediately replied: "We have no law among us whereby to punish any for only declaring by words their minds concerning the things and ways of God." Consequently, the Quakers came to this colony in increasing numbers, and as their numbers increased became quite prominent in civic affairs.

Rhode Island's 1663 Charter pointedly gave Rhode Island something no other colony had—religious freedom—while at the same time it protected the state's right to punish those disturbing the "civil peace"—a clause that perhaps tempered Williams' concern about the Quakers.

> That our royal will and pleasure is, that no person within the said colony, at any time hereafter, shall be any wise molested, punished, disquieted, or called in question, for difference in opinion in matters of religion, [that] do not

---

[111] This and subsequent quote from James, *History*, p. 55.

actually disturb the civil peace of our said colony; but that all and every person and persons may, from time to time, and at all times hereafter, freely and fully have and enjoy his and their own judgments and consciences in matters of religious concernments.[112]

★★★

Rhode Island's tolerance, however, did not mean that all its Quakers would escape persecution, as we shall see in the case of Anne Marbury Hutchinson, her sister, Catharine Marbury Scott, and their mutual friend, Mary Dyer.

Few seem to be aware of the fact that Catharine was the youngest sister of the better-known Anne, and nearly as strong-willed in support of her religious beliefs. That both sisters should be such staunch and radical religious believers is not surprising since their father, Rev. Francis Marbury, was a "vigorously dissenting minister, a man so contentious that his bishop declared in a rage that he was 'a verie Asse, an idiot, and a foole...By my troth....I thinke he be mad, he careth for no bodie.'"[113]

Anne was the third and Catharine the last of fifteen children by Francis Marbury's second wife, Bridget Dryden. Bridget was the sister of Sir Erasmus Dryden, grandfather of the poet John Dryden. Catharine never really knew her father who died in 1610/11, about the time she was born. In addition to Bridget's fifteen children, there were three others in the household birthed by Francis's first wife, Elizabeth Moore. We know nothing of the childhood of these eighteen children, nor anything of them besides Anne and Catharine.

---

[112] Quoted in Conley, *Liberty*...,p. 26.
[113] Smith, p. 39. She is quoting from John Winthrop's journal..

4. Antinomians & Quakers

We do know that when Catharine wrote "John Winthrop, Jr., governere at Harvard in New Inglesland," on April 17, 1658, [114] she was a Quaker and her crusading zeal was apparent. Her letter indicates that "I have writ to thee before," but she does not know if it was received. She declares that she writes

> out of true love and pity to thee, that thou maiest be free, and not trobled, as I have heard thy father was, upon his death bed, at the banishment of my deare sister Hutchinson and others. I am sure they have a sad cup to drink, that are drunke with the blod of the saints: O my friend, as thou lovest the prosperity of thy soull and the good of thy posterity, taike heed of having thy hand, or hart or tounge lifted up against these persons that the wise yet follish world in scorn calls quaikers; for they are the messengers of the Lord of Hosts, wch he hath in his large love and pity sent into this parts, to gather together his outcasts and the distressed of the children of Israell; and they shall accomplish the worke, let the rage of men be never see great: taike heed of hindering of them, for noo weapen formed against them shall prosper. It is given to them not onely to believe, but to sufer, &c., but woo to them by whom they sufer.
>
> O my friend, try all things and waiy it by the balance of the sanctuary: how can you try without hearing of them? For the eare tries words as the mouth tasts meat. I dare not but beare witnese against the unjust and cruell lawes of my countrymen in this land: for cursed are all they that cometh not out to help the Lord against the mighty: and all that are not with him are against him, &c,. Woo be to ym that gather and not by him, & cover with a covering and not with his spirit, wch woo I desire thou maiest escape.

Catharine was described as "of unblamable conversation, a grave, sober, ancient woman of good breeding;" her sister, Anne, as a woman "of fiery spirit

---

[114] Quote of letter that follows found in Clark, Bertha W. (typed carbon, p.10: listed under "Genealogies")

with remarkable confidence and self-assurance;" Anne's husband, William Hutchinson, as "'of very mild temper and weak parts...wholly guided by his wife,' who confessed himself to be 'more nearly tied to his wife than to the Church.'" However, his "'parts' were not so weak but that he was able to sire fifteen children by Anne" (the same number her mother had).[115] Considerably older than her sister, Anne's story comes first; Catharine's and Mary Dyer's come later, intertwined with that of Christopher Holder.

☆☆☆

Anne Hutchinson, a follower of the Rev. John Cotton's preaching in England, came to Boston on the *Griffin* in 1634 with her husband and their children, after Rev. Cotton had left because of religious persecution. She had married William Hutchinson, a well-off merchant, in 1621 when she was twenty-one years old, and he had acceded to her desire to move to America, regarding his wife as "a dear saint and servant of God." For the next three years after their arrival in Boston, the Hutchinsons lived across the street from John Winthrop. During that time, Anne was quite popular as a trained mid-wife/nurse, and generally thought highly of'.

As she went house to house attending the women, Anne gradually gathered a following who looked up to her for leadership, and, largely at their insistence, started holding weekly religious services in her home. The clerics, initially, did not frown upon these meetings, even as the numbers of women attending grew to as many as fifty or sixty. They included Mary

---

[115] Smith, p. 39. Other sources put the number of children at 11 and at 12; perhaps some counting children who died at birth or early-on, and others not.

4. Antinomians & Quakers

Dyer who was later described as "notoriously infected with her [Anne's] errors."[116] With no men in attendance at the meetings, it took some time for them to become aware of just what Anne was preaching at her meetings. But gradually, as word seeped out of her controversial interpretation of the Bible, Boston's religious leaders came to regard Anne as a threat to the community, calling her an "American Jesabel," who used "skill and cunning" to win over followers.[117]

At first the attack on Anne came obliquely with an attack on her brother-in-law, John Wheelwright, who overtly supported her and himself delivered what the clerics called "incendiary sermons." Despite two separate petitions to the court on his behalf, signed by as many as forty of the town's leading citizens, the civil court found him guilty of spreading seditious doctrines, his sermons called "manifest heresie" and "notorious blasphemy." When he refused to change his ways, he was disfranchised and banished.

Despite the court's repeated warnings to Anne to change her ways, she refused. Thus it was that on November 7, 1637 she went on trial, charged with "traduceing the mi[niste]rs & their ministry in this country." The trial last several days as Anne vigorously defended herself, but the official record describes it briefly thus:

> "Shee declared volentarily her revelations for her ground, & that shee should bee delivered & the Court ruined, with their posterity, & there upon was banished."

It was Governor Winthrop who ordered her "banished from out of our jurisdiction as being a

---

[116] Haley, Old Stone Bank, Vol. II, p. 23
[117] Despription of Anne's trials that follows, including quoted descriptive phrases, and quotes by Rev. Cotton and from the public record, can be found in Norton, *Founding Mothers*....,pp. 361-397.

woman not fit for our society." But since it was then mid-winter, they did not actually expel her untill the following Spring.

In March 1638, at a time when she was not entirely well and was less able to put up an energetic defense, Anne additionally faced a church trial. This presumably was to decide whether her church membership should be nullified.

There had been a sexual overtone even during the civil trial, but they became even more distinct during this trial. There was a manifest fear that a "community of women" would lead to adulterous behavior, or worse, Lesbianism (though the word itself was never used). The Rev. Thomas Shepard declared:

> "She is of a most dayngerous spirit and likely with her fluent Tounge and forwardnes in Expressions to seduce and draw away many, Especially simple Weomen of her owne sex."

In the end, Rev. John Wilson gave the final verdict:

> "From this time forth to be a Hethen and a Publican and soe to be held of all the Bretheren and Sisters of this Congregation."

Later, Anne's judges felt it was proof from God that they were right in having banished her when they learned that her follower, Mary Dyer, had suffered a still birth with Anne in attendance, and then she herself suffered the same. Rumors persisted that the babies had been "deformed monsters."

Seventeen of those who had signed the petition of support for John Wheelwright were also "disfranchised and disarmed." Included amongst them were Phillip Sherman, who had left the Congregational Church and later became a Quaker; William Dyer whose family had

4. Antinomians & Quakers 87

become close friends with the Hutchinsons soon after their arrival in Boston; William Hutchinson, her husband; John Clarke, a recent arrival who had supported Anne all during her trial; William Aspinwall, John Underhill and John Wheelwright himself. The latter three, unlike the others, eventually became reconciled with the Massachusetts government and returned there. Meanwhile, taking advantage of the time allowed them by the courts before their forced departure from Boston, a number of the petition-signers met at William Coddington's house.

There, John Clarke wrote for them the "Portsmouth Compact" that laid out freedom of worship as the cornerstone for governing their new settlement. Later, in Aquidneck, Sherman, another of those present, an educated man and skillful penman, showed himself to be a man of "intelligence, wealth, and influence, and [was] frequently consulted by those in authority."[118] This group's foresight in laying out a government in advance was quite unlike Williams and his group who made no such plans for a new settlement before their departure from the Bay colony. In general, this group was better educated than the men who had left with Roger Williams. Also, unlike Williams who had left in great haste, they had time to prepare for the move.

After leaving Boston, the Hutchinson group of eighteen or so first stopped in Providence and won Williams' support. Roger liked Anne, even though not entirely in agreement with her religious views, and extended to her his belief that "all had a right to speak when they chose and say what they wished. 'Because, if it be a lie, it will die; and if it be true, we ought to know it.'"[119]

---

[118] *Genealogies*, V. 1, p. 787.
[119] Haley, Old Stone Bank, Vol. II, p. 22.

At the same time in March 1638 that Williams got his written deed from Canonicus and Miantinomi, already discussed, he helped the Hutchinson group, headed by Coddington, to obtain theirs. For 40 fathoms of white 'wompi' beads, they received the island of Aquidneck with its surrounding marshland and grasses all the way from Portsmouth at the northern end (where they first established their homes) to Jamestown at the southern. It may have been the group's request for Williams' help with the Indians that had prompted him to seek his deed.

A year later, dissension among the founding group on Aquidneck led to the departure of the Dyers, Clarkes, Coddingtons and a number of other families for the southern end where they settled Newport. After a period of rivalry between the two settlements, they agreed in March 1640 to reunite.

Even during the time they had lived in separate settlements, Anne Hutchinson and Mary Dyer remained close friends, continued to visit each other, and continued to share the same religious beliefs that had prompted Mary to boldly "walk out with Anne, in the presence of the whole congregation, when the Boston Church had first cast Anne out." [120]

After her husband died in 1642, Anne left with her servants and the youngest eight of her children. Some say she just wanted a change, but Randall Holden suggested she moved because she feared that even in Rhode Island, she might not be able to avoid persecution by "vengeful Bay authorities."[121] She went first to Long Island and then to Pelham Bay, a thriving and prosperous community. Unfortunately, however, this settlement was on ancient Indian land, and the Indians had expressed their intention of killing all the

---

[120] *Genealogies*, V. 1, p. 287.
[121] Norton, *Founding Mothers...*, p. 397.

4. Antinomians & Quakers

white settlers on it. And so it was that on an August morning in 1643, Indians suddenly emerged from the woods, hatchets raised, and started butchering Anne (then 52 years old), her children and her servants. Seeing the flames from Anne's burning house and hearing the screams, neighbors left by boat. When they later returned, they found only charred bodies.

Anne's eight year old daughter, Susanna, out picking blueberries at the time, luckily escaped the carnage, but was captured by the Indians and lived with them for some three years, before being ransomed by the Dutch at Albany and returned to friends in Boston. In December 1651 she married John Cole, the only son of Samuel Cole the innkeeper. Father and son had come here from England while John was still a child. [There is no mention of his mother.] John and Susanna (who bore eight children) moved from Boston to Narragansett country in 1664.[122]

Some blamed the Bay Colony's General Court for Anne Hutchinson's death, others celebrated, feeling she got what she deserved. Thomas Welde expressed this opinion in his book, *A Short Story of the Rise, Wane and Ruin of the Antinomians* (1644):

> I never heard that the Indians in these parts did ever before commit the like outrage upon any one family, or families; and therefore God's hand is the more apparently seen herein, to pick out this woful woman, to make her and those belonging to her an unheard of heavy example of their cruelty above others.[123]

In Providence, Anne's long-time friend, Mary Dyer, determined to continue carrying her message to the world, conducted a service for Anne at her sister Catharine's home. Four of Anne's five remaining

---

[122] Account found in Cole, pp. 83-84 & Plimpton, pp. 97-98
[123] Quoted in Holliday, p. 47.

children, the only ones who had escaped the carnage by their absence from New York, attended. (Susannah was then still a captive of the Pequot Indians.) One of the children, Edward, served in King Philip's War, was wounded, and died August 19, 1675. His daughter, Anne, later married Samuel Dyer, son of Mary and William Dyer.

✮✮✮

As for Mary Dyer, throughout her life she did hold firmly and fearlessly to religious beliefs she had first heard boldly expressed by Anne at the meetings in her home. In effect, Richman, in his history, blames Anne for Mary's self-destructive behavior. He states that "under Anne Hutchinson, her preciptress, Mary became so infatuated an individualist, so relentless a challenger of theocratic pretensions, that she can hardly be regarded as possessed of perfect balance." [124]

Maria (Mary) Barrett, born in 1610/11, married William Dyer on October 16, 1633 at St.-Martin's-in-the-Field in London and came to America with him soon after. William, born in 1609, had been a milliner in London's New Exchange when he and Mary married. Little is said of what he did after they emigrated.

The Dutch writer Gerald Croese described Mary as "a person of no mean extraction and parentage, of an estate pretty plentiful, of a comely stature and countenance, of a piercing knowledge in many things, of a wonderfully sweet and pleasant disposition, so fit for great affairs that she wanted nothing that was manly except only the name and sex."[125] She was also described as "comely of stature and countenance, of a piercing knowledge, of a wonderful sweet and pleasant

---

[124] Richman, p. 43.
[125] Haley, Old Stone Bank, Vol. II, p. 23.

4. Antinomians & Quakers

discourse."[126]

These descriptions help very little in trying to understand why Mary suddenly left her husband and six children (Charles, less than a year old) and returned to England, mid-winter 1650, the most perilous time of year for such a trip. Impulsiveness and homesickness seem inadequate explanations. That she had just weaned Charles and felt it a good time for a break from domesticity does not seem much more compelling. A lengthy, very colorful political explanation can be found in the appendix of William Allan Dyer's *A Dyer Genealogical Record.*[127] Briefly it claims that Mary was of royal blood, in line for the English throne, and suggests she may have known this and precipitously decided, on her own, to go to England, after she heard that King Charles I had just died. [*Could Mary's son, Charles, have been named after this King?*] Alternatively, this account suggests she may have heard of his death from friends in England who urged her to come quickly. Even though we know little of Mary's first year in England, it is a story any English historian would have trouble giving any credence.

The first we know of Mary in England was her fascination with the *Seekers*, headed by George Fox. This was a small group of independents who believed the Christian church had lost its way and thus rejected the regularly constituted churches. They believed no person was authorized to administer any church ordinance, and were seeking the coming of the "Great Head." Meanwhile they claimed religious liberty and sought revelations as to the true church, ministry

---

[126] Chapin, Sketch 27.
[127] For a full account of this explanation, see the Appendix in Dyer, William Allan.

and sacraments.

When Fox, soon after, formed the more lasting Quakers, Mary, like many of the Seekers, followed him. It must have had an especial appeal to strong-willed, independent women like Mary Dyer, Catharine Scott and her sister, Anne Hutchinson, because it was the only faith that, from the beginning, recognized women in the ministry, and, in general, gave them an equal part with the men. Mary was determined to meet Fox, its founder, in person before returning to America.

Mary had been in England for seven years when she finally succeeded. And it was January or February 1657 when she finally set sail for home, possibly unaware of Massachusetts' punitive laws against the Quakers. She was still in England in July 1656 when the Friends first appeared in New England, brought to Boston from Barbados by two females. This event gave rise to the first of a long succession of cruel and sanguinary laws against them in the province of Massachusetts, and in all the colonies in New England, excepting only the colony of Rhode Island.[128] No explanation has been forthcoming to explain exactly how the authorities knew of Mary's beliefs, but, in any case, as soon as she stepped off the ship, she was arrested and jailed, along with a friend, Anne Burden, who was coming to America to settle up her deceased husband's estate. Somehow Mary's reputation must have preceded her: "her apparent character and vigorous expression of the same, no doubt caused her [then, and later], to be looked upon as a formidable opponent of the orthodox Puritans."[129]

For two and a half months after their arrest, Mary and Anne Burden "remained incommunicado in their darkened cells with boarded up windows....[Mary] had

---

[128] Staples, *Annals*, p. 420.
[129] *Genealogies*, V. 1, p. 287.

4. Antinomians & Quakers 93

never known such darkness, dampness, and chill....Every night as [she] lay on the prickly straw bedding, she wondered how she was going to get word to William of her whereabouts. She was finally able to slip a letter out through a crack to someone outside the jail. It took a long time for the letter to reach William Dyer in Newport."[130]

When the letter finally did arrive, Mary's surprisingly faithful and forever supportive husband, promptly showed up in Governor Endicott's office and succeeded in persuading him to release her after posting a bond and agreeing, on his honor, "not to lodge her in any town of the colony nor to permit any to have speech with her on the journey." Massachusetts ordered that Mary never again return. [Nothing more is said of what happened to Anne Burden.]

After an absence of seven years, Mary Dyer discovered the family's farm, and her children, had both grown enormously. Samuel was twenty-two, already married to Anne Hutchinson, the daughter of Captain Edward Hutchinson and Catherine Hamby; granddaughter of her beloved friend, Anne Hutchinson. Mary's daughter, Mary, was seventeen, Will, sixteen, Maher, eleven, Henry, nine, and Charles, seven.[131]

Mary Dyer was at once restless, unable again to assume a motherly-housewifery role and to remain silent as the court demanded. She felt her family had done well without her during her years in England; her children had not suffered even while their father was also away (suggesting they must have had excellent domestic help or relatives who cared for the children). As for William, he must have loved Mary very much to have been (and continue to be) so tolerant of her neglect.

---

[130] Plimpton, pp. 137-138
[131] Listed, with no other information, in *Genealogies*, V. 2, p. 560 & *A Dyer Genealogy Record*.

Many men then (and even now) obtained divorces on lesser grounds than a seven-year abandonment of a wife's "rightful duties". Mary appreciated her husband as the remarkable man he was and knew she could depend on him again if she resumed her protests of Massachusetts' treatment of Quakers. Their relationship was certainly unique as he, apparently, right to the end continued to love and respect Mary.

And so it was when Mary heard in September 1659 that a number of her friends, including Christopher Holder of Providence, were again in prison in Boston, she refused to maintain the silence Massachusetts had demanded of her; she was determined to visit Boston once more to protest.

☆☆☆

As for Christopher Holder, his actions were not only about to lead Mary Dyer once more into trouble with Massachusetts, but, earlier, they had similarly led Catharine Scott and her children into trouble. Holder was an educated, well-off man, a convert to Quakerism in its earliest days. In August 1656, at age twenty-five, he had come to Boston from Gravesend, England with seven others, all eager to spread their religious views. Their arrival came only a few days after women missionaries (presumably the two Barbados women mentioned previously) had been driven out of town. Before the Holder group were allowed to disembark, "officers of the colony had come aboard and searched their boxes for 'erroneous books and hellish pamphlets.' Then they were thrown into a foul prison, kept there for eleven weeks, their personal belongings being appropriated by the jailer for his fees, and after this sent back to England on the *Speedwell*, which had

4. Antinomians & Quakers 95

brought them." [132] They had trouble returning because heavy fines were then being imposed on all ships transporting Quakers.

Finally, in June 1657, Holder succeeded in persuading the captain of the *Woodhouse*, built by a Quaker, to transport him back to America. Again he was arrested by the Massachusetts' authorities and banished to Rhode Island, but September found him back in Salem. He was attempting to preach at a regular church service, when he was "haled back by the hair of his head and a glove and handkerchief thrust into his mouth." Undeterred, the next day Holder proceeded on to Boston where he was again arrested and given thirty stripes to be administered all at once by the hangman with a knotted whip; the hangman "fetching his stokes with the greatest strength and advantage he could, to cut the flesh and to put them to suffering...the cruelty of which was so great, that a woman, seeing it, fell down as dead."

> The stocks and the pillory, stripes at the whipping-post or at the tail of an ox-cart, fines and imprisonment, branding and mutilation, banishment and death upon the gallows, were meted out with shocking barbarity to unresisting victims, who exhibited a constancy and a heroism in suffering never surpassed in the history of the world. Many were imprisoned, some for years. Some were reduced from comfort to penury by the fines imposed upon them. Some had their ears cut off, and the law provided for boring the tongue through with a hot iron. Two were ordered to be sold into slavery to pay their fines, and large numbers were mercilessly whipped. Neither age nor sex was spared. [133]

---

[132] See Clark, Bertha account for quotes and the information about Holder (6typed pages).
[133] Rogers, pp. 4-6.

BE031231 "Whipping Quakers in Streets," ©Bettmann/CORBIS

Following Holder's whipping, he spent nine weeks in an unheated jail during the cold winter season. He had no bed or straw, and for the first three days no food. Despite the conditions, Holder managed to write and get circulated a "Declaration of Faith" that so

4. Antinomians & Quakers

angered the authorities that they ordered he be whipped twice a week, beginning with thirty lashes, three more to be added each week, each stroke drawing blood. He had received 357 lashes before he was finally, near the end of November, released with the warning

> that if he and his friends "attempted to preach there again their tongues would be bored through with hot irons."

Holder was then put on a ship to be returned to England, but 1658 saw him back in Barbados and the islands where Quakerism was spreading rapidly; then back in Sandwich, Massachusetts where he was again arrested and suffered thirty-three lashes before again being banished to Providence where he found refuge with Richard and Catharine Scott—and presumably became enamored of their daughter, Mary, whom he would subsequently marry. It is probably about this time in 1658 that Catharine wrote the letter to Winthrop quoted earlier. Another letter "to the Honnored General Courte now Assembled at Boston," dated July 12, 1658, was from "the humble Edward Hutchinson," Catharine's nephew. This suggests that it was during this time that Catharine was arrested and held in prison for a time. The letter reads:

> That whereas yer petitioner had an Aunte came into this jurisdiction who was Apprehended as a Quaker and dealt with accordingly, and abiding in the house of correction for not paiment of her fees: The courte I supose can not but apprhend it no smal trouble to me to have her abide there for ye not paiment of a smal some, I tould her I would pay it rather than she should ther Abide, but she refuseing to goo out if I should doe soo, neither was she wiling to goo without the three Quakers in prison, I was forced to deposit for al these ffees in Mr. Rawons hand, upon his condition that if this court did judge these fees due by law wch was demanded ...then there the keepr might have it, but if this court judge them not due then to be returned to me.

> Yer petitioner therefore humbly prayes this Honrd Court to pass these laws wch concerne the house of Correction together with the first law in the first books and give yer resolution herein, and I hope I shal be wilingly satisfied with your resolution, and for ever owne my selfe to be bounde to prayer.

A note on the side suggests they approved the fees and her release. However, persecutions did not stop, but became even more widespread. Despite this, even while staying with the Scotts, Holder continued preaching in Rhode Island and at various places in the Massachusetts Colony, sometimes making converts, sometimes being arrested. After one of these arrests, Holder had an ear cut off as punishment. Catharine Scott became infuriated on hearing of it, and, with her daughter, Patience, then eleven, went to Boston to comfort him, only to be arrested themselves.

> When Patience was brought to trial, The Court duly considering the malice of Satan and his instruments by all means and ways to propagate error, and disturb the truth and bring in confusion among us, that Satan is put to his shifts to mke use of such a child, not being of the years of discretion, nor understanding the principles of religion, judge meet so far to slight her as a Quaker, as only to admonish and instruct her according to her capacity and so discharge her to Captain Hutchinson [Patience's first cousin] undertaking to send her home...[At her trial] some of ye confest that ye had many children, and that they had been well educated, and that it were well if they could say half as much for God as she could for the Devil....It was mid-September when the child was taken home.[134]

As for Catharine, she was committed to Prison and given "Ten Cruel Stripes with a three-fold-corded-knotted-Whip, with that Cruelty in the Execution, as

---

[134] See "Richard Scott and his Pedigree", p. 14. Also, Clark, "Scotts", p. 14.

4. Antinomians & Quakers   99

to others, on the second Day of the eighth Month, 1658." It did not seem to matter at her trial when some stressed, in an attempt to help her, that "some of you knew her Father, and called him Mr. Marbury."[135] Nor had it helped when others pointed out that "she had been well-bred and had so lived;" that she had been married for twenty years and was "the Mother of many children."[136] Moreover, Governor John Endicott warned her *that ye were likely to have a Law to Hang her, if she came thither again.*" To which Catharine answered: "*If God call us, woe be to us, if we come not; And I question not, but he whom we love, will make us not to count our Lives dear unto ourselfes for the sake of his Name.*" He then said: "And we shall be as ready to take away your Lives, as ye shall be to lay them down."[137]

> One historian noted, "The whip used for these cruel Executions is not of whip cord as in England, but of dryed Guts, such as the Base of Viols, with three knots at the end, which many times the hangman lays on with both his hands, and must need be of most violent torture and exercise of the Body."[138]

It is hard to imagine the commitment these people must have had to their religion. Imprisonment, whippings, dismemberments and threats only seemed to induce more Quakers to flaunt Boston's laws. By early October, seventeen more Quakers could be found in the Boston jail, amongst them, again, "Holder, the mutilated." Fortunately for them, the Court was hesitant to hang them all. And so it was

---

[135] Her father was "the Rev. Francis Marbury of London, and her mother was a sister of Sir Erasmus Dryden, Bart., grandfather of John Dryden the poet." Rogers, p. 12.
[136] Catharine had four daughters and a son.
[137] Rogers, pp. 10-11.
[138] Peckham, p. 171

that Mary Dyer would once more defy the Boston authorities and go to visit them.

★★★

En route to Boston after hearing about Holder's new imprisonment, Mary Dyer broke off her sixty or so mile trudge through the wilderness with a stopover at the Scotts' house in Providence. Having been subjected to a whipping herself, Mary knew that Catharine Scott would understand her mission. And when Catharine's daughter, Mary, heard that Christopher Holder, her by-then betrothed, was one of the men being brutalized at the jail, she wanted to go too, as did their friend, Hope Clifton (who also later married Holder). So anxious were they, that they walked the distance to Boston where all were arrested as soon as they arrived.

Mary Scott, Hope Clifton and several of the others were released on November 12th after five weeks in jail, first being admonished for "their disorderly practices and vagabond like lie in absenting themselves from their family relations and running from place to place without any just reason." They were then ordered to "depart this jurisdiction within five days, which if they fail in shall be committed to prison to be proceeded with as the law directs." Others, both men and women, perhaps because they had been previously admonished, were ordered to be given varying numbers of whippings. William Robinson, Marmaduke Stevenson and Mary Dyer, because they had previously been banished, were condemned to die on the morning of October 27, 1659.[139]

When Mary's husband heard of her arrest and sentence, he wrote a "pathetic letter to the

---

[139] See Clark, Scotts, p. 14.

4. Antinomians & Quakers

Massachusetts authorities" dated August 30, 1659. It reads, in part:[140]

> Though wet to the skin, she was thrust into a room wherein was nothing to sit or lie upon but dust. Had your dog been wet, you would have afforded it a chimney corner to dry itself...but alas, Christians now with you are used worse than hogs or dogs...

His letter goes on to talk of his visits to dissenters in the Tower of London and prison while he was there. It then continues:

> Hath not people in America the same liberty as beasts and birds have to pass the land or air without examination?...It is not to be forgotten the former cruelties you used towards her when she came from England, having been tossed at sea all winter, but a little refreshment that had by cross winds at Barbados, yet as soon as come into Harbour shut up in prison and there kept... for no transgression at all, only that Mr. Bellingham then, as now, said she was a Quaker....
>
> Where your law or rule to keep a man's wife from him seven or eight weeks and a mother from her children, in a capacity of a close prison, which admits of no baylement?...so saith her husband, W. Dyer, Newport, this 30th August, 1659.

When Mary Dyer and the two younger men approached the site of their execution in October 1659, a rope was already strung from a great elm near the Frog pond. "The crowd was so great that the bridge between Boston and the North End broke," and the magistrates, fearing the force of public opinion against hangings, had "provided a force of militia to quell any disturbance or attempt at rescue." [141] What none of them knew, nor did Mary, was that even though her husband's letter had failed to free her, her son, Will, Jr.,

---
[140] *Genealogies*, V. 1, pp. 291-292.
[141] Booth, *Women*, p. 3 & Haley, Old Stone Bank, Vol. II, p. 24.

had succeeded. But first, he and the Governor had agreed on a plan to so frighten her that she would never again return to Boston. She was to be on the gallows with the two men condemned with her and so watch their hanging close-up, unaware she was not to suffer the same fate.

> Mary Dyer, seeing her companions hanging dead before her, stepped up on the ladder. Her skirts were tied around her feet. The halter was slipped over her head and lay limp on her neck. Her face was then covered with a handkerchief which the minister, John Wilson, had lent the hangman. As she stood on the ladder awaiting that final moment of death, there was suddenly a stir in the paralyzed crowd. A white horse came galloping across Boston Commons headed for the gallows. Its rider was wildly waving his hands and crying 'Stop! She is reprieved.'...Mary's feet were loosened, and the rope removed from her neck. When Wilson's handkerchief was removed she was startled to see her son Will holding the reprieve from Governor Endicott.[142]

When they bid her to come down, she stood still, saying "she was there willing to suffer as her Brethren did; unless they would null their wicked Law, she had no freedom to accept their reprieve, but they pulled her down," [143] forced her to get on a horse and accompanied her as far as Rhode Island's border.

In the next several months Mary spent a good deal of her time on Shelter Island teaching religion to the slaves and Indians who gathered around her. But then she saw a published copy of the *Apologie* written by the Rulers of Boston to be sent to England vindicating their barbarous proceedings against the innocent; using "her case to soften the public opinion which had arisen against them because of the other two

---

[142] Plimpton. P. 170
[143] *Genealogies*, V. 2, p. 562

4. Antinomians & Quakers 103

hangings." It infuriated her to read their claim that she had "accepted her life, promising or consenting that she would depart their Jurisdiction in a few dayes and return no more." She concluded: "thus do they make lies their refuge, and add iniquity to sin."[144]

[144] *Genealogies*, V. 2, p. 562 & Haley, Old Stone Bank, V. II, p. 24.

Mary Dyer was so angry that in April 1660 she left Shelter Island to go to Boston once more to protest.

By horse, by ferry and by foot, often having to traverse through unknown Indian territory, Mary made the long trip from her home to Providence where she spent a few days with her friends, the Scotts, before continuing on to Boston. Mary knew she could trust Catherine and her family even as she saw Catherine's fear, knew she felt she was "headed straight for the lion's din."

On May 27, 1660 Mary's husband wrote once again to Governor Endicott:

> I have not seen her above this half-year, and therefore cannot tell how, in the frame of her spirit, she was moved thus again to run so great hazard to herself and perplexity to me and mine; and all her friends and well-wishers, so it is from Shelter Island, about by Pequot, Narragansett, and to the town of Providence she secretly and speedily journeyed and as secretly from thence came to your jurisdiction. Unhappy journey, may I say, and woe to that generation, say I, that gives occasion to grief and trouble to those that desire to be quiet, by helping one another, as I may say, to hazard their lives for I know not what end, or to what purpose.[145]

This plea by Mary's husband seems feeble compared to that written earlier, but no plea probably would have helped her this time anyway, since Mary seemed determined to die. Another offer was made to free her if she would leave and come to Boston no more, but she refused, saying, "In obedience to the will of the Lord I came, and in his will I abide faithful to the death."[146]

On June 1, 1660, aged forty-nine, she was hung on Boston Common about nine o'clock in the morning.

---

[145] *Genealogies*, V. 2, p. 563
[146] *Genealogies*, V. 2, p. 563

4. Antinomians & Quakers

Field describes the event quite poetically:

> ...like a moth flying back to the candle, which has already scorched its wings, Mary Dyer returned to 'the bloody town of Boston', to protest against the unrighteous laws under which her companions had suffered death, and was herself in turn executed on the gallows, on the first day of June.[147]

One person who reviled Mary when she went to execution was the Rev. John Wilson of Boston. He had been the pastor when Mary and William arrived there in 1635 and joined his church. Their first child, Samuel, was baptized in this church on December 20, 1635.[148] But Mary's death may not have been in vain. After her hanging, such an outcry of protest arose that it was taken up by the Quakers in England who persuaded King Charles II, in 1661, to order no more hangings of Quakers in Boston. The hangings did then stop, but it was not until 1672 that Quakers were finally allowed to preach there without arrest.

The same year Mary was hanged, George Fox visited Rhode Island. How delighted Mary Dyer would have been had she lived to see him there; succeeding as he did in converting a goodly number of its citizens to his ideas. Roger Williams was less delighted, never having approved of the Quakers. He respected their right, any man's right, to worship as they wished, but, nonetheless, loved "to argue his side of any question and win others over to his way of thinking." And so, even though he was by then over seventy years old, he spent a whole day paddling alone to Newport in his canoe, not arriving until midnight, determined to debate Fox in person. Their debate lasted for three days, after which they adjourned and "came to

---

[147] Field, V.2, p. 106.
[148] *Genealogies*, V. 1, p. 281.

Providence, where the discussions were completed, both sides claiming victory."[149]

Sometime after Mary's death, William Dyer married a second time to Catherine (last name unknown), with whom he had a daughter, Elizabeth. An interesting side-note on William is a lawsuit he lost in 1684 and 1685 which shows his own religious intolerance. "A public officer, [William] had seized the estates of eight Jews for 'alienage,' but the verdict was rendered for the defendant Jews. The Jews petitioned the General Assembly for relief. It voted that they 'might expect as good protection here, as any stranger, not of our nation, ought to have, being obedient to the laws.' As the Jews had been most useful residents largely engaged in commerce at Newport for more than thirty years, their questionable position under the law shows the generally eccentric treatment of this remarkable race."[150]

About the same time that Mary Dyer made her last trip to Boston, Catharine Scott embarked for England with her daughter, Mary, and Christopher Holder. Two months after Mary Dyer was hung, Mary Scott married Holder: on August 12, 1660, at Olveston in the county of Somerset. "In a public meeting of the people of God" they agreed to "live together in mutual love and fellowship in the faith till by death they were separated." After they returned to America, they made their home on Patience Island and Mary gave birth to two daughters, Mary and Elizabeth. These few happy years came to an end, however, in January 1664/5 when Mary died giving birth to Elizabeth. After this, Holden married Hope Clifton, their long-time mutual friend. They moved to Newport where they were living when Hope, too, died on

---

[149] Haley, Old Stone Bank, Vol. III, pp. 73-74 & p. 84.
[150] Weedon, pp. 118-119.

4. Antinomians & Quakers 107

January 16, 1681. She had given birth to seven children, all but one, possibly two, dying in infancy. Holder then returned to England where he suffered several more imprisonments (for what reason is not stated) before his own death in 1688.

At the time of Catharine Scott's jailing and whipping in Boston, she clearly was a devout Quaker, but some time after that, possibly while in England, Catharine stopped going to Quaker meetings for a considerable number of years. However, it is believed she was again a Quaker in good standing at the time of her death since her death is listed in the Quaker records in Newport. Catharine was in her seventies when she died in 1687, eight years after her husband.

By the time they died, their five children were all grown and married to Quaker men: Mary, as we have noted, to Christopher Holder; Hannah to Walter Clarke; and Patience to Henry Beere, master of a sloop running between Providence and Newport. Deliverance married William Richardson, and their only son, John, later married Rebecca Brown. Tradition has it that John was mortally wounded by an Indian while standing in the doorway of his own house at Pawtucket Ferry. He died in 1677.[151]

---

[151] *Genealogies*, V.2, p. 824

5. Cocumscussoc & R I's Second Charter

We now return to Cocumscussoc and the charter. Since Roger Williams's return from England after obtaining the 1644 charter for Rhode Island, the family had been living at Cocumscussoc. But when the town again insisted he make a second trip to obtain yet another charter (more on this will follow), Williams felt compelled to sell his holdings there—which, presumably, included the family's home, acreage, and probably Goat Island—in order to provide for his family while he was gone.

Richard Smith, who had established a post nearby about the same time as Williams had started his, purchased it for £50. Smith had already bought out Edward Wilcox, who also had established a post near the Smith's and Williams's. These three holdings were now combined into one large plantation that Smith passed on to his heirs, at least in part, for many generations. Remnants of it still exist today, representing the last remaining plantation in Rhode Island.

✯✯✯

The writer now digresses to tell something of the interesting history of the Smith's at Cocumscussoc, and especially that of their women.

After Richard Smith's son inherited the Cocumscussoc plantation, his wife, Joan, used the Gloucestershire recipe she had brought with her from England to replicate England's famous Cheshire cheese using milk from their cows. It was so popular and of such a high quality that it was adopted by all the neighboring wives—and in the ensuing years was "marketed as Narragansett cheese both at home and even abroad"—a very early business initiated and

5. Cocumscoussoc & RI's Second Charter

carried on by a woman.[152]

Then around 1691, Abigail Updike, the wife of Smith's grandnephew, Ludovick, proved her pluck at a time when all the men were away. Single-handedly, she confronted a band of Indians, "pointing out that all were in a like plight, that the danger and distress to whites and Indians were the same. Her appeal succeeded in pacifying them." On yet another occasion, "she and her household defended the mansion against attack, and actually fired, through loopholes in the solid shutters, upon the savages until they were repulsed." Abigail, clearly, was not intimidated by the Indians even in threatening situations, but more than that, she must also have had a real regard for them. She is said to have used "her considerable knowledge of medicine in treating the ills of both the Indians and her own slaves."[153]

The mansion at Cocumscussoc, of course, was not generally under attack, and Abigail was noted primarily for her grand balls. On one night of especial note, the mansion was especially beautiful "with its many lights shining out over the water beyond the lawn." The music sounded "while the guests from Boston, Providence and Newport danced merrily—'Pea Straw,' 'Lady Hancock' and 'Boston Delight'." Then whispers began to spread as to why Hannah Robinson, from a neighboring plantation, 'the most beautiful girl in the American Colonies,' had mysteriously not yet joined them.[154]

Later they learned that Hannah had only pretended to set off for the ball. Instead she had eloped and married Peter Simons, a union her father, Rowland Robinson, violently opposed.

---

[152] Woodward, p. 27.
[153] Woodward, pp. 56-57.
[154] Haley, Old Stone Bank, Vol. II, p. 27

Robinson was one of the richest of the Narragansett planters, the eldest son of Deputy-Governor William Robinson. "In 1741 he married Anstis, daughter of a wealthy Boston Neck farmer,...and in 1746 moved into "the beautiful and stately mansion about a mile north of the old South Ferry." This was also the year their first child, Hannah, was born.

In contrast, Peter, a Frenchman, was the son of a man who had been tried and acquitted for piracy. At the time Hannah and Peter met, he was a teacher of music, dancing and French at a select school in Newport where Robinson had sent his daughter for a short time. They fell madly in love and insisted on continuing to see each other despite her father's disapproval. On one occasion when Robinson came home unexpectedly while Peter was calling on her, Hannah thrust him into one of the house's many cupboards, "where he remained safely hid until she had received her father's good-night kiss and the coast was clear for his departure." On another occasion, a terrible scene followed Robinson's catching Peter in their garden, and, thereafter, ordered that anytime Hannah walked or rode out, she must be accompanied either by a member of the family or a trusted servant. Hence, the need for help in planning her elopement the night of Abigail Updike's ball.

The guest list was so extensive for the great ball planned at Abigail's estate (about eight mile north of Hannah's home) that Robinson felt he could not deny Hannah permission to attend. And so it was, on the evening of the ball, after affectionate good-byes to her family, Hannah set out on horseback with her sister, Mary, and their slave-servant, Prince.[155] At a spot agreed upon, Peter awaited her, and, ignoring those with her, "the lovers dashed away to Providence,

---

[155] Of Robinson and Prince we'll hear more later; another story.

5. Cocumscoussoc & RI's Second Charter   111

where they were married....The year of Hannah's marriage does not appear to have been recorded in any account found of her life, but it is said that she lived for many years in Providence."[156]

Some have claimed that Peter was a gambler and a villain who neglected his wife after their marriage, and, his discovery that Hannah's "wealthy father did not come to her aid." But others deny this. "Robinson offered a large reward for the names of the person or persons who had helped her to elope, but no one would inform him," including Hannah, despite his demands that she do so if she wanted to reconcile with him. It would seem that his self-imposed stubbornness caused unnecessary suffering for them both: Robinson, despite his anger with his daughter, would walk from room to room touching objects that had been Hannah's, settling down only after he found her cat. "When he believed himself unobserved, he was seen to press the little beast to his heart, while tears ran down his cheeks....but he firmly resisted his wife's entreaties that Hannah be sent for to return home."

"They had come to know that she was in a sad condition in Providence....Because of the hardships she had suffered, and the desertion of her husband, for whom she had sacrificed so much, Hannah was now heart-broken, poor and ill." Despite her mother's pleadings, her father would agree only to send her servant, also named Hannah. It was not until his daughter was near death that Robinson finally saw her, and in tears gave her money and sent servants to retrieve her home. When she died shortly after and a servant was asked the cause of her death, she said: "Nuthin' ail Missus Hannah. Dis world wer ony jes too hard for her, and di poor chile die ob de heart break."[157]

---

[156] Haley, Old Stone Bank, Vol. II, p. 60
[157] Haley, Old Stone Bank, Vol. II, pp. 61-62

Others have ascribed a less poetic ending to her life and one that did not include a reconciliation with her father, stating only that she died of tuberculosis after about nine years of marriage. Some also believe that Hannah left an eight year old daughter, despite fact that Robinson mentioned no such child in his will—this explained by the belief that he retained his bad feelings against his daughter, right up until his death, for defying him and marrying Peter.[158]

☆☆☆

We now return to Rhode Island's need for a second charter. It had been hoped that the 1644 charter would end the state's border disputes with Connecticut but skirmishes continued, as well as the controversy between William Harris and Roger Williams over the dividing line between Pawtuxet and Providence. After Coddington somehow managed to receive a charter that established Newport as a separate town and him as its "ruler for life," attacks on the authenticity of that first charter, which lacked the royal seal, increased. Both charters could not be valid. Things got so ugly that the only solution seemed to be another trip to England to secure a new royal charter that would finally confirm Rhode Island's borders and its right to exist.

And so it was that in 1651 Roger Williams reluctantly agreed to a second trip, again promised £100 by the town for his expenses. But the only record of any payment for either of his trips appears in the notes of the town treasurer for the period between

---

[158] More can be found of this complicated love story and other connections with the Bowen family in Clauson, pp. 36-40. Also a long, slightly different version in Haley, Old Stone Bank, Vol. II, pp. 59-62.

5. Cocumscoussoc & RI's Second Charter

1649-1652: Roger paid £18 and his wife £5 "since he went to England."[159]

Roger Williams was accompanied on his second trip by John Clarke, representing Newport and Portsmouth, and William Dyer, Secretary of the General Assembly, to serve as secretary. Clarke's wife, Elizabeth, also accompanied them; her eagerness to see family and old friends in Bedfordshire, tempered, no doubt, by a bit of trepidation. She had reason to fear her wealthy father would not be pleased to learn what her life in this new country of America was like. At the time he approved her marriage in 1634, he thought she was marrying an up-and-coming English physician. As for William Dyer (not even mentioned by many historians when writing about this trip), he was especially eager to be going along since he hoped to persuade his wife, Mary, who had been in England for a year already, to return home with him. Of course, we know he was unsuccessful.

Roger Williams, having left his wife, Mary, the money he received from the sale of his trading post, helped pay his own expenses during his three-year stay in England by giving lessons in Hebrew, Greek, Latin, French and Dutch. "Williams was so genuine a scholar that the learned poet, John Milton, liked to talk and read with him, and learn Dutch of him. Mr. Williams taught foreign languages in the modern way. 'Grammar rules begin to be esteemed a tyranny,' he says. 'I taught young gentlemen, a parliament man's sons, as we teach our own children English, by words, phrases, and constant talk. I have begun with mine own three boys...others are coming to me.'"[160] *Note he*

---

[159] Staples, *Annals*, p. 87.
[160] Miner, Lilian, p. 37.

says nothing of teaching his daughters the same.

On October 2, 1652, despite the turmoil raging in England at the time, the group was successful in getting the Coddington charter at least suspended "until further direction be given."[161] Dyer, having given up on his efforts to persuade his wife to return with him, had agreed to return home to dispatch the news. After ten weeks at sea, he arrived in Newport on February 18, 1653.

Roger Williams was next to return, in the spring of 1654. Perhaps he missed his family and felt that John Clarke could complete their mission just as well without him. Earlier Williams had written to the towns of Warwick and Providence pleading for them to consider that he was a father and husband who "longed earnestly to return with the last ship, but who could not leave so long as needed. He then continued:

> If you conceive it necessary for me still to attend to this service, pray you consider if it be no convenient that my poor wife be not encouraged to come over to me, and wait together on the pleasure of God for the end of this matter....I write to my dear wife my great desire for her coming while I stay, left it to the freedom of her spirit because of the many dangers; for truly at present the seas are dangerous.[162]

It was another year before Roger in fact returned, and Mary had not joined him. Even if she had desired to do so, she would have found it difficult to leave the children, and would not have wanted to take them with her, subjecting them to such a hazardous sea voyage. It's clear from Roger's letters how devoted he was to Mary, how much he missed her, how concerned he was when she was recovering from a "dangerous sicknesse"

---

[161] Field, History, V. I, p. 92
[162] Haley, Old Stone Bank, Vol. III, pp. 54-55.

5. Cocumscoussoc & RI's Second Charter   115

(unspecified). In one letter he wrote his "dear wife":[163]

> Dearest Love and Companion in this Vale of Tears....My dear Love, since it pleaseth the Lord so to dispose of me, and of my affairs at present, that I cannot often see thee, I desire often to send to thee. I now send thee that which I know will be sweeter to thee than the Honey and the Honey-combe, and stronger refreshment than the strongest wines or waters, and of more value then if every line and letter were thousands of gold and silver...I send thee (though in Winter) an handfull of flowers made up in a little Posey, for thy dear selfe, and our dear children, to look and smell on, when I as the grasse of the field shall be gone, and withered....

According to an entry in Governor Winthrop's Journal, Roger also bought Mary at least one new dress while away. The entry reads: "Mrs. Williams wore a new gown and a somewhat expensive one."[164] *(Where Roger got the money for such is not clear since he was, supposedly, tutoring in order to pay his expenses while in London?)*

Mary had good reason to miss Roger, too, and certainly must have looked forward to his letters, but we may wonder who read them to her, a necessity we assume since she was illiterate. *We may also wonder where Mary and the children were living during Roger's stay in England, since he had sold their home in Cocumscussoc? Had they resettled in Providence before he left? What, in fact, had happened to their original Providence home when they moved to Cocumscussoc? Was the money he left Mary from the sale of his trading post enough to last the three years Roger was absent? Who tended Mary and the children during her unnamed illness that worried Roger? Did she have help with the children, house, farm and stock during his absence?*

---

[163] Kimball, pp. 49-50
[164] See Anthony, Bertha Williams, p. vii.

Surely Thomas Angell had long-since ended his term of indenture to Roger. *Could Roger possibly have made an Indian available to help her out?* At one point he did have at least one Indian servant: records show that in May 1649 the Colonial Assembly "granted him leave 'to suffer a native, his hyered household servant, to kill fowle for him in his piece at Narragansett about his house.'" [165]

Without letters from Mary, who could only have written through an intermediary since she was illiterate, histories answer few of the questions raised. But few doubt that Mary was a loving and devoted wife who believed in Roger and selflessly encouraged his expression of his beliefs—even if she did not always agree with him. Mary's sacrifices are pointed to as examples of her "very fine character. Before her marriage she was accustomed to a life of comfort, but adapted herself to new conditions and was a courageous and competent mother,—reared all her six children while many children in other families died."[166]

★★★

When Roger Williams returned to Rhode Island early in the summer of 1654, he was dismayed at the dissension he found going on among the four towns—Providence, Newport, Portsmouth and Warwick. He set out to persuade the fractious populace on the mainland and on the island to agree to unite and finally was successful. However, despite this initial agreement, it still took until 1658 before the four towns agreed to embrace a single government, all reluctant to give up their independence. Newport was especially reluctant, since it was outpacing all the other towns in wealth and

---

[165] Woodward, p. 14.
[166] See Anthony, Bertha Williams, p. vii.

5. Cocumscoussoc & RI's Second Charter

growth. The town's residents were shipping hogs, cattle, sheep and maize all over the world in exchange for items the colonists wanted and hitherto had had to do without. Prosperous Jews were coming from Manhattan and settling there; in 1763 building the first synagogue, Touro, in the new world. (It remains as the only synagogue still surviving from the colonial period.)[167]

It was another nine years before John Clarke and his wife, Elizabeth, returned to America. Clarke had been handicapped in getting the new royal charter by the struggle taking place between the King, the House of Commons and religion, under the aegis of Sir Oliver Cromwell, the "Protector." After King Charles II finally prevailed, Clarke still had to witness the hanging of Sir Harry Vane[168] (who had been Rhode Island's chief advocate), before he was finally able to curry sufficient favor with the King to obtain the desired charter; he had to convince him that support of this "Lively Experiment" was a "profitable investment." And flawed though it might have been, the 1663 royal charter, largely written by Clarke, held fast, with only occasional amendments, until the state adopted a constitution in 1843.

---

[167] Information found in Plimpton, p. 121.
[168] Vane had been Governor of Massachusetts when Anne Hutchinson was tried and banished, but had returned to England and it was mainly through his influence that Williams had been able to secure the first charter. At the time of this second visit, Williams spent much of his time at the Vane estate where he met many of the powerful figures of the time he needed to talk to. Vane was then virtual head of the English Navy, directing its attacks against his nation's enemies. [He must, however, have fallen out of favor for his opposition to the king's positions.] Haley, Old Stone Bank, Vol. III, p. 54.

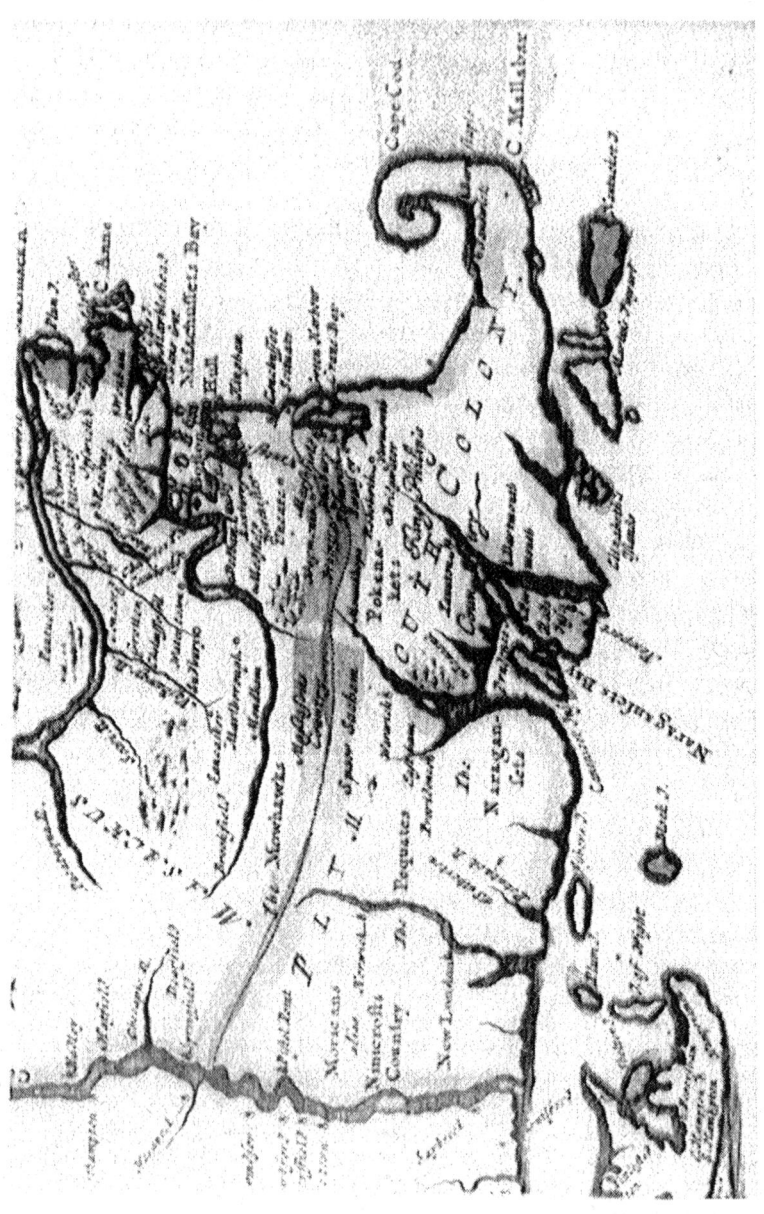

5. Cocumscoussoc & RI's Second Charter   119

It is notable that the name accorded the state in this charter—"The Colony of Rhode Island and Providence Plantations in the Narragansett Bay in New England, in America"—more accurately reflected its true status than had that in the earlier 1638 charter: The charter arrived in Rhode Island on November 26, 1663, contained in a "golden box," to much rejoicing.

> The complete instrument contains a little more than six hundred words. The highly ornamental heading is a complicated composition of heraldic symbols, fancy scroll work and pen flourishes, and this design work extends down the left hand side of the charter face about half way. Within the huge initial letter C of the name Charles appears a portrait of the royal author, and, according to the picture, Charles II sported...long, wavy tresses of raven locks, parted in the middle, [that] flow down over His Majesty's plump shoulders....[169]

The charter "mandated annual elections for all at-large officers of the colony; provided for the raising and governing of a militia; and established acceptable boundaries (which included the Pawcatuck River as the western line of demarcation)"[170] Even so, boundary disputes continued until 1747, especially with Connecticut which still sought to annex the Narragansett country.

The 1663 charter's most unique inclusion, which existed in no other charter, was the clause that used the Declaration of Breda:[171]

> Our royal will and pleasure is, that noe person within the sayd colonye, at any tyme hereafter, shall bee any wise molested, punished, disquieted, or call in question, for any differences in opinione in matters of religion, and doe not

---

[169] Haley, Old Stone Bank, Vol. III, p. 57.
[170] Conley, *Liberty*...,p. 19
[171] James, *Clarke*, pp. 82-83

actually disturb the civil peace of our sayd colony; but that all and everye person and persons may, from tyme to tyme, and at all tymes hereafter, freelye and fully have and enjoy his and their owne judgments and consciences, in matters of religious concernments,...they behaving themselves peaceablie and quietlie, and not useinge this libertie to lycentiousnesse and profanesse, nor to the civil injurye or outward disturbance of others.

Because it spells out religious liberty, just as had the Portsmouth Compact Clarke wrote earlier, some historians say Clarke should be "considered the Father of this state" rather than Roger Williams whose earlier charter did not, specifically, mention religious liberty as is generally thought.[172] In any case, one hundred and twenty-eight years later, one can see the influence this charter had on the Bill of Rights signed on December 15, 1791.

> Congress shall make no law respecting an establishment of religion, or prohibiting the free exercise thereof; or abridging the freedom of speech, or of the press; or the right of people peaceably to assemble, and petition the Government for redress of grievances.

---

[172] Letter by Moses Brown, quoted by Bicknell, V. 1, p. 283.

6. King Philip & Queen Weetamo

With the new 1663 Charter in hand, it was hoped that both Rhode Island's internal and external disputes over borders would end. But they continued right up until King Philip's War forced the men, even William Harris, to put aside their disagreements at least temporarily.

Small skirmishes had repeatedly broken out in New England between the Indians and white settlers for a number of years, increasingly fueled by the Dutch continuing to supply the Indians with more and more guns. By mid-1675, it seemed more and more likely that a full-scale war was inevitable.[173]

King Philip, after whom the war took its name, was the son of Massasoit, the great Sachem of the Wampanoag Indians. This tribe had at one time been subordinate to the Narragansetts, along with the Nipmucs, Aquednecks and Niantics. Massasoit had always been friendly with the settlers and the relationship had served him well in strengthening his tribe. But Philip resented the encroachment of the whites on what had been his father's land, "forcing them further and further back into their hunting grounds." He had repeatedly witnessed atrocities committed by the whites; a hunter had captured an Indian squaw and ordered her "torn to pieces by his dogs.... Bounties were placed upon the heads of all young and defenseless redmen, $130 being paid for the scalp of an Indian boy and $50 for that of a squaw."[174]

Then, after the death of Massasoit, the whites, suspecting a plot against them, ordered Alexander,

---

[173] Varying details of this war can be found in Haley, Old Stone Bank, V. I, pp. 22-24, V. II, pp. 34-36 & 40-44, & V. III, pp. 66-72.
[174] Haley, Old Stone Bank, V. II, p. 41

Philip's older brother who had replaced their father as sachem, to Plymouth. He died while there, and Philip believed the colonists had poisoned him. Taking over as Sachem, "he gathered together all his allies among the brow-beaten tribes and struck blow after blow on the English settlements." He began to "pounce upon unprotected farm-houses, burn, plunder, murder and then disappear into the forest." [175] Williams attempted to end the series of skirmishes peaceably by treaty, but failed. Perhaps by then he was too old to still be effective, or perhaps it was just that all the Indians with whom he had been so friendly had died.

The first killing of a white occurred at Swansea on June 24, 1675. There was much confusion as the colonists unsuccessfully pursued Philip, but generally found only deserted wigwams.

Rhode Island, at first not involved, was drawn into the struggle as "old men, women and children and the wounded and feeble of the tribes whose warriors had entered the field under Philip poured into Rhode Island seeking protection and shelter from the Narragansett chiefs and their people. These homeless unfortunates were fed, clothed and treated with kindness; the sick were nursed and the wounds of the disabled warriors were tenderly bound up by the Narragansett squaws."[176] It was only after the United Colonies of New England [which did not include Rhode Island] demanded that the Narragansetts turn over Philip and his subjects to them, that the Narragansetts, until then neutral, "turned away from their life-long white friends in Rhode Island and elsewhere, and placed them[selves] on the side of the fighting tribes." As a result, "on November 2, 1675, the United Colonies of New England

---

[175] Quotes in this paragraph from Haley, Old Stone Bank, V. II, pp. 41-42.
[176] Haley, Old Stone Bank, V. III, p. 68.

6. King Philip & Queen Weetamo

declared war against the Narragansetts."[177]

"About the middle of the following month, one thousand well-armed white troops reached the village of Wickford, Rhode Island, bent on seeking out the Indian stronghold somewhere in that vicinity."[178] They suspected Philip was being sheltered there and when the head sachem, Canonchet, refused to give up him up, the bloody battle of Tower Hill—also referred to as the Great Swamp Fight—took place on December 19, 1675.

The colonists attacked the Indian fort, "largely a group of wigwams surrounded by a rude hedge fence of dead bushes."[179] They reached it by way of a path the Indians had made through the thick dismal swamp. "Over the frozen ground and through the gap, the troops leaped into the fort about noon. After about three hours of fighting, someone set the hedge on fire, which soon engulfed the whole encampment. ...No mercy was shown to any one"; the shrieks of those caught in the burning wigwams could be heard above the roar of the flames. "The whole swamp was a scene of horror." Estimates indicate that as many as 300 Indian warriors were killed in that battle, as well as 400 of their women and children; another 450 were taken prisoners. Sixty-eight whites also were killed, and 150 wounded. Many of the colonists who survived died on the trip back to Wickford, from where they'd started; a trip through ice and snow that was worse for them than the fighting had been. "Many men fell from exhaustion and were left there to die by their helpless companions."

With all the great Indian sachems now dead—

---

[177] Haley, Old Stone Bank, V. III, p. 68
[178] Haley, Old Stone Bank, V. III, pp. 69
[179] Quotes in this paragraph are from Haley, Old Stone Bank, V. I, pp. 23-24.

Canonicus, Mascus, Miantanomi, Mexanno and Canonchet—Queen Quaiapen "gathered together the pitiful remnants of her tribe—those who had managed to escape during the Great Swamp Fight. They lived in hiding in [what became known as] the Queen's Fort. Late in June, 1676, she left the fort with the rest of her tribe and set forth on an expedition towards the north….They had only proceeded a little way when they were attacked on Sunday morning, July 2nd, by a roving band of Connecticut horsemen, who were on a warlike excursion through Rhode Island, and completely massacred."[180] Of the 238 Indians, not one escaped.

"In the following month of August, William Harris wrote in commemorating the tragedy: 'A great counciller of ye Narragansetts, & spetially of a great woman; yea ye greatest yt ther was; ye sd woman called ye Old Queene…'"[181]

During the various Indian raids which preceded and followed the Great Swamp fight, Rhode Island's settlers tried to fortify their houses, fearing, especially, for the safety of the women and children. Some fled to the "island of Rhode Island" (Aquidneck) and others to Long Island. Pawtuxet was raided, its corn and hay burned, sheep, cattle and horses driven off; houses were burned near Wickford; only part of the walls remained of what had formerly been Williams' trading post. Warwick was nearly destroyed, its citizens fleeing *en masse*. In Providence, twenty-seven men, out of a population of 500, are listed as "stay'd and went not away", including Roger Williams. However, they were unable to prevent the burning of its houses—twenty-nine were burned on March 30, 1676;

---

[180] Haley, Old Stone Bank, V. II, pp. 43-44.
[181] Haley, Old Stone Bank, V. II, p. -44.

6. King Philip & Queen Weetamo 125

most of Towne Street wiped out, and many of the town's records destroyed.

A letter exists, dated April 1676, that purportedly was written by Roger Williams to his brother, Robert, who lived in Newport. It tells of Roger's meeting with the Indians at the very time of this rampage. Roger displayed real anger that the Indians are allowed this to happen. He referred to one Elizabeth Sucklin, a Quaker married to Thomas Sucklin, who was killed with a hammer as she was "preparing to goe from Her own Hous [at the Southern end of town] to A Fort but delaying." He noted that even as he was talking to the Indians, he could see smoke rising "from my Daughtr Mercies House in the Woods." [At the time, Mercy Williams Waterman, his youngest daughter, was the widow of Resolved Waterman] The letter goes on to tell Robert that he proclaimed to the Indians: "In this Hous of mine now burning before mine Eyes hath Lodged kindly Some Thousands of You these Ten Years." [This may well have been his trading post/house rather than the one in town.] "They knew many times I had Quenched fires between the Bay and them, and Plimoath, and Quiniticutt, and them." [182]

William Harris, whose farm was next to William Carpenter's, gave another account of an Indian attack. He reported that in January 1676, following attacks on Rehoboth and Providence, about 300 attacking Indians burnt Carpenter's "outbuildings, corn and hay, and drove away 180 sheep, 50 head of cattle and 15 horses." [183] The defenders were able to extinguish the fire set to his house, but were unable to prevent the death of his son, William, Jr. and a servant, possibly a

---

[182] *RW Correspondence*, pp. 717-728. Includes efforts to and problems in authenticating the letter.
[183] This and subsequent quotes of Harris's account are from *Genealogies*, V. 1, pp. 44 & 552.

negro slave. Following this onslaught, Harris is quoted: "And then went to Patuxet & ther burnt some houses and an empty garrison and fought against another, and shott fire upon arrows forty or fifty but ye English put them out, and in ye night time went ther way...."

Two months later an even greater number of Indians descended and, in Harris's words, "burnt all ye houses in Warwick all in Patuxet and almost all in Providence and the inhabitants are gone some to one place and some to another." During one or the other of these attacks all the buildings on the Harris farm were burnt, his son Toleration and a servant were killed.

☆☆☆

Because Mrs. Mary White Rowlandson's account of her experience while held captive by the Indians during this period is so unique, it bears recounting here even though she was not from Providence. Her diary appeared in print in 1682 under the title, *The Sovereignty & Goodness of God, Together, with the Faithfulness of His Promises Displayed*. Dexter says "Mrs. Rowlandson makes no pretension to style, and displays no learning save in the Bible; but she writes clearly and forcibly, in vigorous and idiomatic English. She was a close observer, and gives valuable information in regard to the habits of the Indians"[184]— especially those of its "upper-class" women. *Unfortunately, we do not learn if or how Mrs. Rowlandson's exposure to and survival in an alien culture changed her self-perception; whether she changed; whether she added new ideas and skills to her role of wife and mother.*

Mrs. Rowlandson, as she is generally referred to, was born Mary White in Somersetshire, England about

---

[184] Dexter, p. 133.

6. King Philip & Queen Weetamo 127

1635 and came with her family to Salem, Massachusetts while still very young. Later, they moved to the then-agricultural village of Lancaster, Massachusetts where she married Joseph Rowlandson, a Congregational minister. During the war "the town was alarmed by rumors of an impending attack by the Indians, and Mr. Rowlandson went to Boston to beg help from the Council. On February 10, 1675/6, while he was there, the attack took place. The entire town was burned to the ground, many of the inhabitants killed, the rest, about twenty, captured. Among the captured were Mrs. Rowlandson and her three children, fourteen, twelve, and six years old. Mrs. Rowlandson and the youngest child had both been wounded, and the little one died on February 19th. The two older children were not allowed to stay with their mother, and she saw them only a few times during her captivity."[185]

For three months the captives were forced to follow the Indians "on long marches through northwestern Massachusetts and southern New Hampshire and Vermont," as they were fleeing from pursuing English troops. Perhaps feeling encumbered by so many captives, they sold Mrs. Rowlandson and her children to Quinnapin, closest to Philip, and his wife, Queen Weetamo, sister of King Philip's wife.[186] Weetamo, whose name means "sweetheart" in the Indian language, was

---

[185] Dexter, p. 131 & Ulrich, p. 227 & 174. Ulrich, unlike other accounts, places Rowlandson in Barre, Vermont at the time of capture—"women, children, the old, the sick and the lame" abandoned by the men who went off to fight an approaching force of the English army. The place and event she describes most likely occurred during the time Rowlandson was forced to follow the Indians, as described by Dexter.

[186] Where they were camped at the time is never stated, but it seems reasonable to suppose it was in Rhode Island since Mrs. Rowlandson was eventually released in Newport, which was not her home.

quite a remarkable woman in her own right; said to have inherited her personality from her father.

> "She also inherited her mistrust of the English" whom he had no use for. "Legend has it that she had six husbands," little known of the first, but the second was "with Wamsutta, the eldest son of Massasoit." Their life together was stormy. "Court records show that she entered a complaint against Wamsutta for selling land she claimed was hers and not paying for it.
>
> When Wamsutta died, Weetamo didn't play the part of a mournful wife. She married again and lived in Pocasset...and became known for her lavish entertaining. Many Narragansett Indians were invited to her parties and her next two husbands came from that tribe. Everyone admitted that she was very beautiful and also very vain....[187]

Mrs. Rowlandson's comments on Weetamo would bear this out. She wrote:

> Bestowing every day in dressing herself, near as much time as any of the Gentry of the land: powdering her hair, and painting her face, going with Necklaces, with jewels in her ears and Bracelets upon her hands. When she had dressed herself her work was to make Girdles of Wampum, and Beads....She was always attended by maids.[188]

Viewing herself as a slave, Mrs. Rowlandson served Weetamo and Quinnapin in a housewifely capacity and put her trust in God for her survival. Actually, her situation was much improved over the forced marches which had entailed such as wading in water "up to the knees, and the stream very swift, and so cold that I thought it would have cut me in sunder." Afterwards, "I sat down to put on my stockings and shoes, with the tears running down mine eyes, and many sorrowful

---

[187] Old Stone Bank, "RI Portrait in Sound"
[188] Quoted in Church, pp. 209-210 & Rider, p. 11 (Mrs. R's narrative, pp. 40-46)

6. King Philip & Queen Weetamo

thoughts in my heart, but I gat up to go along with them."[189]

In her diary Mrs. Rowlandson describes her mistress, Weetamo, as a proud and independent woman. Ulrich in her account of Mrs. Rowlandson in *Good Wives* suggests Rowlandson did not admire this quality, but rather in "rejecting pride [for herself], was projecting it upon her captors, finding personal redemption but no charity for her enemy in the humiliation of captivity."[190]

Mrs. Rowlandson apparently struggled with cold and hunger during the entire time of her capture [hungry at least partly because she found it difficult to eat wild meats], and seemingly cared little about the suffering of the Indians in the camp. "When a 'savage' extended human sympathy, she could only attribute it to Providence. When Weetamo's baby died, she observed that now there would be more room in the wigwam." [191] But it is not at all clear that Mrs. Rowlandson felt, as Ulrich suggests, that Indians were by definition "atheistical, proud, wild, cruel, barbarous, brutish...diabolical creatures...the worst of the heathen."[192] She was far more ambivalent than that in her attitude to her captors—and they in regard to her. She wrote:

> I have been in the midst of those roaring lions, and savage bears, that feared neither God, nor man, nor the devil, by day and by night, alone, and in company; sleeping, all sorts together, and not one of them ever offered the least abuse of unchastity to me in word or in action.[193]

---

[189] Dexter, p. 132, quoting from Rowlandson diary.
[190] Ulrich p. 230
[191] Ulrich, p. 229.
[192] Ulrich, p. 227. She is quoting Charles H. Lincoln, *Narratives of the Indian Wars 1675-1699.*
[193] Rider, p. 13 (from Mrs. R's Captivity, p. 51)

A ransom of £20 was finally raised through the auspices John Hoar of Concord and she was released at Newport on May 3, 1676 after eleven weeks and five days as a captive. The big farewell dinner they gave her suggests some sort of rapport had developed between Mrs. Rowlandson and the Indians. As part of her description of the event, she wrote:

> There were eight dancers, four men and four squaws; my master and mistress being two...[My mistress wore] a Kersey coat covered with girdles of wampum from the loins upwards. Her arms from her elbows to her hands, were covered with bracelets; there were handfuls of necklaces about her neck; and several sorts of jewels in her ears. She had fine red stockings, and white shoes, her hair powdered and her face painted red.[194]

A short time after her release, her two children were also released for a ransom of seven pounds. Soon after that, her husband "received a call to the church at Weathersfield, Connecticut, where he died suddenly in 1678. The church, which had already given the family a house and furniture, then voted Mrs. Rowlandson an annual allowance of thirty pounds. The date of her death is not known." [195] What her husband had been doing during the three months of his wife's captivity also is not known, but one surmises he had continued preaching in his former church in Lancaster, Massachusetts.

Within three months of Mrs. Rowlandson's release, the war was over.

> In July, King Philip...was with Quanopen, and Weetamo, near Taunton, [Massachusetts]. They were attacked by Capt. Church, and all scattered. Philip's wife, and son, were captured, and both sold as slaves. Quanopen was captured, and taken to Newport, where he was tried, and shot, on the

---

[194] Rider, p. 11 (from Mrs. R's Narrative, pp. 40-46).
[195] Dexter, p. 133.

6. King Philip & Queen Weetamo   131

20th of August. Philip fled to Mount Hope, where he was shot, August 12th, and Weetamo, while crossing the Taunton river on a raft, alone, was drowned, thus came to an end all these people.[196]

Not all dismiss Weetamo quite so easily. Some credit her as an active participant in the War, and some even believe she lived on.

> When the King Philip's War broke out, she was visited by the Englishman, Captain Benjamin Church, who thought the queen [a title she had a right to as the wife of a Sachem] might be persuaded to take the side of the English. Never was he more mistaken.
> She not only rejected the side of the English, but ordered some of her subjects to show the captain what her warriors were capable of when it came to fighting. Not all of her subjects agreed with her methods...many of them, discouraged by the apparent hopelessness of their cause, left her. But the queen never wavered. From her three hundred fighting men, her tribe was reduced to twenty-six warriors, her luck was running out. The colonist tried to track her down. She managed to escape but they found her later. They said she had drowned, but the legend of the Sachem Queen lives on. She's still talked about as far away as the white mountains in New Hampshire [where] there's a trail [named after her]...just as there's one in Rhode Island called the Wampanoag Trail."[197]

Whatever Weetamo's fate, the war finally ended in August 1676 when King Philip was slain in a swamp by an Indian allied with the whites.

But the white man's own barbarousness and desire for revenge had not ended. Philip's body was "drawn and quartered and his head placed above the stockade at Plymouth as a warning to other potential rebels."[198]

---

[196] Rider, p. 12
[197] From Haley, Old Stone Bank, "R.I. Portrait in Sound"
[198] Conley, *Liberty...*, p. 198

Death of Philip.

Several thousand Indians had died in the war trying to rid their land of whites, as did more than six hundred whites fighting to keep their land. Most of the

6. King Philip & Queen Weetamo

captured Indians were sold into slavery either at Cadiz or in the West Indies. Philip's wife and his nine year old son were among them.[199]

Some of the Indians were bound over to the colonists as indentured servants for terms of years. One writer has poignantly observed:

> [The Indians] decline was totally due to the coming of the English, the enervating effect of white civilization being disastrous to these people whose strength lay in the pursuit of a simple existence. It seems tragic that they who were such an integral part of the forests they loved, had to perish. They never fully realized just what it was they were fighting. It was not the whites in themselves but white civilization, ...inevitable in it consequences. [200]

Roger Williams was a member of the committee formed to decide what to do with the considerable number of Indians captured by Providence's defenders. Miner reflects that "you can see the clear head and warm heart of Roger Williams...in the milder than common treatment" decided at a town meeting in August 1676. "The committee put the captives up for sale to the townspeople. But they limited the time of servitude to varying periods of years depending on the age of the individual Indian." These varied with servitude prescribed until the age of thirty for those under five at the time, eight years for those then between twenty and thirty, and "as they can be sold" for those already thirty and over.[201]

He quotes Judge Staples on the prices paid:

> For Indians, great and small, £8. Two for 22 bushels Indian corn. Two, in silver, £4.10. One, in silver £2.10. One, 12 bu. Indian Corn. One, in wool, 100 lbs. One for three fat sheep.

---

[199] Church, p. 209-210.
[200] Haley, Old Stone Bank, V. II, p. 36.
[201] Miner, Geo., p. 22

Thirty-six were sold and the proceeds divided among the town's defenders. Williams reminded the conquerors that "the most High delights in mercy," and that the slaves should be treated as "to make mercy eminent." [202] Nonetheless, in approving their sale, we must conclude that Williams, like most everyone else at the time, accepted slavery "as a necessary part of the social pattern." [203]

A brief note in the records, dated August 29th, is tantalizing in its sparsity as it tells of the Williams' son, Providence, returning his mother to Providence in the same manner he had removed her during the war:[204]

> By God's Providence it seasonably came to passe that Providence Williams brought up his mother [Mary] from Newport, in his sloop and *cleared the Towne by his vessel of all the Indians to the great peace and Content of all the Inhabitants.* (author's italics)

The Narragansett and Wampanoag Indians who escaped death and capture sought refuge with the Niantics who had abstained from taking part in the war; this group, collectively, eventually became known as the Narragansetts.

One can only wonder how many women, white and Indian, were left widows, how many were able to remarry; how many had to live in temporary shelter as burned homes were rebuilt, how many were hungry as crops were replanted. For the white women, it was like starting over. For the Indians, it was more like an ending to the simple life they had always lived; most of their land now belonged to the white settlers.

With the War over, quarrels over Rhode Island's boundaries resumed; those over the Pawtuxet Purchase not ending until 1712.

---

[202] Miner, Geo., p. 36.
[203] Bartlett, p. 5.
[204] Kimball, p. 97. (General information, pp. 87-97).

7. Mary, Roger & their Children

As previously noted, Roger was already old at the time of the King Philip's War, and his participation in the disposition of the Indians captured during that war must have been one of his last acts on behalf of the colony he had founded. Mary, of course, was getting along in years, too, further aged by the burdens of child-rearing in the most rustic and trying of circumstances.

One can only speculate as to just when they moved in with their son, Daniel, and his wife, Rebecca. *Perhaps they had felt old age creeping up on them and had reluctantly left their own home; or, another possibility, their home on Towne Street had been one of those the Indians burned during the war and they felt unable to start over at their age.* In any case, we know they spent their last years in Daniel and Rebecca's home.

Mary died first, in 1676 (the same year the War ended) or 1677, age about sixty-seven or sixty-eight; the historians unable to determine either her birth or death dates with certainty. After her death, Roger must have missed her greatly, and wrote to a friend in May 1682 of sitting by the fireside at his son Daniel's house, with his children and grandchildren around him, "old and weak and bruised...with lameness on both my feet." As he looked back on his life, he wrote, "It hath pleased the Most High to carry me on eagles' wings through mighty labors, mighty hazards, mighty sufferings."[205]

Roger died six or seven years after Mary, sometime between January 16 and May 10, 1683, age about eighty. The only proof of the date is a letter from John Thornton to Samuel Hubbard at Newport which states: "The Lord hath arrested by death our ancient approved friend Mr. Roger Williams." The last time his name

---

[205] Kimball, pp. 136 & 144, Arnold, Samuel G., V. 1, p. 476 and Miner, Lillian, p. 38.

appears in official records is in October 1682.

Kimball in her book, *Providence in Colonial Times,* stated that it was unknown where Roger Williams was buried, but Woodward, in *Plantation in Yankeeland* states, without qualification, that he was "interred on his own lot east of his residence just off Benefit Street" (the site of the Dorr mansion). After telling us how much Roger admired apple trees, Woodward goes on to say:[206]

> In the course of years a giant apple tree grew beside the grave and overshadowed it. When nearly two centuries later, in 1860, it was decided to open the grave to transfer the remains to the North Burial Ground, the principal object discernable in the midst of the dust was a large root, curiously shaped along the lines of the human skeleton. Nature in her slow, inexorable manner had converted the founder's venerated bones into a part of the apple tree. The root was reverently removed and preserved.
>
> No true likeness is known to exist. But along with the man-made suppositional statues and portraits, which are legion, nature's unique relic —the root of the apple tree— reposes in the museum of the Rhode Island Historical Society, a symbolic reminder to successive generations of the founder's physical presence in these parts three centuries ago.

Neither Woodward nor Kimball mention Mary. *Did they not know that in the grave adjoining Roger's, preservationists found what they thought to be Mary's remains?* They found "a wonderfully preserved lock of braided hair, a surprising discovery since the graves were then more than 170 years old." And so when "the dust was carefully gathered up and placed in a proper receptacle" to be taken to the North Burial Ground and deposited in the Stephen Randall tomb," it included the

---

[206] Woodward, p. 47.

7. Mary, Roger & their Children

remains of Mary too. And so it was the remains of both Roger *and* Mary that were moved once again in 1939, placed in a small bronze casket and interred in the solid stone base of the Roger Williams Memorial.[207] After such loving thoughtfulness, *why is there no recognition of this on the base, nor of Mary's role in establishing Providence?* In a letter by Moses Brown in 1830, he quotes friends of Williams as having described him as "a strong-minded, self-conceited, persevering man, making an unusual character for a man of talents and education." [208] *We can only ask, And what of Mary?*

★★★

Mary and Roger successfully raised six children to adulthood, their marriages combining to produce thirty-one grandchildren and fifty-two great-grandchildren. We know very little about the children, nothing, really, of their childhood, but a brief overview of the little we do know of them follows.[209]

MARY (1633-1684)

Mary, Mary and Roger's oldest daughter, born in Plymouth, Massachusetts, married John Sayles in 1650. They made their home on Aquidneck Island where Mary bore seven children before her death in 1684. She was the only one of Roger's children not to outlive him. Both she and her husband are buried near Easton's Beach, in Middletown, Rhode Island. In tracing their descendants we find ties to the Greene, Olney, Angell, Jencks and Whipple families.

---

[207] Miner, Lillian, pp. 38-39 and Haley, Old Stone Bank, Vol. IV, pp. 58-60.
[208] Letter quoted in V. 1, Bicknell, p. 283
[209] The major part of the lineage that follows comes from Anthony.

FREEBORN (1635-1709)

Freeborn, the Williams' second daughter, born in Salem, Massachusetts, married Thomas Hart about 1656. He was a shipmaster who preferred "the lively port of Newport" to Providence, and so they made their home there. Freeborn was pleased when Hannah Scott, just married to Walter Clarke, also moved to Newport. Freeborn must already have known Hannah, since their families were neighbors on Towne Street in Providence, and probably friends despite their differences in religion.

Walter Clarke was a strong Quaker like Hannah Scott. His first wife, Content Greenman, had died the year before at age thirty, leaving Walter with three young children. Then, just four years after Freeborn and Hannah became neighbors, Freeborn's husband, Thomas Hart, died, leaving Freeborn with four young children.

Then, in 1681, Walter Clarke's second wife, Hannah, died,[210] leaving him again a widower, now with seven children: Mary from his first marriage, now seventeen, and six others by Hannah. Needing more than ever a mother for all these children, Clarke asked the now-widowed, Freeborn, his friend and neighbor, to marry him, and so she did in 1683. That meant Freeborn was taking on the no-easy-chore of mothering eleven children (her four, his seven, though both of Clarke's male children died young). Hopefully, this was a less onerous task for her than it might have been since the children had been neighbors and playmates for most of their lives.

The marriage of Freeborn and Clarke offers an example of the complicated ties that marriages created between families of the early settlers. In this instance, Clarke became both Samuel Cranston's uncle and his

---

[210] The author of *Mary Dyer of RI*, Horatio Rogers, is a descendant of the Scotts through Hannah.

7. Mary, Roger & their Children

stepfather-in-law——for Samuel Cranston's mother was the sister of Walter Clarke, and Samuel's wife, Mary Hart Cranston, was the daughter of Freeborn and Thomas Hart. And with that marriage of Samuel Cranston and Mary Hart goes one of the most intriguing stories of the early days.

Soon after their marriage, Samuel left to go to sea.[211]

> Hearing nothing from the young sailor for several years, the family gave him up for dead, and [Mary], in due time, accepted an offer of marriage from a Mr. Russell of Boston. ...All plans for the wedding had been arranged, the day and hour for the ceremony were near at hand, when the long lost Samuel arrived in Boston on his way home. His wanderings had taken him to many lands and a long imprisonment in Algiers, where pirates held him captive, had delayed his return and prevented communication with his family.
>
> On his way from Boston he happened to learn of the wedding scheduled for that very night, and, although Samuel traveled with all possible speed, the guests were already assembling when he wearily approached his home in Newport. The whole setting, filled with dramatic tension, found the returning wanderer going to his own kitchen door, where he sent word to his wife, through a servant, that 'a person was there who wished to speak to her.' She came to the door and found the strange sailor who announced that he had news of her husband, still alive and on his way home...[After repeating the assertion], to convince the distracted lady of his message he raised his cap and pointed to a scar on his forehead. Instantly she recognized her husband, and the rest of the story can be imagined.
>
> The day was probably spoiled for Mr. Russell of Boston, and the gathering of friends and relatives very likely gave Samuel Cranston a golden opportunity to relate his thrilling story of adventures, sufferings, escapes and shipwrecks....Thereafter, Samuel Cranston attached

---

[211] Haley, Old Stone Bank, Vol. III, pp. 77-78.

himself to the merchant class as a goldsmith, and began a long career as a leader in civic activities.

As for Walter Clarke, he became a widower once more in 1710 when Freeborn died. Soon after that he took a fourth wife, Sarah Gould, widow of John Gould and daughter of Matthew and Mary Prior. Most if not all, of Freeborn's and Walter's children were grown by then, and there is no indication that Sarah and Walter had more. Sarah survived Clarke and inherited "his worldly goods." Before his demise, however, Walter Clarke was, amongst other things, governor of the colony six times and deputy governor twenty-three times.

PROVIDENCE (1638-1683)

Providence was Mary and Roger Williams' third child and first son. Said to be the first white child born in Providence, they named him thus because of "God's goodness" to them. As an adult, Providence moved to Newport where he was a shopkeeper, shipmaster and merchant, carrying trade between that town and Providence in the same sloope used to carry his mother and siblings from Providence to Newport during King Philip's War. Whether he also was involved in the slave trade we do not know, but we do know he once transported "three barrels of rum, one hundredweight of sugar, one panier, and 'one Collow for a horse'" on consignment for Captain Arthur Fenner.[212] Trade in rum, of course, was closely tied to the slave trade, and early-on Providence Williams was one of those who had requested land for a wharf in Providence. He died in 1686 at the age of forty-eight, never having married.

MERCY (1640-1705)

In 1659 when she was nineteen, Mercy, the

---

[212] Kimball, pp. 227-228.

7. Mary, Roger & their Children

Williams' third daughter, married Resolved Waterman.[213] During their eleven-year marriage, she bore five children that connected the family to the Rhodes, Harris and Arnold families. The lineage of their son, Resolved Jr., is especially hard to follow because he and his first wife, Anne Harris, had two children they named Resolved (3rd) and Mercy; then, Resolved (3rd) married another Mercy (last name not noted).[214] Some claim their son, Richard, married Anne Waterman, his cousin, which would complicate relationships with that family, but even the existence of Anne is questioned by others.[215]

We learn something of the household of Mercy Williams and Resolved Waterman from what was *not* in the inventory of Resolved's possessions when he died in 1670—no silver, no crockery or glassware, not even a "bottle," no clock nor book, even a Bible. It did record pewter, iron and brass, and the luxury of a "warming-pann," "looking glass" and "4 chairs," rather than the more common wooden settle. Resolved left his considerable property to his sons and two grandsons, with the stipulation that his wife, Mercy, "was to have the use of all these lands during the minority of the three children." [216]

On April 10, 1677 (seven years after Resolved died), Mercy married Samuel Winsor, the only son of Joshua Winsor.

---

[213] Resolved's father, Richard Waterman, had come with his family to Providence in 1638, the same year Resolved was born. Richard was one of the thirteen originally granted land by Williams, perhaps some of it being in Warwick since he is said to have been one of Warwick's first settlers.
[214] Anthony, *Roger Williams...*, Rhodes, *Genealogy &Genealogies* V.2, p. 416
[215] See Jacobus & Waterman
[216] *Genealogies*, V. 2, p. 416--419

In order to pay off the money borrowed to pay for his passage to Boston from England, Joshua had spent several years as an indentured servant to John Winthrop in Boston before coming to Providence. Roger Williams had heard about Joshua's religious-related conflicts and worked out an arrangement with Winthrop for him to come there as his indentured servant (the second time we have noted Roger having such). In 1640 (the same year Mercy was born), Joshua completed his two years of service and became a freeman. He then purchased a home lot and six acres of pasture land on the town's west side. His wife's name remains unknown, but aside from their son, Samuel who married Mercy, it is known they had three daughters—Sarah, Susanna and Mary—all of whom settled in Boston after they married.

Samuel, said to have "a taste for good living," was among the first to have a wharf in Providence, and was also a farmer, wheelwright and Elder in the Baptist church. He and Mercy had three children, two of whom became ministers. One, Samuel, Jr., in 1733 became pastor of the Providence Baptist Church, almost a century after Roger Williams' brief tenure. In sharp contrast to his grandfather, he remained as the church's minister for twenty-five years. He and his wife, Mercy Harding, had two sons who also became ministers.

Both Mary Williams and Samuel Winsor died in September 1705 and were buried somewhere near the Providence city water-works in Cranston[217] (their graves presumably since moved).

JOSEPH (1643-1724)

Joseph, the Williams' third child and youngest son, was born, as previously noted, in 1643, six months

---

[217] *Genealogies*, V. 2, p. 425, 428 & 431.

7. Mary, Roger & their Children 143

after Roger sailed for England. On December 17, 1669 he married Lydia Olney, youngest daughter of Thomas, Sr. and Mary Small Olney. They were married by Lydia's brother, Thomas, Jr. and afterwards moved into a dwelling-house built on the twenty acre lot they had received as a gift from Roger. It was located across from what became the Elmwood Avenue entrance to Roger Williams Park.[218] Joseph was "a cooper by trade, made wheels, hoops, tubs and pails, a wood worker but not a carpenter." He was thirty-three when he received citations for valor and skill for his service in King Philip's War.[219]

When Lydia's father, Olney, Sr., died, he left his son-in-law "all my part in the yoake of oxen which is between us." The remaining cattle, together with his "moveable goods," were to be "equally divided into three parts, of which 'Liddea Williams' was to receive one." Olney's will went on to enumerate in detail all his belongings; the total of his estate being valued at £78.9.5.[220]

The lineage of Lydia and Joseph's daughter, Mary, has been questioned. According to Bertha Williams Anthony, Mary married Obadiah Brown (son of John, son of Chad, one of Providence's first settlers) and they had three children: Chad, Amey, Mary, and probably a fourth, John Jr., born in 1703. [221] This would provide a direct link with the notable Brown family. However, a later genealogy of the Brown family indicates that the last name of the Mary who married Obadiah is unknown, casting doubt on this linkage. (Both

---

[218] The house was torn down in 1886.
[219] Anthony, Bertha Williams, p. 161
[220] Kimball. pp. 85-86.
[221] From "The Chad Brown Workbook." This genealogy also has Obadiah's wife as Mary, but leaves her last name as unknown. Therefore, it leaves it in question as to whether the Williams' and Browns' families were related.

genealogies name the same children.)

Lydia and Joseph also provide an interesting link to a "beloved" part of Rhode Island's history. Their son, James, is the progenitor of the line to Betsy Williams of the famous "Betsy Williams Cottage." She was born in 1790 to Mary Waterman Williams and James Williams of the 5th generation, making Betsy the great great great granddaughter of Mary and Roger Williams.[222] When Betsy died in 1871, she left her farm of about one hundred acres to the city of Providence, to be called Roger Willliams Park. Since then the city has added over 300 acres. It is in this park that many have visited "Betsy Williams Cottage," built about 1733 by her grandfather, Nathaniel, for her father.

By the time Joseph Williams, Sr. died on August 17, 1724, he had acquired considerable property. He left his son, Thomas, 330 acres of land at Rocky Hill, "where he now dwelleth," but Thomas died only 10 days after his father. Undoubtedly these lands then went to Thomas's own seven children, all but two being boys. Joseph, Sr. left Joseph, Jr. one-half of the land at Masipauge, about 130 acres, adjoining to the house where he then lived. To James he gave 200 acres of land at Rocky Hill that adjoined that of his brother, Thomas. James also got one-half of the homestead farm, and adjoining acres that included the house where he and Lydia lived.

His will contained a proviso that left his "loving wife," Lydia, the "common, benefit and use of that

---

[222] Betsy, James[5], Nathaniel[4], James[3], Joseph[2], Roger[1]. Betsy's mother was also a descendant of Roger Williams. Betsy, who never married, was not regarded as beautiful but had Titian red hair. In her later years neighbors regarded her as rather eccentric. She then was living with her sister, Rhoda, who had become blind and died before Betsy. See Anthony, Bertha Williams, p. viii. This same account gives 1771 as the date the cottage was built, but this seems entirely too late to be accurate.

7. Mary, Roger & their Children

Roome in my said House call the outward Roome wherein I now dwell, during the term of her naturl life." He also left her "the bed 'wherein I usually Lodg with all the furniture thereunto belonging. All the other moveables, together with all cattle, sheep, swine and house kind he gives to James, he to pay all debts, and provide 'all things his mother shall have neede of and that are necessary for an antiant woman dureing the full term of her naturall Life.'" Lydia survived her husband by only twenty-three days, dying on September 9, 1724.[223]

They, along with many of their descendants, were buried on the homestead farm they shared, located on what is now Elmwood Avenue, across from Roger Williams Park; like so many others, their graves, presumably, since moved. The homestead survived for over two hundred years before being torn down in 1886 to make room for improvements. Some historians regard Joseph as the most distinguished of the Williams' children, having served in King Philip's War, as deputy in the colonial assembly and as town councilman and assistant.[224]

DANIEL (1641-1712)

Daniel was the youngest child and second son of Mary and Roger. Of him, his father once said when hearing Daniel described as "a hard labouring, industrious man": "*Ah! My son Daniel is like a hog under a tree of acorns, very industrious in eating them but never considering whence they come.*" Daniel, who seemed unconcerned with matters spiritual, made his living dealing in Providence real estate. The letter he wrote on August 24, 1710 conveys somewhat mixed feelings about his father and *his* real estate dealings.

---

[223] *Genealogies* V.2, pp. 578-582 & Kimball, p. 143-144
[224] Kimball, p. 143-144.

After more-or-less chastising his "friends and neighbors" for accepting land grants from Roger without compensation, leaving him impoverished in his old age, Daniel continues with a question: "Can you find such another now alive, or in this age?" He then continued:

> He gave away his lands and other estate, to them that he thought were most in want, until he gave away all, so that he had nothing to help himself, so that he being not in way to get for his supply, and being ancient, it must needs pinch somewhere. I do not desire to say what I have done for both father and mother. I judge they wanted for nothing that was convenient for ancient people, &c. What my father gave, I believe he had a good intent in it, and thought God would provide for his family. He never gave me but about three acres of land, and but a little afore he deceased. It looked hard that out of so much at his disposing, that I should have so little and he so little. ...If a covetous man had that opportunity as he had, most of this town would have been his tenants, I believe.[225]

On December 7, 1676, Daniel married Rebecca (Rhodes) Power, the widow of Nicholas Power 2nd who had died the year before, killed in King Philip's War. Rebecca was the daughter of Zachariah and Joanna Arnold Rhodes and granddaughter of William Arnold. After their marriage, Rebecca and Daniel went to live in the Power house on Towne Street. Before Daniel died on May 14, 1712, leaving Rebecca a widow for the second time, they had seven children. Daniel was the only one of Roger's children who named a son after him.

Daniel's will makes clear he had done quite well for himself even though he had not received from his father the amount of land he thought he should have. Daniel left his son, Roger, two forty foot lots plus the homestead lot on Towne Street, next to Nicholas Power, "provided

---

[225] *Genealogies*, V. 2, p. 571

7. Mary, Roger & their Children

he disturb not his mother Rebekah Williams of her reasonable privilege and benefit in said dwelling house and premises during her natural life." He left his daughter, Patience, a home lot on Towne Street he had bought from Richard and Ann Waterman, as well as "his negro girl named Ann, four cows, and all the goods that she hath in her chests and trunks or that part that her mother condescends to." He left other tracts of land to his sons, Providence and Joseph. The will does not mention the eldest son, Peleg, presumably because he had already received a liberal share of the estate.[226]

In addition to Daniel's slave girl, Ann, his wife had two slaves, Jack and Hope, which she gave to Providence when she died about 1727. Another slave, Genne, she gave to Patience stating: "It is my will that Genne shall not be a servant during her life except she commit some fact that may give just cause, or some other like reason: so I leave it with my daughter Patience to deal Christian like by her." *So we may ask, Just how involved in the slave trade were Daniel and possibly others in the Williams family?*

---

[226] *Genealogies*, V. 2, pp. 574-576. Also, Kimball, p. 142.

8. Prosperity & Commerce

By mid-1700, Providence had become more prosperous, and with it had come much improved housing, a real boon for the mothers and wives who had strugggled so hard initially to make a comfortable home for their families under the most adverse of conditions. What is perhaps surprising is that, for the most part, for some time, even those who began to build well-pointed two-story mansions, often with gables towards the street, still built them on the narrow lots along Town Street rather than "a stone's throw up the hill" on the acres of land available there. "It is almost as if the houses huddled together to keep warm. It couldn't be money alone; the owners ordered beautiful carpentry work for their paneled and corniced interiors [and] spent money on lovely woodwork, even though niggardly land space gave them little privacy. Solid paneled window shutters were utilitarian indeed."[227]

Most often, the houses were now built at least partially of brick, the ceilings supported by massive beams. Many had a double chimney near the middle with rooms of varying size around it. Some, instead, had four chimneys, one on each outside wall of the four downstairs rooms—a kitchen and living room to the right of a spacious entry hall and the parents' bedroom and a guest room to the left. Stairs led to rooms under the likely gambrel roof where the children were bedded, and, above them, typically, was a loft, reached by ladder or steep staircase, for the servants.

Those who made their living on the sea prospered more than the average farmer or mechanic and they

---

[227] Miner, *Angell's Lane*, p. 63.

8. Prosperity & Commerce　　　　　　　　149

had the most distinguished houses and more furniture of good quality than others in the community. In furnishings, Kimball notes that by the late 1830s a distinction is made between square, oval and round tables. She goes on to say:

> 'High-back' chairs appear. One well-to-do 'mariner' left a 'Cannister of Tea' of one pound, ten shillings value, and two 'flowered Bottles.' Four years later we find that ancient mariner, Captain Abraham Angell, of the Rainbow, possessed of 'Chinia Tea Cups and Plates,' and a large assortment of 'China Punch Bowls.' In the adjoining cupboard were ten silver spoons, glass beakers and wineglasses, and a teapot. *His [this writer's italics]* well-stocked kitchen-closet could also boast two 'Coffe mills.' A neighbor's sideboard was resplendent with 'six Tea spoones & Tongs & strainer.' These, together with '2 Large silver spoones,' were estimated at £9, and their owner was likewise the proud proprietor of a tea-kettle.[228]

Another who prospered at sea was Major William Crawford who "had a large house with 'an East chamber, a northwest chamber, a Great Chamber, a West Chamber, a garret, a Greate Roome, a Bed Roome, a Dairy, lean-to, and Kitchen, as well as warehouses for salt and for Tum, a shop and a back shop.'" [229] Others who built famous houses during the later 1700s were Nicholas, Joseph, John and Moses Brown, John Merritt, and Edward Dexter. These fine houses often contained beautiful woodwork—paneling and hand carving—in mantelpiece, cornice, and staircase.

> A family might own silver—a spoon or two, a pair of buckles, even a cup or porringer. Women carried fur muffs; men, gold or silver headed canes and silver watches. Chairs became common; cooking utensils varied. Candle moulds, coffee mills, pepper boxes, and nutmeg graters rejoiced the

---

[228] Kimball, p. 257.
[229] Miner, Lillian, p. 104

housewife. She had warming-pans, tin and pewter to replace her wooden trenchers, and, finally, painted Queen's ware and glass. She might have a negro cook, while still devoting herself to preserves and pastry. In her house she now had window-glass, clocks, brass or iron and irons, bird-cages, flower-pots, looking-glasses, and carpets imported or American....She fed her family on fine flour instead of on the coarse corn meal that Roger Williams praised. She bought for them mustard from Yorkshire, and dressed them in 'English piece goods of every kind that can be made use of'...."[230]

Samuel Sewall of Newport talks of ordering goods for his daughter from London, once requesting: "A true looking glass of the newest fashion if this fashion be good, as good as you can buy for five or six pounds. Two pair of brass candlesticks, not slighting, of the newest fashion."[231] Candlesticks were still essential for lighting, but preferably also were decorative.

Colonel Nicholas Power's "spacious homestead on the Towne Street" certainly reflected his prosperity, having followed his father-in-law in accumulating wealth at sea. As Kimball notes:

> [It] was graced with the smiles and blushes of five gay girls, and must have welcomed many a jolly party within the 'greate lower room'...His was one of the earliest, if not the first, house in Providence to be provided with a 'dining room'. Among the 'dineing room furniture' was an oval table of a size to accommodate fourteen chairs and 'a Leather Cheair,' doubtless that for the Colonel himself.[232]

It is interesting that most accounts of furnishing attribute ownership to a man, even in cases where the items are clearly women-oriented. This leads one to speculate whether this is because married women had

---

[230] Miner, Lilian, p. 109
[231] Levin, p. 28
[232] Kimball, p. 240

8. Prosperity & Commerce 151

no right to ownership of household items, or if it is just one more example of historians' proclivity to dwell on the men and exclude women from their accounts.

In any case, we do have one list of "furniture for housekeeping;" made in March in 1796 by one Alice Carpenter. Her purpose for making the list is unknown. A copy is included.[233]

---

[233] Available from the RI Historical Society, RIM, vol. 1, p. 131.

The less well off, which no doubt represented the majority of Providence's citizens, did not have the luxurious homes as those just noted, but instead generally depended on the wife's dowry to provide almost all their home's furnishings. Ironically, however, their smaller homes, easier to heat, were often more comfortable during New England's cold winters than the mariners' larger, more expensive ones.

Whether a house had a fireplace on each of the four outer walls or a central chimney with rooms grouped round it, these bigger houses were a challenge to heat. Samuel Sewall in his diary "describes his wife being unwilling to receive a visitor in the parlor because there had been no fire lighted there during the day, and even though her husband had just lit a fire, only the chimney was warm, so they received the visitor upstairs 'in my wife's chamber.'" At another time Sewall alludes to having "lit the fire in the chamber at six a.m. so it would be warm enough for guests by midafternoon," whom they were entertaining to dinner. He also refers to instances of his ink freezing and of the water being too frozen for laundry.[234]

It was both costly and back-breaking to provide sufficient wood for the huge fireplaces needed for heating and cooking. Some have estimated "it would have taken all the wood from one acre of trees each winter to heat the average house." As for the work involved, "even if you did not cut down the trees yourself, there would still be a tremendous amount of labor involved in getting the wood into the house and into the fireplace....[accordingly] few rooms were heated and living arrangements were altered in the winter."[235]

☆☆☆

---

[234] Levin 27-28
[235] Levin, p. 29

8. Prosperity & Commerce

Servants were also becoming more common by the mid-1700s. Initially, most all the colonists were poor, and few could have afforded this luxury, but by then both slaves and those indentured by the courts as servants were available and affordable, as well as the daughters of poorer families who were hired out to supplement their income. Often poor children and orphans were taken on as apprentices, the indentured boys and "excess" sons more often than the girls. They were apprenticed to shoemakers, blacksmiths, shipwrights, cordwainers, coopers, weavers, tanners, tailors, joiners, blockmakers, riggers, and mastmakers in the town—all growing occupations by the mid-1700s.[236]

The exception for girls were those apprenticed to learn the weaving trade which took fourteen years. One such was Jerusha Sugars who, on January 11, 1708/9, was taken from her mother by Thomas and Hannah Joslin when she was only about one year old. The Joslins were "carefully her to keepe" and to "learne the said Jerusa Sugars the art and mistry of a Tailor, well and sufficiently to make apparill both for Men and Women and to learne her to Read well." She was to "receive sufficient board, lodging and apparel for a servant," and, at eighteen, was to "receive two sufficient sutes." The Joslins were to pay Jerusa's mother "£8 in silver and 40s. in a yearling heifer. The payment was changed January 20 to £10 silver."[237] We can only hope that Jerusa learned the trade and later prospered as did some women in the mid-1700s. Martha Nicols was paid 20s. for "making one gound." Joanna Dugglass, a single woman, in 1764 was paid 72s. per week for eleven weeks for "sempstry." Amy Shearman had one

---

[236] Ulrich, p. 43.
[237] Miner, Lilian, p. 69 & Weedon, p. 113, quoting *Early Rec. Prov.*, Vol. V, p. 18..

pound in cash to pay for "making her Bonet."[238]

Betsy Metcalf was one of those fortunate girls whose parents had sufficient income without apprenticing her, but who was clever enough to learn on her own to make bonnets and profitably sell them.[239] She was born later in the century, in 1786, to Lucy Gay and Joel Metcalf, an artisan, tanner and currier. Betsy left us a letter and a sort of memoir/diary, both written after the fact. In them, she describes in some detail how her bonnet business came about, but begins by noting that when old enough to write she was sent to "Means School." There, she tells us, she was "too neglectful" and without sufficient patience "to attain the art." Betsy was eager, instead, to read and study and do "Figures" (a critique in itself of the schooling offered girls).

Betsy's memoir then describes how, the day in 1798 when she was twelve and home from school sick, she started trying to "braid straw bonnets." Though she did not do so herself, apparently an aunt living with the family kept urging Betsy to keep at it even when she found the learning-process tough-going. Betsy records that it took her several months before she felt she could "make a bonnet which would do to wear." But with perseverance, Betsy adds, she learned all kinds of braiding "by seeing the English bonnets." Then, after her sister also learned, "we had considerable of a manufactury."

Their first customer, after their work became known by the public, was "Sally Richmond who lived next door." After that, word gradually spread over the country and "for two or three years, was very profitable. I could frequently make 1 dollar per day." [the letter states,

---

[238] Weedon, pp. 286-287
[239] All information and quotes are from Baker, Betsy Metcalf, memoir/diary and Letter.

8. Prosperity & Commerce

sometimes $1.25]. "I received much commendation and praise which not a little flattered my vanity." After that there was too much competition and the price was too low to make a profit.

In any case, Betsy was worried about her vanity. She criticizes girls becoming so "obsessed in the apparel of their own making, they have purchased the vanities of Europe and brought dress more in fashion when it was quite enough so before....I hear gentlemen say that it is almost impossible to get a girl to do housework in the country, they are so engaged in braiding straw." Betsy clearly asserts that house work and babies come first.

One wonders if this last assessment was made by the twelve to fourteen year old she then was, or came later, looking back.

After the original memoir, Betsy responds to a request for more information about her straw-bonnet-making business in a letter dated February 11, 1858. In it she goes into great detail about the whole process of bonnet-making, and adds that she taught others for free and did not get a patent though told she should. "I told them I did not wish to have my name sent to Congress."

When Betsy was fourteen and her business no longer prosperous, she returned to the public school just opened in her district by the Baptists. Her father, Joel Metcalf, who was on the Town Council, had always been a strong advocate for public schools. He even neglected his own business to work on the town to approve and repair such schools— "finally seeing four, accommodating 150 scholars." Betsy continued at school until she was seventeen, studying geography and grammar and excelling as first in her school. Betsy tells us that when the school committee visited, which they were wont to do every three months, the students displayed their work "with as much pride as if we were Monarchs of an empire."

Betsy concluded her account with an assessment of reading habits. "I was never fond of reading novels, though they are the most fashionable, especially among the female sex." She adds that after her father "bought a right in the town library," she "began to read History...Ancient History particularly.

Later Betsy taught school in Dedham, Massachusetts for a brief time before marrying a Dedham man, Obed Baker. By the time Betsy died on February 14, 1867, aged 81, her contribution to the establishment of a thriving new bonnet-making industry in New England had been duly noted. Betsy had at least four brothers and four sisters.

✯✯✯

Toward the latter part of the 17th century, Providence began to turn away from a land-based economy and toward the sea. It would not be inaccurate to conclude that Pardon Tillinghast started the trend when he requested, in 1679/80, "a little Spott of Land against his dwelling place...for the building himselfe A store house with the prieveladge of A whorfe Alsoe." Arthur Fenner followed with a similar request for a "Spott of ground." By 1681 five lots of "forty feet square by the water side" had been laid out. Soon there appeared dozens of wharves and warehouses owned by a considerable number of Providence's settlers: Thomas Harris, Samuel Winsor, Samuel Whipple, Thomas Hopkins, Zachariah Field, Providence Williams, Peter Place, Ephraim Pray, John Whipple, Jr., Thomas Olney, Thomas Olney Jr., James Ashton and Daniel Abbot, Jr. When Gideon Crawford, an already experienced merchant, arrived in 1687, he "gave stability and due direction to the rising trade." Prior to this the more populous Newport, with its three

8. Prosperity & Commerce

shipyards, had been the Colony's undisputed headquarters for its importing and exporting trade.[240]

Gideon Crawford was an immigrant from Scotland, who, on April 13, 1687, married Freelove Fenner, daughter of Arthur Fenner, granddaughter of William Harris.[241] Somehow he had managed to meet and win the heart of Freelove (or at least her agreement to marry him) only months after he settled in Providence, having come to America as a result of his relationship and friendship with Governor John Cranston. By the time Gideon died on October 10, 1707, he had acquired considerable wealth, "chalking up a record of acquisitiveness without many scruples."[242] Gideon left Freelove his whole property until such time as she died; after that to be divided between their two sons, William and James; their two daughters barely mentioned.

After Gideon's death, in addition to raising their four children, Freelove carried on his mercantile business "with great energy, accumulating a large property."[243] James, in his history, *Colonial Rhode Island*, stated that she "was as close to being a merchant as any man in town." When Freelove died on June 1, 1712, amongst other things, she left her son, William, her part in the sloop *Dolphin*, and each son, a part of a sloop in process of being built and rigged by Nathaniel Browne with money from the estate. To each of her daughters, she left £100 in money and various other goods.

William and John both married Whipple daughters, and though they both died fairly young, they had already accumulated large estates. When William died

---
[240] Kimball, pp. 129-130 & Field, p. 395.
[241] See Arthur Fenner Family Tree in Appendix. Also that of William Harris.
[242] James, *History*, p. 262.
[243] *Genealogies*, V. 1, p. 331.

in 1720, his inventory amounted to £3,551.19.1, the largest yet recorded in Providence. Before John died on March 18, 1718/19, he had built the "Crawford House," west of the old Canal Market, where he and his wife, Amey, were accustomed to "a luxurious style of living." He also owned several vessels in addition to real estate. His personal inventory amounted to £1,614.02.11, not as large as his brother's but still amazingly large for the time.[244] John and Amey Crawford's son, John, Jr., also entered the mercantile business, and on a voyage to the West Indies in December of 1746, he was lost at sea and never heard from again. He had a daughter, Amey, a mere infant at the time, who later married John Carter.[245]

☆☆☆

By 1704, commerce in Providence had increased to the point that a grant was sought to locate a warehouse on the "the east bank of the river, west of the city street," but the town was not yet ready to relinquish long-established customs. It responded to the request with a resolution declaring that "the said neck of land and every part thereof shall be and remain continually in common." The resolution explained that if a warehouse were built there, "the cattle swimming across the river would have no place to land, nor would those who forded the river." It had long been the custom for people to cross by foot at low tide, or "with Cannooes & Boates, Riding & Carting & Swimming over of Cattell from side to side; & the Streame often times Running so swift..."[246]

It was seven more years, in 1711, before this

---

[244] *Genealogies*, V. 1, p. 331
[245] Biographical, pp. 251 & 249
[246] Early Records, Vol. IX, p. 89

8. Prosperity & Commerce 159

resolution was voided and Nathaniel Brown, a shipbuilder formerly of Rehoboth (now East Providence), was given a grant to build ships on a part of this land. He had moved to Providence, as had so many before him, after religious trouble in Massachusetts.[247] Since a wooden fourteen foot wide bridge had finally been constructed that year between the town and the Weybosset side, the town no doubt felt a landing for cattle crossing was no longer needed. This bridge had been constructed so that one section could be removed to accommodate the passage of ships now engaged in commerce. At the same time, a highway was built from the westerly end of the bridge that became known as Weybosset Street. For use of the bridge, strangers had to pay a toll, but not the town's citizens—a new source of revenue.

There had actually been a bridge connecting the town with the meadows on the Weybosset side as early as 1660, but it was "so poorly built that it came to mending in less than two years." [248]

The town was unable or unwilling to pay the amounts needed to keep it in repair. "In 1668 Roger Williams offered to maintain the bridge 'with God's help,' providing each family furnished one day's work and he be allowed to charge strangers toll. After four years the General Assembly repealed Mr. Williams' grant" [249] and this bridge was abandoned—that would be a year after the new bridge was built in 1711, and so not needed.

But the 1711 bridge was not to last either and a replacement was built in 1738. At the same time, Towne Street was widened and became known as the Town Parade. Then, in 1744, a fourth Weybosset Bridge

---

[247] Haley, Old Stone Bank, Vol. I, pp. 30-31
[248] Miner, Lilian, p. 68.
[249] Wilson, p. ix.

replaced this one with a substantial 18 foot wide version.

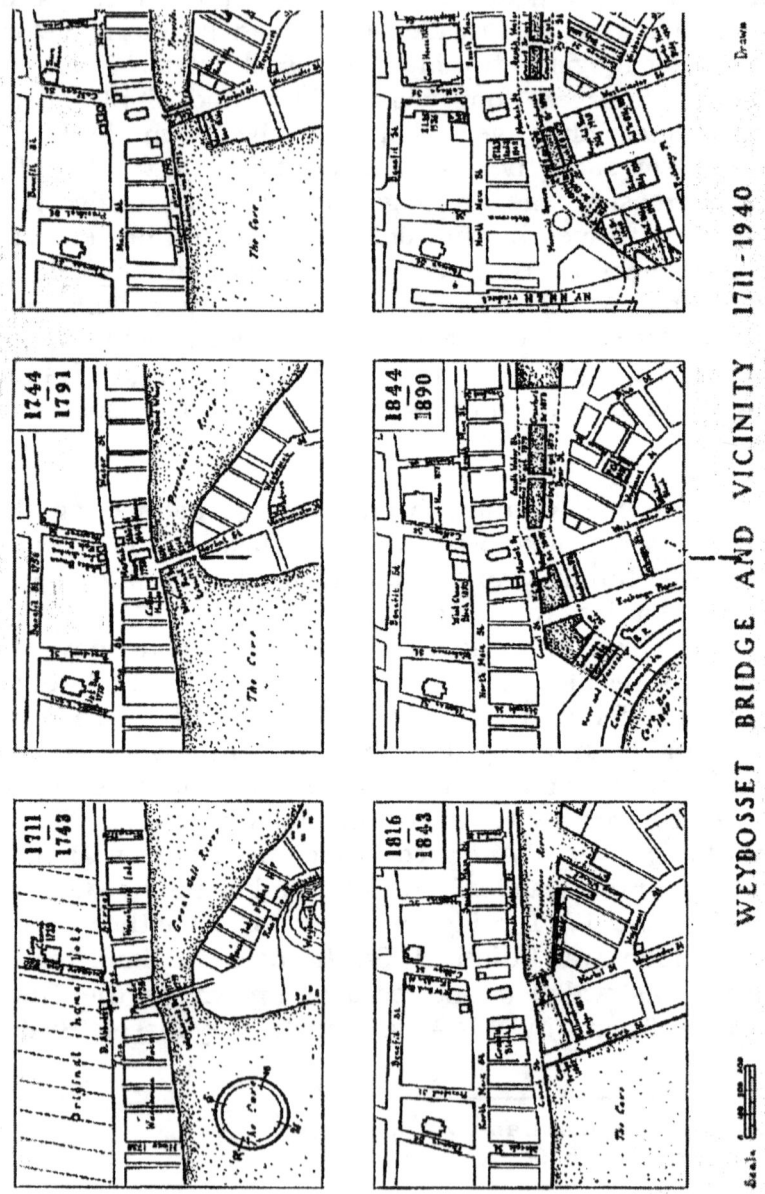

8. Prosperity & Commerce

This bridge was followed by a fifth in 1764, 22 feet wide and 150 feet long; a sixth in 1792, 56 feet wide and 120 feet long; a seventh in 1816, 95 feet wide. It included, for the first time, a 22-foot wide sidewalk. Yet two more replacement bridges were built in 1843 and 1888, by which time the town also had three additional bridges.[250]

During its history the Weybosset Bridge has been the site of everything from "a fish market to a whipping post. In 1767 one victim of the latter was sold for one year."[251]

☆☆☆

In 1708, Governor Cranston had this to say of the change from farm to sea taking place in Providence:[252]

> The land on said Island being all taken up and improved in small farms, so that the farmers, as their families increase are compelled to put or place their children to trades or callings, but they [children's] inclinations being mostly to navigation, the greater part betake themselves to that employment. So that such as are industrious and thrifty...get a small stock beforehand, improve it in getting a part of a vessel as many of the tradesmen in the town of Newport also dothe for the benefit of their children that are bred to navigation.

At first the move away from a living built totally on "improvinge the wildernesse" was slow; one hundred forty men out of a population of 7,181 earned their living as seamen. But after the arrival in Providence in 1711 of the shipbuilder Nathaniel Brown, possibilities rapidly expanded—more and bigger ships were added to the then-existing twenty-seven sloops and two

---

[250] See Cady, pp. 13-21 for a complete story of the sequence of bridges with illustrations (reproduced above).
[251] Arnold, Samuel G., p. x.
[252] Coughtry, p. 9.

brigs, thus enabling merchants to make greater use of the seas than had previously been possible. Trade with the West Indies and with the other colonies grew apace. In fact "the whole economy of life in the plantation was stimulated and developed by the shipbuilding" and "the population of the colony trebled itself in the first quarter of the eighteenth century....A new industry applying native materials and employing a variety of workmen increased the wealth and stimulated the intelligence of a community in equal proportions." [253]

"Everywhere, youngsters were perfecting themselves in the intricacies of knot-tying and splicing; enterprising landlubbers were found buying and packing merchandise sought by ready buyers in distant ports; the women went from house to house, seeking news of their own husbands or sons who might be mentioned in a neighbor's letter," eager to hear of loved ones, fearful they might be lost at sea, never to return.[254] The sea would certainly bring Rhode Island wealth, but it also brought tragedy to many families.

"By 1750 even farmers were investing hard-earned savings in seagoing ventures the way people today invest in the stock market, hoping that their ship would come in loaded with profitable wares. Even so, expanding trade and prosperity did not come easily. Merchants had always to take risks, to look for ways to cut corners, and to make use of every conceivable loophole in the navigation acts and other imperial trade regulations. "The word most commonly used for that kind of cutthroat competition was *enterprise*, and Rhode Island had an abundant supply of that commodity. It was a trait that at last united them in spirit to the rest of New

---

[253] Kimball, pp. 129-130, Field, p. 395 & Weedon, pp. 122 & 193-194.
[254] Haley, Old Stone Bank, V. III, p. 103.

8. Prosperity & Commerce 163

England and America. By entering into the mainstream of imperial trade after 1710, Rhode Islanders became considerably less exceptional."[255]

☆☆☆

Pardon Tillinghast, in asking the town for its first wharf in 1679/80, could hardly have realized what momentous changes were about to occur in Providence. A cooper by trade, he was born in 1622 in Sussex England and came to Providence as a young man. He prospered as a business man and for some time was chief amongst the shippers. He also was active in the affairs of the Baptist church where he became an elder, and, despite much opposition, a strong advocate for paying the Baptist clergy (which was already happening in the other denominational churches).

In 1711, by then sufficiently wealthy and tired of having to hold their religious services outdoors or in various homes, Pardon presented the congregation with its first meeting house near the corner of what is now North Main and Smith Streets—"for the Christian love, good will and affection which I bear to the church of Christ in said Providence," It was a "rude and unsightly" building, with what has been described as a "hay-cap-like" top and a central chimney with a roof opening to let out the smoke. Nonetheless, it allowed the church to be heated, unlike most churches of the day—congregants having to bring with them a heated brick to put at their feet to ward off chills.

In 1726 this church was replaced by a "worthier sanctuary" that served the congregation until just prior to the Revolutionary War (1774/5), when it was replaced by the present church with its tall, graceful spire. Known as the First Baptist Meeting House, this oldest

---

[255] McLoughlin, pp. 61-62.

Baptist Church in America is generally regarded as "the most perfect specimen of colonial church architecture standing... The design was conceived by Joseph Brown from drawings published in a 'Book of Architecture' by James Gibbs, a pupil of Sir Christopher Wren." The original church bell, cast in London, weighed 2,500 pounds, and bore this inscription:

> For freedom of conscience the town was first planted,
> Persuasion not force, was used by the people,
> This church is the eldest and has not recanted,
> Enjoying and granting bell, temple and steeple.

In the spring of 1787 the bell was broken and subsequently recast at Hope Furnace (by then built by the Brown brothers and named after their mother). The church's crystal chandelier came from England in 1792; a gift of Hope Brown, daughter of Nicholas Brown Sr., in memory of her father who had died the year before. The chandelier was first lighted at the time of Hope's marriage to Thomas Ives who was associated in business with her brother, Nicholas 2nd. It initially burned candles, then in 1884 was fitted for gas, and, finally, in 1914, for electricity.[256]

As for the elder Pardon Tillinghast, who had provided the Baptists with their first permanent place to worship, he had married Sarah Butterworth of Rehoboth, Massachusetts in 1653 and they had three children.[257] Sarah died in 1660, probably without having had the pleasure of knowing her seven grandchildren. Four years after Sarah's death, on February 16, 1664, Pardon married Lydia Taber of Tiverton. She bore nine children from whom

---

[256] Kimball, p. 132, Field, pp. 89-90, & Haley, Old Stone Bank, Vol. IV, p. 98-99.
[257] Information on genealogy and will are from "Pardon Ancestors and Descendants."

8. Prosperity & Commerce 165

descended seventy-four grandchildren.

Pardon died in 1718. His will, which named his second wife, Lydia, as executrix, left his son, Joseph, "part of his dwelling lot, and all his riches and interest after his wife's decease"—an unusual allocation since Joseph is not his oldest son (John is by the first marriage, and Pardon, Jr. by Lydia). But to Pardon, Jr., he apparently left only £50, the same as to his sons, Philip and Benjamin. To each of his five daughters he left £10, and, to each of his grandchildren, five shillings. Curiously, his three children by Sarah Butterworth are not mentioned even though they were all still alive. Pardon's wife, Lydia, died in 1720, two years after her husband.

Whether left a substantial inheritance or not by his father, Philip did well, most likely in the shipping trade. He built a home for himself and his wife Martha Holmes "of almost fabulous magnificence. Its dimensions are reported as being about forty by thirty feet; it was two stories high, with a kitchen in the basement and an extra half-story above the attic. Both main stories were divided into four rooms, and the furnishings were such as to make the colonists gasp. There was a 'great room' on the first floor, which was sixteen feet square and eight feet in height. In this the ceiling was made of paneled woodwork, and paneling was used to decorate other parts of the room also. The great fireplace was highly ornamented, and the chairs upholstered with leather...in those days the colonists hardly dared dream of such wealth."[258]

Philip and Martha's son, Benjamin, carried on in the shipping trade. When Benjamin died in 1726, he left his heirs his third of the ownership of two sloops, warehouses "replete with 'coco, salt, sugar, molasses Rum and other Spirits', and sundry ship goods." At

---

[258] Haley, Old Stone Bank, V. I, p. 31

least part of Benjamin's estate went to Colonel Nicholas Power 3rd (his sister Mercy's husband). This was the second marriage of Nicholas 3rd; his first had been to Mary Haile of Swansea, Massachusetts.

The Tillinghasts, including its women, must have continued in the mercantile business for generations for in the family papers we find a letter dated March 18, 1807 in which Lydia Tillinghast (perhaps a granddaughter or great granddaughter of Pardon and Lydia) gives Capt. Robert Gray power of attorney to collect from John L leCuesta monies owed "for ninety five Barrels Tar left in his hands by Capt. Benjamin Tayler, Master of *Snow Susan* April 1802." Lydia further gives him permission to collect it in produce.

Lydia wrote a more homey letter to her son on December 26 (the year omitted) that begins with expressions of her worries at not having heard from him for so long, but, she adds, she is "comforted today by thy letter," and she hopes "thou will be able to leve that place by the brige." [Lydia's use of thee and thou leads one to believe she was a Quaker, such use being their custom.]

Lydia goes on to say she would have sent her son some of her home-made preserves but was afraid he would be gone by the time they arrived. Near the end, she notes that "Grandmother is as well as can be expected" and comments on others in the family. She signs the letter, "Your affectionate and Loving mother Lidia Tillinghast." The attachment to the letter again suggests her involvement in the family's business. It is a report of sales by an auctioneer that includes 3 barrels cyder for 11 shillings, varying amounts of cheese sold, and 30 gallons cordial, £1.16.3.

★★★

8. Prosperity & Commerce

The Grandfather of Nicholas Power 3rd [259] (who married into the Tillinghast family) was Nicholas Power, the elder. He had been one of the thirty-eight signers of a "compact for good government" in 1640. When the elder Nicholas died in August 1657 "by reason of extreme sickness and sudden death," he left no will, which gave local officials the right to determine the division of his estate. They gave his wife, Jane, "the dwelling house and half the cellar that she built, with house lot, &c., and at her decease, her son Nicholas 2nd was to have the house and lot, and her daughter Hope, other land." But Jane had other ideas.

For the next ten years, while the children were still young, Jane successfully managed her husband's estate despite the town elders looking askance. Then, when the children were about to reach maturity, enabling them to claim most of the estate for themsleves, Jane went to the town and asked them for a more generous share than they had initially alloted her. Impressed as they were with her 'industrye,' they agreed. And so, for ten years Jane Power had shown her independence, and, in the end, got what she felt was rightfully hers.[260]

Of Jane's death, we only know it was after 1667. The Power's youngest child, Hope, only seven when her father died, later married Rev. James Clarke of Newport [perhaps the brother of Dr. John Clarke, since his will mentions a brother, but not by name].

Nicholas 2nd married Rebecca Rhodes, daughter of Zachariah and Joanna Arnold Rhodes. The house he built for Rebecca and his family on the west side of Town Street included a great lower room, dining room,

---

[259] Unless otherwise noted, the information and quotes regarding the Power family are from the Powers, Franklin, *Genealogical Record of the Power Families* & from *Genealogy* V. I, pp. 704-709.
[260] An account can be found in Norton, *Founding Mothers*, pp. 148-149.

kitchen, bedroom, little bedroom, chamber NE, chamber NW, chamber South, and garret, besides warehouse, cooper's shop, etc.

After Nicholas 2nd died in 1675, during King Philip's War "by a shot from the command with which he was serving," his wife, Rebecca, married Daniel Williams (a marriage already noted).

In 1701 Nicholas Power 3rd, who was a merchant of some note in Providence, bought a house from Daniel Williams in the lower end of town. (Daniel by then had married Rebecca Rhodes, the widow of his father.) Mary Haile of Swansea, Massachusetts was Nicholas 3rd first wife. They had only one daughter, Mary, before she died, possibly in childbirth. Nicholas 3rd then married Mercy Tillinghast, Pardon's daughter (already alluded to as the sister of Benjamin). It was their daughter, Hope, who became the mother of the famous Brown brothers of whom we will hear more later. When Nicholas 3rd died in May 1734, his will made his wife, Mercy, and his son, Nicholas 4th, executors. Numerous legacies were left to Mercy and to both his married and unmarried children. His inventory amounted to £1751.13.3. Mercy did not die until November 13, 1769, aged ninety-one.

Interestingly, there began another tie with both the Tillinghasts and Browns when Nicholas Power 4th, a merchant and distiller, married Anne Tillinghast, daughter of Philip and Martha Holmes Tillinghast. One of their daughters married into the Joseph Brown family. In 1743, Nicholas 4th, his wife, and his mother, Mercy, sold to Captain John Brown of Newport, for £3,300, "ten acres and barn therewith, a six acre orchard, and 'dwelling house wherein I now dwell,' warehouse, still, &c." [261]Where they then lived is not stated. After he died in 1744, the inventory of his belongings totaled £1042.9.6 and included books, silver

---

[261] *Power Family*, p. 20.

8. Prosperity & Commerce

money and a watch among other things.

The 5th Nicholas Power was also a merchant, and a ropemaker. After he married Rebecca Corey, they "received a deed from her father of dwelling house, &c. providing care was taken of grantor's wife if she outlived him." Also of note, in 1781 he "manumitted and set free" his negro man, Prince.[262]

The 6th and last of the Nicholas Powers at various times sold liquors, dry goods, and groceries in his store on Cheapside near the Baptist Meeting House. In 1842, he erected a tombstone on the long-neglected grave of his affectionate mother, Rebecca Cory, who had died on October 29, 1825:

> Can storied urn or animated bust
> Back to its mansion call the fleeting breath?
> Can honor's voice provoke the silent durst
> Or flattery sooth the dull cold ear of death?[263]

His own grave was in the North Burial Ground; that of his wife, Anne, and their daughters, Sarah Helen and Susan Anna, near by.

☆☆☆

Another of those who early-on obtained wharves was Thomas Hopkins, Sr. We must assume he is the same Thomas Hopkins who was the oldest of the three children of William Arnold's sister, Joane, who came to this country with the Arnold family group in 1635. [There is no mention of his father, William Hopkins, which makes it unlikely that he ever came to America.]. Sometime later, Thomas was allotted home shares at the south end of town, and later still, as the population spread, additional land ten miles further out in what is now Lincoln. He made this his home until he fled to

---

[262] *Power Family*, p. 21.
[263] *Power Family*, p. 23.

Long Island during the King Philip's War, never returning. By the time of his death, the elder Thomas had over 1,000 acres of land. The parents of his wife, believed to have been named Elizabeth, is in dispute. Thomas and Elizabeth had at least two sons, William 2nd and Thomas, Jr. who "stayed and went not away" during King Philip War.

Thomas Hopkins, Jr. made his home in the outlying area around Providence.[264] In 1698, he married Mary Smith, daughter of Elizabeth and John Smith, mason. When Thomas, Sr. died and left his estate to the elder brother, William (per the laws of primogeniture), William gave his title to Thomas "in consideration of the mutual love and affection between [us], and for other good causes." William Hopkins, Jr. continued to live on the initial home lot of his father. In 1650 he married Abigail, widow of Stephen Dexter, daughter of Sarah and John Whipple.

To digress: John Whipple was also a man of some prominence in Providence—an inn-keeper, trader, surveyor, carpenter, member of the town council, member of the General Assembly and a principal legal practitioner. In 1680, the town granted him perhaps its first license to "keep a house of Intertainment" (to serve liquor). The Whipple Inn, established at the foot of what later became Constitution Hill, "had only two rooms and no place to put up travelers," as did later taverns, but it did have "pewter basins, quart pots, pint pots, gillpots, glass bottles, and other dishes" which were then very scarce.

The following description of tavern-keepers, called "a picturesque lot," probably applies, at least in part, to John Whipple.[265]

---

[264] *Genealogies*, V. 1, pp. 479-482.
[265] Haley, Old Stone Bank, Vol. II, pp. 92-93.

8. Prosperity & Commerce 171

> Usually stout, good-natured, good-looking, and well-dressed, they were prominent public figures, enjoying all sort of confidences, public and private, leading the singing in the meeting houses, running ferries, teaching the children of travelers, serving on the legislature or town council, acting as recruiting officers in times of war, as storekeepers, surveyors or story-tellers. Some were frugal and thrifty, some mean and penurious, while others were extravagant. Some were of bitter dispositions, but, as a rule, they were jolly enough.

Of John Whipple we also know he was one of those who "stayed" during King Philip's War. He was given the title Captain, and after the war was amongst those appointed to sell the captive Indians, receiving at least one himself.

Sarah and John Whipple had eight sons, one of whom, John Jr., married Mary Olney and then Rebecca Scott. Two letters we have of Rebecca's confirm, unintentionally the subordination a wife felt to her husband, at least as far as money is concerned [the following italics are authors].[266]

The first is a brief note, dated June 21, 1692, that Rebecca wrote to her husband in Newport, clearly at a time when she was away from home. She attached an account of items she had purchased with **his** money. "I have paid £12.5.0 of **your** £13, no more, but more love to you and my children and also I rest your loving wife, Rebeka Whipple."

The longer letter Rebecca writes to her husband a few days later suggests her absence from home has to do with an unspecified illness, whether fatal or not we do not know, since the date of her death is not noted. Her letter is especially interesting for what it reveals about medical practices at the time—and how taken for granted they were:

---

[266] Letters available in manuscript section of RI Historical Society.

> Loving husband my love to you and my children hoping you are all good. I am under the doctors hand I have some incuragmont I hope. [She then names doctors who] need thirty shillings now and thirty more when he has done the cure. I must be loss blood before I can come home. I have been blooded once. Pray inform Waite Brown from Doctor Colman his advice to her [regarding Robert]: take crabs scalloped or roasted if they be biganuf then soak them and bake [*becomes unreadable by this person but continues about an alternative of getting*] ten bushels of Indian corn of John Smith miller. [*Again unreadable, the final reference is to Mr. Crawford and Olney, and then*] Pray them not to fail Robert.

At the end, without further explanation, Rebecca refers to 2 bushels wheat; ground ginger "hard to get" and "half *your* money all gone." It continues:

> When Simon Davies comes in send your anser whether you will have mollasos and rum pray send down some money *if you please* and love to all at Newport, June 27 1692. Your loving wife Rebekah Whipple.

To return to Sarah and John Whipple: In addition to their eight sons, they had three daughters, one of whom, Abigail, married Stephen Dexter. It was Stephen's grandfather, Rev. Gregory Dexter, who printed the first edition of Roger Williams' book, *Key into the Language of America*, while Roger was in London in 1643. Afterwards, in 1644, Gregory Dexter returned to America with Roger Williams.

☆☆☆

Another family involved in trade comes to light as the result of a preserved, difficult-to-read, eighty-page diary by Julia Bowen Martin whose short life extended

8. Prosperity & Commerce 173

only from 1779 to 1808.[267] Her father was Ephraim Bowen, Jr., a merchant and soldier who was born in 1753, died in 1841. Julia's grandfather, Ephraim Sr. (1716-1812), was a doctor in Providence. Julia was only thirteen when her mother, Sarah Angell, died and her father married Sarah Whipple.

She was about twenty when she wrote the diary that extends from April to August 1799. In it she frequently mentions her parents, grandparents, uncles, aunts, cousins, brothers, sisters, half-brothers and half-sisters; the relationship of some of those mentioned still not clarified. In April, Julia describes chores which were probably common in her life; perhaps also the lives of most young women at the time:

> "Rose at eight, after breakfast rubbed the handirons &c clearstarched some handkerchiefs, in the afternoon Ironed two muslin gowns and several handkerchiefs. Sat lolling out of the window after I had made my room tidy." On other occasions, "Thank Heavens the quilt is done & never were mortals gladder," and "made a cockade for George Washington." *[Would this have been when the President visited Providence?]* In another vein, "Made a frugal repast composed of chocolate and some crackers."

A month later, on June 12, 1799, Julia writes: "The news of the French defeat by the Austrians is confirmed—had dreadful dreams all night of the French invading us."

In August, Julia gives a vivid account of meeting a black, perhaps for the first time:

> "We all went to a famous fortune teller just arrived in town, a black man, we walked down beyond the new Presbyterian Meeting House, I found him quite on the hill, in a negro house. I was ushered up Chamber first. I was prodigiously frightened at first, but my fears soon

---

[267] This diary available in the manuscript section of RI Historical Society.

subsided. I saw a monstrous fat black man. His face from his nose up, full of notches..." [She then describes the fortune.]

Her earlier run-in with a sailor in May did not seem as pleasant, but Julia certainly does seem to be the venturesome sort.

"I took Esther with me, we stopped at a tavern to ask where a woman lived who spun for Grandmama A—we saw four sailors pass us there...as we went uptown we overtook the four sailors again, who said something to us, & hallowed...we took no notice of them till one of them got up behind the chaise. I took the whip and struck him several times. They then hallowed as loud as possible bringing al the men to their shop doors. After lugging heartily we went round the square."

Writing about a picnic in July, Julia once again reveals a young woman with few inhibitions who enjoys life.

Attended wild drunken picnic at a local riverside location called Cold Spring. "Betsey Brown, Sophia Smith & Sarah Howell were quite tipsy. After we had dined we sang several patriotic songs..." Most of the girls ended up falling in mud, and ended up in various states of undress; "I was almost naked."

Julia regularly attends church and in July muses on the subject: "My soul feels too large for its confinement as if striving to break loose. Teach me, O God, and be my guide thro this life..." She also mentions occasionally going to the theater, and reading three volumes of *Clermont* and part of Hume.

In April, Julia expresses her fears that she is not accepted in the best society. This may just be a temporary pique, because her appearance at Moses Brown's wedding suggests otherwise. She writes: "Invited [the richest, most popular girls in town] to visit me on Wednesday, among them Miss A[lice]

8. Prosperity & Commerce   175

Brown, who never honored me, but promised to do me the honor." Alice did visit as promised, but regarding the others Julia says, "it is unaccountable to me, that Sally & Betsey have not visited me...I am determined not to go there again, until they have visited me."

Regarding that wedding on May 2, 1799 at the Quaker Meeting House in Providence, Julia wrote:

> Bride and Groom rose and Moses of the said Friends takes Phebe Lockwood to be my wife, promising to be unto her a loving and faithful husband till it shall please the Lord by death to separate us. She said the same and the ceremony was over.

She follows this entry on the same day with the comment: "Went to tea at one of Browns in afternoon."

Julia only briefly mentions the man she would marry in 1803, John Martin. Only two years later Julia died of "the fever;" this brief statement in her obituary giving us the only clue as to why she died before her twenty-sixth birthday.

9. Slaves

It was the prospect of making large profits that gradually drew Rhode Island merchants into the slave trade. Initially the Caribbean Islands served as markets for the colony's small export trade in lumber and provisions which they traded for molasses to produce rum. This, however, was very "low profit." By adding slave trade to the equation, large quantities of their rum could be sold at a relatively high price in an overseas market where there was little competition. They could then "purchase slaves cheaply [in Africa] and sell them dearly, primarily in the West Indies," in exchange for the molasses needed by the Rhode Island distillers. The distillers then "furnished the colony's merchants with a saleable item for the coasting trade."[268]

©All Rights Reserved: Courtesy of Rhode Island Black Heritage Society

The trade had its risks (fierce storms and capture by privateers amongst them) but the profits were high. For instance, the weather might eliminate all profit from

---

[268] Coughtry, pp. 20-21

9. Slaves

such a venture as was the case with Captain Cleb Godfrey in 1738 when lightening struck the sloop he commanded. "The crew escaped in the longboat, but the many slaves on board were lost." And two years later, when a sloop under Captain Polypus Hammond was wrecked by the weather, all fifty-five of his slaves drowned, while "the captain with eight of the crew took to the longboat. They were six days at sea, 'without Victual and Drink,' but got safely to the West Indies." [269] Clearly the slaves were not a captain's first concern even thought losing them meant a financial loss.

A strong healthy slave, costing £4 to £5 in rum or iron bars, could be sold in the West Indies, at a price ranging from £30 to £88, for work on the sugar plantations. The "so-called 'refuse' blacks could be sold at home or in other ports of the colonies....Most Rhode Island blacks were taken from the 'refuse' persons lists," usually bringing from £15 to £25.[270]

Some were drawn into the trade who should not have been; one such Capt. Eddy, his Father and Uncle. They "risked the fruits of many a year of hard & honest Industry & the hopes of two large families of Children" in the hopes of "doubling their Capital in one voyage." Instead, the man entrusted to bring him the slaves disappeared, his brig was condemned, most of his crew perished "thro' want & sickness" & Captain Eddy sought "a passage back to his friends after having lost almost every farthing of their property & his own." This left him with a desire for revenge; a desire to return to Africa to "seize every man woman and child...till he had paid himself."[271] *Hopefully, his family, presumably now impoverished, were able to prevail upon him not to even*

---

[269] Hawes, p. 149.
[270] RI Short Story Club, "Slavery in the RI Colonial Period", Rae Vaule, p. 68.
[271] Hawes, p. 144.

consider such an unwise undertaking.

Jay Coughtry documents in his appropriately titled book, *The Notorious Triangle*, that between 1709 and 1807, Rhode Islanders made 934 slaving voyages carrying 106,544 Africans to bondage in the New World. "As the trader acquired wealth, he would send ship loads with rum directly to Africa so that by 1750 Newport had become the leading American slave port with Bristol second and Charleston, South Carolina third." Providence was a lesser participant (see tables and graphs following).[272] The distillation of molasses and sugar into rum quickly became Rhode Island's most important industry; in Providence the still-houses were along Towne Street. So it is not surprising that the sugar or 'Molasses' act of 1733, passed by the House of Commons [in England], that laid a heavy duty on products imported from foreign islands into the northern colonies, was the beginning of troubles that eventually ended in the American Revolution.[273]

In 1708, before the slave trade really took hold in Rhode Island, the census recorded 426 blacks (nearly all from Barbados, a few enjoying free status), out of a total population of 7,181 [Providence's population, 1,446]. By 1755, at a time when Providence's population totaled only 3,159 and Newport's 6,753, the number of slaves in Rhode Island peaked at 4,697. Rhode Island was said to have the largest percentage of black slaves per population of any of the Middle Atlantic or New England colonies, negating the claim of many at the end of the 20th century that Rhode Island had few slaves. Furthermore, James believes there were even more black slaves than given in the official records, justifying his assertion in a footnote: "there was no incentive for

---

[272] Stewart, p. 5.
[273] Weedon, pp. 221-222 & Coughtry, pp. 27-28

9. Slaves

the citizens anywhere in the colony to make known the number of their slaves, who either were or might become taxable property."[274]

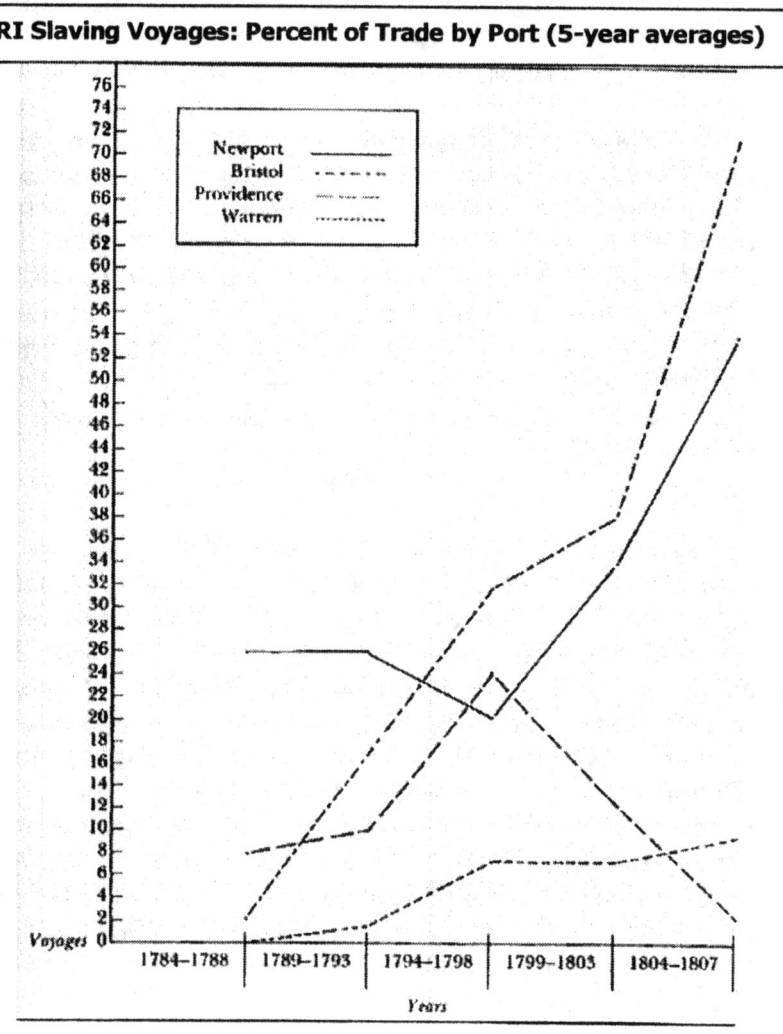

[274] Conley, *Liberty...*, p. 199 & RI Short Story Club, "Slavery in the RI Colonial Period", Rae Vaule, p. 67. Also, Bartlett, p. 9 & James, *History*, p. 255.

On the eve of the Revolution, Rhode Island recorded its Indian population as almost 1,500, but the intermingling between blacks and Indians had, by then, produced so many of mixed ancestry it is difficult to know just who was included in that number.[275] Bartlett points out that with both blacks and Indians sharing similar menial labor and social positions, the reason for the intermingling is obvious. "Moreover," he writes, "as the eighteenth century progressed and some masters began to free their Negroes, they were looked upon as good husbands by Indian women who had been brought up in a civilization in which women did all the drudgery. Consequently, more than one Indian woman purchased a Negro's freedom that he might marry and support her." [276]

★★★

Although Thomas Windsor is credited with having brought the first African slaves to Rhode Island in 1696 on his ship the brigantine *Seaflower*, Rhode Island's General Assembly had legalized slavery as early as 1652. However, that law had limited slavery to ten years, and involved, primarily, the exportation of Native Americans. Interestingly, the colony in its "Reports to the British Committee for Trade and Foreign Plantations denied any such involvement."[277] As for the *Seaflower*, of forty-seven slaves on the ship, fourteen were sold in Rhode Island for about £30 each (some accounts put the number sold there at only four); the rest were taken to Boston.

---

[275] James, *History*, p. 231
[276] Bartlett, p. 11.
[277] RI Short Story Club, "Slavery in the RI Colonial Period", Rae Vaule, p. 67. One might also ask why a denial was necessary!

9. Slaves

RI Slaving Voyages to Africa, 1709-1807

Year	Voyages	Slaves	Year	Voyages	Slaves
1709	1	116	1761	15	1574
1714	1	140	1762	18	1726
1717	1	143	1763	18	2021
1725	3	349	1764	27	3193
1726	2	232	1765	16	1885
1727	1	116	1766	15	1686
1728	2	232	1767	16	1883
1729	1	116	1768	20	2534
1731	2	232	1769	19	2274
1732	6	697	1770	18	2038
1733	8	914	1771	15	1864
1734	6	549	1772	23	3469
1735	8	965	1773	20	2285
1736	13	1511	1774	25	2940
1737	10	1162	1775	4	628
1738	10	1162	1785	5	542
1739	13	1449	1786	7	827
1740	6	697	1787	7	878
1741	5	581	1788	7	599
1742	6	697	1789	8	864
1743	5	581	1790	10	939
1744	6	697	1791	7	861
1745	8	232	1792	8	1094
1746	2	349	1793	14	1591
1747	3	349	1794	17	1924
1748	2	232	1795	10	1177
1749	9	1046	1796	32	4244
1750	4	349	1797	21	2105
1751	15	1608	1798	11	1026
1752	11	1255	1799	19	1090
1753	10	1184	1800	19	1824
1754	11	1082	1801	10	929
1755	12	1165	1802	17	2044
1756	17	1833	1803	11	1680
1757	7	851	1804	23	2637
1758	10	1077	1805	51	6576
1759	6	651	1806	47	6253
1760	7	661	1807	26	3184
			Total	854	106,544

It was the end of 1707 before the next African slaves were brought to Rhode Island via Barbados, selling for roughly the same price. Thereafter, "nearly every vessel returning to Newport from the West Indies brought a few slaves." A duty, imposed on these imports between 1707 and 1732 (when it was repealed), paid for paving Newport's streets and repairing its bridges. In 1769, Newport had twenty-two distilleries and was the principal slave port and mart in New England, remaining so until the latter part of the 18th century. "Forty or fifty vessels were then engaged in the traffic and nearly all her merchants were interested.... The commerce in rum and slaves afforded about £40,000 per annum for remittance from Rhode Island to Great Britain. ..."[278]

"Captain William English of Newport wrote to his employers, Jacob and Aaron Lopez, from the Gold Coast of Africa in 1773 that he could trade 'two hundred gallons [of rum] for men and 180 for women' and in some cases '195 for men and in proportion for women.' The rum cost 18 to 25 cents a gallon to make, while the slaves brought $250 to $400 in Havana, Charleston or Newport."[279]

In one important respect, Rhode Island differed from the slavers of England. For example, "the deck plan of the 320-ton English slaver *Brookes*, shows 450 slaves packed together in prone position on two separate levels in the between-decks compartment....Rhode Island vessels, on the other hand, averaged only one hundred tons, and rarely exceeded two hundred." They deliberately "restricted their trade in slaves to smaller craft, in order to reduce the time spent on the disease-ridden African coast. They collected cargoes of only seventy-five to one hundred fifty slaves quickly, and thereby minimized the threat of sickness and death to slaves and crew alike."[280] These smaller craft and the smaller numbers of slaves also made the notorious "middle passage," which lasted from five to twelve weeks, both easier and safer for all concerned.

---

[278] Field, V. 2, p. 401.
[279] McLoughlin, pp. 64-65
[280] This and following paragraph, Coughtry, p. 7.

9. Slaves

Plan of an African Ship's lower Deck, with Negroes in the proportion of not quite one to a Ton.

GIRL'S ROOM.

WOMEN'S ROOM.

BOY'S ROOM.

MEN'S ROOM.

"THE above plate represents the lower deck of an African ship, of two hundred and ninety-seven tons burden, with the slaves stowed in it, in the proportion of not quite one to a ton.

"In the men's apartment, the space allowed to each is six feet in length, by sixteen inches in breadth. The boys are each allowed five feet by fourteen inches; the women five feet ten inches, by sixteen inches; and the girls four feet by twelve inches. The perpendicular height between the decks is five feet eight inches.

The men are fastened together, two and two, by handcuffs on their wrists, and by irons riveted on their legs. They are brought up on the main deck every day, about eight o'clock; and, as each pair ascends, a strong chain, fastened by ring-bolts to the deck, is passed through their shackles : a precaution absolutely necessary to prevent insurrection. In this state, if the weather is favourable, they are permitted to remain about one third part of the twenty-four hours, and during this interval, they are fed, and their apartment below is cleaned ; but when the weather is bad, even these indulgences cannot be

R R—*Store Rooms.*

"On Rhode Island vessels, slaves were quartered above, as well as between decks, and spent some time each day topside in the open air." They were typically segregated by sex and age: "men were confined in the hold; women and children might be placed there, too, but were occasionally housed at one end of the main deck behind a specially built barricade...Weather permitting, it was customary to feed and bathe slaves on deck, procedures that involved bringing all slaves topside in several shifts, and removing at least part of their shackles. It was fairly common aboard Rhode Island slavers to find women, children, and even a few men at various times roaming about the main deck partially or completely unchained."

These practices were self-serving in that the ship captains were aware of the "relationship between overcrowding, poor hygiene, and disease" and knew their profit depended on the arrival of their ship with as many healthy slaves as possible. "In the final accounting, it was 'mortality' that determined the size of profits and losses...." This said, the captains were not well prepared to fight the inevitable diseases that broke out during the middle passage. The so-called medical supplies included items such as "gum camphor, pulverized rhubarb, cinnamon water, mustard, and betters." They also "found many medicinal uses for rum, which was strong enough to mask additives, and was in plentiful supply." The best that can be said for these medicines is that they were unlikely to harm a patient, "at least not in small doses. All things considered, the surprising fact is not that 12% of the slaves died during the middle passage, but that 88 % lived."[281]

James DeWolfe, a notorious slaver, pinpointed

---

[281] Coughtry, p. 145, 150 & 153.

9. Slaves

slave deaths as "the biggest threat to the bottom line when he noted the loss of fifteen slaves aboard the *Juno* in 1796, and concluded matter-of-factly that 'the mortality was the ruining of the voyage.'" [282] Perhaps he was also remembering an earlier trip in 1790 on the barque, *Polly*. He was returning from Africa to the West Indies with 127 slaves, when "a woman slave came down with what the captain and crew took to be smallpox." When her condition worsened, Captain DeWolfe decided he had to get rid of her to prevent the others from being infected. The crew, however, declined his request to throw her overboard, so the Captain himself, "lashed the slave in a chair, bound a handkerchief around her eyes and mouth, and hooked up a tackle." She was then lowered into the water. At a later hearing, DeWolfe reportedly said he was sorry to have lost such a good chair. He escaped being charged with murder after the crew testified he had no choice but to rid the ship of her, but the lack of prosecution greatly upset members of Providence's Abolition Society. As for DeWolfe, it is said that the incident "occasionally haunted his career and even embarrassed his beautiful daughter in Washington society years later when he was serving as United States Senator from Rhode Island." [283] Perhaps his conscience was pricked, thus explaining a later order to his managers in Cuba to "exercise 'all' humanity in treating the slaves, particularly pregnant women."

Suicides, attempted and successful, also had to be contended with, no matter how "kind" the captain might be in respect to the African captives' welfare. Women especially, driven by despair, attempted suicide "by refusal of food; in response slaving captains often resorted to forcible feeding, and special equipment for

---

[282] Coughtry, p. 146
[283] This and following quote from Hawes, p. 183-184.

this purpose was developed and carried." [284] Nathaniel Briggs on his vessel reported a woman he "believed went over Board and nobody seen her."

> How many others contemplated such solutions is unknown. Women, of course, were helpless targets of the crews' sexual desires ...Curiously enough, the only reference to sexual assaults on slaves by Rhode Island seamen documents a failed attempt. Such attacks were undoubtedly frequent, but on the ship *Mary*, at least, they were not sanctioned by the captain, and were not always successful. A notation in the ship's log on June 6, 1796, explains: 'This morning found our women slave Apartments had been attempted to have been opened by some of the Ships crew, the locks being spoiled and sundered.'
>
> Ten days later Captain Sterry stripped Officer More of his rank and privileges for sleeping in the slave room, commenting that he was 'no longer fit Companion for the Cabin.' Sterry, and there were certainly others like him, frowned on abuse to their valuable human charges, sexual or otherwise ....[However] not all slaves could count on having such conscientious commanders, and the trade may well have attracted more sadists than saints. Wanton cruelty, however, was undoubtedly not the norm on the majority of Rhode Island vessels."[285]

The outcome of the slave sale that culminated the voyage depended on many things: "arrival time, quantity and quality of slaves already at market, status of the local crop, local currency and credit conditions, general health and makeup of the slave cargo...The average price of slaves—young and old, male and female, prime and sickly—ultimately governed whether ledger lines were tallied in red or black."[286]

Names of women colonists associated with the

---

[284] Hawes, p. 136.
[285] Coughtry, p. 160.
[286] Coughtry, p. 165.

9. Slaves

slave trade *per se* are limited to ships' names, often those of the owner's wife or daughter, but of these there was a plethora: *Ann, Betsey, Fanny, Hope, Lucy, Elizabeth, Freelove, Mary, Marygold, Nancy, Polly, Sally, Sukey,* and *Three sisters*. This does not mean, however, that the women did not benefit from it, both directly, by purchasing slaves to be their servants, and indirectly, by the wealth thus accrued enabling them to purchase luxuries not previously affordable.

Slave traders regularly retained a select number of blacks. Sales of those brought to Providence generally took place at the Crown Coffee House, located opposite the Court House. Most of these ended up as domestic servants or doing outside work such as clearing forests or laboring on the farm lands in the Narragansett country. The more fortunate ones, through apprenticeships and work alongside their masters, became experienced "sailors, shipbuilders, iron workers, coopers, waiters, carpenters, butchers, tailors, tanners, goldsmiths, bricklayers, plasterers, blacksmiths, rope makers, fishermen, rum makers, [and] weavers.... *Slaves were a valuable and essential part of the labor supply.*"[287] [writer's italics]

> In 1708, North and South Kingstown had about eighty-five slaves, but in 1738 South Kingstown owned the most slaves and was reputed to be the richest town in Rhode Island. Between 1748 and 1749, one out of every five persons was a slave and by 1755, the ratio of blacks to whites was one in three. As late as 1782, the proportion was one in six. *Providence was not an important slave-holding area until 1748 when she ranked second to South Kingstown* [writer's italics].[288]

---

[287] RI Short Story Club, "Slavery in the RI Colonial Period", Rae Vaule, p. 69.
[288] RI Short Story Club, "Slavery in the RI Colonial Period", Rae Vaule, p. 67.

By far the largest number of "blacks and Indians, and their offspring of mixed blood, who were enslaved, labored on South County plantations or in the homes of wealthy merchants in Newport, Providence, and Bristol."[289] By 1718 most of the manual labor on Rhode Island's plantations was done by slaves—by 1730, an estimated one thousand were working on Narragansett farms. Slavery had become an essential part of life on the plantations and almost every person of any means owned at least one slave. There still were a few independent white laborers, but most work, especially that out-of-doors, was done by slaves.

According to Weedon in his history, "the average price of a mature and able negro man was about £50;" of a woman, about between £10 to £40, more valued when used in house service. "Young negroes appear to have been valued at relatively low prices. In 1710, one negro of 17 years, one boy of 4 years, one girl of 2 years, were lumped with a cart, yokes and tools at £93.18." [290]

These plantations varied in size from five to ten square miles; Robert Hazard, one of the most prosperous, "had seventeen thousand acres and grazed four thousand sheep....The farmers were said to keep about an equal number of slaves and horses. Negro women were usually kept in the dairies."[291]

☆☆☆

Slave traders were looked upon as successful business men, enjoyed the highest social positions, held the highest offices, enjoyed trust and responsibility. Owners and traders were governors, members of Congress, of the House of Representatives, of the

---

[289] Conley, *Album*, p. 42 & Stewart, p. 5
[290] Weedon, pp. 140 & 143
[291] Bartlett, p. 10

9. Slaves

Senate; they were scientists, philanthropists, elders of the church, and founders of Rhode Island's early institutions. Such evidence confirms that "no stigma was attached to the ownership or traffic in slaves before the revolution. Slaves were classed the same as any other product—they could be bought, sold, traded, given away, or left as a vital part of a man's estate." [292]

Wills of Rhode Island's citizens often named slaves and their value. For example, Daniel Williams's will mentioned one, his wife's, two; Col. Nicholas Power, when he died in 1734, mentioned four; and Gabriel Bernon, when he died in 1736 also mentioned four (valued at £500). There were many others who also left slaves as part of their estates, especially those owning the large plantations in the southern part of the state.

As for Gabriel Bernon, either in his will or earlier, he was responsible for emancipating one of the better known freed slaves: Emanuel (Manna) Bernoon. Manna bought a house and lot in 1769 and his wife, Mary, sold "liquor without tippling on the premises for four years, competing on a ten-shilling license with Captains, Colonels and Esquires." Manna, for his part "established the first oyster house on Towne Street near the location of the subsequent custom house....Manna sought the heart of the softening town by way of a gratified and contented stomach....Best of all was his jolly smile as he clinked glasses in the midst of descendants of Roger Williams and William Harris." [293] Other of Gabriel's slaves must have passed to his descendants for records show an "Eve Bernon, a single woman,...[later] freed her negroes, Amey, and [Amey's] son, Manny;" and ordered that "if they should be sick, or through accident unable to support themselves, they should be maintained by

---

[292] RI Short Story Club, "Slavery in the RI Colonial Period", Rae Vaule, p. 69
[293] Weedon, pp. 224-225

her relative Allen and the Crawfords." [294]

Another unnamed freed slave couple saved enough to return to Africa where their two hundred or so pounds in savings would make them rich.

★★★

Tradition has it that "conditions of slavery were milder in the Narragansett country than elsewhere," with some indication that in some households they even shared meals with the family. "There may be some truth in this claim; ...a few records present a system of requiring each slave to perform certain tasks—tend so many horses or sheep, make so many cheeses per day—beyond which the slave had no further duties." For instance, "each female slave on Robert Hazard's plantation was in charge of twelve cows and expected to make twelve cheeses daily."[295] This type of management allowed slaves to use their remaining time as they pleased, and some raised crops for market. "Something of a slave society developed, with an annual festival in June reminiscent of the Roman Saturnalia...."[296]

Rowland Robinson, owner of one of Rhode Island's largest plantations, is said to have been most compassionate toward his twenty-eight slaves, treating them kindly, and never selling them. The story goes that after watching the arrival from Africa of one group of slaves, "poor, sick, weary and frightened black creatures coming down over the side of the vessel, Robinson became weak at the sight and never again sent to Africa for labor." There was at least one exception to his supposed declaration of no more slaves from Africa

---

[294] Weedon, p. 343.
[295] Bartlett, p. 10.
[296] James, *History*, p. 256.

9. Slaves

when he gave in to the plea of his prized houseservant, Abigail.[297]

> Abigail had been a Queen in Africa, and, once reconciled to her new home in this country, she begged her master to allow her to go back to her native land, find her son, an African Prince, and bring him back with her to this land of plenty. So Mr. Robinson permitted her to go and provided for her comfort on the journey. And back Queen Abigail came, bearing with her the young man, who became Mr. Robinson's especial body-servant, and he was always called "Prince."

Could this be the same stubborn, not so compassionate, Rowland Robinson we met earlier in the sad story of his daughter, Hannah's elopement on the night of Abigail Updike's ball? It was this same Prince who led her to the place where she was to meet her lover. Given Robinson's seeming obsession in learning who had helped his daughter, one must wonder what he said or did to Prince after his return home that evening and told his master of Hannah's elopement. Even to speculate on an answer must depend on whether we believe this story of Abigail and Prince; on which ending to the Hannah story we believe; on which description of Robinson we find most credible. Some have described him as "relentless, unforgiving, harsh" (and so he seemed with Hannah), while others have claimed that he was "impetuous and over-bearing" but "nevertheless had a fine, generous and forgiving spirit."

Not everyone agrees that the "conditions of slavery were milder in the Narragansett country than elsewhere." In South Kingstown, for instance, which had such a large number of slaves, there was a code that provided that "if any Negro slave was caught in the

---

[297] Haley, Old Stone Bank, Vol. II, p. 67.

house of a free Negro, both would be whipped. No outdoor gatherings of Negroes were allowed, and no Negro could own livestock of any kind under threat of thirty-one lashes. ...In 1750 [Rhode Island] passed a law which provided that any white householder who allowed any slave to enjoy 'dancing, gaming, or any other diversion whatsoever' should be punished by a fine of fifty pounds or one month in jail. If a free Negro was found guilty of such a crime, he was dispossessed and sold back into slavery." [298]

Bartlett, in fact, says that *life in the Narragansett country "resembled the plantation life in Virginia more than the typical rural existence in New England"* [author's italics].

In sharp contrast to the restrictions placed on slaves enjoying themselves, their work left their owners free to cultivate a "graceful social life....Every house worth its salt had a ballroom; and during the Christmas celebrations, the gentlemen of Narragansett, wigged and powdered, outfitted in scarlet coats, lace ruffles and silk stockings, escorted their ladies, handsomely dressed in brocade and high-heeled shoes, their hair cushioned high, to dance the minuet at celebrations which frequently moved from mansion to mansion and lasted several days." [299]

More can be learned of their wealth and belongings by looking at the inventories of the Hazards. When Sarah died in 1740, "her equipment was worthy of her station and her personal estate of £5,324.12. [But] the comparative wardrobe of this husband and wife, enjoying what they wanted, shows clearly that the men dressed better than the women. Mrs. Hazard's clothing at £59.12 was less than half the value of her husband's. In jewelry she excelled, though the outlay was not

---

[298] Bartlett. p. 14.
[299] Bartlett, p. 10

9. Slaves

excessive. Her gold necklace and locket cost £6.10. Apparently gold rings were more often worn by men than by women. The snuff box was a necessity; for nearly a century ago everybody, men and women together, took snuff. The lady's riding horse, saddle and bridle cost £70.12." [300]

Ads in the *Providence Gazette* appeared from time to time confirming both the presence of slaves in Rhode Island homes, and the fact that they were neither passive nor content.

> 1/8/1763: Yesterday a Negro man belonging to Mr. Edward Bosworth, of this Town, as he was going forth to his Labor, fell backwards on a Stone lying at his master's door, which fractured his Skull, and he expired in a few moments.
>
> Also on 1/8/1763: To Be Sold Only for Want of Employ: A likely spry health Negro boy, about Ten Years of Age: Inquire of the Printer.

Another ad was placed that year by the slave trader, Mark Anthony DeWolfe of Bristol. He advertised for a runaway slave who escaped from his service. Following a full, detailed description, he offered four dollars and expenses to anyone who returned him.

Despite what some Rhode Islanders in the year 2000 want to believe, it seems clear that slavery once loomed large in Rhode Island, Providence not being an exception. And if we remember Bartlett's statement that Narragansettt plantations resembled more closely Virginia's plantations than New England farms, we might better understand blacks' present-day objections to the continued use of Plantations as part of Rhode Island's name.

---

[300] Weedon, pp. 168-169

10. The Brown Family

Many of Rhode Island's citizens got rich on the backs of African blacks—men, women and children. Some profited directly from the trade, others indirectly—shipbuilders, the pitch industry and textiles; even the Slater Mill which depended on cotton from the south. Amongst those who thus became rich was the Brown family, not exactly typical Rhode Islanders, but almost certainly typical of the growing numbers of its wealthy—and so the descriptions of some of the Browns, and especially of their wives and daughters, that follow, are also representative of this wealthy group.

The progenitors of the Brown family in Rhode Island were Chad Brown and his wife, Elizabeth Sharpurowe. Though they eventually acquired a home lot on Towne Street, no explanation has been forthcoming as to why they were not included among the initial thirteen who received land grants. Chad and Elizabeth had with them their eight year old son, John, when they sailed from England on the ship *Martin* in July 1638. Soon after, they proceeded to Providence.

Before Chad died in 1650, he "drew up the list of the home lots and the meadows from which our knowledge of these properties is obtained." [301] He also played a leadership role in drawing up a government plan for the town and was the first elder of the Baptist Church where he was ordained a pastor in 1642.

After Chad died, Elizabeth remained on their home lot, as provided for in his will. When she died in 1672, the home lot passed to their sons, John and James; four other sons either deceased, or, presumably, inherited other property. Chad and Elizabeth were both

---

[301] Kimball, p. 38

10. The Brown Family

buried on their home lot (which was then customary) near the corner of the old Court House on College Street. In 1792 they were moved to the North Burial Ground by the town.

Chad Brown's son John sold his portion of the Towne Street lot to his brother, James, who in 1723 sold a portion of it to Daniel Abbott. Daniel Abbott, however, did not keep the lot for himself but, with his wife, Mary, deeded it to a group of Congregational ministers for the purpose of erecting a meeting house (where the Court House now stands at the corner of Benefit and College Streets). Another portion was sold in 1746 to John Checkley, a missionary preacher in the Narragansett area. When he died in 1754, he left his share to Henry Paget, an Irishman and member of King's Church, who had married his daughter. After Paget's death in 1772, his portion of the Towne Street lot went to the Arnold family. It was over a hundred years later before any part of this Chad Brown property returned to the Brown family. Then, John and Moses Brown purchased a portion and presented it to Rhode Island College (later Brown University) at the time of its move to Providence from Warren (discussed in a later section).[302]

It is rather ironic that in the year 2000, Chad Brown's name is primarily associated with one of the poorest housing developments in Providence.

✯✯✯

Two of Chad and Elizabeth's great-grandsons are of especial significance in creating the Brown dynasty: James 2nd, born in 1698 to James and Mary Tew, and his brother, Obediah, born in 1712. They were the first of the Browns involved in shipping—first in coastal trading, then actively in slave trading, and, finally, with

---

[302] Kimball, pp. 176, 264.

the West Indies. Little is known of the four other brothers and three sisters.[303]

JAMES BROWN, HOPE POWER & OBADIAH BROWN

The grandson, James, brother of Obadiah, married Hope Power. Hope was born in 1702, the daughter of Nicholas 3rd and Mercy Tillinghast Power (both mentioned earlier). James and Hope had one daughter, Mary, and five sons: James 3rd, Nicholas, Joseph, John and Moses. Tradition has it that their slave nurse, old "Mamie," used to call the boys to breakfast by singing out "Johnnie, Josie, Nickie, Mosie, come and eat your puddie 'Lassie.'"[304] If for no other reason, the truth of this story is questionable since it, like most historians, ignores the brother, James. He did not die until 1750 by which time the next oldest son, Nicholas, was already twenty-one.

James 2nd became a merchant like his father, James, and "his sloop, *Mary,* [sailing in 1736] enjoyed the dubious distinction of being the first slave-trading vessel to sail from Providence."[305] [Newport had been the main port until then.] It was captained by John Godfrey, assisted by James's younger brother, Obadiah. "[They] obtained [their] cargo of slaves and sold them in the West Indies, returning to Providence with coffee, cloth, cordage, and salt." Hawes states that he was not tempted to try this trade again, and that none of the Browns were involved in slave voyages for the next twenty-three years. Instead, James opened a shop on Towne Street, importing and

---

[303] They are referenced in the genealogies but no information about them has been ascertained. A brother Joseph is mentioned as one of the executors of the father James's estate. Perhaps all the other children died young. There is also no other information about the sister, Mary, of the "famous four" Brown brothers.
[304] *Gowdy Collection: Vol. 17, "52 Power Street."* RIHS library.
[305] Hedges, p. 5

10. The Brown Family

exporting a variety of commodities. But he must have made at least one other sea-faring trip, perhaps to the West Indies rather than to Africa, for on August 23, 1737 he wrote his wife, Hope, advising her regarding the business in case he should not return.[306] He also is concerned about the trustworthiness of his business partners or workers. In part he wrote:

> My Dear if you follow these Directions whilst I am gon You may do wall:...if you should look on them once in a while they will do no harme in your Bisenes. I trust no man one paney worth of aney thing...take all the Care you Can that your estate is not stolen from you...
>
> Comfort Carpintor is to have 296 gallons of Rum [from the stillhouse] after he's pd off the Balance on the Book first.[307]

James owned and operated a number of enterprises, including distilleries and a slaughterhouse, and he invested in real estate, engaged in the maritime insurance business, and loaned money at interest.

Obadiah, fourteen years younger than James, had been his brother's apt pupil, and after James died in 1739, took over most of his businesses. Obadiah was on a voyage to the West Indies when he received word of his brother's death, and after he returned to Providence is said never to have sailed again. However, in 1759 he did finance the *Wheel of Fortune* on a slaving venture despite the fact that it was the middle of the Seven Years' War. Insurance was costly and French privateers were capturing many vessels along the African Coast. His records indicate that the ship arrived safely on the Windward Coast, but a notation in his Insurance Book then notes: "Taken." This appears to have been the last slaving venture of the Browns until after Obadiah's death in 1764.

---

[306] Hawes, p. 155.
[307] RIHS manuscript (See "Resources")

James's will had provided for his wife, Hope, and she also was to collect the monies owed him until their sons came of age. It is unclear why Obadiah became *loco parentis* to James' and Hope's five sons, then aged fifteen to less than a year, since Hope was still very much alive; in fact lived until she was over ninety. Another curiosity is the lack of mention of James' and Hope's only daughter, Mary, who was eight at the time of her father's death. Whatever the children's actual legal situation, Obadiah undertook training the boys (hopefully, Hope did the same for Mary), as his brother had him, and apprenticed Moses when he reached the age of thirteen—at which time Moses left school.

JAMES BROWN, SON OF HOPE AND JAMES

Hope's son, James [the third generation of James Brown's], took over as head of the family in February 1745 when he reached his majority. According to their father's will, each of the five sons was to get a fifth of his estate when he turned twenty-one, an extra sum going to James as the eldest.[308] However, on February 15, 1750, this James died off the coast of York, Virginia, on board the sloop *Freelove*.

NICHOLAS & RHODA (JENCKS) & AVIS (BINNEY) BROWN

Historians often ignore James, presumably because he died fairly young, and refer only to the "famous four" Browns. Nicholas was the oldest of these four, born in 1729. Therefore, after his brother James's death, he took over as head of the family and of the Brown enterprises. In 1762 Nicholas married Rhoda Jencks, who was the daughter of Joanna Scott and the prominent merchant and justice, Daniel Jencks.

Rhoda and Nicholas had ten children but only

---

[308] There is no mention of their sister, Mary. Had she died young?

10. The Brown Family

Nicholas, Jr. and Hope (mentioned earlier as giving a chandelier to the Baptist Church) lived to adulthood. Brown University was named after their son, Nicholas, Jr. (no doubt a sizable donation led to the name-change in 1804).

Hope was named after her grandmother, but also after a sibling that died before she was born. When that child drowned before her fourth birthday, it must have been a heart-wrenching experience, especially for Rhoda. The then-common practice of naming a child after one who has died seems almost cathartic, but also an effort to keep alive at least a memory of the lost child.

In 1781, Rhoda and Nicholas's surviving daughter, Hope, wrote a letter to her father while at school in Newport. It is quoted, in part, for the glimpses it gives us of the education and concerns of the wealthy young ladies of her day:

> Must beg Mama will be so good as to send me some Cake a little better than what I brought with me as it will be my Dancing Day to Morrow Week & I must find Tea & Cake, Mrs. Wilkinson is much pleased to find how little I have lost in my Writing & Spelling in so long an absence but thinks I lost greatly in my Sempstring, which she does not so much regard, as she holds the other Branches of my Learning. when I wrote to my Grandmama I did not expect to have wrote you, but Mr. Mumford who is the Bearer of this & had the Care of my Trunk & Basquet, did not go up to Providence Yesterday as He intended, which has aforde me Time to answer Your Letter. The good advice it Contains I hope to adhere to.
>
> Please to give my Duty to my Mama. Love to my Brothers & sister, Miss Molly Powers & Miss Sally Hudson, & Compts to Miss Stillman, in which Mrs. Wilkinson joins me as She recollects having the Pleasure many Years past Traveling from New port to Boston in Company with that Young Lady at a Time she was over burthend with the Care of a Brood of Young Chickens. believe I have not forgot any

of my Connection, if I have must beg my Papa will be so good as to recollect them for me & offer my Respects & Love were they are due. Accepting a Large portion Himself from His Truly Affectionate & Dutiful Daughter.

In another, briefer letter to Dear Mama, also written from Newport on December 26, 1781, Hope thanks her mother for sending the Cake and sugar plumbs. A postscript from Mrs. Wilkinson, head of the school, acknowledged "Payments by Mr. Nicholas Brown." The items are interesting for what they reveal about costs and subjects taught, even a glimpse at wearing apparel:

> for Dancing Musick, £0.12.0; for the writing Master, 13 Weeks @ 16, £0.17.4; for Board Etc., Discounting three days. She was absent, 13 Weeks @ 21/, £13.13.0; 4 pr. Cotton Hose @ 12/, £2.8.0. It shows a Balance Due of £15.2.4

A later letter from AB Wilkinson to Nicholas includes the following—and explains Hope's earlier request of her mother for a cake:

> I have ingagd a very good Fiddler to play for the Misses one Afternoon in a Week, by which means they will improve in their Dancing & have the Advantages of useful exercise. Every Miss takes Her turn to pay the Fiddler which is half a Dollar & treat the other Misses with Tea & Cake for that Day, having liberty to invite two or three Misses of their particular Acquaintance. I hope Mrs. Brown & Yourself will approve of the Method, which must beg you will be so good as to Communicate to Your Brother Brown & Govr Bowen, to whom please to make my best respects as also to Their Worthy consorts, after offering Sincere Regards to Yourself & Mrs. Brown do with best Wishes Acknowledge myself Your Friend & Servt.

Soon after Nicholas' wife, Rhoda Jencks, died, on December 16, 1783, Nicholas wrote a four page letter to Avis Binney describing her last illness and death in

10. The Brown Family

great detail. He tells Avis how much her recent visit had rejuvenated his wife and how much he regretted not having urged her to stay on, for after her departure Rhoda's spirit again collapsed. Avis had been a family friend for some time, and, by 1785, Nicholas was urging her to marry him; a proposal she was apparently resisting. In May he wrote Avis an eleven-page love letter in tiny, almost impossible to read, script. Deciphering a phrase here and there, Nicholas suggests they may be "destined to seek the Kingdom of Heaven together." Throughout the letter, Nicholas makes clear his belief that what comes, good and bad, depends on God's will.

On September 9, 1785, Avis and Nicholas married. Avis was the daughter of Avis Engs (b. 1720, d. 1779) and Capt. Barnabas Binney. The Captain owned his own vessel and traded to Demerara where he owned plantations and had slaves. He also had a store attached to their home in Boston. An interesting item appeared in the *Boston Gazette* on September 17, 1770:[309]

> Strayed from Boston, on Tuesday the 7th instant, a small yellow cow with short horns, the tops of which are sawed off; she had a slit in her right ear, her 'tets' are very small, who ever shall bring said cow to Capt. Barnabas Binney, opposite the new South meeting house, in 'Seven Star Lane,' shall be well rewarded for taking her up.

In 1788, we find from a diary by Susanna (Susan) Lear, then about eighteen, that Avis Brown had been to Philadelphia, which, presumably, is Susan's home. She is returning to Providence with Avis with whom she is staying during her visit in Providence. Also making the trip are Avis's sister-in-law, Mary Woodrow Binney, and Mary's daughter, Mary, then about five or six. Mary was the youngest of the four

---
[309] Binney, p. 27

children of Mary Woodrow and Dr. Barnabas, the Captain's son who served as a surgeon during the Revolutionary War.

Avis Brown outlived her husband, Nicholas, by sixteen years: Avis died in 1807, Nicholas in 1791. They almost certainly never had any children and Avis never married again. Judging by a letter his niece, Sarah, wrote to her brother, James, on June 10, 1791, Nicholas's death must have been rather sudden and while he was away from home. She wrote:

> We received last Saturday the melancholy news of Uncle's death, the manner in which he died is truly affecting and must have shocked his friends around him much more than if he had died in his bed, the loss of so good a man is great indeed but we must console ourselves with the Idea that he is now perfectly happy. Poor Hope, my heart aches for her, she most assuredly is the greatest sufferer, and has real cause for affliction, pray write me directly and inform me how she is, Heaven I hope has endowed her with fortitude to bear up under this severe trial.

There is another curious short letter from Avis to her nephew, James, dated only 1791, that reads: "Though too deeply affected with the loss of my best friend [her husband?] to enjoy the melon, this endearing mark of attention from you, my heart feels as I ought. May you ever love me for your dear Charles sake." [*Sarah's husband, Charles?*] Signed, "Aunt Avis Brown."

Hope Power Brown died almost exactly a year after her son, Nicholas, on June 9, 1792, aged ninety years and six months. An entry made by Susan Lear in her diary on June 3, 1788, suggests that Hope, near the end of her long life, may have been living with at least one of her sisters. She wrote:

> Went to see Mrs. B's mother and sister, two old ladies. The mother is 88 [*must have been 86 if these dates are*

10. The Brown Family

correct] years old. Her countenance and manners so interesting that I loved her the moment I saw her. The old lady is quite helpless and cannot get out of her chair without the assistance of some kind arms, not withstanding which, there is such an appearance of cheerfulness and resignation in her whole behaviour that it is impossible not to reverence her.

She had been dearly loved by her children and grandchildren who always referred to her as "Mother Hope."

JOSEPH & ELIZABETH (POWER) BROWN

The third brother, second of the "famous four," was Joseph, born to Hope and her husband, James, in 1733. In 1759, Joseph married his cousin, Elizabeth, daughter of Nicholas Power 4th and Anne Tillinghast.

While Joseph showed little interest in the family business, Elizabeth assumed both clerical and administrative responsibilities, especially in their spermaceti candle-making side of the business.

The introduction of these candles which used whale oil for the wax was a great boon to housewives, simultaneously relieving them of making less effective candles and brightening up their previously gloomy homes. For the first time reading, sewing, and other such activities could be done even after sunset. Credit has been given to more than one source for the introduction of the spermaceti candle-making process: (1) brought to Newport around 1745/46 by Portuguese Jews escaping from religious persecution abroad; (2) closer to home, Dr. John Vanderlight, married to Mary Brown (*a rare mention of the "famous four's" sister*), is given credit in the *Chad Brown Memorial* genealogy. It reads:

> In connection with his brothers-in-law, he engaged in the manufacture of candles, having brought with him from Europe a knowledge of the Dutch process of separating

spermaceti from its oil.

Unlike Elizabeth who became directly involved in the business, Joseph pursued any number of other interests. Having become quite informed about architecture, he joined with John Howland and Stephen Hopkins in designing the First Baptist Church, the Providence National Bank building on South Main, Market House and a number of other buildings, including his brother John's house on Power Street. As an amateur astronomer, Joseph observed the transit of Venus in 1769 with imported astronomical instruments, and thus gave the name to Transit Street in Providence. He also was sufficiently knowledgeable about "experimental philosophy" [today's Physics] that Brown University appointed him as a professor in that subject after it moved to Providence.[310]

JOHN & SARAH (SMITH) BROWN

In 1760, at age twenty-four, John Brown (the fourth brother, third of the "famous four"), married Sarah Smith, daughter of Daniel and Dorcas Smith, Quakers. For the next twenty-eight years they lived in a brick house on Water Street (perhaps at the corner of Towne Street), described as 40 x 36 feet with the Lot, wharf, and stores adjoining Thomas Halsey's House on one side, his brother Nicholas's on the other. Records show that in the 1760s John and Sarah bought chairs and mirrors, among other things, from Philadelphia, Newport, and Boston—items which had been exceedingly scarce in Rhode Island.

All of Sarah's and John's children were born in that house: two sons and three daughters—Sarah, Abigail and Alice. One son did not live to adulthood, and the other, James, never married, and continued

---

[310] *Gowdy Collection: Preservation Society House Histories*, p. 96.

10. The Brown Family

to live in the family's Power Street house until he died in 1834. He must not have heeded his father's advice, quoted below, on mate selection, or perhaps took it too much to heart!

On October 15, 1782 John wrote to his son, James, then in Philadelphia. First discussing various business matters, he then advises James at length about choosing a wife:

> If you should Incline to Form any Lasting Connection with a young Lady Either at Phil. Or ElseWare, or whenever this Inclination may happen, I have to Begg, beceach and Intreat, that it be in the best Family and that she be not only Possessed with a good Education but that her Natturall Disposition and Manners Joined with her other Vertuous Quallifications cannot Fail to make her Perfectly Agreeable to Your Parents Sisters & Friends, and in point of Fortin if she Possesses or if her Parents are Living and will settle on her £20,000 Philadela Currency I will Immediately Double the amount on my son—but above all Let the Lady be of a Vertuous Carrector and an agreeable Disposition a Calm and Unruffled Temper tho Spritely & Agreeable, Wishing you may find such a Carrictor with the Addition of Every thing Else which is most agreeable to Yourself, in the Course of a Few Years, I subscribe mySelf Your Parent.

Somehow the same undertone of criticism found in James's letter from his father, underlays the mix of doubt, disbelief and praise found in James's letter to his sister, Sarah, on March 28, 1785:

> I have not yet been able to ascertain the author of a piece of Poetry said to be yours, which Mr. Smith handed to me. Should it be yours I warmly congratulate you on the Perfection you have arrived at in so sublime an art, nothing could exceed my surprise on being told it was a production of my sister but I shall not be much mortified if Mr. Smith denies his assertion...

Based on a later letter dated January 3, 1791, that Sarah wrote to James, it would seem that she, like her Aunt Elizabeth, Joseph's wife, took as interest in the Brown business even in her youth. In it, she discusses the fact that "our river is entirely frozen for nine miles," she goes on to comment that with "4 of our vessels in great distress to get up, they walk to the shores."[311] Continuing, Sarah adds:

> They talk of launching a 5th [ship], but I don't expect they will;...yesterday although it was Sunday they had 80 men at work...

Sarah again shows her interest in her father's ships in a brief diary entry written on April 25, 1796 when she was twenty-three. It suggests a comfortable familiarity with the rough and smelly area through which she must pass with a friend to get to the *George Washington*, used in her father's China trade—wharves, ropewalks, a distillery and the family's spermaceti candle-making factory.

> M.A.A. and myself walked to India Point, the ship G.W. haul'd down the river. The dragoons and 3 companies paraded.

---

[311] This apparently was not the worst freezing seen in the Bay. In 1740 the ice extended far enough out from the Rhode Island shoreline for a person to drive a horse and sleigh from a point near New York all the way to Cape Cod. Near Fall River the ice measured between 25 and 30 inches thick and it must have been equal to that at the head of the Bay nearer Providence. On February 25, 1741 a wedding guest made the trip all the way across the Bay from some point on the South county shore to Common Fence Point.

"...[The people] must have sufferd greatly in spite of the fact that safe and short ice lanes brought certain points closer in respect to travel." They surely had to huddle closer than ever before the fireplaces of their still simply built homes. Then, too, "deep snow drifts and zero weather meant neglected cattle, shortage of home provisions, sickness, extreme discomfort, and isolation." Haley, Old Stone Bank, Vol. III p. 99.

10. The Brown Family

©All Rights Reserved: Courtesy of Rhode Island Black Heritage Society

Perhaps it was this very interest that led, eventually, to her marriage to Charles Herreschoff, one of her father's partners, in July 1801. Because Sarah left us a diary, we will learn more of her later.

☆☆☆

Returning now to the parents, Sarah and John Brown. In June 1788 they became the first "to leave [their] old house on the thickly settled Towne Street" and move to their "new mansion on the hill, [on] hitherto open land along southern Benefit Street" (at the corner of Power Street). It had taken two years to build. When our diarist, Susan Lear,[312] saw it in May while visiting in Providence, she called it the "most elegant building in America." After other visits later that summer, she elaborated:

> The house is very large and furnished in the most extravagant manner. Tis built after the plan of some of the

---

[312] Mentioned earlier when she was visiting from Philadelphia, staying with Avis Brown.

noblemen's seats in England, and far surpasses any I have seen. ...It far surpasses any idea I ever had of grandeur and elegance. The family have but just moved in and have not got it completely furnished. We were taken from the cellar [*was this one of the earliest homes with a cellar?*] to the top of the house. My eyes never beheld such a prospect as we had from the top of it...We stayed there nearly three hours and so hearty was their welcome that I wished to take up my abode there.

All the bedrooms on the upper floors had "massive fire-places, no two alike. Mantels, doorways, dadoes and cornices from top to bottom [were] exquisitely chiseled from enduring wood in classical patterns, both ornate and conventional." John's brother, Joseph, had died before even the cornerstone of the house was laid but the "dimensions, floor-plans, rises, elevation, scales and decorative motifs had all been worked out by him before his death." [313]

John Brown must have been unusually prosperous as early as 1780 because that year he bought two country houses "for entertaining and family retreats." One was "Spring Green Farm" the other, "Poppoersquash," better known as Point Pleasant. They eventually became the "destination of the household goods and furnishings of 52 Power Street shortly after the death of [their] daughter, Sarah Brown Herreschoff, in 1846."[314]

★★★

Abigail, another of Sarah and John's daughters,

---

[313] Quotes in this paragraph are from Haley, Old Stone Bank, Vol. IV. pp. 106 & 108.
[314] Quotes and information about John Brown's houses and the weddings are from Levin, pp. 61, 67, 69-70 & 75. Also from a personnal letter to this author from Henry A.L.Brown, a descendent still living at Green Spring Farm.

10. The Brown Family

had set January 1788 as the date she would marry John Francis, another of her father's partners. At the time, the *Providence Gazette* described Abigail as "a young lady whose truly amiable disposition and engaging manners cannot fail to adorn and dignify the connubial state." Even though her father's house on Power Street was not yet complete, Abigail wanted the wedding to take place there and her father, proud of her and of his house, agreed, opening four of the rooms for the occasion. We are fortunate to have accounts of this gala event preserved in two very different letters written to Mrs. Abigail Goddard (wife of the newspaper publisher) by two of the bridesmaids, Elisa Bowen and Anna Bowen.[315] They bring to life an occasion and the fun they had, rescuing the participants from the stiff and stale portrait we may have of our ancestors.

Anna describes it this way:

> The ball was given at the new house, which is almost finished. As they had no furniture in it, they only sent a dozen or two of chairs in and for the rest we had long benches covered with green cloth, which looked extremely well. You know the east end of the house is divided into two original rooms. As those below were unfinished, we danced above both rooms—and a merrier crew I never laughed with.
>
> We behaved with tolerable decorum till about eleven, when we sat down to a good substantial supper of meats and chocolate. After which somebody proposed a cut-out jigg. I forget who began it, but a ring was instantly formed round the actors, and every creature that never cut a caper before now tried the suppleness of their feet...never were such shouts—such bursts—such acclamation as when the elder gentlemen and the novices stepped in. They were in a moment surrounded by girls who were

---

[315] From the Henry A. L. Brown collection on deposit at the RI Historical Society.

struggling to dance nearest them...As true a bustling frolic as ever you saw.

When the novelty of jiggs was over, we played blind man's bluff—and Col. Nightingale made a great deal of fun by throwing himself in the way of the blind man, who happened to be O. Brown, in the drollest mixture of male and female dress. One of the ladies who had been caught refused to be blinded, and so we returned to country dances again...The bride looked the very goddess of tranquil and compleat felicity. A sweet and gentle smile enlivened her expanded countenance, and modest tenderness glowed on her cheek when she turned her eyes on her beloved friend. He, poor fellow, is very far from well—but I have hopes that now all doubts and suspense are at an end [*sounds like they had a tumultuous relationship leading up to the marriage*], they will both enjoy returning health among their accumulating blessings.

Elisa has this to say of the occasion:

After a week spent in the most tedious ceremony of dress, etc. I have a moment of calm which I will fill with the recital of the occupations of the last week, and anything else that swims on the surface of my mind.

Last Tuesday evening witnessed the union of my two friends Francis and Abby. I was present and officiated as bridesmaid in unison with Miss Francis and Stillman...

On Friday Mr. Brown gave a smart ball at this house on the Hill. Indeed it will be a most elegant place. We have four rooms lighted up on the second story—one for supper, another for cards, and two for dancing. We danced in the large chamber of the hall and continued through the doors into the next room, which made the whole length of the house.

The rooms are already genteel, but will be elegant when finished and furnished. Two of the largest and most elegant mirrors I ever saw ornamented the rooms. Standing in the door which is in the middle of the partition you are just in the line with them, so that at the head of the dance you can look down through a variegated

10. The Brown Family

crowd of sprightly dancers, and if you are a little elevated above the common race of mortals or chance to be made so by high heels or long feather, you can then have the pleasure of contemplating your image and seeing it reflected 52 feet. So at the foot of the dance you may do the same. The effect was charming to look in and see such a moving multitude.

I had the honor of dancing with the bridegroom in consequence of my being one of the bridesmaids. Yesterday closed the duties of the bridesmaids. This occupation brought instantly to my mind the occasion on which I first assumed it. Those reflections diffused a shade of melancholy over me, which I was obliged to shake off to fulfill the duties of my station...Well, this is the second time I have been bridesmaid, and I think 'tis or ought to be my turn next to be a bride.

After John Francis died in 1796, Abigail and her two children moved back in with her parents on Power Street. John, Jr. continued to lived there with his mother until her death in 1821, after which he married his cousin, Anne, daughter of Nicholas Brown.

Alice has not undergone the same scrutiny by historians as have her sisters, Abigail and Sarah, perhaps because her family disapproved of her marriage to James Mason, and the birth of their daughter, Abby, the day following, a much greater shame to a family then than it is today.

As for their father, John Brown, Miner describes him this way: "In partnership and independently he is shrewd, long-headed and venturesome, his shipyards line India Point [*where the Seekonk River flows into the Providence River*]; sloops, brigs and finally full-rigged ships lie off his wharves. Distilleries and iron-forgers, candle works and a glass factory are on his books—and always trade and venture and excellent returns fill his robust days."[316]

---

[316] Miner, Geo., p. 67.

During the Revolutionary War, John Brown supplied ships and gunpowder to the colonists, and, in 1787, was the first to set sail from Rhode Island waters for China. In 1799, then in his sixties, he served two years in the U.S. Congress. It should also be added that John was by far the most persistent slave-trader of the "famous four" brothers.

MOSES BROWN, THREE WIVES & TWO CHILDREN

Moses, the youngest of the "famous four," an infant when his father died in 1739, and only a few years past his maturity when his Uncle Obediah died in 1762/3. After Moses had completed his apprenticeship with his uncle, his uncle had made him a full partner in the enterprise he had formed, separate from that of Nicholas, Joseph and John. But after Obadiah's death, Moses merged it with his brothers' business operations as "merchants, ship owners, importers and exporters, storekeepers at retail and wholesale, investors in iron ore and foundries, forgers of cannon and anchors, makers of spermaceti candles, and distillers of good New England rum."[317] About the same time, probably at the instigation of his brother, John, talk was resumed of again entering the slave trade. Hence , the ill-fated trip to Guinea was arranged. The *Sally*, of which we will hear more later, was to depart from Newport that summer of 1764; the proceeds intended to finance the establishment of the Hope (Pig Iron) Furnace, named after their mother.[318]

Most historians when writing about Moses Brown skip from his apprentice-ship, to Obadiah's death in 1763, to his taking over of Obadiah's business, and, possibly, to his marriage to his cousin Anna in 1764. Henry Chace is an exception. He leaves no doubt that Moses and the other young men of the town, many of

---

[317] Miner, Geo. P. 64.
[318] Hawes, p. 155.

10. The Brown Family

them "closely related with family ties and common interests," enjoyed a full social life before their marriages, perhaps also as young married couples.[319] This would have been, roughly, during the decade leading up to the Revolutionary War, from about 1760 to 1770.

It was a time when tavern-keepers were typically showmen, and their taverns places where young and old gathered to "dance the old square dances and minuets. The music supplied by a viol, flute, fiddle, or spinnet was weak, but once the spirit of the gathering was aroused, the singing voices carried on the tunes....In every respect, the taverns were the center of town and community life," including places to hold town meetings and to "discuss revolt prior to the Revolution." [320]

The Olney Inn was no exception and it is there that Chace relates that Moses Brown, William and Jabez Bowen, and the Fenner, Corlis, and Olney boys arranged "assemblies" in the manner of Boston and Newport. They were attended by the four daughters of Obadiah Brown, the Paget girls, Polly Olney, the tavern-keepers daughter, and probably others. The occasions were joyous with music and dancing filling the evenings; perhaps when resting they discussed the likelihood of war with Britain. On occasions when "chums from Boston" came to the "assemblies," there seem to have been sparks of jealousy. Particularly infuriating was the time when the Bostonians tried, "with the aid of some local young men, *not in the swim*," to arrange one of these occasions themselves. The Providence boys responded by turning a "cold shoulder" on any of the young ladies "who had the temerity to attend."[321]

---

[319] See notes in Chace papers (RIHS Manuscripts).
[320] Haley, Old Stone Bank, Vol. II, pp. 92-93.
[321] Quotes are from notes in the Chace papers (RIHS manuscripts).

Nonetheless, it was at one of these assemblies at the Olney Inn that William Palfrey from Boston first met Polly Olney, and managed to engage Moses Brown as a go-between in Palfrey's pursuit of her.

Early in 1761, when their romance began, "Palfrey was employed as a clerk in the establishment of Nathaniel Wheelright" in Boston. He was described as "an agreeable person with a frank and generous expression of countenance, great gayety and heartiness of disposition, a fund of anecdote, a seasoning of original wit, and a somewhat sedulous attention to dress as well as to manners." Polly was the "charming and strangely facetious daughter of Joseph Olney," who had carried on the favorite Olney Tavern of his parents.[322]

Letters preserved at the RI Historical Society tell of the ups and downs of their romance, perhaps typical of the day, at least among the wealthier families.[323] It started when Palfrey met "several damsels," at the Olney Tavern, while being entertained by Moses Brown during a visit to Providence on business. On his return to Boston, on March 16, 1761, he wrote Moses:

> Please remember me to Jo. Olney and my best complement to all the Ladys who I had the honr to be acquainted with at Providence. Especially the dear Polly, tell her more than I can express at present. I believe I must make you a confidante in a certain amour that shall be nameless.

Nearly a month later, on April 13, 1761, Palfrey

---

[322] Haley, Old Stone Bank, Vol. II, p. 84. Joseph Olney, born in 1706 and died in 1777, was a descendent of Thomas Olney, an original settler, through his son Epenetus, James, Joseph. See Olney Family Tree.

[323] All quotes are from the original letters, except as noted.

10. The Brown Family

writes again explaining that he has been too busy to write and is fatigued from the trip back to Boston.

> Enclosed you have a letter for Polly which I doubt not you will be kind enough to deliver her, in as private a manner as the nature of the thing will admit of. I must confess a correspondence with the fair sex is vastly agreeable to me. Especially with one who I have so great a regard for as I have for Polly. I am very sorry that I was obliged to leave Providence before I had an opportunity to settle the affair with her as I was deprived of the pleasure by her being gone to one of the Neighbors a visiting, however, hope I shall have another opportunity soon.

On August 7, 1761, Palfrey writes Moses, clearly upset. First he had heard from reliable sources that Polly was to be married the following week to a Mr. Bowers of Swanzey; then he was told by friends they knew nothing of this, but rather that Polly was being courted by Moses Brown. He asks Moses if this is true, so he can "retreat with honour" and urges a reply by return mail "that I may know how to regulate my future proceedings. I hope sincerely that I shall find there is nothing in that report. I shall rely upon your friendship in the affair."

In his reply Moses explains that Polly had merely been visiting in Swansea and that Dr. Bowers had returned with her. Moses went on to disclaim any interest in Polly, himself, and to suggest, further, that he'd heard Palfrey was courting someone in Boston. In Palfrey's reply on August 31st he declares he never really thought Moses was undercutting him, and explains about the Boston lady in question:

> I assure you that [your imputation] is false and that the story arose from much the same source that yours did, being a particular friend and very intimate acquaintance of Mr. Cazneau, a young attorney in this place I used frequently to be with him at his father's house. Consequently got acquainted with his sisters, who

> I us'd sometimes to take a walk with, and once or twice carried them with some other Ladies to a play from which the story arose in the Tattling Town of my courting her, but I have not been near the house for some time past.

Depending on the account by Richman (and a brief note by Chace) at this point rather than the originals (which were all but illegible), there was no further contact with Moses Brown until February 20, 1762. Then, in a long letter, Palfrey recounts the pangs he's suffered trying to see Polly. According to Chace Palfrey made the trip from Boston to Providence on horseback and when he found she wasn't at the Olney Tavern, he got a fresh horse and continued on to Newport "where he found her at a dancing party with other Providence people, including Moses Brown. In the morning they all rode back to Providence together. Meanwhile, the coquettish Miss Polly, with the aid of Moses, artfully evaded the declaration of the unhappy and disconsolate William who returned to Boston after a ride of 150 miles."[324] It was then, according to Chace, that Palfrey wrote the long account of his feelings to his friend Moses.

> What was he to do? He contrived, by the aid of Polly's brother 'Jo,' a neat stratagem. A certain Miss Paget was to invite Polly and himself to her home 'in the Evening & take an oppor'y of Leaving us together.'

On this occasion he only got a cool rejection by Polly, and the admonition "to think no more of her." Palfrey thereafter returned to Boston, deeply humiliated and stopped writing to her. Then, on April 16, 1762, Palfrey informs Moses that Polly has made a journey to Boston.

> Polly is this minute gone out of the Store, having come

---

[324] The quotes in this paragraph from Chace's notes (RIHS manuscripts). The rest from Richman, as stated, pp. 166-170.

10. The Brown Family

in with another young Lady to buy some Silks...She did not seem to be quite so much upon the Reserve as usual.

He apparently met her at a ball where she still seemed "Exceeding Shy & behave'd with an Air of Distant Reserve." He closes his letter to Moses denying rumors that he had "deceived Polly during the whole affair", and declaring "he had always dealth with her honorably, and, if in doubt, Moses Brown might show this letter to her." Moses replied that he believed Palfrey.[325]

At this point, Palfrey did turn his attentions, with some seriousness, to Miss Cazneau.

Returning from Richman to the original letters, we learn that on April 20th Palfrey wrote Moses, clearly then courting Miss Cazneau, that the latter had inadvertently seen Moses' letter concerning Polly and "from Curiosity Natural to her Sex," had opened and read it, but fortunately without any consequences. Palfrey goes on to express his appreciation of Moses' "wishes for our mutual happiness" and adds:

> Miss Cazneau is a fine young Lady & every way Calculated to render the marriage State agreeable.' I hope my friend Brown has made a choice, and wish he may meet with one every way suitable to his Taste.

It's only a week later, on April 27th that Palfrey again writes Moses, now having learned from a friend that Polly said her "air of Coquetry" at their last meeting had been because "she thought it would have looked odd for a young Lady to say Yes so soon." Palfrey adds:

> I suppose she thought I should not take No for an answer. However upon the whole she told M Flagg that if there was any misunderstanding between us she was very sorry for it, and I hope to see her soon.

---

[325] Haley, Old Stone Bank, Vol. II, p. 86.

Palfrey goes on to say he hopes they can "still have a friendship."

> [I] would be sorry to have her ill-will and sincerely wish her Happy in some Clever man who may be able to give her all the satisfaction her heart can wish. I am sorry I was not acquainted with her temper and disposition before as it would have prevented all that has happened.

Apparently Polly's trip to Boston, referred to earlier, had not been in vain since on August 25, 1764, this item appeared in the *Providence Gazette*:

> Tuesday evening last, Mr. Thomas Greene of Boston, merchant, was married to Miss Polly Olney of this town, a young lady who has real merit, added to a beautiful person, to grace the connubial state and perpetuate its felicity.

A year later Palfrey married Miss Cazneau. Palfrey went on to serve on George Washington's personal staff during the Revolutionary War. But his apparent demise came in 1780 when "he sailed out of Delaware Bay, on the *Shillala* to fill his last appointment, [as Consul-General to France], but neither he nor the ship were ever heard of again." Other than the fact that Polly and Nathaniel had no children and that Polly had a second husband, John Timmins, a Boston merchant, we do not know what became of Polly nor of Mrs. Cazneau Palfrey.[326]

☆☆☆

In 1764, the same year that Polly married Thomas Greene of Boston, Moses Brown also married—his Uncle Obadiah's daughter, his cousin, Anna (Nancy) Brown. And it was that same year their daughter,

---

[326] Quote from Haley, Old Stone Bank, Vol. II, p. 86. A Genealogy of the Greenes in Massachusetts note that the eighth generation of Thomas Greenes (born 12/24/1729) "married Mary Olney, of Providence, RI, and died without issue." p. 52.

10. The Brown Family

Sarah, was born. Their only other child who lived was Obadiah Moses, born in 1771.

After Anna died in February, 1773, following a prolonged illness, Moses began to suffer from depression and melancholia which continued periodically for the rest of his life. Anna's death had come only a short time after they'd both started attending the Quaker religious services, and so Moses became increasingly involved with the Quakers after her death. This perhaps helps explain the affect visiting her grave had on him in November 1773, when he "meditated long and prayerfully...to know what the Divine will was concerning him."

Later, when "speaking of his bereavement to a friend, he said: 'I saw my slaves with my spiritual eyes as plainly as I see thee now, and it was given me as clearly to understand that the sacrifice that was called for of my hand was to give them their liberty.'" [327] It was soon after that, on November 10, 1773, that "Moses signed a deed freeing all his slaves. Of those freed, six were given one acre plots on Moses' farm, while the other four were able to support themselves through their trades." He resigned from all the Brown businesses and "from that day forward became the most powerful opponent of slavery in Rhode Island...."[328]

But slavery still ran deep amongst the Browns. Not only did his brother, John, remain involved in the trade, but so did the husband of Anna's sister, Phebe. Phebe's husband ran this ad in the *Providence Gazette* on October 18, 1777:

> Run away from John Fenner, of Gloucester, a negro man named Yockwhy, about 28 years of age, 5 ft. 8 inches high, marked on both cheeks; had on and took with him a light cloth-colored homespun coat, with wooden buttons,

---

[327] This and prior quote from Richman, p. 170.
[328] Quotes from Bartlett, p. 18.

breeches of the same color, blue serge jacket, pair of good leather breeches, a fine Holland shirt, a fine tow shirt, a new pair of thread stockings, one pair of new dark worsted stockings, one pair of wite ribbed yarn do., one dark silk handkerchief, one linen do, one good castor hat without loops, one felt do., one pair of shoes with strings, one pair of silver sleeve buttons. Whoever will take up and secure said negro, and return him to his master, shall hav six dollars reward All masters of vessels are forbidden to carry off said negro at their peril. (signed) *John Fenner*.

Several thoughts may occur to the reader of this ad: the detail in the description; a question as to the nature of the "marks" on his cheeks (a slave branding?); and a wonder at the amount of clothes he had. (Master allocation? Probably not stolen or ad would have said so.)

As for Moses Brown, his house at Wayland and Humbolt Avenues became a major stop on the underground railroad. Providence lay on the route that ran from New Bedford (where the escaping slaves arrived by ship) to Fall River and then to Rhode Island. From there the slaves would "continue their zig-zag route and move on to the more northern parts of Massachusetts....Traveling toward the North Star under cover of darkness, a fugitive slave would reach Rhode Island and find shelter for a period of time. It might be for a stay of only one night, but often the shelter and the moral and financial assistance stretched out for months." Another stop on the underground railroad in Providence was Bethel A.M.E. Church, founded in 1795, which, according to tradition, was visited by Harriet Tubman. Other Rhode Island stops were located in Central Falls (the Elizabeth Buffum Chace House), Westerly (the Charles Perry House), Pawtucket (the Daggetts & the Pidge Farm), and Newport (Isaac Rice Homestead, the Touro

10. The Brown Family

Synagogue & the home of George T. Downing Block, who came from New York City to Newport where he became its most prosperous black).[329]

Moses Brown went beyond offering his home as an under-ground railroad stop, also helping blacks in need of financial assistance. One such was Peggy Harrison, a former servant, who wrote to him from Boston in 1804 seeking money "so that I can give my mite" to help with preaching. There were other letters from her asking help because "the times is so hard," and, later, because "my husban he is old." The last letter was from her daughter, Ann, informing Moses that her mother had died. "She was very willing to die and go to the Lord above and she desired me when dieing to let you know of our distresses." Moses helped pay for the "expense of the burying and the debts she owed." Right up until he died, Moses "persisted in his efforts to improve the condition of the colored people in the state." [330]

Deeply religious, Moses had been troubled by the family's involvement in the slave trade ever since the brig *Sally* had made its ill-fated trip to Guinea in 1764 with Esek Hopkins as Captain. [He later became first Admiral of the US Navy]. Clearly intended to restrain slaves, the brig had been equipped with "seven swivel guns, one cask of powder, 40 'hand Cufs,' 40 'Shekels,' three 'chains,' two pairs of pistols, eight 'small Arms,' thirteen 'Cutleshes,' one dozen 'pad Locks,' and one pair of 'Blunder Bursers.'" [331]

The log that Captain Hopkins kept throughout the venture offers proof that captured Africans did not come peaceably; that filling even a small ship was not

---

[329] Yeaton, pp. 6-7 & Blockson, pp. 201-208.
[330] Bartlett, p. 23.
[331] Hawes, p. 129

always quick and easy, as suggested earlier; and that bartering was an important part of the trade. Hopkins was on the Guinea Coast nine months. On January 16th Hopkins records that three flasks of rum were exchanged for "bringing back on board" a runaway slave; on the 31st more was given for the return of two other runaways. The Captain also used some of the slaves for bartering even before leaving Africa— on February 18th he traded "4 slaves 2 men 2 women" for 270 iron bars; then, "a Small garle Slave" for a profit of four bars. Next came "4 Slaves 2 old woman & 2 old man" in exchange for 240 bars. Other slaves were lost by death; twenty by August 20th when the *Sally* was ready to leave the Guinea Coast with its remaining 167 blacks. At least one woman by then had "hanged her Self between Decks"

Letters to the Captain from Nicholas Brown and Company suggested that "he go to Charleston; if the market there were unfavorable, he might try Virginia. In either case he was to 'get what Hard Cash' he could." Later, noting glutted markets there, he advised the Captain to go to Barbados or Jamaica.

Already replete with problems, the return trip of the *Sally* presented still more. Deaths ensued as soon as Captain Hopkins set sail. On August 21st "1 garle Slave Dyed," on 25th "one boye slave Dyed," on 27th "2 women and 2 boys dyed", later "3 boys & 1 garle." Further, perhaps as a consequence of these deaths, a revolt ensued. The Captain reported when he got to Antigua "an uprising of the Negroes on board ship and its suppression brought heart-breaking results. The surviving Negroes were 'so disperited' that 'some drowned themselves, some starved and others sickened and died.' Eighty-eight of the slaves were dead and the remaining were in a 'very sickly and disordered manner.' The *Sally* had traded her cargo of rum for tragedy, disease, and death.....The records show that on

10. The Brown Family

December 20, 1765 there occurred the 109th death....Only 24 [slaves] are known to have been sold...." [332] The voyage was a financial disaster for Nicholas Brown and Company, costing them two thousand pounds sterling, and believed to be the worst voyage ever undertaken from Providence.[333]

The Brown brothers seem, for the most part, to have taken the financial loss with equanimity (indicating more than anything just how wealthy they were by then), writing to Hopkins: "We need not mention how Disagreeable the Nuse of your Luseing 88 slaves is to us & all your Friends, but your Self Continuing in Helth is so Grate Satisfaction to us that we Remain Cheirful under the Heavy Loss of our Ints."[334] Apparently, it was only Moses who remained haunted by the disaster it represented for the captured Africans, though it is believed that neither Nicholas nor Joseph, in addition to Moses, ever again participated in the slave trade part of their numerous businesses. In contrast, John was undaunted by the loss and continued in the slave trade even after it was made unlawful. Even as late as 1800, "as a Representative in Congress from Rhode Island, he spoke against a bill designed to reinforce the federal statute of 1794 prohibiting citizen participation in the foreign slave trade....[He was] one of only five Congressmen who voted against the bill."[335]

★★★

Moses outlived his first wife Anna, and then his second, Mary Olney, daughter of Richard Olney.[336] Mary

---

[332] Quotes not cited are from Hedges, pp. 78-81.
[333] Coughtry, p. 146.
[334] Quoted in Hawes, p. 155.
[335] Hawes, p. 156.
[336] Mary and Polly Olney, about whom we previously heard so much, were approximately the same age, their fathers both

was a fellow Quaker Moses married in 1779. They had no children during their eighteen years together. After Mary died in 1799, Moses married a third time, the widow Phebe Waterman Lockwood (the wedding we have already heard mentioned by Julia Bowen in her diary). After Phebe died in 1809, Moses remained unmarried until his death in 1836 twenty-seven years later.

Moses son, Obadiah Moses, also actively opposed slavery like his father. He sponsored free blacks and helped them find employment, helped them financially, backed them up in legal disputes, and helped educate them. He also sought to free slaves kidnapped from cities and seaports along the coast and held by southern slave traders in camps in the deep south.[337]

After Obadiah Moses had married Dorcas Hadwen of Newport, and his daughter, Sarah, had married William Almey, Moses established his son and son-in-law, along with Samuel Slater, in the cotton manufacturing business. It's curious that this is the only reference found to Sarah, providing us with no knowledge of where she lived, how she spent her time, even when she died. More is said of Obadiah Moses, including the fact that Moses bought him a brick house, giving him the title to the property "on account of the love and affection I have," and he and his family lived there throughout their lives. After these actions on behalf of his children, Moses retired to his farm several miles outside of Providence where he was living at the time of his death.

When Obadiah Moses preceded his father in death

---

descendants of the pioneer settler, Thomas Olney, Sr., and both their fathers owned taverns in Providence. See *Olney Genealogy*, pp. 20-21. Polly is the nickname for Mary, same as her "cousin"; perhaps why she came to be called Polly.

[337] This and some other information on Browns from the R I H S's "Brown Family Paper Project, first draft."

10. The Brown Family

in 1822 at age 52, Moses lamented: "my beloved son, in my old age, on whom I was looking to lean." [338] Not having had any children, Obadiah Moses left his "dear wife Dorcas [Hadwen] Brown" a life annuity of $3,000. Title to their house went to his niece, Anna Almey [this must have been his sister Sarah's daughter and the bequest suggests Sarah had died by then], but to Dorcas he gave "the use and improvement of my Dwelling House for Herself and Family, which it is my Wish may be kept up therein as long as she may think proper, and that it be made a comfortable home for her and my Friends during her life..." Five months later his niece, Anna Almey, deeded the house, lot and outbuildings to her Aunt Dorcas. Dorcas lived four more years, leaving her property to her two nieces, the Hadwens [her brother's children]. She also left spoons to her sister, Ruth Williams, and the curtains to her bed to her sister Mary Hadwen [who must never have married]. Dorcas died four years after her husband, on May 15, 1826.[339]

---

[338] Miner, Geo., p. 93, quoting Moses.
[339] Miner, Geo., pp. 95-96.

11. Religion & Slavery's End

In the mid-1700s, at the same time that the slave trade was making many of Rhode Island's families wealthy, there was coincidentally a time referred to as the Great Awakening when revivalism swept through the colonies. This seemed to reinvigorate the Quakers who began actively to oppose slavery, "first urging their members to stop dealing in the slave trade and then putting steady pressure upon them to free any slaves they owned...." One woman was expelled for "encouraging the unmerciful whipping or beating of her negro man servant, he being stripped naked and hanged up by the hands in his master's house." In 1765 another Quaker was expelled for having participated in the purchase and sale of a Negro slave. By 1782 a committee established by the Quakers in the state reported, "We know not but all the members of this [Rhode Island] meeting are clear of that iniquitous practice of holding or dealing with mankind as slaves."[340]

Jemima Wilkinson was not a slave owner but when just eighteen was "disowned" by Rhode Island Quakers during the Awakening for quite different, but easily understandable, reasons.[341] To begin at the beginning.

One of twelve children, Jemima's mother died when she was eight, and her father worked such long hours to support his large family that the children were largely ignored. Left without guidance, discipline or schooling, Jemima became willful, crafty, and deceitful, and regularly avoided her household duties. Exceptionally

---

[340] McLoughlin, pp. 78-79 & Bartlett, pp. 15 & 19.
[341] Jemima's story & the quotes that follow are from McLoughlin, pp. 79-80, Weedon, pp. 300-301 & Haley, Old Stone Bank, pp. 50-52

11. Religion & Slavery's End

beautiful and vivacious, "dress, amusement and pleasure were her sole considerations.... She would not think of going to a party unless she could be dressed better than any other girl there. Needless to say she never suffered for lack of male admirers.

"In 1774 she suddenly abandoned her gay life and became deeply interested in religious subjects. She studied the Bible, remained quietly at home, neglected her dress and ceased competing with the rival beauties of the neighborhood. She kept in retirement for two years, when she began to pretend illness and finally went to bed....She professed to have strange visions and visitation from white figures and celestial forms which she would point out" to those who now kept watch on her day and night.

After a period of seeming lifelessness, Jemima claimed to have "been to heaven and to have become a new Christ on earth," demanded her clothes, dressed and went about in perfect health. "Her friends were astounded by her arrogant assumption and the great change in her voice and manner. At church the following Sunday, Jemima collected the congregation under a tree during intermission, and harangued them eloquently on the depravity of sin and the beauty of holiness. Then began her career as head of the self-styled sect she created, the 'Universal Friend of Mankind'."

As Jemima began to travel around New England on horseback "holding large meetings which she addressed in a very eloquent and persuasive manner," seeking converts to this new sect, she was a very imposing figure, fair, with "dark and brilliant eyes, her auburn hair falling on her shoulders in three full ringlets, her voice clear and harmonious....She wore a white beaver hat, sides turned down, a full, light drab mantle; a unique underdress and cravat around her neck."

"A few weak men, and a greater number of silly women and children became her disciples," some even leaving their families behind to follow her. "The acquiring of money being her chief object, she managed to ensnare several wealthy persons who found their association with her both costly and disastrous." One such was William Potter, "chief justice of the county court, with a large estate easterly from the present village of Kingston.... He built for her and her followers an addition to his 'already spacious mansion,' containing fourteen rooms." She lived with him there for six years, "controlling master, household, and the income of the good property." Eventually, the Judge lost everything in bankruptcy.

Jemima claimed to work miracles, accrediting any failures to lack of faith. "In one instance she connived with a young girl who was to feign serious illness during which she was attended only by Jemima. The girl was to simulate death and go through the usual form of a funeral. Jemima was to walk beside the coffin on the way to the cemetery invoking divine aid, and at the proper moment, by a pre-arranged signal, the supposedly dead girl was to give a sign that she was returning to life. The coffin would then be opened and the miracle accomplished." It was only after the girl's sister convinced her that the scheme was blasphemous, that Jemima had to abandon her stunt.

"Jemima was entirely unscrupulous and overbearing," and ruled her converts with an iron hand, punishing one "garrulous Sister" by ordering her to "keep silent for three days. But although her mouth was sealed with wafers and rags she persisted in laughing frequently and the punishment was not a success." Jemima carried on her Ministry from the end of 1776 until July 1819 when she died, aged sixty-eight, following a long illness during which she suffered greatly, but refused any medical care. At the time of her death, Jemima was living in the small community she had founded in 1790 in western New

11. Religion & Slavery's End

York. She had never returned to Rhode Island.

✯✯✯

Another Rhode Island woman, Sarah Haggar Osborn, a member of the first Congregational Church in Newport, also caused quite a stir during the period referred to as the Great Awakening. After her husband died, she started teaching school, trying to support herself in the manner of many single or widowed women. But it paid so poorly that she also took in boarders, and caused quite a stir amongst the parents when she sought to raise the school fees charged her pupils. Sarah persevered and other teachers followed her example, but she "bore the blame for them all," and, in the end, was "forced to rescind the increase." Sarah consoled herself with the thought "that she was not 'indulging in a covetous worldly mind.'" [342]

Later Sarah married and started a women's prayer group that met in her home. Then, in 1765, she boldly allowed slaves to attend, again creating a public outcry. "Newport slaveholders feared she was spreading 'disturbance or disorder' among their servants" and claimed she was "keeping a Negro House." "But within a few months her onetime critics started to applaud her efforts, for they quickly discovered that many formerly recalcitrant slaves had 'reform'd' under her influence...".

Criticism increased again, however, when attendance at her revival meetings spread beyond women and children and attracted men. She was warned to stop, as "men were more qualified than she to be spiritual leaders." They hinted that "she could better devote her time to appropriately 'feminine' tasks." Sarah continued to resist these pressures at least until 1769 when she stopped her "private praying Societies Male and Female." Nonetheless, she apparently retained her

---

[342] Norton, *Liberty's Daughters*, pp. 140-141

influence in the church, because, in 1770, she was the deciding influence in the selection of Reverend Samuel Hopkins as minister, despite a majority of the congregation preferring his opponent.[343]

Sarah's success in winning over approval for her inclusion of slaves in her prayer group may have contributed to their increasing admission to the white man's churches. This idea of "equality under God" that came forth during the Awakening gave the poor, black slaves and Indians hope. The Rev. Doctor Ezra Stiles even presided over the marriage of Caesar Lyndon, a free slave, to Sarah Searings. But "many pastors wrote the words *black* or *Indian* after their names, indicating that equality before God did not mean social equality."[344] Even Roger Williams felt this way. "In 1637 he congratulated John Winthrop on God having placed in his hands 'another drove of degenerate seed.'"[345]

Not all ministers, nor their wives, were inclined to give any recognition to the humanity of slaves. Dr. James MacSparran, one of the most prominent and beloved ministers in Narragansett, wrote in his journal for August 29, 1751:

> I got up this morning early, and finding Hannibal had been out...I stript and gave him a few lashes till he begged. As Harry was untying him, my poor passionate dear [wife] saying I had not given him eno., gave him a lash or two, upon which he ran.

"Hannibal was finally found and secured, so the doctor wrote, with 'Pothooks put about his neck.' A few days later the Negro was again beaten; he again

---

[343] Norton, *Liberty's Daughters*, pp. 129-132.
[344] McLoughlin, p. 77
[345] RI Short Story Club, "Slavery in the RI Colonial Period", Rae Vaule, p. 69.

11. Religion & Slavery's End

ran away and was returned by one of MacSparran's parishioners, together with a plea that he be more lenient to his slave."[346]

In 1722 the Rev. MacSparran and Hannah Gardiner had married. She was only seventeen at the time, "a beautiful and gifted member of a powerful family, allied by marriage to the even more influential Robinson and Hazard families [both, as we've seen, amongst Rhode Island's biggest slave owners], and the young preacher found himself welcomed and adopted into the highest social circles of the Colony. His young wife possessed exceptional qualities of mind and heart which especially fitted her to be [MacSparran's] intimate companion and, in 1755, after her tragic death in London, he writes of her as 'the most pious of women, the best of wives in the world.'"[347] The praise and approval accorded both this husband and wife serves to emphasize the low esteem in which they, their friends and relatives, held black slaves.

☆☆☆

Many, if not most, Rhode Islanders "shared the general social prejudice against blacks, and it did not initially occur to them that anything in their struggle for the 'the rights of Englishmen' applied to the slaves in their midst." However, as early as 1768, "a writer in the *Providence Gazette*, insisting that freedom was the inalienable right of every man, attacked the colonists for their inconsistency in complaining of denial of their natural rights by Britain while keeping slaves themselves." "And as the rhetoric of the Revolution moved to the higher place of 'inalienable natural rights' and the claim that 'all men are created equal,' it became

---

[346] Bartlett, p. 15.
[347] Haley, Old Stone Bank, Vol. II, p. 53.

increasingly difficult to justify the institution of chattel slavery."[348]

The Quakers made slavery a topic of fierce debate at the Continental Conventions during the War of Independence but the paragraph that pledged that Americans would purchase no more slaves after December 1, 1774 did not become part of the law. Rhode Island's General Assembly, too, failed to forbid slavery when the first attempt was made in 1770.

But in February 1784, shortly after the Treaty of Paris was signed,[349] it did pass a bill that provided that "all children born of slave mothers after March 1, 1784, were to be considered freeborn citizens. However, they were to remain in the hands of their mothers' owners, who were to be compensated for the loss of their 'property' by binding them out to service and taking their wages until they reached the age of twenty-one." Of course, slaves born prior to March 1st remained slaves for life.

The part of the bill that would have outlawed the slave trade itself had been deleted before passage, primarily through the efforts of John Brown and John DeWolfe.[350]

---

[348] McLoughlin, p. 105 7 & Bartlett, p. 19.

[349] In this treaty, signed on September 3, 1783, Great Britain formally acknowledged American independence and also made peace with the French, Spanish and Dutch with whom they had been fighting over borders for years: the French and Indian Wars, 1689-1763 (the struggle between Britain and France for control of the Continent); King William's War, 1688-97; Queen Ann's War, 1701-13; French and Indian raid on Deerfield, Massachusetts in 1704; and King George's War, 1745. These wars were actually an asset to the colonists in two ways: firstly, Great Britain's preoccupation allowed the colony more freedom to develop in its own way; secondly, the years of fighting drained and weakened Britain's military rendering them easier to defeat in the War of Independence.

[350] McLoughlin, p. 106.

11. Religion & Slavery's End

Staples presents the case of Jacob Shoemaker, late of Providence, to demonstrate how conflicted members of the Assembly apparently felt over the issue. Since Shoemaker had died intestate, they had to decide the disposition of his properties. Hence, on the one hand, they felt "bound to enforce the law of the colony for the benefit of the creditors of the deceased," but, on the other, they did not want to "participate in any gain to be derived from the unwilling labor of their fellow men."[351]

> [He] hath left six negroes, four of whom are infants, and there being no heir to the said Jacob, in this town or colony, the said negroes have fallen to this town by law, provided no heir should appear. Therefore, It is voted, by this meeting, that ...they do hereby, give up all claim of right or property in them,.... And it is hereby recommended to the town council, to take the said negroes under their protection, and to bind the small children to some masters and mistresses. And in case there should not be personal estate of the said Jacob Shoemaker, sufficient to pay his just debts, it is further recommended to said council to bind out either, or both, of the adult negroes, for that purpose.

The Quakers, especially, led by Samuel Hopkins, Stephen Hopkins, James Manning, Henry Ward and Moses Brown, redoubled their efforts to get a stronger bill passed, "saturating the Rhode Island press with essays, poems, and articles illustrating the moral evils of slavery and the slave trade's role in perpetuating that institution." [352] Their persistence paid off when, in November 1787, Rhode Island's General Assembly passed an act prohibiting the importation of Negroes into the colony; a fine to be levied on any Rhode Island vessel's owner caught engaging in the slave trade.

---

[351] Staples, pp. 236-237.
[352] Coughtry, p. 205

Enforcing the law was not so easy, as noted when a jury refused to convict such a prominent citizen as John Brown even when he was caught "red-handed."

Not surprisingly then, blacks were still arriving in the state, subject to indenturing if not outright slavery. As late as November 1800, the *Providence Gazette* ran an ad stating:

> ...a number of black Men, Women and Children new here and others expected are to be bound out by this Council, men and women for a term of years—male children until they are 21 years old and females until they arrive to the age of eighteen. All persons desirous of taking indentures of such people to apply to this Council as Soon as may be.

And so Frederick Douglass declared that the so-called emancipation laws "had merely transformed people of color from slaves of individuals into 'slaves of the community.'"[353]

Rhode Island was one of the worst offenders in complying with any of the anti-slavery laws. Between 1803 and 1807, fifty-nine Rhode Island vessels, coming from Newport, Bristol and Providence, carried 7,958 slaves into Charleston. As late as 1818, they were still evading the law and still transporting Africans for sale.[354]

Even after the federal law prohibited the slave trade in 1808, "business was carried on quite openly by ships out of Bristol, where a common remark of departing seamen was that they were off to 'catch some black birds.'" Some of these traders must nonetheless have had pangs of conscience because one is quoted as saying, in later life, that "sometimes [he] had to put

---

[353] Mellish, p. 85-86
[354] McLoughlin, pp. 106-107 & 142. (Bartlett says approximately *forty thousand* were brought into Charleston between 1804-1807. p. 9.)

11. Religion & Slavery's End 235

down his morning cup of coffee because he seemed to see blood on the surface of it, and when he saw it he remembered his throwing a slave with small pox out of a boat, and chopping off his hands with an axe when he tried to pull himself back over the gunwale."[355]

Various additional pieces of federal legislation followed that of 1808 until passage of the 1820 Act "which made slaver pirates subject to the death penalty." This undoubtedly expedited the move away from slave trading that already was underway. "Even in the 1790s, when maritime commerce was still king in Providence, her merchants began diversifying, withdrawing risk capital from marine ventures and ancillary industries, and reinvesting in the fledgling state cotton industry."

The gradual shift taking place from commerce to factory was revitalizing "local economies within the Providence orbit and throughout the state." This fundamental economic transformation of the whole society from merchant capitalism to manufacturing underlay whatever "the personal, psychological, economic, and legal reasons of individuals who relinquished" their slaves and the slave trade. "By the 1820s, the [slave] trade had become archaic adventurism," [356] and most of the nation had become obsessed with settling the West.

By 1807, most of Rhode Island's slaves had been freed, but that did not mean they were free of "prejudice and oppression in every sphere of life. They were segregated in the churches, kept out of the public schools [after earlier admitting a few], denied employment in the textile mills, and finally, in 1822,

---

[355] Bartlett, p. 9.
[356] Coughtry, p. 235-237.

denied the right to vote."³⁵⁷ "Many were confined to domestic work;... considered poor business risks and of course could not get capital to establish a business in the trade they knew best."³⁵⁸ Too often they were left idle; called lazy by the whites who shunned them. It was not until May 1843, that Rhode Island's state constitution absolutely forbid slavery.

---

³⁵⁷ McLoughlin, pp. 107108
³⁵⁸ RI Short Story Club, "Slavery in the RI Colonial Period", Rae Vaule, p. 73.

12. Newspapers: Goddards, Franklins & Carters

Besides the shift from farm to sea, other changes were occurring in Providence early in the 18th Century. It greatly expanded in size as well as population, well beyond its original four square acres. Gradually most of the early homesteaders along Towne Street moved outwards to the north and west, replaced by newcomers. New houses, new shops, and new taverns appeared in the town; Market House, a firehouse and a library were built. Churches were also added—Kings Church, the first Anglican church in Rhode Island, and a Presbyterian and Congregational church—but none of these without considerable opposition from the dominant Baptists and the Quakers, both of whom were doing their own expanding. The Friends built their still-used Meeting House on Meeting Street in 1727, and the Baptists built a series of meeting houses as already noted, the final one holding an amazing 1400.

Then, mid-century, Providence gained its first newspaper. In June 1762, Sarah Updike Goddard lent her son, William, £300 to set up Providence's first printing house.[359] By then widowed, Sarah no doubt had inherited money both from her well-off father and from her husband.

Described as "a lady of remarkable business ability and literary gifts,"[360] Sarah was born about 1700 at Cocumscussuc (now Wickford, Rhode Island). She was one of six children (five daughters) of the prosperous Lodowick Updike, a descendent of Richard Smith whom we met earlier when he bought out Roger Williams at Cocumscussuc. Sarah was tutored at home in "Greek, Latin, French, and 'several branches

---

[359] Dexter, p. 171.
[360] *Biographies*, p. 249.

of mathematics."[361] Later, she tutored her own children, teaching them to read, write and cipher, and to enjoy Shakespeare, Pope and Swift, the writers she herself enjoyed.

On December 11, 1735, Sarah married Dr. Giles Goddard of New London, Connecticut, a practicing physician and postmaster, probably having met him while visiting her sister, Esther, who lived in New London. After Dr. Giles died in 1757, Sarah moved to Providence with their two children: Mary Katherine, born June 16, 1738, and William, born on October 20, 1740.

William was seventeen when his father died, and half-way through a seven-year apprenticeship as a printer. He completed it in 1761, on his 21st birthday. William was fortunate to have apprenticed under two men, James Parker and John Holt, whom many regarded as better printers than either William Bradford, of some prominence at the time, or Benjamin Franklin.

With his training complete and his mother's help, William bought at least one printing press and several fonts of type, and arranged for supplies of paper, stationary, forms and books to be shipped either from England or from one of the colonial mills. His first printing job, in mid-August, was a handbill announcing the storming of Morro Castle by the British, and, at about the same time, a playbill for a theater troupe announcing its first-ever appearance in Providence.

"[The theatre] was patronized by the elite of the city, but in some quarters the objections were almost fanatical....What the conditions were like is shown somewhat by notices in the [Newport] newspaper requesting gentlemen to keep off the stage and maintain strict decorum throughout a funeral performance." The

---

[361] Lancaster, p. 5

12. Newspapers: Goddards, Franklins, & Carters

presence of rowdyism is confirmed by an indignant notice, expressed rather quaintly, reading as follows:

> A reward will be given to whoever can discover the person who was so very rude as to throw eggs from the gallery upon the stage last Monday, by which the clothes of some ladies and gentlemen in the boxes were spoiled, and the performance in some measure interrupted.[362]

The company continued to play after being forbidden to by the Town Council. Later, however, the General Assembly enacted a law, personally executed by the Sheriff, which put an end to the theatre in Rhode Island until after the Revolution.

In 1792 actors again came to Providence, even though they knew Rhode Island had a prohibitory law: they were counting on its repeal, knowing that the majority favored the theatre. "On December 10, 1792, the Town Council took action. It made no move to repeal the law, but granted certain liberties, and agreed neither to prosecute nor uphold any prosecution of the players," on condition that every fifth night the proceeds would be given to the sheriff and placed in the town treasury. The theater called their performances "lectures," and referred to them as "Comic Lectures", "Moral Lectures" (tragedies) and "Humorous Lectures" (farces). "It was open twice a week while a play was running....[but] since seats were not reserved, servants were sent early to occupy them till their masters and mistresses could come. Between the acts the servants brought in trays of wines and sherbet bought at a theatre bar. Playbills bore requests for no smoking."[363]

For a time performances were given in the rear part of McLane's Coffee House, but "influential citizens" got together to raise monies for a permanent theater.

---

[362] Haley, Old Stone Bank, Vol. I, p. 59
[363] Miner, Lillian, p. 114.

Construction started on August 6, 1794 and the first performance of "The Child of Nature" took place in the magnificent new structure on Westminster Street on September 3, 1794. "So great was everyone's interest in the theatre that the carpenters all gave up their other occupations and devoted their time exclusively to work on the new building until it was finished."[364]

However, judging from a letter Sarah Brown wrote her brother, James, sometime after this, not everyone was happy with having a theater in Providence.

> Everything is resuming its former gay appearance. Their Assemblies and every other amusement except the Theater present themselves. There is a very strong party against the theater. They even have proposed having that elegant building sold for some better purpose, as they term it. I pray they may not succeed thou' it will probably make no difference to me.[365]

Other amusements of the time, perhaps some of those referred to by Sarah, were, mostly for the young men—ball-playing in the lots, shooting at poultry or a mark, wrestling, and jumping. There were also weddings and "at times muster days in small parties with young women," followed by a dance. "At harvest time, [the young people] would go miles to a husking, as the farmers generally would at that time make merry." Other gatherings "sound as much like work as play...bush cuttings, stone-wall bees, chopping bees, house raisings, spinning, quilting and husking bees." There was not yet hockey to take advantage of the 1740 winter — "a hard one, with much snow—the ice solid from Providence to Newport."[366]

On October 20, 1762, William put out his first

---

[364] Haley, Old Stone Bank, Vol. I, p. 76.
[365] Letters in Manuscript section at RI Historical Society
[366] Miner, Lillian, pp. 114-115, & Staples, pp. 603-604

12. Newspapers: Goddards, Franklins, & Carters

edition of the four-page weekly, the *Providence Gazette and Country Journal*, in a building "opposite the Court House." He calls his readers who support the paper, "publick-spirited" and assures them the paper will be "as entertaining and as generally useful as possible." With the Seven Years' War then going on between England and France he also tells his readers that "Every Thing that relates to the Honour and Interest of our Country, and the Humiliation of our Enemies, must be peculiarly interesting; and as such, they shall be carefully inserted in this paper."[367]

The *Gazette* at once became competitive with the *Newport Mercury*, and soon William's mother and sister were not only keeping house for him, but also "helping set type, manage the business and run the shop where books and printed forms were sold."[368] With numerous well-off relatives living in Providence, especially on his mother's side, William now expected to have an entrée into the "best" of its families and to lead a prosperous life.

The *Gazette* was replete with news from abroad, as promised, as well as shipping news, useful information on crops, and ads for the sale of houses, Indian corn and various merchandise. There were also ads of a personal nature:

> 1/29/1763: Whereas my Wife, Freelove Staples, hath eloped from me, and hath refused to live with me: These are therefore to forbid all persons from keeping her, or her Child, thinking to have pay of me, for I will not pay any Thing for their keeping: And I also forbid all Persons from trading with, or trusting my wife Freelove, on my Account, as I will not answer any Debits of her contrasting. [Signed: Jonathan Staples, Cumberland, 11/20/1762].

Another ad in the same issue of the *Gazette* seemed

---

[367] Miner, Ward L., pp. 26-27
[368] Lancaster, p. 5

simultaneously to seek someone to start a school for dancing in the Town, and to object to the prospect. Both Puritans and Quakers frowned on dancing, believing it to be a serious evil. The paper also carried one writer's long response to the ad, quoted in part:

> I was surprised to see some ludicrous Thoughts and Observations, calculated to set that commendable diversion in an unfavorable Light, by endeavoring to show the destructive consequences of Dancing schools in every Place where they are encouraged. ...Upon impartial observation Examination, we shall find but little Room for many numerous Reflections which the Author of this Piece has felt at Liberty, by such false insinuations, to eclipse their innate nature: For to them we are indebted for the Politeness and engaging Behavior which constitutes the Pleasures and Felicities of a Civil Life.
>
> In Regard to Dancing, it is an Amusement neither faulty in itself, nor [not readable] and I dare say the Gentleman that speaks so bitterly against it, knows very little of the Matter but by hearsay, and is prepossessed against it by mere Prejudice; other wise he could not... blame an Art that can change a Romp into a polite Lady that can give a genteel, free Air, to the most awkward Creature imaginable; in fact, an Art that is capable of working Wonders:—and instead of that ridiculous Formality, for which some, of both sexes, are so peculiarly remarkable, they will become Masters and Mistresses of Qualification, that must render them easy to themselves and agreeable to all around them.

The letter continues, proclaiming the merits of dancing in "civilizing" and molding the young into worthwhile citizens. Near the end, the writer suggests women's superiority over men, pointing out that Foreigners often remark that "the industry of the Women of this country surpasses the Economy of the Men; and in Fact there are but few Points in which the Ladies seem to be inferior." The letter ends with a warning:

12. Newspapers: Goddards, Franklins, & Carters 243

[T]o conclude as Excess in all Things is condemnable, to Dancing or any other innocent Recreation, or even the most useful Employments in Life, ought not to be without Bounds, or engross too much of our Attention from more exalted Pursuits, which, on all Occasions, we ought to guard against, till we cease to be. [Signed, Philathea]

For some time the *Gazette* received letters for and against a dancing school, some suggesting a spinning school would be more useful, but soon after a dance master did come to Providence.

In July 1763 William Goddard announced the relocation of the paper above a book shop where "subscriptions, advertisements and letters of intelligence for this paper will be thankfully received." However, Goddard was having a hard time collecting for subscriptions (seven shillings per year). He ran an item in the paper on April 26, 1763, requesting "those persons who have generously favored with their custom, and are in arrears for the first half year of this Paper, to pay the same as soon as convenient, that he may be the better enabled to serve them for the future."

About the same time in 1763, at the request of Benjamin West, Goddard published Providence's first Almanac. It supplied prophecies on the weather, "weather judgements," and listed main roads, with distances, leading in any direction from Providence to other cities and towns. It also had "quotations and extracts from the English poets plentifully scattered through its pages, while moral observation, maxims and proverbs are wormed in among the weather forecasts, sessions of courts and aspects of the planets." Quaint sayings included: "choose a companion for his good behaviour rather than for his purse," "beauty consists more in good actions than in colour," and "the usurer is the greatest Sabbath breaker because his plough goeth every Sunday."[369]

Finances, nonetheless, continued as a problem, even though such as "tallow, wood, wool and other articles of country produce" were accepted by Goddard in lieu of cash. When the British imposed the Stamp Act early in 1765, things only got worse, especially so after Goddard became involved in the Stamp Act agitation, and in arguments between patriots and loyalists. As a consequence, in May 1765 William suspended printing of the paper with the announcement that "his Hopes ha[d] vastly exceeded his Success." and left Providence for New York. He could hardly have anticipated the imposition of the Stamp Act on March 22nd that had resulted in his closing the paper when he had optimistically moved his printing office only three days before to a more prominent location opposite Nathan Angell's 'Sign of the Golden Eagle,' and next door to Knight Dexter, Esq., on what is now North Main Street. [Across the street from where William lived after his late-life return to Providence.][370]

With things looking bleak for his paper, William had accepted an offer from his old apprentice masters, Holt and Parker, to join them in New York. But his mother and sister, Mary Katherine, both having spent many long hours assisting William, and both now skilled printers themselves, were determined to continue his business. Sarah set about forming *Sarah Goddard and Company*, the *Company* consisting of her daughter, Samuel Inslee (possibly steered to Providence by William), and a few journeymen and apprentices.

A year after William's departure, on August 9, 1766 (five months after the Stamp Act's repeal), the first edition of the revived paper appeared under

---

[369] Haley, Old Stone Bank, Vol. IV, p. 62
[370] Miner, Ward L., p. 46. Information also found in *Printers*, pp. 9-13

12. Newspapers: Goddards, Franklins, & Carters

Sarah's by-line. For reasons unknown, Inslee did not stay long, but also departed for New York. However, his replacement in August 1767 by John Carter, who came from Benjamin Franklin's office in Philadelphia, proved fortunate.

Sarah also continued her son's effort, started with three other men late in 1764, to open a paper mill in Providence. They sought to circumvent the need to have paper shipped from England, something that became even more important after Britain began imposing various taxes. The four men advertised for rags— "linen, sail cloth and junk"—that would make such an undertaking possible, but it had not yet come into being prior to William's departure. Sarah ran a similar ad in her first edition of the *Gazette*, offering different amounts for different sorts of rags. Her offer included the statement that she would take the rags "in Pay for the *Providence Gazette*, if brought when payment should be made, in lieu of Cash."[371] In another announcement Sarah declared that "one-half of the subscription price was to be paid on receiving the first paper and that 'provisions, grain of any kind, tallow, wood, wool and many other articles of country produce' would be accepted instead of money."[372]

In taking over the printing business from her son, Sarah had assumed a role in Providence much like that assumed by Ann Franklin in Newport after her husband James's death.

☆☆☆

James was the older brother of Benjamin Franklin. He had moved his printing business from Boston to Newport in 1732, following a period of imprisonment

---

[371] Miner, Ward L., p. 40
[372] *Printers*, p. 12

for criticizing the governor in print. His first paper there, the *Rhode Island Gazette*, came out on September 27th. After he died in 1735, Ann, whose maiden name is unknown, then took over his printing business, publishing pamphlets and supplying blanks for the public offices. While she was in charge, Ann also revived the *Rhode Island Almanac*, which her husband had first printed in 1727. From 1739 to 1741 Ann wrote, edited, and printed it, "thereby becoming the first woman in America to produce an almanac, in addition to being the first female printer."

During this time, while her son James was away in Philadelphia apprenticing under his Uncle Ben, Ann had the help of her two daughters. From their early years, their father had instructed them in printing and they had spent considerable time working in the printing house. Both were regarded as "correct and quick compositors,... sensible and amiable women."[373] After James finished his apprenticeship in 1748 and the firm became "Ann and James Franklin," Ann helped start the weekly newspaper, *The Newport Mercury*. She remained an active partner until 1757 when she retired. After James suddenly died in 1762 [shortly before the appearance of the first edition of the *Providence Gazette*], Ann, by then sixty-five, again stepped in. But soon after that, she became too ill to continue her work on the paper and her partner, Samuel Hall, took over its publication.

Ann died late in 1763, having outlived all her children. Ann's obituary read, "She excell'd most of her Sex."[374] Two hundred years later, in 1963, Ann was inducted into the Journalism Hall of Fame at the University of Rhode Island.[375] It is hard to understand

---

[373] Dexter, p. 168.
[374] Lancaster, p. 4
[375] *Women*, p. 4, Dexter., pp. 168-169 & Richman, pp. 131-132.

12. Newspapers: Goddards, Franklins, & Carters

why this honor was not also accorded Sarah Goddard.

✯✯✯

In the August 15, 1766 edition of the *Gazette* (Sarah Goddard's second), this item appeared, at least partially perhaps, celebrating the end of the Stamp Act several months before:

> Yesterday, a few gentlemen in this town made a great feast for the poor. There was a general invitation of all the objects of this liberality, besides a special invitation to many. A hog of 120 lbs. was provided, half a sheep, and a lamb, and other provisions, at Carpenter's Point.
>
> It was a picnic on a large scale, and unique, as it respects guests. The place has seen many parties since, but probably none more replete with pleasure than this.

An August 30th edition of the *Gazette* published what was then thought to be a witty and entertaining poem, but it might also be construed to reflect the role of women who were less able to become financially independent as had Sarah and her daughter.

> Of all the experience, how vast the amount,
> Since fifteen long winters I fairly can count;
> Was ever poor damsel so sadly betray'd,
> 'For to live to these years, and still be a maid.
> Ye heroes triumphant, by land or by sea,
> Sworn votries to love, yet unmindful of me;
> You can storm a strong fort, or can form a blockade,
> Yet ye stand by like dastards; and see me a maid.
> Ye lawyers so just, who with slippery tongue,
> Who do what you please, or with right or with wrong;
> Can it be or by law or by equity said,
> That a charming young girl ought to die an old maid.
> Ye learned physicians, whose excellent skill,
> Can save, or demolish, can cure, or can kill;
> To a poor forlorn damsel contribute your aid,
> Who is sick, very sick of remaining a maid.

You fops I involke not to list to my song,
Who answer no end, and to no sex belong.
Ye echoe's of echoe's and shadows of shades,
For if I had you,—I might still be a maid.[376]

By May 1768 William Goddard had moved from New York to Philadelphia, and, in partnership with Joseph Galloway and Wharton, was producing the *Pennsylvania Chronicle*. Despite the fact the *Providence Gazette* was then doing well, on that date the two partners persuaded Goddard that he should sell his Providence shop and concentrate on the Philadelphia paper; in exchange, they promised to find a nice home for his mother in Philadelphia and a store for her to sell books and stationary. (*Why was the Providence paper still his to sell? Did it have to do with laws affecting women's right to ownership?*)

When William wrote his mother of the plan, she swiftly replied that as her life was nearing its end, she had no desire to leave old friends and start anew in a new place. But William persisted, and on a subsequent trip to Providence, without his mother's consent, "he relinquished his postmastership of Providence and sold the print ship and the *Providence Gazette* to John Carter...for $550."

Hence, in November 1768, Sarah and Mary Katherine had no choice but to move from their beloved Providence to Philadelphia—*so much for a son's consideration of his mother and sister for all they had done for him from the time of his first newspaper venture.* His one small gesture of appreciation was to oblige his mother's request that he move a small press into her new home so she could do the printing of blanks and small work while he did the big jobs. However, for reasons unexplained, this so angered his partners that Sarah

---

[376] Miner, Ward L., pp. 57-58 quoting from *Gazette*.

12. Newspapers: Goddards, Franklins, & Carters

returned the press to the shop.[377]

Sarah did not like Philadelphia and wrote her sisters in New England:

> I have been much indisposed this winter yet through the goodness of God I am in a better State of Health then I have been for Sometime when I first came to this City the Air and Climate did not Seem to Agree with me if I Stay I hope it will become more Natural...Katey is now under preparation for the Small Pox and Expect her to be inoculated Some day this week.[378]

Sarah died on January 5, 1770, after only fourteen months in Philadelphia. The *New York Gazette* wrote a long obituary that reviewed much of her life, beginning with her background. In conclusion, it noted:

> Her uncommon attainments in literature were the least valuable parts of her character. Her conduct through all the changing trying scenes of life, was not only unblamable but exemplary; a sincere piety and unaffected humility, an easy agreeable cheerfulness and affability, an entertaining, sensible, and edifying conversation, and a prudent attention to all the duties of domestic life, endeared her to all her acquaintances, especially in the relations of wife, parent, friend, and neighbor. The death of such a person is a public loss, an irreparable one to her children.[379]

As cruel as one might rightly accuse William of being with his mother, he was to extend it further to his sister. He quarreled regularly with other newspaper men, and finally broke with his partners, which left him with bills he refused to pay unless they paid their share. In 1772, this landed him in debtor's prison from

---

[377] Quoted by Miner, Ward L., pp. 84-87
[378] Quoted by Miner, Ward L., p. 87.
[379] Dexter, pp. 171-172 (includes information about her daughter) and Lancaster, p. 5.

which he continued to attack his partners, accusing them of having been successful in politics through crooked maneuverings. He remained there for three or four weeks before his former partners made him a loan "sufficient to extricate him from the Iron hand of Oppression" (perhaps feeling that despite his attacks on them they were responsible and he should not have to suffer further imprisonment.) Meanwhile, his sister, Mary Katherine, had taken charge of the printing shop, assuring that the *Chronicle* continued to appear on schedule.

On release, William moved his shop to a better spot "across the street from Philadelphia's chief center for gossip among seamen and merchants and tradesmen of the town."[380] But during the winter months of 1773 and 1774, as William paid less and less attention to the *Chronicle*, and spent time in Baltimore trying to get a shop started there, Mary Katherine was, in essence, publishing his Philadelphia paper. For a short time the two papers overlapped, but on February 8, 1774, William discontinued the *Chronicle*, "thanking his subscribers and friends" and expressing "his gratitude for their patronage and support 'amidst the Rage and Wildness of Party, the Insolence of Office, the gigantic Strides of arbitrary Power, and the more dangerous Plots and Manoeuvres of secret Conspirators.'" It was generally agreed that, for all his faults (and without recognition of Mary Katherine's contribution), Philadelphians were losing "their best-edited newspaper before the Revolution."[381]

Mary Katherine followed William to Baltimore, and on February 17, 1774 took over management of the *Maryland Journal*, while her brother, throughout that

---

[380] Miner, Ward L., p. 103.
[381] Miner, Ward L., p. 110.

12. Newspapers: Goddards, Franklins, & Carters 251

winter and the next, traveled up and down the coast in an effort to establish and strengthen a postal system free of the British. Mary Katherine continued the *Journal* quite successfully for the next ten years, right through the Revolutionary War and is credited with having printed the official copies of the Declaration of Independence. Her paper was referred to as "a journal second to none in the colonies in interest;" Mary Katherine, herself, said to be "an expert and correct compositor of types."

Perhaps after an independent postal system was finally adopted by the Continental Congress on July 26, 1775, William felt his mission accomplished and wished once more to start printing the paper. At any rate, on April 3, 1781, Mary Katherine wrote in her *Journal* that she had heard there were designs to open another competing paper to hers "with a View to diminish her Business, and compel her to quit."[382] Mary Katherine was tired of the controversies that always revolved around her brother, and did not desire him to interfere with her own "hard-earned prosperity." Perhaps he adhered to her wishes for he formed a partnership with Eleazer Oswald and for some time they stuck to running the paper mill they had established in Elk-Ridge Landing.

A coolness now prevailed between brother and sister, despite the fact that both were doing well. Mary Katherine was doing so well that on March 14, 1783, she expanded her *Journal* from a weekly to twice a week. Gradually, however, William began to assert himself into the paper, until on January 2, 1784, his name appeared on the colophon: "Printed by William and Mary Katherine Goddard, at the Post-Office on Market Street." [383]Four days later his sister's name had disappeared.

---

[382] Miner, Ward L. p. 178.
[383] Miner, Ward L., pp. 180-181.

Ousted as she was, Mary Katherine tried to "retain her customers by publishing her own almanac, in direct competition with her brother," but she lost out in that too.[384] And yet another blow was to hit her.

Mary Katherine had become the Postmistress of Baltimore, the first woman in this position in the United States. She also continued as proprietress of a bookstore, no longer connected with the print shop and newspaper, and in 1784 established a delivery service in 1784. But in 1789, new Postmaster General, Samuel Osgood, removed her as Baltimore's Postmistress, asserting that "since Baltimore was to become the district office for the whole of the South, more travelling might be necessary than a woman could undertake. Despite a petition from 230 leading citizens of Baltimore, George Washington refused to overrule Osgood's decision, so Mary Katherine had lost the two jobs she liked best."[385]

Mary Katherine "died aged 78 in 1816, with only a slave woman [Belinda Starling] in attendance," never having married nor reconciled with her brother. Her will does not mention her brother, but gives Belinda her freedom as a reward for all her years of care and affection. She also left Belinda "all the property of which I may die Possessed all which I do to recompense the faithful performance of duties to me."[386]

Before William returned to Providence permanently in 1792, he had returned several times to visit friends and relatives. One such time was May 25, 1786 when the *Gazette* reported that this prosperous forty-five year old had married Abigail Angell, an heiress after her father's death in 1785. Born on December 3, 1758,

---

[384] Lancaster, p. 7.
[385] Miner, Ward L., pp. 193-194 and Lancaster, p. 8.
[386] Miner, Ward L., p. 194 and Lancaster, p. 8.

12. Newspapers: Goddards, Franklins, & Carters

Abigail was considerably younger than her new husband and a descendent of two of Providence's oldest families—the eldest daughter of Mary Mawney (Pardon Tillinghast was Mary's Great-Great Grandfather) and the late Brigadier-General James Angell (a descendent of Thomas Angell, who had come to Providence with Roger Willliams). The *Gazette* described Abigail as "a Lady of great Merit, her mental Acquirements, joined to a most amiable Disposition, being highly honourable to her Sex, and are pleasing Presages of connubial Felicity."[387]

After the wedding, John Carter, who had remained a family friend after taking over the *Gazette*, wrote to "Miss Katy," hoping that "the affectionate qualities of Abigail would serve to bring together the brother [William] and sister [Mary Katherine]." Carter described Abigail and William's wedding thus:

> The wedding took place at Col. Bowen's Villa, three miles from town, on Thursday afternoon, the 25th, at two o'clock....There were present [twenty-seven guests, including John Carter]. The bride was clad in an elegant white Lutestring, and made a charming appearance: she behaved like herself on the occasion, though the solemnity of the ceremony caused a momentary embarrassment ....Col. Bowen's good lady being out of health, the pageantry of a public celebration was purposely avoided; but though the guests were few in number, mirth and conviviality prevailed. Excepting my own, it was the most pleasing scene of the kind I ever attended, your absence being the only alloy. On the two following days they were visited by all the genteel inhabitants of Providence, and tomorrow they leave Col. Bowen's to reside by invitation at Mr. Whitman's [Abigail's sister] till their departure for Baltimore, which will take place too soon.

He goes on to say that Abigail's father left his four

---

[387] Miner, Ward L., pp. 184-185.

sons and two daughters a generous inheritance, her part "estimated at about 2500 Dollars." Carter added that even had she been destitute "such a wife [as Abigail] would prove a fortune in herself." He urges Miss Katy "with all the warmth of my heart, an immediate settlement of every matter in dispute between you and your brother." In conclusion, Carter advises Mary Katherine that Abigail is bringing with her a portion of the wedding Cake for her to put under her pillow, and "we hope [this] may induce pleasing dreams."[388] Possibly Mary Katherine mellowed a bit after this, but as we have noted she never actually reconciled with her brother

Soon after Abigail moved with William to Baltimore, she wrote Carter complaining about "the want of fish." He replied that she should "be a good girl, bear in mind the interesting word obey, eat your 'hominy and pone' with a contented mind."[389]

Meanwhile Goddard got into another of his quarrels with a printer, this time over the almanac trade. Abigail "must have had several doubtful moments about the gentility of the newspaper profession" as she read some of the scurrilous invectives that filled their columns. She may also have been upset when "in January 1787, Benjamin Franklin made an attempt through a Baltimore agent to collect the sixty-pound bond of almost twenty years before that Goddard and his sister had signed." William made an equivocating reply probably never intending to pay "this particular debt, despising Franklin as he did."[390] It is not clear that he ever did pay it either.

In 1789 he and Abigail began talking about his retiring and their returning to Providence, but after an agreement with Abigail's brother, James, that made

---

[388] Quotes from letter are from Miner, Ward L., pp. 185-186
[389] Miner, Ward L., p. 186
[390] Miner, Ward L., p. 190.

12. Newspapers: Goddards, Franklins, & Carters

him a partner, the Goddards lingered on for a number of years, splitting their time between the two cities, usually staying with relatives when in Providence. It was during one such stay in June and July of 1790 that their first child died after a long illness. Then on November 29, 1790, they had the first of their five children who lived to adulthood—Ann Elizabeth. After their second, Mary Angell, was born on May 24, 1792, Abigail began to be more insistent about their moving to Providence permanently. And so it was that in August William sold his share of the partnership to James and also collected monies owed him.

However, after paying off his own debts of £2500 and £500, there was little left. Consequently, in order for them to live there, Abigail had to use her share of the inheritance she had received from her father to purchase her siblings' share of the family estate. Even though the house, located in what is now Johnston, was rather small and old, built about 1680, it included a two-hundred-and-fifty acre farm. Abigail loved entertaining and their guests included Moses Brown, a friend who managed their finances for them, and John Carter, who now also frequently saw William in town visiting what had once been his printing shop.

While the Goddards lived in this country retreat, Abigail bore three more children: William Giles, their only son, who became editor of the *Rhode Island American*, and a professor of moral philosophy at Brown University from which he had graduated in 1812; Abbie Angell, born early in 1795, of which little is written; and Sarah Updike, born June 9, 1796. By 1803, feeling cramped in their three-bedroom house, and, in any case, wanting to be in Providence nearer their friends, they made their final move to a house at the corner of Main and Thomas streets. William died there in December 1817, aged seventy-eight; Abigail in December 1845, aged eighty-seven.

Though William Goddard alone is credited with starting Providence's first newspaper, and no one disputes that he was a fine newsman, it would seem that his mother and sister should share the credit, for it was they who resurrected it when he gave up, and who kept his various newspaper ventures going when William was away, concerned with other matters.

★★★

After John Carter bought the *Providence Gazette* from William Goddard, he combined the paper's printing with a post office, and located them on the south side of Meeting Street across from the new Friends Meeting House. There he erected a "substantial, three-story structure that was destined to be known as Shakespeare's Head," retaining Goddard's trade-mark illustration of the "Bard of Avon" on the paper's masthead. Carter also "painted or carved the head of William Shakespeare on a sign suspended from a high post in front of the building." As a place that also sold books, it became a "politically exciting" gathering place during the War for Independence. He continued to supply "the mechanics of publicity for his community...until [February 12,] 1814 when he retired and died."[391]

On May 14, 1769, the same year Carter built "Shakespeare's Head," Carter and Amey Crawford (great granddaughter of Gideon and Freelove Fenner Crawford) married. If their home was not within this new three-storied building, it must have been nearby, and it was there that Amey bore nine children. Interestingly, her daughter Huldah's arithmetic books from her school days is preserved, as is daughter

---

[391] Haley, Old Stone Bank, Vol. IV, p. 68.

12. Newspapers: Goddards, Franklins, & Carters

Rebecca's copybooks from 1791 when she was thirteen, and her diary for the year of 1794 when she turned sixteen. Diary entries suggest that, at the time of writing, Rebecca was living with one of her sisters, perhaps Ann, who was the oldest of the nine children. Several entries note "dinner at Momma's (8/24), "went up to mother's" (9/15), or "Mamma's for tea."[392]

Unfortunately, even though Rebecca faithfully wrote in her diary daily, it is so teeny-tiny that even with Rebecca's teeny-tiny hard-to-read-handwriting, she does not have enough space to elaborate on how she spends her time. Nonetheless, we learn something of the day-to-day-life of an adolescent, probably typical of what we might now call a middle-class, perhaps upper middle-class, family.

After noting that she started dancing school on April 4th Rebecca follows with numerous entries that note either "dancing school in the morning" or "spent morning at lessons." Following the April 21st entry—"in the afternoon began to go to Mr. Larned school"—there are a number of entries noting "to Larnd School in afternoon."

Every Sunday, Rebecca records going to church "all day"; once she noted going to Quaker meeting with A. Dexter to hear a preacher. Despite this regular church attendance, on August 22nd, "musing on her 16th birthday", Rebecca writes: "still find my mind illy stord for the year but my next may I devote more to my maker and my work."

Rebecca also spent considerable time sewing. It is probably on those days she notes, "spent day at home". During March she tells us she starched and mended stockings, worked on clothes for her younger sister, etc.; on July 23rd, "finished the body of my shift"; next day, "trimmed my white hat with lace"; on

---

[392] Diary is in manuscript collection at RI Historical Society.

August 5th, "made sleeves for my smock"; and on October 26th, "ripd up my hat and alterd it".

There are frequent references to tea, and many references to A Dexter. One of the early entries, March 18th, notes "all the girls drank tea with me except A Dexter." On May 9th, "A Dexter called in to see me a few moments"; on May 10th her Mamma refused to let her go to Moses' home, Green Spring; on May 13th, "A Dexter spent day with me at home".

On July 16th, Rebecca notes that "little Moses [her nephew] is very ill"; the next day, "Moses breath his last."

Near the end of the diary, the number of references to "parties", usually in the afternoon, increases—especially noting those to which she was not invited. On July 10th, "Went to party in afternoon;" on August 7th, "No invitation to the party"; on August 15th, "I was angry I had no invitation to the party;" on September 11th, "Waited all the morning in expectation of an invitation to the party but was disappointed."

The final entry in Rebecca's diary is on December 30, 1794 : "A little snow; went to play at the Coffee House."

In addition to her diary, Rebecca left numerous undated notes, affirming for us that invitations to tea were frequent—"Miss Brown requests the pleasure of Miss Carter's company to take tea tomorrow afternoon." [*Requests of all sorts were then made in writing, delivered by hand, sometimes with the request to wait for a reply. There were no phones, no E-mail, not even a post office, to speed things along.*]

> Mr. Caleb Bowers: Compliments wait on Miss Carter I request the pleasure of attending her to the Cadet Ball on Monday evening.
>
> [At bottom] Miss Carter regrets extremely.
>
> My Dear Rebecca I hope Mr. Garrish saw you safe home

12. Newspapers: Goddards, Franklins, & Carters

last Night. The poor fellow seems to be Quite in the figgets to had this note to your Ladyship. I hope you Intend to favor me with Agreeable Company to Baptist meeting this Afternoon. If you will go I will call for you with the greatest Pleasure. [Signed Abby Dexter]

Other notes found in a miscellaneous file at the Historical Society offer some insight into the kind of apparel young girls cared about, and suggest that borrowing between the women was common.

> Will my dear Sister oblige me with loan of the Handkerchief She had on the first evening I called—it appeared to be wrought with purple sewing.
>
> Will you my dear Rebecca be so obliging as to send me your bonnet to try to make one by? Yours most affectionately A. Chace.
>
> I am quite ashamed my Dear Rebecca to send my gown. It is very dirty as you'll see...yesterday in a great hurry I altered it to wear to the Assembly and tried to make something of it. Different from what I had worn before. Do excuse it. I do not often muss my clothes to look quite so bad. It is the only fashionable dress I have. Yours in heart, Amelia.

In September 1801, Rebecca married Amos Throop Jencks, son of Freelove Crawford and John Jencks. Amos was a merchant who died in Cuba in 1809, only eight years after their marriage. He left her with two young sons: Francis Carter, only two years old, and Amos, Jr., born the same year as his father's death. They also had a daughter and two other sons who died young.

After Rebecca's mother died on December 18, 1806, at 63 years of age, Rev. John Lynn Blackburne delivered the sermon at her funeral held on January 4, 1807 at St. John's Church in Providence. The following excerpts, quoted from his thirteen-page sermon written in small elegant script, tell us not only how many people felt about Rebecca in life, but also reveal the commonly held attitudes toward death. It is difficult to imagine today such a lengthy funeral service as this must have been.

> We may rest assured that when we die, our bodies shall be laid in the silent grave, yet, it will not be long 'eer this corruptible shall put on incorruption, and this mortal shall put on immortality.
>
> Child of my heart, may the afflicted parent exclaim, while she bends her head over the untimely grave and drops a pitying tear on the insensible coffin. Child of my heart farewell; for thee I mourn; nature must indeed feel the parting pang! Thou art torn from me, and the anguish of separation is, as if one should tear by violence a limb from my body! My heart bleeds at the very thought! But I submit to necessity with chearfulness; because my religion teaches me to turn my views from earth to yonder regions of Glory, where with an eye of faith I see thee partaking of the bliss of Saints, and cloathed in the vesture of immortality. Thou can't not come to me, but one comfort still remain, I shall go to thee.
>
> In every condition life, [Amey] was a pattern to her sex, appeared mistress of those peculiar qualities which were required to conduct her with honour, and never failed to exert them in their proper seasons, to the utmost advantage. She was careful without anxiety, and frugal without parsimony. A solicitous attention to the Partner of her life and to the education of her Children engrossed all her care, and no pains were spared in the cultivation of the minds of the latter. In a word, she was truly good, wise and christian like; and died a faithful member of the Protestant Episcopal Church. Her virtues live in the faithful memory of her friends and time itself cannot obliterate the impression they have made on the hearts of mankind.
>
> Shall we permit our fears of dying to frustrate all that our dear redeemer hath done and suffered for us? No, my friends, we know indeed that it separates us from our

12. Newspapers: Goddards, Franklins, & Carters

bodies for a reason, but only that we may receive them far more pure and glorious....It's soon born again; it rises up invested and adorned with a beautiful cloathing. And if God so cloathe the grass of the field, which today is, and tomorrow is cast into the oven, shall he not much more cloathe us, who are of greater value than they?

Make peace with God, be at peace with your maker, be at peace with your conscience. Prepare rationally and cheerfully for your own death, that when disease, or accident or violence shall destroy the life of your bodies, your souls may be received into the bosom of your Father and your God...where mortality shall be known no more; where all tears shall be washed from off all eyes, and all our troubles and sorrows shall have an end.—Now, unto God the Father, God the Son, and God the Holy Ghost, be ascribed as is most due, all honour, glory, majesty and dominion, now and evermore. Amen.[393]

---

[393] Complete sermon in manuscript section of RI Historical Society.

13. Women, War & Independence

During the 1700s, Providence had become a prosperous manufacturing and commercial center, its prosperity based primarily on trade with the West Indies, and especially with England, their best customer (even early-on, one year's business with them amounted to £20,000, a vast sum at the time). So it was not surprising that its men loudly objected when England started interfering, beginning in 1763. The women no doubt protested just as loudly, if not as publicly, when they saw their house moneys threatened and the possibility of no longer being able to have such items as "fine linen" that now regularly arrived from England.

For the most part, however, Providence merchants were able to avoid the armed British vessels sailing up the down the New England coast, trying to prevent goods entering without paying the proscribed revenues: their shops remained full of both the staples colonists needed and many of the luxury items as well.

This being the case, for a while Rhode Island was reluctant to act. But not acting did not mean the colonists did nothing. Goddard's involvement in Stamp Act agitation after its passage by the British on March 22, 1765 has already been noted; Benjamin Franklin was in England trying to persuade the British they should not impose such taxes until the colonies were represented in Parliament; citizens in Newport were so angry they hung a number of Tories in effigy; and in Providence women formed the "Daughters of Liberty," given that name by Dr. Ephraim Bowen.[394]

---

[394] Dr. Bowen was the father of Julia Bowen Martin whose diary was quoted earlier. And earlier in his life, Dr. Bowen had been the rejected suitor of the beautiful Hannah Robinson, Mrs. Ludovick Updike's niece, whose story we heard before. We might well surmise that Hannah would have had a happier life if she had stuck with the good doctor instead of eloping with Peter Simons, as she did.

13. Women, War & Independence

Dr. Bowen "invited eighteen young ladies from prominent families to spin from sunrise to evening to prove that the colonies could produce their own yarn....The ladies were given a dinner by the doctor after the spinning. The next meeting was held at the courthouse because the group was so large."[395] Once again women were seen walking through the streets, many carrying spinning wheels, on their way to these spinning, sewing, quilting, and knitting bees where they welcomed the opportunity to indulge in "enlightened conversation" while they worked.

It was as if they had returned to colonial times; most women having given up making their own clothes. Instead, they bought cloth from abroad and utilized seamstresses or tailors to make their clothing. They certainly were no longer limited to one dress, unlike the early pioneer women who often "owned only one dress at any given time." Some had even had to wear "the same dress for several decades. Clothing was mended, cut down, restyled, and finally cut up for rags or bedcoverings. ...the dress of the typical colonial woman [had] consisted of a coarse linen or cotton chemise covered by a bodice of homespun cloth or leather that was loosely cut and sometimes laced in front. The chemise was the basic article of under-clothing [and often the only underclothing] worn by women of all classes until well into the nineteenth century...Skirts were full and fell only to the ankle. For added warmth, a woman might wear two or three petticoats under a wool skirt, or she might wear a petticoat alone without a skirt."[396]

As the Daughters of Liberty continued to meet, "stories about spinning bees, which had been both rare and relegated to back pages of the *Providence Gazette*,

---

[395] Simister, p. 28.
[396] DePauw, p. 48

suddenly became numerous and prominently featured."[397] One such article described an occasion when "a number of young ladies, daughters of liberty and industry, assembled at the Rev. Mr. Rowland's with their spinning wheels, and at night presented him with 1,020 knots of thread."[398] At another time, Eleanor Fry of Greenwich was said to have "spun seven skeins on knot linen yarn in one day,...enough to weave twelve linen handkerchiefs."[399] These numbers reflect the fact that on many occasions the women turned their task into entertainment by having a competition.

Additionally, the women boycotted British products —paper, sugar, glass, silk, linen, wine and tea. They now drank a comparatively odious home brew of herbs instead of the banned tea. (It has been suggested that this was the beginning of the American switch to coffee from the previously preferred tea of the English.)

Concerned that the boycotts were a threat to their trade with the colonies, British merchants persuaded the British Ministry to repeal the Stamp Act, as they did on March 18, 1766 after only one year. Providence outdid even Newport in celebration, drinking more toasts and ending with a grand ball. Dr. Bowen escorted the Daughters of Liberty to the ball, described as "elegant; 'the most brilliant appearance of ladies this town ever saw...' Skyrockets were 'played off' near the courthouse in the evening and thirty-two toasts were drunk, 'loyal, patriotic and constitutional...under a discharge of seven, five and three cannon, accompanied with the sound of drums, trumpets and the loudest huzzas of the loyal multitude...'"[400]

---

[397] Norton, *Liberty's Daughters*, p. 166
[398] Staples, p. 617.
[399] Earle, *Home Life*, p. 185.
[400] Simister, p. 28.

13. Women, War & Independence 265

With the Stamp Act's repeal, tension with England was temporarily reduced, but it did not last long. Only a year later, in 1767, Britain passed the Townsend Act, taxing numerous of the colony's imports.

On the Monday afternoon of July 25, 1768, Rhode Island citizens again gathered to protest, this time under the shade of a huge elm tree in front of Olney's Tavern. It seemed that all of Providence was there as well as many from the surrounding countryside and some from as far away as the Province of Massachusetts Bay. They were there to dedicate the elm tree as the "Tree of Liberty." Silas Downer delivered "an animated discourse, pointing out the terms of colonization of the first planters of these colonies. A declaration of our rights and a particular enumeration of our grievances, together with a designation of the means of redress."[401]

Some apparently feared to express publicly the feelings they freely expressed in private about the British, but young Silas, a Son of Liberty, had no such reservations about "twisting the tail of the British Lion." He was a Harvard graduate in the class of 1747, number 25 in a class of 28, at a time when students were ranked by their social standing rather than their merit. Married to the young widow (undesignated) of a Providence man, and living "in a small house at Muddy dock on Weybosset Street," he was often employed by the courts to write legal papers.

By 1770, Ben Franklin, still in England, was so disillusioned with his efforts to stop Britain's taxing the colonies that he wrote back to Boston predicting violence that would end either in "absolute slavery in America or

---

[401] Quotes and account of Liberty Tree celebration in this and following paragraph are from Chace notes found in manuscript section of RI Historical Society.

ruin in Britain by the loss of her colonies..." [402]

At the time, Rhode Island was still trying to collect an old debt owed them for artillery stores they had furnished for Britain's Crown Point expedition in 1756 while Britain was in a struggle with France for North American supremacy. So, in 1771, the General Assembly sent its personable attorney general, Henry Marchant, to England to see if he could resolve the matter before things got worse. In June 1772, while Marchant was still there, the *Gaspee* affair occurred.

When the *Gaspee*, a British revenue schooner, had arrived in the Narragansett Bay, it posed a real threat to Rhode Island's thriving local trade and its rampant smuggling activities intended to avoid the British taxes. Led by John Brown, a group of Providence's most prominent merchants, including, Samuel Whipple, Ephraim Bowen, Benjamin Page, John Hopkins, John Mawney, Turpin Smith and probably others, conspired with Capt. Abraham Whipple to do something. On the night of June 10th a group of about sixty men met at Sabin Tavern and proceeded under the Captain's leadership to the eight long boats that were to take them to the *Gaspee*. Shortly after midnight the first shots were fired, wounding William Dudingston, the ship's commander, before boarding and taking the surprised crew. After ransacking the ship, they torched it and took the captives to shore in Warwick.

The event barely made the Saturday, June 13, 1772 edition of the *Providence Gazette* which devoted its entire front page, and much of its second, to a report on the Revolution in Copenhagen planned by the Queen Dowager of Denmark. Page three had two short articles (reproduced above) related to the Gaspee: one reporting the incident, the other by the British offering a reward

---

[402] RIHS publication, *Rhode Island History*, Henry Marchant's Journal, 1771-1772, p. 40.

for the capture of the "perpetrators of the said affair."

PROVIDENCE, June 13.

Monday last a Sloop from New-York arrived at Newport, and after reporting her Cargo at the Custom-House, was proceeding up the River on Tuesday. The Gaspee armed Schooner, then lying near Newport, immediately gave Chace to the Sloop, crowding all the Sail she could make; but the People on board not being acquainted with the River, at Three o'Clock in the Afternoon she ran on Namquit Point, near Pawtuxet. About Twelve at Night a great Number of People in Boats boarded the Schooner, bound the Crew, and sent them ashore, after which they set Fire to the Vessel, and destroyed her. A Pistol was discharged by the Captain of the Schooner, and a Musket or Pistol from one of the Boats, by which the Captain was wounded, the Ball passing through one of his Arms, and lodging in the lower Part of his Belly. He was immediately taken to Pawtuxet, and we are told is in a fair Way to recover.

We hear that one Dagget, belonging to the Vineyard, who had served the before mentioned Schooner as a Pilot, but at the Time of her being destroyed was on board the Beaver Sloop of War, going ashore a few Days since at Narraganset to a Sheep-Shearing, was seized by the Company, who cut off his Hair, and performed on him the Operation of Shearing in such a Manner, that his Ears and Nose were in imminent Danger.

MR. *TOLES* begs Leave to inform Gentlemen and Ladies, that labour under the Misfortune of the Loss of their Teeth, that he makes Teeth of the best polished Ivory, and sets them in the neatest Manner, so as to become serviceable to the Speech, Features, and eating their Food.—He makes no Doubt of giving Satisfaction to those who choose to favour him with their Commands. He is to be spoke with at the House of Mr. JACOB WHITE-MAN, on the West Side of the Great Bridge.

FLOUR by the Barrel, White Beans, and a Parcel of excellent Cheese, to be sold by

JOHN UPDIKE.

BY THE HONOURABLE
JOSEPH WANTON, ESQUIRE,
Governor, Captain-General, and Commander in
Chief, of and over the English Colony of Rhode-
Island, and Providence Plantations, in New-Eng-
land, in America.

WHEREAS on Tuesday, the Ninth
Instant, in the Night, a Number of People,
unknown, boarded His Majesty's armed Schooner
the Gaspee, as she lay aground on a Point of Land,
called Namquit, a little to the Southward of Pawtuxet, in the Colony aforesaid; who dangerously
wounded Lieutenant William Duddingston, the Commander, and by Force took him, with all his People,
put them into Boats, and landed them near Pawtuxet; and afterwards set Fire to the said Schooner,
whereby she was entirely destroyed.

I have therefore thought fit, by and with the Advice of such of His Majesty's Council as could be
seasonably convened, to issue this Proclamation,
strictly charging and commanding all His Majesty's
Officers within the said Colony, both Civil and Military, to exert themselves, with the utmost Vigilance,
to discover and apprehend the Persons guilty of the
aforesaid atrocious Crime, that they may be brought
to condign Punishment. And I do hereby offer a Reward of One Hundred Pounds Sterling, Money of
Great-Britain, to any Person or Persons who shall
discover the Perpetrators of the said Villainy, to be paid
immediately upon the Conviction of any one or more
of them. And the several Sheriffs in the said Colony are hereby required forthwith to cause this Proclamation to be posted up in the most public Places
in each of the Towns in their respective Counties.

Given under my Hand and Seal at Arms, at
Newport, this Twelfth Day of June, in
the Twelfth Year of the Reign of His Most
Sacred Majesty GEORGE the Third,
by the Grace of God King of Great-Britain, &c. Anno Domini 1772.

JOSEPH WANTON.

By his Honour's Command,
HENRY WARD, Secretary.

13. Women, War & Independence

To the participants it was an act to protect the interest of Rhode Island's merchants, to the British it was an act of treason and they wanted the miscreants caught and transported to England to be tried. Though no one ever turned in the participants, the affair accomplished little for the colonists and did complicate relations with Britain. It had occurred just when the final decision regarding payment of its debt to Rhode Island was to be made by the British Treasury. When he heard of it, Marchant knew that he might as well return home.

Marchant had greatly enjoyed his year in England, had traveled its whole length, visited its factories and theaters, and made many friends, but their politics disgusted him. Catharine Macaulay, who was writing a multi-volumed *History of England,* was an exception. On April 29, 1772, Marchant wrote in his journal: [403]

> I solicited this amiable Daughter of Liberty with inexpressible Pleasure, heightened by the Pleasing Manner in which she recd. Me. We had a Feast of about two Hours Conversation upon Liberty in Genl....She enquired much of American Affairs & is charmed to think There exists in the World two such perfect Commonwealths as Rhode Island & Connecticut. She was desirous of seeing our Charter &c which I promised to gratify Her with.

After Marchant's return to America, they continued to correspond and he was impressed by Macaulay's preference for a democratic republic over that of a monarchy. She urged speedy action to achieve independence.

☆☆☆

---

[403] RIHS publication, *Rhode Island History,* Henry Marchant's Journal, 1771-1772, p. 51.

In 1770, the same year Marchant went to England, Britain repealed the hated Townsend Act, but for reasons unknown continued to tax tea. This led to the famous Boston Tea Party in 1773, but dramatic as this was, it did not end the tax. As talk continued throughout 1774 of reconciliation of some sort with Britain, preparations for war began with independent militia companies established.

In Providence, the Daughters of Liberty continued their boycott, and in 1775 the Continental Congress made it official, mandating that tea should not be used or purchased after the first day of March. The next day, on March 2nd, Providence held its own Tea Party. The women were there in force when the people of Providence, summoned by the town crier, assembled at the market place at five o'clock where "a quantity of India tea will be burnt." He shouted forth that "all true friends of their country, lovers of freedom, and haters of shackles and handcuffs, are hereby invited to testify their good dispositions, by bringing and casting into the fire a needless herb, which, for a long time, hath been highly detrimental to our liberty, interest and health."[404]

> About five in the afternoon, a great number of inhabitants assembled at the place, where there were brought in about three hundred pounds weight of tea...A large fire was kindled, and the tea cast into it. A tar barrel,...newspapers, and divers other ingredients entered into the composition. ...Many worthy women, from a conviction of the evil tendency of continuing the habit of tea drinking, made free-will offerings of their respective stocks of the hurtful trash. On this occasion, the bells were tolled,...Whilst the tea was burning, a spirited son of liberty went along the streets with his brush and lamp black, and obliterated or unpainted the word "tea" on the shop signs.

"English newspapers endorsing the Tea Act were

---

[404] Staples, pp. 244-245.

13. Women, War & Independence 271

thrown into the flames, also the sign from the door of the Crown Coffee House. ...The *Providence Gazette* called the tea 'Madame Souchong' and the burning of it her 'funeral.'"[405] No explanation is given as to why the tea was called "Madam Souchong" or this her funeral, but Staples quotes the paper's account of Madam Souchong, thus:

> She was a native of China, and after travelling into several parts of Europe, where she found great notice among the great and luxurious, she took a trip to America. She came into this country about forty years ago, and hath been greatly caressed by all ranks. She lived in reputation for several years, but, at length, became a common prostitute among the lowest class of people. She became very poor, and her price was so lowered that any one might have her company for almost nothing. The quality deserted her, and by hard living, in log houses and wigwams, her health was impaired. Broken spirits and hysterics seized her, and she died on the first of March 1775, at midnight.[406]

Rather than dying on this occasion as the paper reported, Staples goes on to inform us that Madam Souchong had merely had "a sudden catalepsy seize her...occasioned no doubt by the heavy load of chains for America which the British ministry laid on her shoulders." [*He does not tell us for what reason she was so treated; perhaps the punishment for prostitution at the time.*] Staples continues, stating that Madam had partially recovered by 1776, but it was not until 1783 that she "wholly regained her lost powers." Further, she was still alive when Staples wrote his book (1843?), "as great a favorite as when she first came to this country."

---

[405] Simister, p. 65.
[406] This quote and following from Staples, pp. 244-245 (Same account found in Simister p. 65)

It was little more than a month after Providence's Tea Party that the opening shots of the War for Independence rang out: In April 1775, British soldiers exchanged gunfire with American colonists at Lexington and Concord. Providence's commerce now was too hard hit and its prosperity too threatened to ignore the British interference any longer. As never before, custom's ships became enemy ships, making continued trade dangerous. Whaling expeditions were put in jeopardy, which, in turn, affected candle-making. The General Assembly, meeting on April 22nd appointed a committee to "proportion 2,500 pounds of powder, lead, bullets and flints belonging to the Colony among the several town." They also authorized an " 'army of observation' of fifteen hundred good effective men to be raised and properly armed and disciplined." [407]

Rhode Islanders wanted action and were tired of waiting for members of the Continental Congress to agree, so on May 4, 1776 the state's General Assembly repudiated its allegiance to King George III; retaining, however, its royal charter. Hence it was that Rhode Island, already having declared its independence, took its time in signing on to the Congress's July 4th Declaration of Independence, finally doing so on July 18th ——giving the state two independence days to celebrate should they wish.

No serious battles were fought within Rhode Island's borders during the War for Independence, only a few skirmishes, but the colony nonetheless suffered war-caused disruptions. The legislature authorized the use of "a small fleet of state-owned warships and a large number of privateers and armed merchant ships."

Local militia were called up, and manned forts were established along the entire shoreline with warning

---

[407] Greene, Robert Ewell, pp. ii-iii.

13. Women, War & Independence

beacons to signal danger. "The beacon consisted of a tall mast or tower and a cauldron of tar and logs. Tests of the beacon in Providence were seen as far as Pomfret, Conn." 408 Despite the fact that "Rhode Island had five regiments in service; three in the Continental Army and two in the state," the British by the end of 1776, had captured Newport. "By the end of 1777, half of the available men in Rhode Island were in arms."409

---

408 Levin, p. 8
409 Greene, Robert Ewell, p. iii.

Initially George Washington opposed enlisting blacks in the army, but by 1776, with his forces depleted, he changed his mind, noting that the British already were attracting blacks by offering them their freedom for enrolling. Thus, with his approval, in February 1778 Rhode Island's General Assembly agreed to "enlist every able-bodied negro, mulatto, or Indian man slave" for the duration of the war. They would pay the slave-masters from £65 to £120 each for any of their slaves who enlisted, and promised the slaves "freedom, equality of remuneration and support should they ever come to want, and their own or substitute wearing apparel furnished by their masters."[410]

> [The Assembly] further voted and resolved that every slave, so enlisting, shall, upon his passing muster before Col. Christopher Greene, be immediately discharged from the service of his master or mistress, and be absolutely FREE, as though he had never been encumbered with any kind of servitude or slavery...

Two hundred and ten slaves enlisted, forming the "Black Regiment," designated as 1st Rhode Island. During their five years of active service, they distinguished themselves in the Battle of Rhode Island in August 1778, and participated in battles in Red Bank on the Delaware in New York, in Points Ridge, New York, at For Oswego in New York, near Albany and in Yorktown, Virginia. Many lost their lives. After Christopher Greene was killed in 1781, Jeremiah Olney of Providence assumed command of the 1st Rhode Island, and remained with them until they were demobilized on June 13, 1783 at Saratoga, New York. When they did not receive their promised pay, Colonel Olney declared

---

[410] Greene, Robert Ewell, p. iv & RI Short Story Club, "Slavery in the RI Colonial Period," Vaule, Rae, p. 71.

13. Women, War & Independence   275

"his own faith in 'the Honest intentions of the public to discharge with honor...all the just dues of the army...'"411

The problem was, Congress did not have the power to levy taxes, and bartering in the states was still more common than the use of currency in business and trade. "Earlier in the decade, Congress had considered an amendment to the Articles of Confederation allowing the national government to charge a five percent tax on imports....but amendments required the consent of all the states, which Rhode Island would not give."412

Despite this, in 1778, by order of the Rhode Island General Assembly, the slave-masters were paid in "Continental Loan Certificates." But the slaves may have fared better after an Act in 1785 "directed the town councils, in the towns where the former slaves had

---

411 Simister, pp. 132-135 & Greene, Robert Ewell, p. v.
412 Brookhiser, p. 52.

enlisted, to take care of and provide for the ex-soldiers as they would for any other pauper in their town. The accounts for their maintenance were to be given over to the Assembly and paid out of the general treasury."[413] At least some of the slaves petitioned for pensions, and Greene in the appendix of his *Black Courage* names sixty-two, along with their wives and children, at least seven of whom served in Rhode Island regiments.

In 1790, the federal government agreed to "assume state debts that were still outstanding from the Revolution" in exchange for an agreement that the Capital would be on the Potomac rather than in New York or Philadelphia.[414] Conceivably Rhode Island was then compensated for the debts incurred and the promises that had been made. By that time, it is likely that the transition, which was gradual, from £s to $s was complete. The change first occurred during the War, in September 1776, when the Assembly adopted "the continental denomination of dollars" at the exchange rate of six shillings to a dollar.[415]

After the War, between 125 and 150 slaves who had served were freed, but, regrettably, at least some of them were re-enslaved. Appreciation of their service did not, however, go entirely unacknowledged if the historians are correct in attributing, at least in part, the passing of the anti-slave law of February 1784 (modest as it was) to the people's desire to express their appreciation for the part the blacks played in the Revolutionary War.

★★★

Historians say little of Rhode Island's women during the Revolution, but it was they who took over the running of farms and businesses while the men

---

[413] See Greene, Robert Ewell, p. v. & his Appendix for names.
[414] Brookhiser, p. 80.
[415] Arnold, V. 2, p. 384.

13. Women, War & Independence

were away (and were not always safe in doing so).[416]

Plundering British & Hessian troops in Bristol robbed women of their shoe buckles, gold rings, and handerchiefs.

For some women this kind of responsibility was not a new experience; they had always worked with their husbands running taverns, shops and more; had taken over businesses when widowed or their husbands were away; had served as executrices of estates. A few, such as Betsy Metcalf and heads of Dame Schools, had supported themselves through their own businesses. Others without such experience soon discovered that the skills required were not so different from those required to manage a household.

There were some women who followed the men to their camps; for the most part women who were "desperately poor," or "wives or widows whose farms or other means of livelihood had been destroyed by the

---
[416] Information from Norton, *Liberty's Daughters*, p. 6

British." We know little about them other than they served nobly as cooks, nurses, laundresses, guides, seamstresses, porters, and spies.[417] "General Washington was a great believer in spies and disinformation."[418] Catherine (Katy) Littlefield Greene's story represents, perhaps, the few officer's wives who followed their husbands—husbands whose rank enabled them to provide their wives and children with reasonably comfortable quarters.

Catherine was the niece of Governor William Greene's wife and had been adopted by the Greene's after both her parents died while she was still young. When Catherine married Nathanael Greene in the Governor's mansion in Warwick, Rhode Island on July 20, 1774, she was just nineteen, he thirty-two.[419] Her taffeta gown was rustling on that important day as she descended the stairs into a room filled with the scent of roses. It was the same room where Nathanael had first called on Katy, but it is quite likely they had first encountered each other at one of the parties Nathanael frequented in defiance of his father, a strict Quaker who disapproved of dancing. Not to be deterred, Nathanael often slipped off to East Greenwich, three miles from his home, "to attend beautiful dancing parties, returning home very late. On these occasions he would stop at the woodshed to put a shingle in the seat of his trousers before he went up to his room, lest his father intercept him and give him a sound whipping on his way to bed."

At the time when Katy and Nathanael met, his

---

[417] DePauw, p. 89
[418] Brookhiser, p. 29
[419] All uncited quotes in this account of the Greenes are from RI Short Story Club, "General Nathanael Greene," by Elsa Powel & "Catherine Littlefield Greene", by Alice DeWolf Pardee, pp. 34-44. Other sources of information are found in Haley, Old Stone Bank, V. III, pp. 131-132 & V. I, pp. 40-44 and in Lancaster, pp. 13-18.

13. Women, War & Independence

"heart was caught on the rebound, for he had been deeply in love with the sister of his friend, Ward, who had refused him, and he was suffering from this rebuff until Miss Catherine, the girl who loved to dance, made the 'winter of his discontent' a 'glorious summer.'" [420] He was at once enchanted by the "pretty, vivacious, witty and flirtatious" Catherine, while she, from the beginning, was said to have "idolized her Quaker lover."

After their marriage, Catherine and Nathanael lived in a "charming house" he had built in Coventry, and there he worked with his brother Jacob in the attached-forge until April 1775. It was then that Nathanael left Rhode Island to go to war (another departure from his father's Quaker beliefs), barely having a holiday from the services after that for the next eight years. That winter of 1775/76, both Mrs. Washington and Catherine made the tedious trip to Cambridge to be with their husbands, met and became close friends. At a special camp ceremony that winter, Katy's and Nathanael's first baby was christened George Washington Greene. Later, in March 1777, a daughter was named Martha Washington Greene.

Curiously it was that same month, on March 30th, that Nathanael wrote Katy, without mentioning either her being pregnant or her having just had a baby. He begins by proclaiming about the great distance between them and the few opportunities of hearing from her that leaves him in suspense. What follows gives only the slightest hint that he may know she has recently given birth. If so, his lack of query is strange and his request for her company selfish.

> Eight long months have passed amidst fatigue and toil since I have tasted the pleasures of domestick felicity...I am just returned from Philadelphia. The young ladies of Philadelphia appeared angelick. A few months more

---

[420] Haley, Old Stone Bank, Vol. I, p. 40

Seperation will put my virtue to a new tryal. If you don't wish to put my resolution to the torture, bless me with your company; that is, providing your health and other circumstances favors my wishes. Pray how are you? A line from you will be most agreeable. Give my kind love to all friends.[421]

Later, while the army is camped at Valley Forge during the long severe winter of 1777/78, Mrs. Washington and Katy again join the men, leaving her two children, one still an infant, with relatives. She must have thought the trade-off of leaving "the luxuries of a home for a little hut scarcely larger than that used by the regulars," worth it to be with her husband, and preferable to child care. Clearly Katy enjoyed these visits even if they did involve "going the rounds in bitter and fair weather to carry little delicacies to men who lay sick." As compensation, she had the pleasure of the company of other officers' wives who were there as they "met in Mrs. Washington's rooms to sew and patch the clothes of the soldiers whenever there was anything to patch with."[422] "Two or three times a week the Greenes entertained in the evening. Cards were forbidden and there was not room for dancing, but they could serve coffee and sing. Catherine had learned French...so that she could talk with the French officers....It was at this period that Baron von Steuben's young French secretary, Deponceau, wrote of Catherine that she 'was a handsome, elegant and accomplished woman, whose home was the resort of foreign officers because she spoke the French language and was well versed in French literature.'"

Soon after the signing of the French Alliance, Katy returned home to Coventry for the summer of 1778. From there she could hear the sounds of the Battle of

---

[421] Lancaster, p. 15 citing Greene papers, Vol. 1, p. 50.
[422] Haley, Old Stone Bank, Vol. III, pp. 131-132

13. Women, War & Independence 281

Rhode Island and see the rising smoke. Nathanael was also home briefly that summer before departing for the Hudson River area where they camped during the winter of 1778/79. He had probably already left by October when their third child, Cornelia Lott Greene, was born. At least some of Katy's neighbors did not like Katy's independent ways as evidenced by the letter she wrote that summer to her physician in Valley Forge complaining of the attitude of the blacksmith when she asked him to mend her carriage.

> [When I] told him by way of inducement that I could not stir out until it was done he answered for that very reason he should delay it for home was the proper place for women—that he thought I had better be spinning than riding about,....[423]

In February, 1779, Katy made another long, hazardous journey, with their three children, to her husband's camp in Middlebrook, New Jersey. Even though she had their three children with her this time, it did not seem to curtail her socializing. Just having turned twenty-five, and wearing a lovely gown, she was said to have been as "dainty, pretty and sparkling as crystal."

> As she moved gracefully over the floor, dancing to the strains of lively music played by fiddlers stationed in the hall, Martha Washington remarked how trim her figure looked so soon after the birth of Cornelia (then about three months old). ...She carried a fan and wore a golden locket, containing [Nathaniel's] picture, that had been presented to her by his aides. While their respective mates sat out most of the evening, General Washington danced with Katy again and again, teasing her all the while about having stolen her from her 'Quaker preacher' and betting that he could outlast her on the floor." [They] 'danced upwards of three hours without once sitting down,'

---

[423] Lancaster, p. 16.

Nathanael later wrote, calling it 'a pretty little frisk.'[424]

Obviously her husband was not ignored during that winter's stay in camp for they had a fourth child, Nathanael Ray, in 1780. However, for the next two years, Catherine did not see her husband. Early-on during that time, he wrote her a letter, dated July 8, 1779. He begins expressing "the strong desire I feel to cultivate your happiness makes me embrace every opportunity to write to you." After talking about Mrs. Washington's departure for home, he says that the "feeling manner" in which the General enquires about her convinces him "he had a real friendship for you." Nathanael continues:

> Poor man he appears oppressed with cares and wants some gentle hand free from deceit to soothe his cares. How valuable an honest heart, how pure the pleasure that flows from such society. How many times do I wish for it in vain; when surrounded with such perplexing cares and embarrassed with the wicked devices of ambitious men. It is in this situation that we most sensibly feel the sweet influence of female charms, crowned with virtue and honest...

He concludes by asking her to "Kiss the children for me, and remember me to all friends."

It was the spring of 1781 when Katy joined Nathanael at camp in Charleston, South Carolina, and in 1782, while there, that she bore their fifth child, Louisa Catherine. Nonetheless, right up till the time of delivery, Katy was "the reigning belle, the center of attraction, as the Greenes enjoyed Southern hospitality." Victory celebrations of Cornwallis's final defeat at Yorktown followed soon after Louisa's birth, and after they ended Catherine returned home by boat, too frail (presumably from the recent birth, and

---

[424] Lancaster, p.13

13. Women, War & Independence

with an infant) to make the trip by coach.

Nathanael, alone, on August 15, 1783 started out on the thousand mile trip home on horseback. As he rode through hamlets, towns and cities, crowds came out to hail the hero, bands played and flags waved. He stopped briefly, en route, in Georgia and South Carolina, to examine the gifts of estates these states had given him in gratitude. He was mulling over in his mind plans he had for "a happy life with his wife and children, living in Newport in the summer and on his new southern plantations in the winter." But this was not to be.

Merchants were pressing him for payment for military supplies he had bought for his men during the war, for which he had expected Congress to reimburse him. In an effort to pay them, he gave up the South Carolina estate he had been given and either sold or rented his northern home, but it still was not enough.

It was October 1785 when the family left Rhode Island and moved into the magnificent estate, Mulberry Grove, they had been given by the state legislature near Savannah, Georgia. It had been the home of the Loyalist, John Graham, former Lieutenant-Governor of the state. "Here the prospect did begin to look better for the future...but for the last time Fate intervened." Less than a year after their move, on June 19, 1786, Nathanael died at age forty-four the victim of a sunstroke.[425] He said in his will he had nothing to leave to his family except his good name, having spent from his own pocket all he had to pay for supplies needed by his men during the war. "But Catherine appealed to Congress, and in 1792 the country paid the balance of this bill, about one hundred thousand dollars. A great burden was lifted from her shoulders and she

---

[425] Haley, Old Stone Bank, Vol. III, p. 132

considered that her husband had been vindicated."[426]

Nathanael had left Catherine a widow at age thirty, with five children to raise, the oldest not yet twelve, and Mulberry Grove where she continued to live. However, before settling in, Katy returned north with the children for a visit to her old home, apparently with Phineas Miller accompanying her. He was a Yale graduate who had been employed by Nathanael to help put the estate back into money-making order and also to tutor the children. On her return trip to Mulberry Grove, Catherine met Eli Whitney, a recent Yale graduate, who was on his way to Savannah to a tutoring job. She was quite taken with him, impressed with how he amused her children and mended their toys.

Later, when Catherine learned that Eli had rejected the tutoring job on learning how little his employer intended to pay him, and was considering a return north, she invited him to Mulberry Grove. During his visit, Whitney heard talk of the need for "some sort of mechanical device that would successfully clean cotton." Catherine suggested he use their basement to experiment and Phineas said he would bear the expense involved for a share of the profits should Eli succeed.

> When Whitney believed that he had a practical machine, he called Mrs. Greene to come and watch it in operation. Full of interest and enthusiasm she watched the crude contrivance pull the cotton from the seeds. Overjoyed the two eagerly observed the working of this original cotton-gin, and then disappointment banished their high hopes. The cotton fibers massed against the wires until the teeth of the machine were clogged. Whitney was completely discouraged, but the young widow rushed quickly to the fireplace and, so the story goes, snatched up a hearth brush and with it cleared the wires of the

---

[426] Haley, Old Stone Bank, Vol. I, p. 43.

13. Women, War & Independence 285

clogging fibers. Whitney then constructed another cylinder with a brush attachment and this device practically perfected the cotton-gin, an invention that stimulated cotton cultivation vastly, and rendered profitable the labor of slaves on the plantations.[427]

In the conclusion of a letter to his father in September 1793, he writes that he had succeeded in making a machine before leaving on June 1st —"which may be turned by water or with a hourse with the greatest ease, and one man and a hourse will do more than fifty men with the old machine." Unfortunately the machine was so easy to make, that the patent he and Phineas had been given did not prevent others from making it. To prevent their going into bankruptcy Catherine put up her property for collateral, but the partnership continued in financial trouble so that in 1800 Catherine had to sell Mulberry Grove to pay her tax bills.[428]

Meanwhile in May 1796, Catherine married Phineas in the presence of George and Martha Washington and a few friends. About the same time, Lafayette had persuaded Catherine to allow her son, George Washington Greene, to return to France with him to be educated. He stayed there until Catherine, worried about the "troubles of the French Revolution," sent for him to return home. Shortly after he arrived, he drowned in an accident in the Savannah River, and Catherine never fully recovered from the shock.[429]

After Catherine was forced to sell Mulberry Grove, she and Phineas moved to Cumberland Island, off the coast of Georgia, to a place called "Dungeness." There they started "to grow sugar and cotton using slave

---

[427] Haley, Old Stone Bank, Vol. III, p. 173.
[428] Lancaster, pp. 17-18 citing the correspondence of Eli Whitney, ANR, Vol. III, #1, Oct. 1897, pp. 99-100.
[429] Haley, Old Stone Bank, Vol. I, p. 43.

labor. Three years later, in 1803, Phineas died of blood poisoning at the age of thirty-nine."[430] All the family must have liked him for Catherine's daughter, Martha Washington Greene, who married John Nightingale, named her son, Phineas Miller Nightingale. A letter dated November 23, 1785 describes Phineas Miller this way:[431]

> A young gentleman from Connecticut of amiable qualities, and a mathematical genius equal to any one in the United States. Educated at Yale College, recommended by Dr. Stiles, President of Yale College, and employed by General Greene as a tutor for his children.

There were rumors that Catherine had been unfaithful to her husband during his absences, and divorce was being considered before his death. Catherine also was accused of neglecting her children's education. But Isaac Briggs, a Georgian of some note in his day, who had spent time at the Greene home, called this talk "pure envy and scandal." In a letter written in 1785, he had this to say:[432]

> A lady who is superior to the little foibles of her sex, who disdains affectation, who thinks and acts as she pleases within the limits of virtue and good sense, without consulting the world about it, is generally an object of envy and detraction. She has an infinite fund of vivacity, the world calls it levity. She possesses an unbounded benevolence which but very few possess. The world calls it imprudence. In short, she is honest and unaffected enough that she is a woman—as for the report that she is destitute of maternal affection, paid no attention to the education of her children, I cannot for my life see what foundation there is for it. I am perfectly convinced that she has a great source of maternal affection, and I never met

---

[430] Lancaster, p. 18.
[431] Haley, Old Stone Bank, Vol. I, p. 44.
[432] Haley, Old Stone Bank, Vol. I, p. 44

13. Women, War & Independence 287

with a woman in my life, who had an idea or who had followed a system of education so much to my mind as Lady Greene.

"In August 1814, during the week that the British forces raided Washington and burned the White House, Catherine died at the age of fifty-nine, worn out by law-suits over the cotton gin, and quarrels with two of her children over their shares of the estate. She had been present during revolutionary changes in government, in industry and in the roles of women, and had played a significant role in all three revolutions."[433]

★★★

As for the women left behind, in the midst of the small skirmishes that happened in Rhode Island as elsewhere, it is claimed some took up "hatchets, muskets, farm implements, and even such improvised weapons as pots of boiling lye to defend their homes and families. These women were viewed as sort of an auxiliary to the male militia units..."[434] As we look back now, it may to hard to understand, but at the time, not all those in the colonies supported the Rebels; only 40% at the beginning of the War, and some even helped the enemy. The treatment they received when caught varied.

One man, harshly treated, wrote the sheriff of North Kingstown in 1776 of the house he was warned to quit "on the Saturday next while people are forbid admitting or receiving us into their houses is forceing us to perish in a snow drift..." Another wrote the King's County sheriff: "In my family's alarming situation you will I hope Pardo my addressing a Lr to you...that past a Sentence upon us. The Situation of

---

[433] Lancaster, p. 18.
[434] DePauw, p. 89.

wch in the manner its at Present Pursued must have a fatal and (Pardon me) Inhuman Effect..."

The punishment seemed milder in the case of Mrs. Sarah Slocum and her family "suspected of having communicated intelligence and afforded supplies to the enemy at Newport." The general assembly in 1777 decided that "she and her family reside in such part of the main as are distant not less than two miles from the salt water." In addition to having their property confiscated, Loyalists were imprisoned and banished; at least one was "mobbed by a crowd and murdered," but this, apparently, was unusual. "One Tory was tied to a cart and walked through the streets. One woman was pilloried, had her ears cut off and both cheeks branded."[435]

In general, at the end of the war, the Loyalists were forgiven, the feeling being that they merely held "opinions that everyone else had shared twenty years before" and that they had "reached their decision to become Tories through agonies of indecision." [436]

★★★

In the long run, the Revolution had the side effect of being good for Providence. Until then Newport had been the richer, more populous town. It not only had been settled by a more educated class than Providence, but had benefited greatly by having a naturally protected harbor and immediate access to the open sea. But when war broke out, those very assets made Newport more readily subject to boycott and more vulnerable to occupation by the British. "Its exposed location, the incidence of loyalist sentiments among its townspeople, and its temporary occupation by the British [from 1776 to late 1779] combined to

---

[435] Simister, pp. 217- 218 & 223.
[436] Simister, p. 223.

13. Women, War & Independence

produce both a voluntary, and at times a forced, exodus of its inhabitants."[437] During that period it declined in numbers from 9,209 to 5,532. Providence, meanwhile, became "filled with poverty-stricken refugees," mostly from Newport, and "many a prudent and patriotic citizen removed his family and his valuables to some farm in the back country, or to some inland town less readily accessible for the enemy's headquarters."[438]

Providence had become the wartime capital (and presumably remained so thereafter) and clearly was catching up with Newport in population, money, commerce and wealth. While Newport was occupied, Providence's "merchants and businessmen, deprived of normal commerce, turned successfully to privateering and munitions manufacturing and supply."[439] Newport, in contrast, lost many of its merchants, who, even though Tories, also represented its intellectuals. "The loss of them and of some patriots who had moved away resulted in less vigorous and effective leadership,"[440] and led to a slow recovery even after the end of the occupation.

☆☆☆

In his diary dated August 20th 1776, Theodore Foster, a lawyer and, at the time, Providence's representative in the state General Assembly (he later served three terms in the US Senate), gives us an exact and detailed account of the "Inhabitants of Providence." Foster and Martin Seamans made the count between the 15th and 22nd Days of July A.D. 1776 by order of the Assembly.

Their count included a total of 4,355 individuals

---

[437] Conley, *Album*, p. 48
[438] Kimball, p. 328.
[439] Levin, p. 14
[440] Simister, p. 223.

and 741 families in the town of Providence. It broke down as below:[441]

	Individuals/Families	White Females over 16/under
West Side of River	1,677/310	475/320
East Side of River	2,678/431	684/525

	Indian Females over 16/under	Negro Females over 16/under
West Side of River	2/5	22/24
East Side of River	14/10	74/41

✯✯✯

During the occupation of Newport, both British and American, both men and women, suffered. Stephan Popp, a British soldier, wrote in his journal:

> ...We moved into old, empty, uninhabited buildings. Our quarters were the worst of all, but the provisions were a good deal worse. For seven days each man received 2½ pounds of bread and that was mostly baked of rice and Indian cornmeal. This you could hardly eat for bitterness. Instead of meat we received stinking codfish and that so little that it was just according to the proverb: "For dying too much; for strengthening too little."
>
> On holy Christmas Eve it began to snow and lasted until the 27th. The snow lay upon the ground three or four feet deep. The cold was unbearable. In that cold spell

---

[441] Levin, pp. 22-23

13. Women, War & Independence

nine men of the Brown regiment froze to death and 23 men had their hands and feet frozen.

A woman was found in a hut froze to death with her suckling children in her arms. For the great hunger and cold were alike unbearable. [442]

After it was all over, "the old capital never truly recovered..."

> Soldiers quartered in the public buildings damaged some beyond repair as they like the remaining citizens, struggled to keep warm. Fine old woodwork and family papers, the exotic trees and shrubs in the gentlemen's gardens, anything people could live without, were likely to go into the fireplace. In the Narragansett country, foraging parties from the various armed forces ransacked the land for provisions, while the harried inhabitants fell to accusing each other of favoring the wrong side. Peace seemed at first to restore the old times, but basic economic conditions no longer made a place for Newport's commerce. The smartest men left for New York, Philadelphia, or points south.[443]

The British destroyed as many as five hundred homes. "They slept in beds owned by Newport families; dishes, furniture, linen, books, jewelry, heirlooms, keepsakes, all had become another's property by right of conquest...There wasn't much left in Newport for those who hurriedly returned [after their departure] to rescue what once had been personal property—the British took away all that they could carry including the early town records in manuscript form, but these were recovered some years later."[444]

Despite all this undeniable destruction and suffering, it would seem Newport was still able to

---

[442] Quoted in Booth, *Women '76*, pp. 175-176
[443] James, *History*, p. 265-266
[444] Haley, Old Stone Bank, Vol. III, p. 138.

celebrate in its old style once the French replaced the British as occupiers. With the arrival during the summer of 1780 of "forty-six vessels bearing six thousand Frenchmen, there was a "sudden rebirth of life, joy, spirit; a revival of interest in neighborliness and sociability...Balls and parties were of daily occurrence, and frequently there was dancing in the open air. Dashing French officers led the colonial dames and daughters in a merry whirl as Rhode Island rapidly regained its social feet and set them to perfecting the latest slides and points from Gay Paree." [445]

Richman in his history writes of Rochambeau being "quartered in the stately William Vernon house" and other officers domiciled with equally distinguished citizens. [*How had their homes escaped theft and destruction?*] Richman goes on to tell of the "social resources of Newport...made upon them." [446]

> The beauty and grace of the women—always notable—more than ever were notable now; so much so, in fact, that the French gentlemen who met Polly Lawton the Quakeress [*rejecting the Quaker belief that dancing was evil?*], or Margaret and Mary Champlin, or Mehetable Redwood, or the Misses Hunter, or the Misses Ellery, were apt quite to forego works of soberness in describing their impressions.

A Prince de Broglie left a record describing Nancy Hunter as "the very personification of a rose; she is gay, is always smiling, and has what is very rare in America, beautiful teeth." Of one of the Champlin sisters (undesignated), he says: "She has fine eyes, a pretty mouth, the freshness of youth, a small waist and pretty foot, and a figure that leaves nothing to be desired. To all these advantages she added that of being dressed

---

[445] Haley, Old Stone Bank, Vol. IV, p. 65.
[446] This and the following quotes are from Richman, pp. 238-240.

13. Women, War & Independence

and coifed with much taste, that is to say, in the French style—and of understanding and speaking our language." He left the ultimate tribute for Polly Lawton: "a very goddess of grace and beauty...I frankly confess that to me this seductive Quakeress seemed to be Nature's masterpiece."[447]

The comments on the women's hairstyles by these "gallant Gauls" is amusing; the above as admiring, the following less so: "The hair of the feminine American head is raised and supported upon cushions to an extravagant height, somewhat resembling the manner in which French ladies wore their hair some years ago."

Dances popular at the time were "Pea Straw", "Boston's Delight," Haymaking," "College Hornpipe," Faithful Shepherd," "Innocent Maid," "A Trip to Carlisle," "Freemason's Jig," "Soldier's Joy," and "I'll Be Married in My Old Clothes." As can be seen, the titles were descriptive, and the accompanying dance movements often were designed to act out the subject. Variations of the Minuet, Polka Gavotte, Mazurka, Cotillion and other steps gradually evolved into our Square Dances, or Barn Dances.[448]

One aspect of colonial life the French did not like was the tea they were served. One Frenchman remarked: "I shall weesh to send zat servante to helle for breenging me so much hot vater to dreenk." [*Between the on-going war and boycotts, one wonders where they got the tea to serve.*]

The pleasures of the French occupation also spilled over to Providence. Richman described it this way: "Many a gallant Gaul yielded homage in the old home of Polly Olney to the charms of that coquettish damsel's worthy successors,—Misses Bowen, Miss Waite Arnold,

---

[447] Haley, Old Stone Bank, Vol. III, p. 115.
[448] Haley, Old Stone Bank, Vol. IV, pp. 65-66.

and Miss Sally Church." [449] [Presumably the "old home" referred to is the Inn of Polly's father where she lived at the time of her affair with William Palfrey and before her marriage to Thomas Greene in 1764.]

Not all the French were able to enjoy these entertainments, for a number arrived sick and in need of hospital care. These were quartered in the Old State House and Congregational Church in Newport; "some were sent to Bristol; and about three hundred were transported to Providence and placed in University Hall" which had been "turned over to the French by the Council of War." Classes at Brown had been suspended and University Hall converted into a barracks for the artillery.

---

[449] The bracketed quote inside the Richman quote is from Haley, Old Stone Bank, Vol. II, p. 84

13. Women, War & Independence 295

But these men would not be forgotten come December 24, 1780.

Snow was falling as the more fortunate Frenchmen who had virtually spellbound Newport's and Providence's fair sex with their dazzling uniforms and courtly manners, were celebrating in the tavern room not far from Market House.[450]

> The tunes they sang were familiar to all, but the words sounded strange to the Providence folks who peered through the steaming panes of the tavern windows and who crowded into the room to join the happy Frenchmen. Greetings were exchanged, well wishes extended and toasts drunk...to the pretty girls of Providence.... Then some one suggested that a serenade be given the sick Frenchmen on the Hill; and hardly had the suggestion been offered when an impromptu procession was formed in front of the tavern." Then, after tramping through the mud and slush up the hill, "Frenchmen, Englishmen, officers, soldiers, tavern-keepers, boys, pretty girls and aged patriarchs waited for the signal, and then, as the snow fell lightly upon cockades, bonnets, fur caps and beavers, they sang of Christmas.

That Spring, on March 6, 1781, three months before the French left Newport for Yorktown, General Washington was much honored when he visited Newport to confer with Count de Rochambeau.[451]

> The fleet [lying at anchor in the harbor] thundered a salute [that looked as though the very Bay was on fire]; the general, with Rochambeau unbonneted on his left, walked from Long Wharf between a double line of soldiers [numbering seven thousand] to the State House, and thence to the Count's headquarters in the Vernon house. [The roofs and windows of every house in sight were filled with the fair part of creation. And Oh! The fluttering of handkerchiefs, and

---

[450] Haley, Old Stone Bank, Vol. III, p. 141-142.
[451] Richman, pp. 238-240 & Haley, Old Stone Bank, Vol. III, p. 158

showing of favors.]

In the evening there was an illumination of the town. Later a great ball was given, and Washington, [who thoroughly enjoyed the company of charming ladies, had an opportunity to meet and admire the fairest of the fair among the social lights of Newport's fashionable circles. He chose] for a partner the radiant Margaret Champlain, [noted for her beauty, charm and grace] ...That lady, with a tact that threw the French officers present into an ecstasy of delight, selected 'A Successful Campaign,' [whereupon several of the French officers seized the instruments from the musicians and played for the General and his fascinating partner.]

On March 13th, escorted by Rochambeau for some distance out of town, Washington left Newport to the sound of a thirteen gun salute. He was greeted on his arrival in Providence by a turn-out of the whole population; a crowd of children carrying torches; a discharge of thirteen cannon. He stayed for two nights at the house of Jabez Bowen, and during that time visited with Stephen Hopkins. Moses Brown wrote of the occasion: "I was sitting with him when General Washington alone, called to see him. I sat some time viewing their simple, friendly and pleasant manner... these two great men met and conversed with each other on various subjects." Washington was again wined and dined during this visit and it, too, concluded with a dinner and ball at the State House.[452] The town paid for his entertainment but the only bill published in the *Gazette* was for £2.10.8 against the town for the town's illumination.[453]

---

[452] Located on North Main Street at what is now South Court, and extending back to the then-newly completed Benefit Street. With numerous renovations, it remained the State House until the current one opened in 1901. It then became known as the Old State House; now housing the RI Historical Preservation & Heritage Commission.

[453] Haley, Old Stone Bank, Vol. III, p. 160 & 124.

13. Women, War & Independence

A successful campaign followed Washington's departure, with Rochambeau's army following him westward soon after. On October 14, 1781, Yorktown was taken by assault, with Stephen Olney of Rhode Island commanding a detachment at the head of the storming column.

This was not Washington's first visit to Providence. He had stopped there previously on April 4, 1776, staying in the home of Stephen Hopkins. Hopkins himself was out of town attending the Continental Congress in Philadelphia as Rhode Island's delegate so it became the duty of Ruth, the step-daughter and also the daughter-in-law of Hopkins, to entertain the distinguished guest.

> All the neighbors generously offered Ruth their assistance and freely tendered their services in anticipation of the great responsibility with which she was to be confronted. Friends and relatives alike offered the loan of china, glassware, table linen and other household articles, but Ruth appeared the least perturbed of all concerning the hospitality which the Hopkins home could offer. The house was small, the servants few, and Mr. Hopkins lived in a very plain and humble way. Therefore, Ruth proudly refused all these well-meant proffers with the remark that 'What was good enough for her father was good enough for General Washington.'

Washington arrived on a Friday and left for New York on the Sunday.[454] It would seem it was Ruth's father-in-law, not her husband, who kept her informed with what was happening while they were both away, involved in the war. He wrote her from Philadelphia on June 21, 1775, the year before she entertained Washington in her home:[455]

---

[454] Haley, Old Stone Bank, Vol. III, p. 157
[455] Haley, Old Stone Bank, Vol. III, p. 124.

Beloved Ruth...I wrote you on the 25th of May and gave you an account of our journey hither. Since then I have had an ill turn and two or three fits of fever and ague, but am now well. Your mother has not been well for several days, and is now quite poorly. I hope she will soon be better. George I [her husband?] expected to have seen here, but believe he has gone to South Carolina. Col. Washington will set out from here in a day or two for New England to take command of the Continental Army of which he is appointed Commander-in-Chief. He will be accompanied by General Lee, who also has a command in the army which is taken into the pay of all America. I can give no guess yet when we shall leave this place—certainly not very soon, unless we adjourn to the Northland, which is talked of, but not agreed to yet.

Give my best to all parts of the family, and respects to all who may ask after me. Should be glad to hear from you, and remain your Affectionate Father, S. Hopkins.

☆☆☆

After the War ended, the Daughters of Liberty, the women who had stood-in for the men on farms and in businesses, and all those who had shown their patriotism in so many ways during the war, did not easily shrink back into the traditional submissiveness expected of a good wife. They had succeeded, for the most part, in shattering the generally held belief that women were inferior to men. They almost certainly felt more independent and more willing to question their relationship with their husbands. Conley had this to say on the subject:

In growing numbers after the War of Independence, wives, and also husbands, repudiated earlier tenets that they should endure the afflictions of unhappy wedlock, and they sought instead marital relationships based upon more modern concepts of romantic affection and mutual respect.... I [*the author, Patrick Conley*] believe that the

13. Women, War & Independence

unprecedented wartime involvement and responsibilities of Providence County women, and their varying contacts with liberative Revolutionary ideology, gave many of them their own particular framework of independence.[456]

In increasing numbers, women now were found doing what had previously been regarded as men's work; they were "shopkeepers, teachers, blacksmiths, hunters, lawyers, innkeepers, silversmiths, tinworkers, shoemakers, shipwrights, tanners, gunsmiths, barbers, and butchers." [457] One such, in Providence, was Bridget Treby, involved in selling "dry goods." She advertised the goods sold in her shop opposite the Golden Eagle in Providence, thus:

> ...Irish linens; Sheetings; Holland; dowles; Shalloons; Tammies; plain and spotted Lawns; fine and coarse Cambricks; Silk and Linen Handkerchiefs; Shirting and apron Checks; cross barr'd Stuffs; Cambleteens; Women's Shoes and Goloshes, very near; and Muggs and Tippits of the newest Fashions.[458]

☆☆☆

It would, of course, be many years before women would seek the right to vote and other rights men had long taken for granted. Men still resisted allowing them to "dabble in politics or other public affairs." Husbands might talk to their wives about these matters, even ask their opinion, and long since had entrusted them to run their businesses while they were away—yet they still believed that "the home was woman's sphere and domestic duties her best activities." [459] Hence women were, at most, behind-the-scenes participants in Rhode Island's signing of

---

[456] Conley, *Liberty...*, pp. 235-236
[457] Smith, p. 54.
[458] Dexter, pp. 22-23.
[459] Both quotes from Holliday, p. 142

the Declaration of Independence, and in its final adoption of the federal Constitution after long resistance.

Rhode Island had opposed the constitution first proposed by the Continental Convention, and in 1789 declared itself an independent commonwealth. Just as the towns, earlier, had fought surrendering themselves to a state government, now Rhode Island fought surrendering its independence to a federal government. They were mocked and called names for their intransigence. James Madison called Rhode Island "exasperating," and a group of literati in Connecticut wrote a long poetical satire, quoted here, in part. [460]

> Hail! Realm of rogues, renown'd for fraud and guile,
> All hail; ye knav'ries of yon little isle.
> There prowls the rascal, cloth'd with legal pow'r,
> To snare the orphan, and the poor devour;
> The crafty knave his creditor besets,
> And advertising paper pays his debts;
> Bankrupts their creditors with rage pursue,
> No stop, no mercy from the debtor crew.
> Arm'd with new tests, the licens'd villain bold,
> Presents his bills, and robs them of their gold;
> Their ears, though rogues and counterfeiters lose,
> No legal robber fears the gallows noose.
> ....
> Each weekly print new lists of cheats proclaims,
> Proud to enroll their knav'ries and their names;
> The wiser race, the snare of law to shun,
> Like Lot from Sodom, from Rhode Island run.

Only after a number of changes were made to the document, did Rhode Island in May 1790 finally accept the new constitution, thus ending the taunting by other states and George Washington's snub. Having officially severed itself from the other states in 1789, they had

---

[460] From Conley, *First in War*, p. 29.

13. Women, War & Independence

now actually *rejoined* the union. First in war and last in peace, Rhode Island had adhered to "its tradition of individualism, self-reliance, and dissent."[461]

In August 1790, George Washington, in the company of Thomas Jefferson and a number of others, made a special trip to Rhode Island—going first to Newport for a day where they were saluted and banqueted as on his previous visit, and then to Providence by way of the packet *Hancock*. He arrived there on August 18th.

The visiting dignitaries were greeted with cannon fire, and then, to the accompaniment of church bells and escorted by Governor Fenner, Washington led a long and impressive parade through the streets of Providence to the Golden Ball Inn on Benefit Street where he was to stay.

---

[461] Conley, *Album*, p. 48

After arriving at the Inn, Washington watched from the balcony as the parade continued on past. The *Gazette* reported that "all ages, classes, and sexes were full of sensibility on the joyful occasion, and the brilliant appearance of the ladies from the windows...gave animation to the scene."

"Later in the evening, when the noise and excitement had quieted down, Jefferson accompanied the President on a short walk which took them up the hill to the college where the students had prepared a special illumination of University Hall...[and to an] inspection of the new Providence-built ship, named the *President*." That evening, they attended a sumptuous dinner for two hundred guests at the State House, located just across the way from the Inn. Toasts followed to all those present and many who weren't, ending with a "round to the ladies, the fair daughters of America."[462] The visit, no doubt as intended, "helped cement relations between Rhode Island and the Union", and Washington's "benign presence helped dispel most of the state's lingering doubts concerning the new federal experiment."[463]

It seems likely that "Sally Brown" wrote this undated letter to Sherburne Bowen just after Washington's birthday in February the year following:[464]

> You have undoubtedly celebrated the birthday of the famous farmer from Mt. Vernon may he live to see the happy return to it many years and when time itself shall with him be no more, may every American be truly grateful for his more than human effort to obtain and preserve our Liberty, cherish his name and emulate his glorious example.

---

[462] Quotes and account from Haley, Old Stone Bank, V. IV, pp. 102-104. When Washington came North for his inauguration in 1789, he had avoided Rhode Island.
[463] Conley, *First in War*, pp. 38 & 40.
[464] Letter in manuscript section at RI Historical Society.

13. Women, War & Independence

The "heretic" colony of Rhode Island had managed to preserve its geographic integrity during this period in a way that its neighbors had not—three former colonies had been absorbed into Connecticut in 1662, and the Plymouth Colony into Massachusetts in 1691. However, Providence had changed within its own borders. The territory which once "had included everything north of Warwick, by chunks turned into separate towns. Later Cranston, Johnston, and North Providence lopped off more rural zones, leaving the port city nearly alone in its jurisdiction." [465]

---

[465] James, *History*, p. 265.

14. Schools

A formal Public School system was later coming to Providence than were its churches. Newport, founded after Providence, recorded a public school as early as 1642, Seekonk in 1677 and Swansea at least by 1725; Providence not until 1735, and then the teacher was paid by a "religious society" in England. Providence's citizens pronounced the "worthy art of Learning" to be among the luxuries rather than the necessities of life.[466] Perhaps it was inevitable they should have felt this way as they struggled to carve an existence out of a new land, continued to defend themselves against the Indians, *and* against Connecticut and Massachusetts whose representatives still fought with Rhode Island over borders and still regarded its inhabitants as heretics, rebels and intruders. Further, because many of the early settlers had been driven out of Massachusetts for their varying religious beliefs, Rhode Islanders remained for many years suspicious of any governmental intrusion in their affairs.

This said, the settlers could hardly have been oblivious to their children's education. From the beginning there must certainly have been some home schooling; then perhaps a gathering of all the children in an area in one of the bigger homes—or in a neighbor's capacious barn—usually instructed by the preacher. [*Whether any of the wives, mothers and daughters who came to Rhode Island early-on were sufficiently educated to undertake this role is not known. As has been noted, many of the early settlers, both men and women, were illiterate, signing their names with a mark.*]

Many of the early schools for women were little more than community day care, an extension of the common

---

[466] Kimball, p. 169.

14. Schools

practice of mothers keeping an eye out for one another's children. The women who taught in these so-called "dame schools" were often widows or spinsters—or even young girls, who, not yet married at eighteen, were likely, already, to be looked down upon as "old maids". All these women sought to achieve an independence that would free them from the embarrassment of living with their parents or a brother. However, the pay was "so miserably low that it is a marvel that [those] who maintained these [schools] could keep body and soul together on such fees."[467]

Wills such as that of Zachary Roades in 1662 help us understand why these unmarried women sought independence despite the low pay. Roades left each of his daughters, Elizabeth, Mary and Rebecca, £60 to £80 that they were to receive at twenty-one, or at marriage. But if either "shall Marry or match themselves with any Contrary to ye Mind of their mother or of my two overseers, then it shall be unto their Mother's what to give them, whether any thing or No." Weedon in his history calls them "Independent but not free spinsters."[468]

The very words "spinster" and "distaff" reflect the culture's view of the status of unmarried women. They reflect the fact that spinning and weaving were, for years, the ultimate symbol of the female, quintessentially performed by young, single women. Hence, "spinster" came to mean an unmarried female, and the phrase "the distaff side" came to refer to women in general.[469]

As for the "dame schools", at various times Mrs. LaSalle, the Misses Smith of Bristol, Mrs. Eliza C.

---

[467] Holliday, p. 294.
[468] Weedon, p. 99
[469] Norton, *Liberty's Daughters*, p. 15.

Brenton of South Kingstown and Mrs. Hurley of Providence and others advertised schools for "young ladies" offering classes in Embroidery, Drawing, Painting and Music. An exception was Mrs. Hurley, whose ad indicated that the Rev. Mr. Hurley, presumably her husband, additionally would *explain* "Reading, Writing, Arithmetic, French and English, Grammar, Geography and History." [470]

> The parents who paid to have their daughters educated as ladies did so to assure that they would have the training and polite manners necessary to attract the attentions of young gentlemen. The increasing wealth in America at the close of the eighteenth century permitted men to select wives who would bring large dowries to the marriage and had the ladylike polish necessary to play a role in society....As economic survival became increasingly more difficult for unmarried women, upper-class girls found it ever more essential to attract a wealthy husband. To do so they cultivated the frivolous characteristics of the lady even more assiduously.[471]

Most young girls were taught sewing and embroidery either at home or at these dame schools—fine embroidery representing a status symbol for the rich; fine sewing, a source of income for the poor. Early-on, the women used their own spinning wheels and looms for weaving woolens, linens and cotton, but these were tedious and time-consuming endeavors, so as soon as they could afford it, they hired professional weavers. After Samuel Slater, who had arrived in Providence in 1790, invented a machine that would make thread from cotton shipped from the south, they also ended this as an at-home task. All who could afford it hired a dressmaker to cut and sew fabric.[472]

---

[470] Field, V. 2, pp. 223-224
[471] DePauw, p. 109
[472] DePauw, p. 48

14. Schools

In 1766, Benjamin Stelle moved from Warren, Rhode Island where he had been teaching at the Latin School, to Providence, and opened a school that offered separate sessions for girls and boys. The curriculum for the girls the first year consisted of writing and arithmetic; he added reading the second year. Stelle charged two dollars a quarter for the two sessions that met from 6 to 7:30 a.m. and again from 4:30 to 6 p.m. In between, Stelle offered a separate session for boys. Despite the odd hours for the girls, they, apparently, were fortunate that their curriculum included writing and arithmetic. According to Ulrich in *Good Wives* this was not typical. She writes:

> All of the children were assured instruction in reading, but only the boys were to learn 'to write a Ledgable hand & cypher as far as the Goulden Rule' or 'to write & Cypher as far as ye Rule of three or so far as to keep a Tradesman Book.'[473]

Three years after Benjamin Stelle opened his school accommodating "young ladies," he moved on; possibly expecting again to teach at the Latin School which was soon to relocate in Providence. The pay most certainly would have been better, something he could hardly ignore, since by then he and Huldah Crawford had married (in December 1767) and moved to a house on Towne Street near the home of her sister, Susannah Crawford, and her husband, Captain John Updike.

It was 1770 when the Latin School, along with Rhode Island College (re-named Brown University in 1804), moved from Warren to Providence. James Manning, a Princeton graduate and Baptist minister in Warren, had started the Latin School as a "feeder" for the anticipated opening there of Rhode Island

---

[473] Ulrich, quoting from Joshua Coffin papers. Perhaps Massachusetts' practice differed from RI.

College, chartered by the General Assembly in 1764. The school was unusual at the time for its lack of emphasis on the "practical" and was an unexpectedly huge success. Manning had to "import textbooks from London for his many scholars." [474] The school which became known as the "University Grammar School" moved to a building on College Street at the same time that the college moved to Providence.

Despite the efforts of Newport merchants to move the college there, it moved to Providence after its citizens successfully raised about $15,000 as an endowment, and Moses and John Brown donated the land on which it would be built (referred to earlier). Though established as a Baptist College, from the beginning it admitted men of all faiths, including Jews (then often discriminated against), and so very quickly became the focus of new cultural activity in the town. However, with one exception, women are nowhere to be found in its history until 1891 when Martha Eddy was allowed, from 1784-1785, after her husband's death, to take over his position as steward. This was regarded as a most radical move at the time. The college had graduated its first student in 1765, fourteen year old William Rogers of Newport, and graduated its first class of seven in 1769 while still located in Warren. [475]

☆☆☆

In 1663 (twenty-one years after Newport recorded its first public school), Providence designated one hundred six acres of land for a school, but twenty years later it was pointed out at a town meeting that the lot was still vacant. Noting this, in 1684, William Turpin, an innkeeper who regarded himself as a

---

[474] Haley, Old Stone Bank, Vol. IV, p. 70
[475] Kimball, p. 343, Carroll, p. 20 & McLoughlin, p. 78.

14. Schools

schoolmaster, requested that the lot be made available to him for the purpose intended. But it was yet another ten years before the town finally granted Turpin "a small spot of land [forty feet square] to sett a schoole house," and, at the time of his death in 1709, there was still no such building. Meanwhile, "Turpin had become a popular landlord and town officer. Turpin's Inn on Towne Street was the largest house in the town until the State House was built, and it was a favorite place of meeting for the Assembly and courts....The 'great room' served either for a senate house or dancing hall."[476]

Turpin died intestate. However, the state, in considering what should happen to his estate, gives us a rare, and odd, glimpse at a mother-in-law, that of Turpin's son. She must have been living in a room in the elder Turpin's house at the time of his death. The son agreed she should continue in the room she had been occupying for the remainder of her life, and gave her "one good bedstead, one good feather bed [*an important item at the time*] and bolster," and other bedding. She was also to have "sufficient victuals and drink and washing and suitable attendance. The benefit of the fire to go to and from and abide by it with 'free Recorse to and from said roome.'" She also was to have "£40. Current silver, to be paid £10. Annually for four years. If she be sick so that 'she must Improve a Phisitian [physician],' that charge to be born out of her own estate."[477] *This arrangement sounds as though the mother-in-law was to be provided for, but was to be kept at a distance from the rest of the family.*

☆☆☆

---

[476] Weedon. pp. 219-220
[477] Weedon, p. 125

In 1735, George Taylor, a warden of King's Church, was hired [paid by a religious society in England] to keep a school in "one of the chambers of the Colony House at Providence 'on condition that the glass of said house should be kept in constant good repaier,' and that he should 'erect a handsome sundial in front of said house, both for ornament and use'." Two years later he stated "that he had twenty-three white and two black children under his care."[478]

In 1747, Providence set apart a lot "fronting on the Towne Street, [a school] to occupy eighty feet of the lot, and the gaol to have the remainder, extending over the mud flats to the channel in midstream...bearing witness to the town's solicitude for the mental and moral welfare of its citizens, young and old."[479] Not everyone would agree that such a strange coupling of facilities showed "solicitude", which may explain why the gaol was built but not the school. It was not until twenty years later that a school was finally built on "Meeting Street near the second Colony House. Part of its cost was met by the town, the rest by private subscription. Here, two hours a day were spent 'in perfecting the scholars in reading and properly understanding the English tongue' while what time remained was given over to 'writing, arithmetic, and languages.'"[480]

George Taylor again was appointed to teach at this school with the stipulation, this time, that "the s'd George doth hereby promise, and oblige himself to school or teach one poor Child, such as the s'd Committee shall recommend, Gratis, or for nothing during all sd Term"—others having to pay.

Regrettably, though education of blacks did not end, this lack of segregation in schools gradually did.

---

[478] Kimball, p. 169 & Field, V.2, p. 253 & Carroll, p. 18.
[479] Kimball, pp. 214-215.
[480] Haley, Old Stone Bank, Vol. Iv, p. 69.

14. Schools 311

For example, the ad that appeared in the *Newport Mercury* on March 29, 1773 seems to refer to a school for blacks only.

> Whereas a school was established, several years past, in the town of Newport, by a society of benevolent clergymen of the Church of England, in London, with a handsome fund for a mistress to instruct thirty negro children in reading, sewing, &c. And whereas it has hitherto been found difficult to supply the said school with the number of children required; notice is hereby given, that the said school is now kept by Mrs. Mary Brett, in High street, nearly opposite to judge Johnston's, and is open to all societies in the town, to send their young blacks, to the number of thirty; And, provided, that the number cannot be nearly kept up for the future, the gentlemen to whose care and direction the said school has been entrusted will be obliged to give it up entirely at the expiration of six months. [481]

✯✯✯

John Brown was one of the students at George Taylor's school, leaving for posterity his "Cipher Books" from 1749 and 1752. They include this definition: "Addition Is an Arithmetical gathering of Divers Sums together to Produce one Total." The problems found in the book indicate that the seafaring families, especially, wanted their children's education to be of a "practical nature, based on the needs of the coasting-trade and shop, such as, sums in finding a ship's latitude, finding her Tunnage, the worth of a Tobacco mixture, the rules of barter, figuring the profits of West-Indian cargo, etc." One example:[482]

> Suppose it 45 miles to Boston. How many barley corns will reach there?

---

[481] Field, V. 2, pp. 221-222
[482] Kimball, pp. 216-217.

How Many Sparrows at 10 a Penny will buy a Yoke of Oxen at £10 Price?

Apparently pleased with himself, on one page John noted, "John Brown the Cleverest boy in Providence Town." It can't be missed how different this curriculum was from that offered by the "Dame schools."

By the time John was a parent, at least some schools must have catered to both sexes as suggested by a childhood prank that involved his daughter Sarah (Sally) who was enrolled in such a school in the Narragansett area. Its school master, Robert Noyes, believed in generous use of the rod. Tom Hazard seemed especially to annoy Noyes with his pranks, and, on one occasion, when made to lay out on his desk all the items stuffed in his pocket, they included a bunch of hair pulled from a hourse's tail, two small eels, three live crabs, a piece of beefsteak, one pin hook, one bumble bee, four tadpoles, and one bottom fish. He purportedly was most humiliated on "hearing Sally Brown, his school sweetheart, snicker aloud as he laid these treasures out before the teacher's astonished eyes." On another occasion when Tom arrived at school wet from having waded in a stream he was ordered to hang his breeches on a line outside and was then placed between two girls in his embarrassing condition.[483]

> It happened that he was on precarious terms with both young ladies and one of them improved her priceless opportunity by inserting a pin a half-inch into his bare thigh, making him yell and jump about three feet in the air. For this he [was made to] stand before the whole school reading his primer, his nether parts exposed.

---

[483] Both John and Sally quotes: Haley, Old Stone Bank, V. IV, pp. 69-70

14. Schools 313

Besides the humiliation this must have invoked, it must have given the girls (and boys) a lesson in sex differences as well!

We learn more of Sarah's (Sally's) education from a letter[484] her father wrote to her on March 11, 1786 while she was in Boston either visiting or studying. She was then about thirteen. He remarks that he hopes by now she "dances Prittely" and that she "Play the Harpiscord Equitably", and that she "cypher well" He adds that she is not learning "Latten ... for want of a master....Pray let me intreat your best Exertions that the precasest [precious] Time and Expense may not be in vain." The letter's P.S. asks how long she wishes to stay and sends his love to Sally Foster—perhaps who she is staying with.

Ten years later, Sarah briefly kept a diary, from April to June 1796, that gives us a glance into her life as a young adult. Like many others, she frequently exchanged visits with friends for tea, occasionally worked in her garden—planted asparagus and radishes—and "rode horseback in the square." But the number of diary references to it suggest her special interest was the theater, after it opened the season in Providence with the Comedy, "A Bold Stroke for a Husband" & "The Lying Valet." [The theater's origins in Providence already mentioned in the account of Goddard's first printing of a handbill.]

On June 8th Sarah comments on the excellence of performances of the celebrated tragedy, "The Gamester" and "Spoiled Child." On the 10th, "Pappa accompanied me and Miss Butler to see 'Everyone Has His Fault', the first time little Miss Sully appeared on our stage, an uncommon fair child." On the 13th, "The

---

[484] Letters and diaries are in the manuscript section of RI Historical Society.

Jew" and "The Village Lawyer." On the 15th she sees a repeat of "Everyone Has His Fault" and the new, "The Agreeable Surprize."

On the 17th she comments: "I attended the theatre, with no other view than to see my favorite, Mrs. S. Powel, in the Comedy, "First Love", every time I see this charming woman my esteem and admiration is increased." On the 20th: Mrs. Peck went with me to the Theatre, to see 'Better Late than Never.' Mrs. S. Powel, the Character of Augusta, appeared uncommonly interesting."

Finally, on the 22nd: "Mrs. P so entirely engrosses all my admiration, that I have little left for the rest of the players, instead almost all the pleasure I enjoy at the Theatre is derived from that one woman."

Sarah's diary ends on June 20, 1796 with what sounds like a foreboding comment on Love. The entry suggests that Charles Herreschoff, whom she would eventually marry, may already have been courting Sarah.

> Juliet: my only love springs from my only hate, too easily seen, unknown and known too late! Prodigious birth of love it is to me, that I must love a loath'd evening.

Charles certainly was courting her two years later, on October 30, 1798, when he wrote her from New York while there on business.

> Spare those smiles for your loving little boy, till he comes to tell you that he will not leave you again, that he will never, never love but you.

Their courtship lasted eleven years, continuing by letter even when Charles was away. It seems odd that in his letters he always refers to himself as her "little boy."

Charles came to Rhode Island from Germany in 1790, an accomplished engineer, an excellent linguist and a talented musician. "Because of his versatile

14. Schools

ability he was invited to the home of John Brown almost immediately upon his arrival in the colony, beginning a friendship...that resulted not only in the entrance of the young German into the firm of Brown & Ives but also in his marriage [finally, in July 1801] to John Brown's daughter, Sarah." [485]

But theirs was not a happy marriage. Charles had frittered away much of the family fortune before he committed suicide in a secluded spot in the Adirondeck Mountains in 1819. After Charles' death, Sarah moved back to her father's Power Street house with their two sons and three daughters, as had others in the family in similar circumstances. She remained there until her death on August 2, 1846.

---

[485] Haley, Old Stone Bank, Vol. II, p. 138.

Over the years, Sarah made quite a collection of sheet music that included works by Pleyel, Haydn, Mozart and Beethoven as well as more popular works such as "Little Sally" ("Come buy, who'll buy my woodenware?"). She must have been pleased that her grandson, Lewis Herreschoff, shared her love of music and himself became a composer.

✯✯✯

Returning to the subject of education. "At a town meeting on December 8, 1767, measures were adopted to provide education for the children of all the inhabitants of the place," the girls, at last, to have schools on an equal basis with the boys. "They resolved to build three school houses for small children and one for youth, the cost to be paid from the treasury, and the schools to be placed under the control of a school committee." [486]

Carroll, in his history of *Public Education in Rhode Island* , disagrees with Field's account of the town meeting just quoted. Carroll states that the town meeting *rejected* the two committee reports which had proposed building three schools to accommodate all the colony's children. He goes on to say that only a single school was built in 1770— a two-story structure, the lower floor controlled by the town, the upper by the proprietors (public subscribers). Rhode Island College (alluded to earlier) occupied the upper story of this school, while it awaited completion of its first building, University Hall. The University Grammar School (formerly the Latin School) occupied the lower floor.

Whatever happened at the 1767 town meeting, soon after at least one other school, albeit a private one, was built on upper Benefit Street in the North End of

---

[486] Field, V.2, pp. 254-255

14. Schools

Providence. This "one-story building with a hipped roof and belfry" was named Whipple Hall after Captain Whipple who had donated the land. When it opened, George Taylor, Jr. (*the same George Taylor, the schoolmaster mentioned previously, or his son?*) was in charge of the upper grades and Sally Jackson the lower. "About forty pupils attended, the tuition being four shillings sixpence apiece." [487]

Since female teachers are rarely mentioned in accounts of these early public schools, one may surmise that Sally Jackson obtained her position because she was the daughter of Stephen Jackson, referred to as "schoolmaster" in the histories. Further, beginning in 1762, the Jackson family was living on Benefit Street on land Stephen Jackson had purchased from Stephen Hopkins. He was married to Anne Boone, who bore him twelve children, one of whom was named Sally. In 1772, Sally Jackson married Tilly Merrick Olney. Whether she continued teaching after that is not known.

Higginson in his *History of the Public School System in Rhode Island* states that in October 1800 four public schools opened in Providence, but they became crowded so quickly that soon after a fifth was opened. However, for the next twelve years attendance remained steady at about eight hundred. A report to the town council at the time as to what the schools should be like is enlightening. A part of it, with some of the soon-after revisions, follows:[488]

> The public schools being established for the general benefit of the community, all children of both sexes admissible by law, shall be received therein and faithfully instructed without preference or partiality.

---

[487] Carroll, pp. 21-23 & Haley, Old Stone Bank, V. iv, p. 69.
[488] Higginson, pp. 22-24

[In a slightly later revision] The instruction shall be uniform, in all the schools, and shall consist of spelling, reading, the use of capital letters, and punctuation, writing, English grammar and arithmetic.

The books to be used are Alden's Spelling Book, 1st and 2nd parts, the young Ladies' Accidence, by Caleb Bingham, the American Preceptor, Morse's Geography abridged, the Holy Bible in select portions, and such other books as shall hereafter be adopted and appointed by the committee. [Added later] The Critical Pronouncing Dictionary of John Walker, Murray's Sequel to the English Reader, Murray's Abridgement of English Grammar, and Dabolls' Arithmetic.

That as far as possible they exclude corporeal punishment from the schools: and in particular, that they never inflict it on females.

That they endeavour to impress the minds of their pupils with a sense of the Being and Providence of God, and the obligation they are under to love and reverence Him; their duty to their parents and masters; the beauty and excellence of truth, justice and mutual love; tenderness to brute creatures; the happy tendency of self-government and obedience to the dictates of reason and religion; the observance of the Sabbath as a sacred institution; the duty which they owe their country, and the necessity of a strict obedience to its laws; and that they caution them against the prevailing vices.

The emphasis on a non-sexist approach is somewhat surprising; the subjects offered are much like those sought by today's "back-to-basics" advocates; and the inclusion of the Bible and references to God would please today's religious fundamentalists. This latter makes one wonder just when in-school references to religion became unconstitutional. Rhode Island's founders who held separation of church and state of fundamental importance, nevertheless took religion's inclusion in the school curriculum for granted. Now we have the

14. Schools

Supreme Court ruling it unconstitutional to display the ten commandments on school property, and for a student to say a prayer before a school football game.

By 1821, there were numerous schools throughout Rhode Island: in Providence there were eight public schools with nine hundred children, and an additional eighty or ninety private schools. A number of these were for boys only, and others for young ladies only [presumably some were for both sexes].[489] After 1838, if not earlier, they did not include blacks and whites together as many schools formerly had; that year Providence formally established separate, publicly funded school systems for blacks and whites.[490]

Providence did not inaugurate its first Normal School for the instruction of teachers, especially those at the elementary school level, until May 1854.

---

[489] Field, V.2, pp. 226-230.
[490] Melish, p. 188

15. Women & the Law

In the following short poem, Roger Williams presents what he perceives as the view held by the Indians of the white settlers:[491]

> Adulteries, Murders, Robberies, Thefts,
> Wild Indians punish these
> And hold the scale of justice so
> That no man farthing leese.
> We weare no cloathes, have many Gods,
> And yet our sinnes are lesse;
> You are Barbarians, pagans wild,
> Your land's the wildernesse.

Probably Field would have agreed with the latter sentiment. In his history of Rhode Island, he wrote:

> The early New England colonists were saints and sinners. The saints were few, the sinners were many. These statements might not be needed were it not that there exists a very common notion that only people of exalted, intellectual and moral quality migrated to these shores during the first half of the 17th century. [492]

Williams, at least in general, felt that justice should be the same for the Indians as for the whites as illustrated by his handling of the angry tribe when one of its own was attacked by "two rascally whites." Williams calmed them by taking the wounded Indian to a doctor and seeing to it that the white would-be murderers were punished.[493]

The men who quickly became the leaders of the new world were, for the most part, men who had voluntarily come here from England because of strong religious and moral beliefs—some well educated,

---

[491] Rider, p. 9
[492] Field V. 3, p. 424.
[493] Miner, Lillian, p. 36.

15. Women & the Law

others not, but sufficiently gifted to rise to positions of prominence. Tradesmen and laborers also came, honest workers looking for a better life; others not so noble, husbands running from wives, wives from husbands, sons and daughters from oppressive parents. There were also a large number of apprentices and indentured servants who came after they "had bound themselves, or who had been bound by others, to periods of service extending over four, six, or even ten years. They were recognized as 'property' by their masters or owners and treated as such....They differed from slaves in but little, save that they were bondsmen by contract, and they could be held in bondage for but a term of years."[494] Many of these had voluntarily accepted bondage as the only way they could afford to come to America; most became honest and welcome inhabitants. But there were also amongst them criminals, thieves, even murderers, who had been given the option of leaving England as an indentured servant in lieu of a far worse punishment if they remained—and many of these reverted to their old ways.

✯✯✯

As early as 1638 Providence prepared for those who would be law-breakers. Members at a town meeting ordered the construction of "a pair of stocks and a whipping post" near what became Olney Street. Stocks, which usually had holes that confined the prisoners' legs, but sometimes also holes that imprisoned the arms, were considered less "plebian" than whippings, but either punishment could be meted out for anything from swearing to horse stealing. However, neither were used as punishment for religious beliefs as happened

---

[494] Field, V. 3, p. 425

in Massachusetts and the Bay Colony.

Those sentenced to a whipping "would be stripped to the waist [and] tied to a post, [while] an executioner checkered their backs with stripes, from which blood flowed at every blow."[495] Occasionally, a whipping might take place at a series of designated spots in town, or with the prisoner bound to the rear end of an ox cart and whipped the number of times ordered by the court as it moved leisurely along. As the town grew, the "blood-curdling screams of the victims" heard at the post in Market Square had become so unpleasant and so disturbing to travelers and business that both the stocks and whipping post were moved from the town's center. In 1685 the town provided Samuel Whipple with lumber to build stocks at or near the east end of the Great Bridge and assigned John Dexter to finish them.

In 1647 the General Assembly adopted a Code of Laws based, in general, on the common and statute laws of England, but added their own imprint of what they thought to be an ideal, immediate justice. The Code detailed the punishments that should be meted out for an array of crimes ranging from high treason, to assault of one's master and of a child on his parent, to suicide, to witchcraft, to burglary and robbery, to rioting, to trespassing, to swearing and so on. [Fortunately, a few years later, because no one in Rhode Island, despite its closeness to Salem, had ever been arrested or tried for witchcraft, it was removed from the Code.]

The Code spelled out that a person convicted of "false weights and measures" for a third time should be sentenced to sit in the pillory—a board supported by an upright post, with holes for securing the head and hands; sometimes the ears were nailed to the

---

[495] Haley, Old Stone Bank, Vol. IV, p. 127.

15. Women & the Law

wood on either side of the head. "This was no fun, especially on a hot day in fly time, or when ripe fruit was within easy reach of small boys." The ducking stool [plunged under water] was used to punish "a common scold, providing amusement for everyone."

The branding iron and cropping of ears or cheeks might be resorted to for more serious criminals such as thieves who became repeat offenders.[496] Thievery was clearly regarded as one of the most serious offenses for in addition to any other punishment a thief was compelled to recompense both the victim and the colony fourfold, and if unable to pay was sold into slavery for a term up to three years. The newspaper would advertise for sale "a cash robber, a sneak thief, or a highwayman," as we might offer to sell our car.

Especially gruesome were the punishments in the Code for High Treason: an offense committed or attempted against the state: **A man** accused by two lawful witnesses or accusers was to be "hanged by the neck, cutt down alive, his entraills and privie members cutt from him and burned in his view; then shall his head be cutt off and his body quartered; his lands and his goods all forfeited. **If a woman**, she shall be drawn upon a hurdle to the place of Execution, and there burnt."[497] Petty Treason included willful murder, especially the murder of or the causing to be killed of a Master, Mistress, Father, Mother or Husband by a servant, child, or wife. *Interestingly, the crime does not refer to men's actions against their wives, children or servants, applying to them only in reference to non-household murders.* For a man convicted of these murders, the punishment was to be drawn and hanged; the convicted woman to be burnt

---

[496] Descriptions from Greene thesis, pp. 12-20. Also see Haley, Old Stone Bank, Vol. IV, p. 52.
[497] *Records of the Colony*, Bartlett, pp. 160-161

alive and the accessories hanged. A man's lands were confiscated on conviction, but the widowed wives and children were "allowed the priviledge of Rent."[498]

Burglary was another crime that exacted death. However, children under fourteen and "persons suffering the pangs of hunger," were exempt from this penalty, evincing "a humanity only too rarely manifested by legislators in that day."[499]

Provisions also were made for slaves, indicating that they did have at least some rights in the courts. "Under the law a slave might be considered as a person....He had the right to life—no master could kill him for any misdemeanor. However, in case of flogging, it was difficult to say just what might have caused death. A slave could not be turned loose to grow old and in want—the master [had to] post a bond of £100 to guarantee that the slave would not become a public charge. A slave might receive property through inheritance or for good behavior. He might use his free time to work for others and thus earn money to purchase his own freedom."[500] For stealing, a slave was subject to being deported or flogged unless the owner was willing to post a bond. [*Deported where? If to Africa, the slave may well have hoped his master wouldn't post a bond!*]

Though many would regard the punishments embodied in this Code, such as those described, harsh by today's standards, many others regard today's long sentences, imposed for such crimes as drug possession, just as harsh. The intent then, in the days before jails and prisons came into common usage, was two-fold: "one, to punish an offender without the pubic

---

[498] *Records of the Colony*, Bartlett, pp. 161-162
[499] Field, V. 3, p. 438.
[500] RI Short Story Club, "Slavery in the RI Colonial Period," Rae Vaule, p. 72.

15. Women & the Law 325

expense of maintaining him [or her] for a long period in jail; and the other, to warn the public against those convicted of heinous crimes by marking them in a way that could be readily recognized." [501]

At the same time the General Assembly adopted the Code of Law in 1647, it also created a judiciary to enforce the Code, most of its early members men of "broad culture" but without any legal training. They included men such as Roger Williams, Samuel Gorton, and John Clarke. It took until 1781 before a clear distinction was made between the legislature and judiciary (both until then hearing cases), at which time it was forbidden for members of either house of the Assembly to sit as justices of the Supreme Court.[502]

The cases that follow suggest that even then "justice" favored the better-off citizen, since most of the convicted, as we shall see, were offered the alternative of paying the state a fine rather than undergoing a punishment such as a whipping. In most of these cases we are not told which sentence was carried out, but clearly for most of the poor, without any money, it was a false choice.

Some distinctions in the punishment of men and women have already been alluded to. There were, in fact, many provisions in the law that were very specific to the women. Conley wrote: [503]

> The rights of women under the colony's laws varied greatly with their status, single, widowed or married, and with the type of case. They could not "participate in the

---

[501] Haley, Old Stone Bank, Vol. IV, p. 127.
[502] Weedon, p. 116.
[503] Conley, *Liberty...*, p. 112. For more detail on the rights of women under colonial law, see pages 111-114

creation, administration, or adjudication of public law." On the other hand, women were active participants in the realm of private law.... Between 1671 and 1729, females were principal litigants in 491 cases, plaintiffs or defendants in 369 civil cases, and criminal defendants in 122 cases at the General Court of Trials....14% of all criminal defendants and 10% of all civil litigants were females.

Women participated in ... all types of actions—debt, property, contract—and, to a very limited extent, slander. All were involved in criminal activity, although men were more likely to be convicted of such violent crimes as theft, assault, and murder. Females were more apt to be involved in cases of receiving stolen goods, illegitimacy, fornication, and infanticide.

Examples of many of these types of cases are forthcoming.

☆☆☆

The first recorded burglary in Providence dates from April 1648 when widow Sayre's house was broken into. [*This most likely was the same widow granted a lot on Towne Street very early in Providence's history.*] An Indian, Wesountup, living in Mashapaug, was accused, as well as a second Indian, Nanhiggan. Both pleaded not guilty, each blaming the other as the actual burglar. Wesountup testified at length against Nanhiggan, claiming

> Nanhiggan took a ladder from the premises of Nicholas Power and set it up against Widow Sayre's house, and was thus able to reach a hole in the gable near the roof, through which he entered; that he put out at this hole a coat of skins and three loaves of bread; that he afterward opened the door and persuaded him, Wesountup to go in and get fire to light a tobacco pipe; that in this way it came about that he, Wesountup, was found and taken in the house.

15. Women & the Law

After other testimony, the court found them both guilty and they were "sentenced to be whipped with twenty lashes well laid on." [504]

Women did not escape the whip either, especially in cases where they were accused of adultery or fornication (especially if a pre-marital contract existed) and adultery. These were "regarded as a serious matter, since it might more readily weaken the bonds of society....The woman who made herself an object of overt sexual attraction to men aroused understandable anxieties."[505]

Court records for 1658 show one Abigail Davice pleading guilty for "liveinge with Edward Richmond contrary to the law of this Collony." She also is guilty of having a "chylde by Edward Richmond" and is ordered "to be whipt or pay Forty shillings...to the Genrl Treasurer."[506] Since the record is mute as to what happened to Edward, we may assume he was not found guilty of a crime.

A similar case in 1666 involves Marie Angell and Richard Arnold. After pleading guilty, in this case *both* were "sentanced to pay forty shillings a peece fine to the Genrl Treasury or to be whipt."[507] We know not in either case which alternative punishment they chose.

Then there was the case of Ann, wife of Peter Tallman (or Tollman), who was accused of adultery in 1665. Found guilty by the General Assembly which heard the case, they sentenced Ann to a fine of ten pounds and to imprisonment until such time as she was given "fifteen stripes at Portsmouth," and an

---

[504] Field, V. 3, pp. 430-431
[505] Smith, p. 52
[506] *RI Court Records*, V.1, p. 45
[507] *RI Court Records*, V. 2, p. 51

additional fifteen at Newport. She applied for mercy but it was denied when she refused to agree to return to her husband. Somehow Ann escaped while awaiting the whipping and was gone for two years before she returned to the colony in May 1667. She was then promptly arrested and again petitioned for mercy. As a consequence, "the fine and one-half of the corporal punishment was remitted, and the remainder, fifteen stripes to be inflicted at Newport, was executed." [508] Additionally, the court record shows she was ordered to pay "six shills Eight pence for Executing the Courts sentance on her, and also she is to pay all chargis and Fees of Court."

A year later, Ann was charged with Fornication "and bienge [being] in Court Cald did not apeere the Court doe juge her Guilty of the Charge. The Court doe Sentance her this beinge the second offence to be twice whipt according to law or pay a fine of fower pounds and pay Court Fees."[509]

After the adultery charge in 1665, the Court had offered Ann the option of returning to her husband rather than being whipped (and presumably before granting him the divorce), but it is not clear he wanted her back—nor that he was, in fact, an innocent party. For immediately after he was granted the divorce, he married Joan Briggs of Taunton. And after Joan's death, Tallman married a third time to a woman called Esther, last name unknown. Before he died in 1708 he had sired fourteen children by his three wives.[510]

Years earlier, in 1649, Peter Tollman was himself in court for owing Ann Elton and her children £300 and the court appointed person was sent to determine

---

[508] Arnold, Samuel G., V. 1, pp. 320-321
[509] *RI Court Records*, V. 2, pp. 57 & 66.
[510] Quote and other information on his marriages from Chapin, #224.

15. Women & the Law

what land of his and his wife's (presumably then Ann), cattle and "alsoe all his negroes" he should forfeit to meet the debt. [He is believed to have been a Dutchman who came to America on the *Dolphin* in 1648, bringing with him three negro slaves.][511] Later, Tollman appears in the court records several times, primarily as a juror, though on more than one occasion (once while foreman of a jury) is charged with breach of the peace. Once he is fined thirty shillings; another time is cleared after "paying fees." [512] "In 1674 he was imprisoned for breaking a Massachusetts law which forbid a person receiving land from the Indians by deed of gift.[513] It would seem that Tollman's record of being on both sides of the law was not unusual; frequently on one occasion men would be the defendant, on another, a juryman. [Women were not jurymen, only men who owned property.]

The penalty the court assessed in 1669 in the case of Will Temberlake and Mary Stockes was more even-handed than it had been in the Tollman's case. They both pleaded not guilty, but the jury found both guilty. Both were then sentenced to be "Kept Close presoner until munday...and then brought forth to Recive one part of that punishment that the Law ha[th] provided and the Court hath sentanced him to which is to be whipt at Portsmouth with fi[fteen] Stripes and after a weecke Respitt to Recive the Licke at Newport and to pay presantly a fi[ne] of Ten pound to the publicke Tresary."[514]

However, "William Temberlake made an Escape from Justice by voyolent breaking the Collony person and he being the principal person in the Transgrestion

---

[511] Chapin, #224.
[512] *RI Court Records*, V. 2, pp. 8-10, 66, 71 & 83.
[513] Chapin, #224
[514] *RI Court Records*, V. 2, pp. 85-86.

and the Court Conceiving it necessary to have him if it may be brought at Last to soffer the Corporall punishment as well as Mary Stockes

> and ther being hue and Cry gone after him to apprehend him and farther the Court takeing into Consideration the grevious Cryes of mrs. mary morris for mercy or some mercy to be Showed to her grandchild (viz.) the aforesaid mary stockes: The Court doe therupon Condescend that the Corporall punishment of mary stockes shall be suspended for a months time or therabout and then shall at the majestrates Discrestion and appoyntment be once sevearly whipt at Newport with fifteen Stripes and shall then have her Choyce to pay five pound or to be whipt soe againe at Portsmouth allwayes proved that Shee pay or Cause to be payd into the gennerall Tresury the fine of Ten pounds..."515

The court responded more leniently to a guilty plea in the adultery case of Margrett, the late wife of Robert Collwell.

> The Court Taking notice of her Ingenioues Confestion Doe therfore Remitt halfe the punishment and halfe the fine Due by the Law for her said offence and accordingly doe Therfore sentance her the said Margrett to be but once whipt and that in the Towne of Newport on munday this Instant being the first day of November [1669] about two of the Clocke at the great gun before Capt morris house with fifteene stripes and to pay alsoe a fine of five pound to the publicke Treasury.516

Sometime after 1750 the penalty for adultery (and polygamy) was changed to include not only a whipping but the culprit also should be "made to sit on the gallows with a rope around his or her neck." In 1797 this law was again changed; the penalty for adultery

---

515 *RI Court Records*, V. 2, pp. 85-86.
516 *RI Court Records*, V.2, p. 82.

15. Women & the Law 331

"a fine of not more than $200, and imprisonment for not more than six months; at the same time one guilty of polygamy was to be set on the gallows with a rope round his neck for an hour and to pay a fine not exceeding $1,000, or to be imprisoned at most two years; and so the law rested until 1838."[517]

The fact that rich and poor alike petitioned for divorce, almost from the colony's beginning, belies the traditional ideal of "provident and faithful husbands bound to loyal, caring, obedient wives." Women most often sought divorce on the grounds of desertion, sometimes with the added claim of abuse or adultery. Less frequently men sought divorce from their wives for desertion. "The least frequent of the categories for which these divorce actions were instigated involved cruelty, gross misbehavior, wickedness, fraudulent contract (i.e., impotency, bigamy), and lengthy absence at sea." An exception was "Sarah Jones, wife of Providence sailor, George Jones, [who] declared to justices that he had left on a voyage shortly after their marriage and now lived with another woman in Norfolk, Virginia." [518]

In the case of Mary Cooke Bowen, the stated grounds for her divorce was desertion by Oliver Bowen, a successful Providence merchant. In the case of Pink Arnold, a destitute black mother, it was cruelty, adultery, and desertion by her husband, Prime, [519] again affirming blacks access to the courts. In Rebecca's case, she told the courts she had "borned" from her husband, David Thayer, "his cruel treatment and his blatant infidelities—even those with the housemaid." One witness testified that David "had boasted to him that 'he would not trier [hire] no maid

---

[517] Field, V. 3, p. 436
[518] Quotes in this paragraph from Conley, *Liberty...*, p.232-229
[519] Conley, *Liberty...*, pp. 226-227

except they would have do with him."'[520] In these cases we do not know if any sort of penalty was imposed on the guilty party.

In 1665, when the General Assembly awarded John Porter a divorce, it at the same time annulled all transfers of his property after the separation until such time as he settled "a satisfactory estate" upon his wife. As noted in an earlier section, the laws then accorded wives, after their husband's death, a right to certain properties until such time as they either married again or died (at which time it usually went to a son). This and the case of Ann Warner that follows suggest wives retained the same right to a property settlement after a divorce (on grounds other than adultery).

We do not know on what grounds, but when Ann Warner in 1683 petitioned the courts for a divorce from John Warner, the court ordered him to "put over" part of his estate for her maintenance and that of their children.[521] This brief allusion to the children suggest that she retained custody of the children. However, records do show that in 1713/4, John bound over his daughter, Susanna, for six years to Thomas Olney, weaver, to learn the "Trade and occupation of a Tailor." Since this is thirty years after the divorce from Ann, perhaps it is safe to assume this is the child from another marriage.

Under the terms of the agreement with Olney, similar in all cases where children were bound over, Susanna was "not to frequent Ale Houses or Taverns except about her Master's or Mistress's business, 'ffornication shee shall not Comitt, neither shall she Contract Matrimony with any Person.' The master was to endeavor to teach her to read, and finally to give her

---

[520] Conley, *Liberty...*, pp. 229-230
[521] Arnold, Samuel G., V. 1, p. 320 & Kimball, p. 108

15. Women & the Law

two suits of apparel This dress was known as 'the freedom suit,' and was often given any minor on coming of age." [522]

The previously noted divorce actions seem not to have been contested. Those that were contested varied in detail and results. One such case:[523]

> Sarah Lyndsay of Providence challenged her husband, Thomas, when he sought a divorce from her alleging periodic desertion and adultery with Thomas Taylor on Hope Island. A divorce was granted by mutual agreement, but only after Sarah denied his charges as "malicious, false, willed and groundless" and accused her husband of constantly displaying a "morose Temper & Bitterness of Heart towards her."

There were also cases of abuse that went before the courts, as in the case of Sarah Herington in 1658 (over twenty years after Joshua Verin was accused of abusing his wife). The Court ordered Francis Durby to "pay five shills for the Breach of the peace to the genrl Treasurer: And doth promise to be A peaceable Behavior towards Sarah Herington and to forbare cominge to her mothers howse and this to be of Force untill the majestrates of the Towne of Warwicke shall see Cause to cleere him."[524]

In the case of Joan Cowdall the wife of John Cowdall of Newport in 1666, it would seem to be Joan who was at fault "for that she did Ausault Beate and Lame the wife of William Wodell. She pleaded guilty and "The Court doe order that [she] be bound by Recognizance with two suffitient Sureties to the peace and good Behavior and to apeere at the next Genrl Court of Tryalls and pay present Fees." At that appearance "The Court

---

[522] Weedon, pp. 214-215, quoting Early Rec. Prov., Vol. IX, p. 5.
[523] Conley, *Liberty...*, p. 233
[524] *RI Court Records*, V. 1, p. 43

doe sentence her to pay a fine of Tenn Shillings to the Genrl Treasury and also pay officers Fees."[525]

☆☆☆

For the most part, treatment of the colony's poor was not codified in the law, but left up to each town; the results were mixed, depending on whether the individual or family were regarded as deserving or not. Take the case of James Bick and his family who had come to Providence from Mendon, Massachusetts in 1688 and become residents by virtue of purchasing land.

> His wife had been a widow before her marriage to Bick, having several children by a former husband for whom Bick undertook to provide. It seems that his way of doing this was unsatisfactory to his neighbors, and complaint was made that they were in want of clothing and other necessaries of life, so that they 'were likely to perish.' They went thus to Jonathan Sprague, their uncle, who applied to the council for advice and assistance. Bick and his wife being summoned before the council did not appear, and the want of the children being present and imperative, Mr. Sprague was advised not to let the children suffer, and it was promised that whatever he might do would be regarded as the act of the council. The relief granted was made to correspond in nature and method with the needs of the case in hand.[526]

Kindliness clearly was shown by the town's people where children were involved. This can also be seen, along with its harshness, in the case of William Garratt who had come, with his family, from Newport to Providence in 1693.

A doubt was expressed by several residents whether

---

[525] *RI Court Records*, V. 2, pp. 51 & 57.
[526] Field, V. 3, p. 393

15. Women & the Law

> they would be able to live without public aid, and the council ordered them to get out forthwith. However, it was December, the cold was severe, and the children would certainly suffer, perhaps their lives be in danger if they were to be just then removed; and the rigor of the order was relaxed so far that the man might not be molested if he should take himself and his family away before the middle of March. The thing was hard, but there is ground for the belief that the difficult conditions of their life made our fathers harder in deed than they were in heart.[527]

This was not always the case, however. The 1760 records of the Providence Town Council contain a long document which bound over "pauper Phoebe Smith and her infant to the service of Eleazer Green for a term of fifteen years and four months." [528]

With no children involved, it was easy for a poor person to be deemed "undeserving" and treated most harshly. Such seemed to be the case with Mary Williams [*presumably neither the wife nor daughter of Roger Williams*].

> When Mary Williams came from Albany to Providence and called a vagrant, "by which we need not understand more than that she was a poor and friendless stranger, though she may have been worse, she was sentenced to be 'whipped five stripes well laid on her naked back at the public whipping post in the said Providence, on the fourth day of September at about eight o'clock,' and to be sent immediately thereafter out of the state by the most direct road toward Albany.[529]

In some cases it was difficult to distinguish the poverty from mental illness. Insanity is first mentioned by Roger Williams in a letter to the town council dated November 11, 1650. In it "he called attention to the

---

[527] Field, V. 3, p. 395.
[528] Conley, *Album*, p. 43.
[529] Field, V. 3, p. 446

'lamentable' case of Mrs. Weston." He requested "the town council take measures to prevent the waste of any little property of which she might be possessed, and that such provision be made for her sustenance as should be necessary. She was presented to the attention of the council as a person reduced to want by mental disturbance, who might be easily overlooked by the constituted authorities."[530]

There is no record of the disposition of this case, but a similar one followed on January 25, 1651 when Margaret Goodwin's case came before the council. John Brown, son of Elizabeth and Chad Brown, was one of the jurors at the inquest after her death.

> She had some property in her own rights. She also had a husband [Adam Goodwin] , who seems to have been unable to support her or unwilling to do so out of his own substance. She was accordingly given into the keeping of six reputable citizens of the town, who should have charge of her person and her estate 'during the period of her distraction,' with power to sell of her property so much as might be needed to indemnify them for any expense that they might incur on her behalf ["and to return the rest of her goods to the Towne"]....
>
> It would appear that the care exercised over her person could not have been extremely vigilant, for a month later she perished.... 'The verdict of us [at the inquest] having made inquiry by what witness they can know of or hear of; we find that so near as we can judge that either the terribleness of the crack of thunder on the 2nd of the third month of 1651, or the coldness of the night, being she was naked, did kill her.' Whether she was killed by lightening or died of exposure the jury was unable to say.[531]

✯✯✯

---

[530] Field, V. 3, pp. 390 & 415--416.
[531] Field, V. 3, pp. 390-391 & 416. Also *Genealogies*, V. 2, p. 564.

15. Women & the Law

In the early 1700s the first almshouse, built in Newport, was intended for both the mentally ill and the poor. In 1738 an effort was made to open a workhouse for the poor in Providence but it came to naught until some considerable years later. It was in Newport's asylum that we find Rebecca Gibbs, "who had lost her reason through disappointed affection, and thereafter had been for thirty years a charge of the town." [532]

> She seemed to be in a sense folded together, her lower limbs being drawn up to her breast so that her knees and her chin met and from this position there was never a change. Her deformity was caused by her having been for several winters shut up in a cell without fire and without clothes, where she had drawn herself as compactly as possible together as a protection against the cold and had so continued till sinew and muscle were unable to relax.

The Colony had a surprisingly enlightened policy toward women who bore illegitimate children, a common occurrence at the time. They became a concern of authorities only if poverty were an issue and they were likely to become an expense to the town.

> When Abigail Curtice, a single woman, who was brought before the magistrates and questioned as to the daughter which had been born to her a few weeks earlier, and had the law read to her, she promptly declared herself competent to provide for her child without help from the town, and cleared all persons from pecuniary liability in the matter, the court declared itself satisfied, dismissed her, and at once adjourned.[533]

In 1693, Rebekah Bullard became an unwed mother in the home of Joseph Jencks, a magistrate. At first Jencks promised to give bond for her but then

---

[532] Fields, V. 3, p. 418.
[533] Field, V.3, p.-397.

failed to show up in court to do so. But because he was a magistrate they laid the blame "at his dore, and not the rest of the Council" and did not order her out of town. [534]

In February 1694, Hannah Hayman, with child, was not so fortunate. She declared she was married to a seaman, and after his departure had become a servant in the household of David Whipple [*This, no doubt, is the same David Whipple, who, unfortunately, was given custody of William Blackstone's son.*] Whipple, in turn, sent her to Thomas Harris, his son-in-law. Neither, apparently, were willing to bond her, so, despite its being "in the midst of a violent snowstorm," she was ordered to "be taken to Justice Peek of Rehoboth, by whom she would be forwarded to Boston."...Even so, she was "thought not so much a sinner as the rather unfortunate victim of ill luck."

These women would be subject to "some gossip among the neighbors, some censure from relatives, and more or less of sympathy from friends generally; but on the whole it was [their] own affair with which when they were not to be any way losers, they need not seriously meddle."...Further, it did not seem to interfere with the mother's chances for "marrying respectably and of moving thereafter in respectable society."[535]

A case in point was that of Providence's prominent citizen, John Whipple, Jr., [*any relation to the above David Whipple?*] who married Lydia (Liddea) after she had an illegitimate son, Job. However, Job fared less well. Lydia's new husband was not as receptive of her

---

[534] Field, V. 3, pp. 396-397 (Quote regarding Rebekah Bullard and Hannah Hayman which follows.)
[535] Field, V. 3, p. 397

15. Women & the Law

son and would not give him his name. Apparently if would be something of a stigma if he took his mother's maiden name as his last name, so after being generally referred to only as "Liddea's son" for some years, he accepted the name Job Liddeason as his name and it was recognized on all his legal papers.

It has been suggested that this name-change may have occurred when he was seven, in March 1696, at the time he was indentured for fourteen years as an apprentice under John Sayles. However, if done at such an early age, it must have been at the instigation of the adults in his life, perhaps John Sayles, since both Lydia and Job had signed their agreement with a cross—"neither being able to write, and the document itself was not recorded by the town clerk till after it had been executed a period of nine full years."[536] Sayles was to give Job "the Nessessaryes to an apprentice doth belong" and to "endeavour to learne him to Read and write." Job had to promise to "keep his master's secrets, not to contract matrimony, or frequent taverns or ale houses, nor absent himself night or day"—all the usual conditions sworn to by an apprentice.[537]

In 1717, in the case of Mary Roolenburg, she was charged with "giving birth to a bastard child." Once previously she had been charged with murdering "a bastard child born of her body," and so there was special concern in this case despite the fact she had been cleared of the earlier infanticide by the General Court of Trials. She was ordered in the new case to "pay a fine of forty shillings or, if unable to pay that sum, to receive fifteen lashes."[538] *We may suspect she was too poor to pay the fine and suffered the whipping.*

---

[536] Field, V. 3, pp. 397-399
[537] Weedon, p. 113, quoting *Early Rec. Prov.*, Vol. V, p. 292.
[538] Conley, , *Liberty...*, p. 112.

The Colony also was not free of murder, a capital offense that was taken so seriously that in one remarkable case in 1706 the punishment was rendered posthumously. Their eagerness in this case was, undoubtedly, compounded by the fact that the accused was a slave. Of course, we know not his motivation, nor the circumstances of his act.

> A slave at Kingstown murdered the wife of his master under circumstances of singular barbarity, and then drowned himself that he might not be taken alive. Two weeks later his body was found on the shore at Little Compton. It was impossible to hang him by the neck till he was dead. He had placed himself beyond the reach of human penalty. Something, however, must be done to deter others from the commission of a like crime.
>
> There was no law for it, but necessity is above law. Evidently the general assembly so reasoned when it ordered 'that his head, legs, and arms to be cut from his body and hung up in some public place near the town, to public view, and his body to be burnt to ashes, that it may, if it plese God, be something a terror to others from perpetration of the like barbarity for the future.' This sentence was duly executed [even though the man was already dead]. [539]

☆☆☆

After 1780, as legalized slavery began to decline, "race mixing" began to increase. In an effort to curb the practice, the Providence Town Council charged an increasing number of blacks with "disorderly behavior" or "disturbing the public peace." The following are examples of those so-charged: "a Certain black Woman, a transient Person known by the Name of Crazy Cate," "Betsy Stanton a black woman," and "Mary Keene,

---

[539] Field, V3, p. 443. The quote within the quote is from Bartlett, pp. 15-16.

15. Women & the Law

transient Mulatto."[540]

> In April and May [of 1800] alone, six different women of color were removed from Providence as "disorderly." Sometimes the accusation was slightly more explicit: Lydia Morgan was removed to Newport for being "a person of bad fame"; Betsy Sisco, a "mulatto girl about fourteen whose conduct is represented to this Council to be such as to make it improper She should be at Large," was incarcerated and, nine days later, bound out to the age of eighteen.
>
> The charge of moral disorder adhered to liaisons between black men and white women as well, but to a lesser extent and often with less severe consequences....Women of color, and sometimes men as well, were frequently required to give explicit evidence of the legitimacy of their family arrangements to public officials.
>
> Women of color were often accused of running "a disorderly house," frequently a euphemism for a brothel but often merely a boardinghouse that catered to a mixed [race] clientele. Public officials only reflected private sentiment; as early as 1782 a mob pulled down the house of Margaret Bowler, alias Fairchild, who had rented the old jail in Providence five years earlier for $1,400 (paper money) a year to use as a boardinghouse. Upon examination by the town council, Margaret listed the occupants of her house as Phoebe Bowen, Betsy Bowen, "another white woman called Debby," Black Bets, and "a Mulatto girl of eighteen or nineteen years." Even though Margaret's yearly rent qualified her for legal settlement and she had been an unfortunate victim of illegal mob violence, the council had her removed to Newport. Again in 1783 and in 1784, Providence mobs destroyed "disorderly" houses of black women.

★★★

Several writers tell us more about Phoebe and Betsy Bowen, two of the above-named roomers. Phoebe

---

[540] Melish, pp. 125-129

appears first in Providence's records in 1769 when brought before the Town Council at the age of twelve for "coming into the town without gaining a legal settlement." Phoebe then claimed to be the daughter of the late John Kelley of Taunton, and to have been living with her married sister in Providence for the past nine years. This apparently did not satisfy the council which voted to reject her "from being an inhabitant," forcing her to return to Taunton.[541]

A year later Phoebe gave birth to an illegitimate son who was given the surname of John Bowen, the man she had married that year when still only fourteen. Bowen was a "foreigner and a sea-faring man" and hence away a good deal. During his absences "she lived with whoever came handiest.... a strumpet if ever there was one." Phoebe had Polly in 1773 and Betsy in 1775. Betsy was seven when Phoebe took her children to live with her in the 'old Gaol House' in the section of town known as 'Hell Huddle' or 'the Devil's Hopyard,' or sometimes 'Hard Scrabble.'" They were living there

> along with sundry notorious women, both white and black, when on a sultry night in July, 1782, a mob actuated by high moral principles and a desire for excitement tore the place down. Phoebe and Betsy were committed to the care of Town Sergeant Bowen. [*Any relation?*]

---

[541] The quotes and account are found in Clauson, pp. 82-84, in Chapin, Sketch #139 & in RI Short Story Club, "That Girl from Providence," Lucile Bruns, pp. 52-57. There is another account of Betsy given by Terhune (pp. 90-114) and repeated in Haley, Old Stone Bank, V. IV that you may want to seek out and read. It is so different from the one given here that the Betsys do not even seem the same person, especially in her early years up to age seventeen. But Terhune gives no sources, such as those quoted here, so it is difficult to substantiate his version. Where the two stories intersect later in Betsy's life, the added information by Terhune is added to the story here for the enrichment it provides. One, finally, however, is left to ask, *Who and What to Believe!*

15. Women & the Law

For the next several years Phoebe tried to care for her children, but several times, when she was brought before the council as a public nuisance, her children were placed in the workhouse, sometimes for several months at a time. Betsy had been there three times before she was seven.

After Phoebe apprenticed her son to Mr. Hopkins, he never returned to the family nor was heard from again. Polly was placed with the Wyatts and Betsy, for a time, was placed with Samuel Allen. In 1786, Phoebe may have learned what had happened to her sea-faring husband if she saw the May 20th edition of the *Providence Gazette*. It reported that John Bowen "being in a small fishing sloop off the Harbour of Newport, was knocked overboard by the Boom and drowned." A year later Phoebe had yet another child, Lavinia Ballou.

Phoebe also married again, to a Jonathan Clarke, who had fought in the War. He already had seven children, all of them constantly in trouble with the Town authorities, and so with threats of jail and flogging hanging over the family, they moved to a hovel on the road to Taunton. They only came into town from time to time to peddle the herbs and greens they collected in the nearby woodsy streams. Phoebe's daughter, Betsy, quickly tired of this life, and left, taking "her charms" to the house of Freelove and Reuben Ballou [*Lavinia's father, perhaps?*]. Freelove was known as a mid-wife of shady reputation where "the canal drivers stopped for a drink and stayed far into the night."

In 1794, by then nineteen, Betsy Bowen, with "Old Mother Ballou" in attendance, gave birth to a son she named George Washington Bowen. The father was unknown, but some speculated it was Reuben Ballou, on the flimsy evidence that he had recorded the birth in an old book of his:

> George Washington Bowen born of Eliza Bowen at my house in town, Providence, RI, this 9th October, 1794.

Since Betsy had named her son after George Washington, and some thought he looked like Washington, rumors spread that he was the father. Betsy would have been fifteen or so when Washington visited Providence after the state's ratification of the constitution, and Betsy quite probably was in the crowd outside the Golden Ball Inn on Benefit Street when he spoke, but that she had any other contact with him is highly unlikely—even though she was known as one of the prettiest girls in Providence and "her life story testifies to her ability and determination to get where she wanted to go from where she was." However, George Washington Bowen was not even born until three years after this event.

Ballou, with whom Betsy was living at the time of George's birth, apprenticed him to Smith Wilbur, a farmer, when he was eight or nine years old (certainly not unusual at the time). Eventually George became a weaver, then learned the baking trade and bought a grocery. He married Anna H. Westcott when he was twenty-five. They had two children. After she died, when he was seventy years old and living on Hewes Street near Benefit, he married Emma A. Loomis.

Whoever George's father may have been, Betsy cared not what happened to him, and soon after his birth she left for New York with Colonel Peter Croix, a former British officer. How she met this "middle-aged Lothario" is not known, but that he had plenty of money would have been sufficient reason for Betsy to run off with him. He installed her in a stately country house, lavished her with costly clothes and jewelry, and introduced her to New York's elite—Alexander Hamilton and Aaron Burr amongst them (Burr destined later to kill Hamilton in a duel). By 1804, Betsy, approaching thirty, still did not have the security of marriage and

15. Women & the Law

decided to use her charm to capture the rich old (about fifty) French wine-merchant, Stephen Jumel, that Croix introduced her to.

MADAME JUMEL.

One story goes that Betsy tricked Jumel into marrying her, feigning she was on her death bed. Then, as soon as the ceremony was performed, "Betsy promptly hopped out of bed and danced around the room, rescued from 'a fate worse than death' by the smile of the church." However, doubt is cast on this colorful story by the fact that St. Peter' Church on Barclay Street has archival records of the marriage on April 17, 1804.

Whatever the truth, Jumel seemed delighted with her "sprightly and entertaining" demeanor and let her will reign in their household thereafter. In 1815, having persuaded Jumel to take her to Paris to live, they sailed on the *Eliza*, named for Madame Jumel. Cordially received by the Bonaparte nobility, the Jumels soon were at the very center of court life at a time when Napoleon was at the peak of his popularity. Betsy had learned a few French phrases from the refugees from Haiti and Santo Domingo who had come to Providence after the uprisings there under the black napoleon, Toussaint L'Ouverture[542]—and used them to mask her lack of education and poor background.

Betsy frequently quarreled with her husband, most probably over money, for Jumel found his wife's extravagances had driven him close to bankruptcy. Consequently, they returned to New York and Betsy, surprisingly capable, took over his finances and found herself quickly and luckily succeeding in one venture after another until they had once more amassed a fortune—which Betsy again set out to spend. She started by buying a big white house overlooking the Harlem River in the city's most fashionable district.

Betsy hired an extravagant number of servants and furnished their new home in a manner rarely seen by New Yorkers—"a marvelously hideous marble-top table given to Papa Jumel by the Sultan of Turkey; a set of chairs that had been Napoleon's; a truly gaudy and cumbrous gold clock, which had been one of the emperor's gifts to Betsy; tapestry and pictures that had once belonged to the Empress Josephine; dining-room

---

[542] After Toussaint's uprising in Haiti in 1793, he conquered Santo Domingo in 1801 after Spain ceded it to France.

15. Women & the Law

furniture that had graced the salle a manger of King Charles X of France; a massive, glittering chandelier, the gift of General Moreau, who had vied with the emperor for Betsy's smiles."

Then, for the 150 acre grounds surrounding their mansion, "the world was scoured by Jumel's merchant ships to secure rare plants and trees...cedars from Mount Lebanon, cypresses from Greece, exotic flowers from South America, roses from Provence."[543]

Once established, the Jumels began to entertain on a grand scale, their guests including Bonapartes they had met in Paris who had since fled to America. Then, one morning in 1830, an hour after Jumel left for work, he was brought home dying. His coach had slipped on ice, turned over, and Jumel had hit his head. Now in her mid-fifties, Betsy wasted no time mourning, but rather began once again to see would-be suitors in her home. However, it was Betsy, apparently, who sought out Aaron Burr when she heard he was in New York practicing law after a period of exile in Europe following his acquittal on charges of high treason.

Burr was then in his late seventies, "wizened, white of hair,...poverty, griefs, bitter disappointments, [having] sadly broken him." He must, nonetheless, have touched Betsy who invited him to be her guest of honor at one of her "renowned dinner parties....The people who had come to stare at him as an escaped arch-criminal went home wholly enslaved by his magnetic charm. Aaron Burr had come into his own again." Soon after, in July 1833, Aaron and Betsy married. But just as Betsy had quarreled with Jumel over money, so did she with Burr—who had taken control of her money in the manner of (most) men at the time. After a number

---

[543] Quotes from Terhune, pp. 99-100. The rest of Betsy's story [but not that of George] is from Terhune.

of separations and reconciliations, Burr died in a Staten Island hotel a few days after their divorce, alone and unmourned.

Again Betsy resumed her gay and flirting ways, and in the summer of 1837 held a mammoth flower fête. Then, in 1853, Betsy again sailed for Paris. Her old friend, Louis Napoleon, recently self-acclaimed Emperor of France, welcomed her and held a court ball in her honor. But now approaching eighty, Betsy's mind was beginning to wander; she was having delusions of being a queen, and thus returned to her New York mansion on a hill where she now "held audiences" rather than "receiving callers." On her annual visits to Saratoga she took with her a retinue of fifty servants. It says much as to just how massive her fortune must have been that despite her extravagances, Betsy had more than a million dollars left at the time of her death on July 16, 1865. She was buried in Trinity Church Cemetery in New York City.

Two years after Betsy's death, her abandoned son, George, on discovering that an illegitimate child could inherit, tried to claim part of the Jumel estate. "There is no reason to doubt that his claim [to be Betsy's son] was true, but the jury in the US Circuit Court at New York [out only a few hours] found against him, and the US Supreme Court reported no error." The initial trial was "the sensation of the day." It was a costly affair and resulted in "a great shrinkage of the Jumel estate. The mansion, which for a time during the Revolution served [George] Washington as headquarters, now is the property of New York City, and in custody of the Daughters of the American Revolution, who house there an interesting collection of Washington relics."

★★★

15. Women & the Law

By 1729, with the state encompassing a larger area and its population reaching nearly four thousand, it found that "prosecuting [its] affairs in the common course of justice" had become an increasing problem. Reflecting this, the colony was 'divided into three distinct and separate counties,' namely, Newport, King's, and Providence; in each of these there was to be 'forthwith erected...one County House, and one County Gaol...for the holding of Courts & Security of Prisoners.' Furthermore, the charge was to be 'defrayed and Paid' by the colonial treasury."[544] Repeated similar orders that each town build its own jail followed, but few complied, partly because they could not afford to do so. There were no regularly collected taxes until 1710, and so when monies were needed for such as "a new jail, a powder house, stronger stocks, a toller, or an extra constable, every one had to chip in to pay the costs"[545]—and everyone may not have been so willing. It was cheaper to use the stocks and whip or to impose a fine than to jail people. It appears that Portsmouth built the first prison, twelve feet by ten, connected to Henry Bull's house for convenience since he was both keeper of the prison and Town Sergeant.[546]

It was not until 1655 that Newport was ordered to build a "sufficient Prison" to be used by all, each town contributing to its costs. By 1696 Providence had decided it needed a jail of its own on the mainland because "there is often times great difficulty and trouble fall upon the Constables and other officers for want of some hou[se] or place of hold to secure prisoners in, until they can have opptye to convey them to the Collonye prison at Newport." [547]

---

[544] Kimball, p. 207.
[545] Haley, Old Stone Bank, Vol. IV, p. 42.
[546] Greene, Richard, pp. 21-22
[547] This and quote in subsequent paragraph from Greene, Richard, p. 26-28

However, there is no evidence that a prison was actually built in Providence until two years later when enough money was finally collected to do so. It was finished in 1699 at a cost of twenty-one pounds and seventeen shillings, exclusive of locks. However, it lasted only briefly, destroyed by a fire sometime before February 1705, evidenced by the fact that at a town meeting on that date it was decided that another jail should be built on the same site as the one that had burned down—on the west side of Benefit Street, near the junction of Benefit and North Main Street. This prison is described as having "two stories, with a garret above, having two rooms on each floor, with a lean-to and a steep roof."

Then, in January 1732, a Court House was completed in Providence with a part set aside for the jail. It was located on Gaol Lane, "so called in recognition of the presence of the gaol, which stood conveniently at hand for the ministrations of judge and jury."[548] But five years later this, too, burned down. However, one year before that, in January 1733, a new jail had already been proposed. Records state:[549]

> ...the old situation at the corner of Benefit and Meeting Streets had proved 'very inconvenient both as to Water and carting Wood,' for it was necessary to carry these requisites to comfort 'some Distance up a Hill,' and in order to mitigate the consequent distress, 'not only of the Gaol Keeper, but the poor Prisoners,' the colony declared itself prepared 'to build a good new Gaol House...of a suitable Bigness,' on condition that the town of Providence should provide 'a good convenient Lot of Land' for the purpose. In 1734 this new gaol was "ready for business," occupying a site on the north side of

☆☆☆

---

[548] Kimball, p. 208
[549] Kimball, pp. 214-215.

15. Women & the Law

When the British forces occupied Newport during the War of Independence, Providence became the recipient of all the prisoners who had, until then, been in the Newport jail. Consequently, it soon became clear that its jail was entirely inadequate in size and certainly not an improvement in conditions. The sheriff, Thomas Rice, as early as 1735 reported that misplaced chimneys caused the whole place to fill with smoke. Four years later he complained that

> ...whereas the vaults (privy) of the Gaol or Prison, in the town of Providence, doth vent themselves under the house, which creates so great a stench, and is become so nauseous that not only the prisoners, but the people residing in the house, cannot long continue there, the place under the said house being so full of excrements.[550]

Despite this, years of controversy followed until 1752 when the proposal was made before the town meeting, referred to previously in the building of schools, that the lot "whereon the Towne Schoole House standeth' be appropriated for the new gaol." The school was to occupy eight feet of the lot, the gaol the remainder, extending over the mud flats to the channel in midstream. Much of the cost was to be met by selling the old gaol site, and the gaol opened in 1753—no better than the old—the wood rotting from the dampness, water overflowing the floors at high tide. The conditions were further exacerbated by "the distilleries, slaughtering-houses, and tanneries in the immediate neighborhood, and the use of open sewers."[551]

Conditions were no better in Newport; women in both locations were housed in the same jail as men, though possibly in separate rooms.

---

[550] Greene, Richard, p. 51
[551] Greene, Richard, pp. 183-184

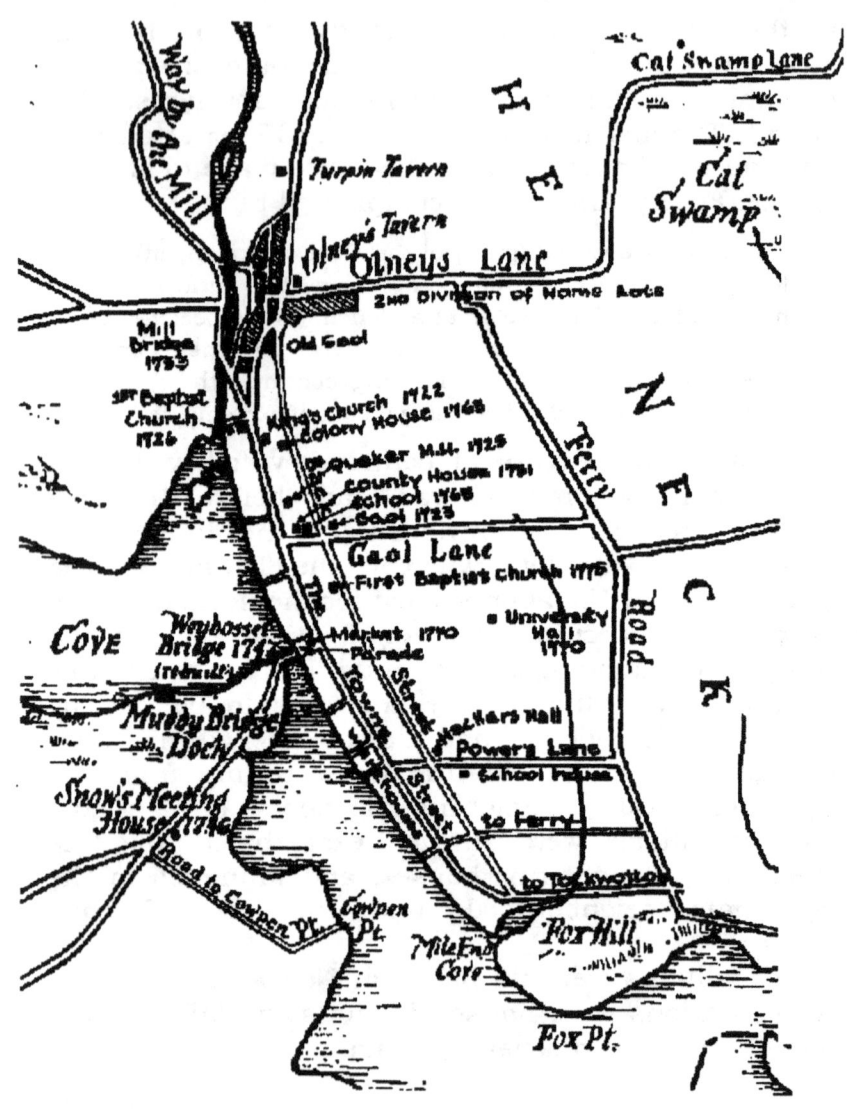

Providence About 1775. (From Cady's *Civic and Architectural Development of Providence*.)

15. Women & the Law 353

Something of the prison experience can be ascertained by a petition for relief from Ester Barbut Keen, apparently an educated woman, confined in Newport in 1754 for reasons unstated.

> ...confined a long Time in this Gaol in a Little Room where she hath only place for a Bed for which is obliged to pay thirty Shillings a Week (her whole allowance by Law) where no fire can be made for want of a Chimney and consequently is forced to sit in The Cold in a Starving Condition; or by the Fire in a publick Room amongst all comers and goers which to a Woman of Tender and Virtuous Education is Worse Than the Confinement itself.[552]

These inadequate gaols had other faults too. "Built of wood and continually in need of repair, it appeared that any desperate prisoner could have found a way to escape without any great difficulty." But one man, Thomas Hammet, "employed more subtle methods than physical force," making use of his helpful wife.[553]

> Hammet having put on his Wife's cloak and Bonnet, knock'd at the door, and the Prison-Keeper letting him into the privileg'd Room, he walk'd through it in View of him and several others, who mistook him for his wife. The Prison-Keeper going immediately to lock the Inner Doors, found his Prisoner was gone, and his Wife and Child left in the Room where he was confin'd. Upon which Notice was given by Beat of Drum in the Town and the Sheriff, with Several Officers of the Militia, rode out on the Island in quest of him, but he is not yet found. This morning the Militia of the Town are in Pursuit of him. The bonnet was thrown over the prison wall last Night.

The report does not reveal whether or not Hammet was eventually recaptured. In general, however, gaolers

---

[552] Greene, Richard, p. 34
[553] Greene, Richard, p. 35

were held responsible for escapes. If it was with their help, they were made to assume the penalties of the escaped prisoner; if a capital offender, the gaoler was fined $3,000 and sentenced to up to six years. If it was just carelessness on the part of the gaoler, the maximum fine was $1,000 and one year in jail. However, the gaoler was given three months to capture an escapee before his punishment took affect.[554]

Providence had appointed its first Town Sergeant in 1651, and he had a number of constables to help him in "chasing thieves, preserving order at town meetings, and holding and feeding prisoners." Since he "took his compensation in the form of fees for services rendered, and sometime accepted a bushel of oats, a fat turkey, or a quart of opened quahaugs in payment," a fine for an escape such as noted above, must have given him an especial incentive to prevent such.

Again in 1792, Providence was considering another jail, but the dithering continued until 1799 when a three-story prison was finally built to replace the old one, at a cost of about $9,000. It was located "at the foot of the Old Court House parade, on the West Side of Main Street, and about 150 feet from it," at what are now the corner of Canal (North Water) and Haymarket Streets.[555] It too, however, was "never satisfactory and always in need of repairs. It became a horrible place and was for years 'a disgrace to the state and a nuisance to the town.'"[556] Nonetheless, it was not until 1838 that it was replaced by a combination state prison and Providence County Jail located at Francis and Gaspee Streets—on the site occupied since 1999 by a luxurious shopping mall named Providence Place.

---

[554] Greene, Richard, p. 73
[555] Greene, Richard, p. 62
[556] Kimball, p. 214 & Field, V. 3, p. 455--457.

16. Doctors & Epidemics

Little has been said about sickness and death in the colonies and most of the early founders were, no doubt, a sturdy lot, but could hardly have escaped common everyday illnesses, infections, gout, distemper, and digestive ills, caused by lack of sanitary conditions and dietary knowledge, to say nothing of the more serious diseases that were rampant in the 1600s and 1700s. Also, there was the constant threat to the children, and consequent worry to mothers, of their getting not only routine illnesses such as colds and diarrhea, but also burns from the fireplaces, measles, whooping cough, diphtheria and intestinal worms. The prayer said by children for generations had an all too imminent meaning for these mothers who all too often lost their children at a very early age.

> Now I lay me down to sleep,
> I pray the Lord my soul to keep,
> If I should die before I wake,
> I pray the Lord my soul to take.

With all this to cope with, it may still have been just as well that there were not too many doctors around during those early years. History records that "more die[d] of the practitioner than of the natural course of the disease." Further, it seems that "the more highly educated the doctor, the faster and more painfully was the patient likely to die. In both England and America surgeons were considered craftsmen, not professionals. ...Whatever the complaint, the aim of the physician was to get out the 'vile humours' that were causing illness....These educated doctors and those influenced by them sneered at the remedies of 'old women,' which were probably no more effective in curing small pox and yellow fever;...however, [unlike many of the doctor's remedies] their treatments would do no further harm and might make the patient more comfortable."[557]

In effect, every pioneer housewife served as "amateur pharmacist, dispensing her specially concocted home remedies for the sicknesses that constantly afflicted her family."[558] They learned from the Indians and black slaves how to identify and find various roots, herbs and plants in the surrounding woods and meadows that were useful for treatment of all sorts of ill. They learned how to make them into medicinal brews, ointments and salves—"salves for sores, soothing syrups for sore throats,...[a] combination of chicken soup and strong ale" to ease pain.[559]

The men were less willing to borrow treatments from the Indians and less impressed by their ability to treat illnesses, Roger Williams no exception. He wrote:

> Their misery appears, for they have not raisin, nor currant, nor physic, nor fruit, nor spice, nor any comfort more than their corn and water, wanting all means of recovery or present refreshing....Their priest, or conjurers, bewitch the people...[and] in sickness comes close to the sick person and perform many strange actions about him, and threaten and conjure out the sickness....the females, young and old, blacken their faces with soot or black earth; when death takes place the men follow the women and blacken with soot their faces.[560]

★★★

Despite the skills of the women in using what they learned from the Indians and slaves, many colonists of both sexes and of all ages died. Historians and genealogists have recorded the early death of many

---

[557] DePauw, p. 36
[558] Booth, *Hung, Strung*, p. 26.
[559] DePauw, p. 36
[560] Williams quoted by Rider, pp. 39-40.

16. Doctors & Epidemics 357

wives and mothers, but rarely have given us a cause. It is quite possible, however, that many died in childbirth, some after having born as many as ten or so children. With women having so many children right from the beginning of the colony, there must also have been women who undertook the role of midwife. One we know of is Anne Hutchinson, both respected and well-trained as a midwife. She successfully delivered one of Mary Dyer's children, even though it was a difficult delivery with the baby turned the wrong way. Mary, in fact, for good reason, was more fearful when John Clarke, a physician, was to deliver another. The first trained (at Edinburgh University) obstetrician to settle in the colonies was thought to be Dr. William Hunter who came to Newport around 1752.[561]

At the time there were "fewer maternal deaths among those women delivered by midwives," than those delivered by physicians—ironically, since physicians felt that they alone were "qualified for internal examinations of the mother. The midwives were not considered 'trained' to reach inside the mother's womb."[562] Nonetheless, it was they who used lard or olive oil on their hands for lubrication to make manual extraction of a newborn easier, while it was not until 1758 that doctors began to experiment with various hand-coverings for the same purpose. Handwashing was not thought of as important.

"It was not until two centuries later that septicemia was diagnosed as one of the major causes of maternal death, transmitted by the unsterilized hands of the physicians."[563] Meanwhile, "when doctors began to crowd out midwives, they were attacked as

---

[561] Information regarding Dr. Hunter is from Garland, p. 3.
[562] Plimpton, pp. 54 and 223. More regarding the political reasons for Mary's distrust of Clarke, p.106.
[563] Plimpton, pp. 54 and 223.

awkward and brutal practitioners. An indignant newspaper editor wrote that the familiarities taken by men in attending pregnant women and those in labor were 'sufficient to taint the Purity and sully the Chastity of any Woman breathing.'"[564]

★★★

John Clarke was one of the earliest physicians to practice in Rhode Island. He was already a trained physician, married to Elizabeth Harges, when he came to this country. Elizabeth's father, lord of the manor of Wreslingworth, Bedfordshire, regarded Clarke as "beneath her," but, as indicated previously, had allowed the marriage in 1634 because he thought Clarke was on his way to becoming "a prosperous English physician." [565] Instead, they emigrated to America where he did practice medicine, but only part-time, because it did not pay enough to support his family.

> Treating fevers and fluxes, coughs and rashes, [for the small and rather healthy population], could not command a sizable income, even when supplemented with fees for attending a few abnormal pregnancies or determining the cause of violent deaths. Probably Clarke went beyond the narrow bounds of an English physician's practice, which consisted mainly of consulting and prescribing and excluded everything in the realm of the surgeon or apothecary. In a raw new community a doctor might have to dress wounds or set bones, mix medicines and sell them as well as prescribe them, possibly even extract kidney stones and abscessed teeth. Nevertheless, in a show of respect for proper professional boundaries, the town of Newport in 1641 authorized a different man 'to exercise the function of Chirurgerie [surgery].'"[566]

---

[564] Smith, p. 55.
[565] James, *Clarke*, p. 4
[566] James, *Clarke*, pp. 17-18

16. Doctors & Epidemics

The date on which Clarke's wife, Elizabeth, died has not been determined, but it is recorded that they had no children. Also, no record was found of the date on which he married his second wife, Jane Fletcher, a widow. This marriage, however, could not have lasted long as she died on April 19, 1672, only two months after giving birth to a daughter on February 14th. Soon after their daughter also died.

A year later, on May 18th, 1673, Clarke took yet another wife, Sarah Davis, whom he had known for some years. Both the Clarke and Davis families were early settlers of Aquidneck. Sarah had recently been widowed by Nicholas Davis, a seaman and fervent Quaker who drowned in 1672, shortly after carrying George Fox, the Quaker leader, in his sloop from Long Island to Newport where he was visiting for a time. The unusual aspect of their union was the cross of religions, something both faiths opposed; she a Quaker, he a leading Baptist. Also unusual, Sarah brought little of material value to this marriage, her now-deceased husband having left a number of debts to pay off. But Clarke seemed only pleased to have her with her five children added to his household, stating that he "at last had the completion of a proper domestic assembly." [567] *We may reasonably conclude from this that the death of Elizabeth and their child had affected him greatly.*

An old family Bible states that "the 20th of the 2d month, 1676, my brother John Clarke, in the night, departed this life in his own house in Newport, on Rhode Island."[568] He left a complex will that protected his wife, Sarah, from his considerable debts [something, presumably, her first husband had not done when he, too, left considerable debts]. His trustees would hold "his farm, the Applegate Neck property, and the house and

---

[567] James, *Clarke*, pp. 96-97.
[568] *Genealogies* Vol. 1, p. 198.

most of the land in central Newport for the support of Sarah during her life. Further, if she lived in the house, she should have the use of the property connected with it, about thirty acres. Regardless of where she lived, Clarke left her his biggest trunk and two beds of her choice, including all the furniture associated with them."

In leaving Sarah's five children more than his own brothers and their children, Clarke reinforced just how much the marriage to her had meant to him. Clarke left her son Simon the waterfront property. "Her three daughters and her other son were to have money when they reached majority or were married, but in any case not before she died. Rather mysteriously, the amounts differed: Sarah Davis would get £40; Thomas, £20; Mercy, £20; but Hannah, only £10."[569]

Sarah, who survived Clarke by sixteen years, remarried a third time, and moved to Hyannis, but she was back in Newport when she died in 1692. After her death, the trustees named in Clarke's will paid her children the sums he had designated for them.

Clarke, like many of the early settlers, had remarried soon after the death of each of his wives, at least some of them recently widowed themselves. This was a common occurrence with both sexes in 17th century New England—"the work to be done to keep a respectable household requir[ed] the partnership of a man and woman...Practical considerations as well as the cultural norms that were absorbed as religious imperatives called for this pair to be husband and wife." Despite its "formularistic quality," on the whole it seemed to work well; love and companionship being a real part of most marriages.[570] (Nonetheless, divorce, too, as we have noted, was not uncommon.)

---

[569] James, *Clarke*, pp. 105-106, and 110.
[570] James, *Clarke*, p. 96

16. Doctors & Epidemics

***

Histories of early Rhode Island name few nurses or women assistants and only a few doctors, the latter at least partly because even those claiming to be doctors had also to undertake other activities to supplement their income. Records of regularly practicing, full-time physicians only begin to appear in Providence after 1700.[571] Until then, the town's people had to turn to Boston for medicines and advice when home remedies proved ineffective, and, perhaps occasionally, the three practicing doctors in Newport may have visited.

John Greene, Sr., a contemporary of Roger Williams, was referred to as a "surgeon," but nothing is said of his practice. Born in 1590, Greene moved with his wife, Joan Tattersall, from Providence to Warwick in 1641. They had married in Salisbury Cathedral in England on November 4, 1619 before embarking for America. She bore six children before dying at Conanicut in 1643, "having fled to that island for safety at the time the Massachusetts troops made their unjustifiable and cruel assault upon the inhabitants of Warwick." [572]

The legitimacy of John Greene's second marriage to Alice Daniels has been questioned, some claiming she was still the wife of Richard Beggerly.[573] The little evidence that is available does not seem to substantiate this: her name on the homelot map does not include "widow," as it does with the other named women allocated lots; and, there are no records of a marriage to Beggerly. Whatever the truth about Greene's marriage to Alice, he did have another marriage later, to Philippi (last name unknown) who survived him.

---

[571] Haley, Old Stone Bank, Vol. IV, p. 44
[572] Hopkins, p. 25-26
[573] Genealogies, V. 1, p. 734.

Captain John Cranston, was, apparently, the first colonist to receive a *license* to practice in Rhode Island. Records of the General Assembly for March 1, 1664 state:[574]

> The Court doe unanimously enact and declare that the said Captain John Cranston is lycenced and commissioned to administer phissicke, and practice chirurgery throughout this whole Colony, and is by this Court styled and recorded Doctor of phissick and chirrurgery by the othority of this the General Assembly of this Collony.

Cranston was born in Scotland about 1625 and came to Newport while still young. There he married Mary Clarke, daughter of Jeremiah Clarke, a prominent Quaker. Their son, Samuel, born in 1659, became Governor in 1698 after his uncle, Walter Clarke, resigned in his favor. His father, John Cranston, also had been Governor: from 1678 until his death on March 12, 1680.[575]

Other doctors who practiced in Rhode Island both before and after Cranston (the earliest practicing only part-time), were John Whipple, called a "natural bone setter," Henry Sweeting, who also made felt hats, John Walton, a Baptist preacher and lawyer, Richard Bowen, who settled in Seekonk in 1676, and the doctors Ephraim Bowen, Sterling, Gibbs, Mawney, Fiske, Jabez Bowen, the younger, and Amos Throop. Those referred to as "eminent physicians" included Joseph Hewes, Ephraim Bowen (b. 1716, d.1812), John Jones, Jonathan Arnold and John Hoyle. There were also so-called "tramp doctors" who claimed to have just arrived from London.

---

[574] Field, V.2, p. 4,
[575] The story of Samuel's seafaring adventures and marriage to the Williams' granddaughter was told earlier.

16. Doctors & Epidemics

Little is known of the practices of most of these doctors. We do know that in 1720, Providence employed Dr. John Jones "to take care of the sick poor of the town and to be paid if he cured them."[576] In 1722, Doctor John Hoyle, practiced as a "Practitioner in Physick," in Providence on the West Side, but his efforts to add a religious centre there were aborted. He was probably also an inn-keeper. Twenty years later, Doctor Henry Sweeting also settled on the West Side. His house was the first built on Weybosset Point. This was not, in those early days, considered an attractive neighbor-hood, but a new community gradually emerged, beginning with his own family. He and his wife, the daughter of Nathaniel Brown, had a son and two daughters, all of whom, when they married, built their homes nearby.[577]

In 1760, though he did not have a medical degree, Jonathan Arnold opened a practice in Providence, and in 1776, after Providence opened the Revolutionary War Hospital of Rhode Island, the Governor appointed him as chief surgeon, a position he retained until 1781. After the War, Arnold served for a time as a member of Congress, then moved to Vermont where he died.[578]

When epidemics broke out in Providence in the 1700s, it is the doctors Bowen, Barnard and Bartlett who are named—and, for the first time, a nurse is mentioned.

★★★

Despite its generally healthy citizens, the colony suffered the ravages of epidemics that broke out from time to time. Still little understood, they perplexed even

---
[576] Miner, Lillian, p. 112.
[577] Kimball, pp. 177, 184-85, 190 & 196.
[578] Bellesiles, p. 637 and Staples, *Annals*, p. 602-603.

trained doctors, created panic and fear amongst the citizens, virtually destroyed many families and disrupted business. Between July and October 1723, something they called "burning ague" took the lives of 18 men, 16 women and nine children. Earlier, in 1690, Small Pox [written as two words at the time] raged. Newport was hit the hardest; very likely the "pestilence" brought there "from some foreign country by a sailor, and the scourge spread rapidly, sparing no class of society."[579] Then, in 1716, it appeared again in several parts of the colony, at which time Newport authorized the building on Coaste's Island of the first public institution for the care of the sick in Rhode Island. "Its purpose was the isolation of smallpox victims. By 1720 it was said to be the best-equipped pesthouse in the colonies."

After another outbreak in Providence in 1751, the General Assembly appropriated funds for its first hospital, built in 1752. Early in the 1700s, Dr. Benjamin Waterhouse, born in Newport, had introduced small pox vaccinations to the Western Hemisphere (meant to induce a mild form of small pox), but they were still very controversial, and at first only the very rich took advantage of them. Many doctors and clergy were strongly opposed, calling the inoculations inherently sinful; as counter to the will of God which brought such diseases upon us to test our righteousness.

But as late as 1772 a legislative act that attempted to legalize inoculations was defeated. Nonetheless, it was that year that the first shots were administered in Providence. Injections were given at "inoculation hospitals," the small pox thus induced lasting about a week or so; the fever relatively mild and the pox mostly confined to the site of injection. However, during this

---

[579] Haley, Old Stone Bank, Vol. IV, p. 44.

16. Doctors & Epidemics

time the recipient was contagious and had to be confined in isolation; hence the hospital stay, or quarantine. However, since the use of these preemptive injections was still limited to only a few, and some of those who did receive the injection were released prematurely while still infectious, smallpox continued to spread in the general community. Widespread use of vaccinations as an effective preventive measure did not occur until 1798 when Edward Jenner discovered that inoculations of cow pox resulted in immunity from the much deadlier smallpox. It was not until 1810 that Providence "employed Sylvanus Fansher to vaccinate the public, the town paying the expense; he vaccinated 4,305 persons and rendered a bill of $233.25, or about five cents for each operation."[580]

Theodore Foster, mentioned earlier, who took the population count and kept a diary during the Revolutionary War, wrote of the time in 1776 that his wife went to what was probably an inoculation hospital—perhaps the hospital Providence had built that year, its second. He gives us some insight into the fears engendered by this disease—and of this husband's reaction to his wife. Oddly, he refers to her throughout as Mrs. Foster, and informs us that she was the Great Grand Daughter of Arthur Fenner and Mehitabel Waterman.[581]

> August 12th, 1776. Monday Morning. Between 7 and 8 O'clock this Morning Mrs. Foster in a chaise with Miss Sally Atwell rode to that part of this Town called Tockwotten in Order to receive Inoculation for the SMALL POX. Wanting to see Doctor Barnard I went to find him and ...found the Doctor making Bandages for the People he was about to inoculate. About 100 Persons were to be

---

[580] Haley, Old Stone Bank, Vol. IV, p. 44
[581] Levin, pp. 14-23.

inoculated this Morning....Between 9 and 10 o'clock Colonel Tillinghast was inoculated and next to him was Inoculated Mrs. Foster. These are the Two first Persons inoculated in Providence by Doctor Barnard. I was in the House when Colonel Tillinghast and Mrs. Foster were inoculated but thinking them to be much farther off than they really were I apprehended myself to be in no danger till I perceived a very disagreeable unusual Smell which giving Me the alarm I immediately Quitted the House....

[*This entry indicates that Mrs. Foster, after her inoculation, stayed in the hospital until she was no longer contagious from the induced Small Pox, a required step if the inoculations were to be effective in stopping the disease's spread.*]

Tuesday, August 13, 1776....I went on to the Common before the Hospital, saw Mrs. Foster for the last Time as I suppose until she recovers of the Small Pox. Being under Some Apprehension that I was exposed to the Small Pox – This Evening undertake to prepare myself for having the Disease. At going to Bed I take a Purgative Pill. [*Why did he not also have the inoculation?*]

Thursday, August 15th, 1776. A cloudy Rainy Day. In the Morning went to Doctor Chace after Physic which I procured and took it at home. Purchased some Watermelons to send to Mrs. Foster at the hospital.

Tuesday Afternoon, 4 o'clock, August 20th, 1776. Miss Nancy Bucklin this minute called up to inform Me that Mrs. Foster is in good Spirits at the Hospital. That she wants a Pair of Shoes. I must now write her a Letter and send the shoes.

I went myself to Tockwotten where I saw and talked with Mrs. Foster at 100 yards Distance.

[Mr. Foster's account ends here, leaving us hanging, but, presumably, his wife returned home soon after.]

☆☆☆

16. Doctors & Epidemics

In 1717, 1791, and in its most virulent form in 1797, there were outbreaks of what was variously called "malignant fever, pestilential fever, putrid fever, and yellow fever." Many of the doctors blamed the outbreaks on "the filthy condition of many parts of the town."[582] There were no covered sewers and the waterfront areas had gradually been filled in blocking natural drainage into the Bay. The streets were full of puddles filled with rain-water, household and shop refuse, grain refuse from the rum-making, from the tanning and candle-making industries, and from hogs kept in cellars of still-houses with yards in the back where they "wallowed and rooted in the slime." The streets were not only stench-breeding, but "disease-ridden rivers of slimy mud and waste matter, and no precautions were taken to protect the well-water supplies in the congested areas from these frightful conditions of surface pollution." [583]

In 1797, at the time of the worst outbreak of yellow fever, 6,000 of Providence's 7,000 inhabitants lived in densely congested districts of the town, and it was in these districts that yellow fever appeared. Those stricken in Providence were attended by Dr. William Bowen (those in Newport by Dr. Charles Bartlett). Records indicate that Mrs. Marcy Piles received $18 for nursing at the hospital and Santealger Hopkins and his wife, $29 for the same.

Accounts list forty-nine deaths during this outbreak in 1797, an average of one per day between August 18th and October 9th. Hundreds of others were broken in health by the spreading scourge. Those who died include many whose names the reader will recognize; e.g., William, Henry, John and Mary Tillinghast; Mary, Joseph and James Arnold [*the dates suggest these would have been of the third generation*

---

[582] Field, V. 2, p. 11.
[583] Haley, Old Stone Bank, Vol. IV, p. 46

from the original settlers]. They also include one Patience Havens, negro woman.[584] Despite efforts by the total community to improve the conditions then-held responsible, outbreaks of yellow fever continued into the next century, compounded at one point by yet another, simultaneous, outbreak of smallpox.

It was at the height of this yellow fever epidemic, 1798, that Providence erected its third hospital "for quarantine of the afflicted. It was high on a hill, overlooking the Providence River; now occupied by Rhode Island Hospital. The epidemic had run it course by 1805" and the 1756, 1776 and 1798 "pesthouses were turned over to the care of sick and injured sailors and came to be known as the Marine Hospital.[585]

Meanwhile, there had been another outbreak in 1800, at which time the Providence paper listed eighty-three names of persons stricken between August 21st and October 8th. Fifty-one of those listed died; thirty-four of them women. Names included William Olney and more of the Tillinghast family—John, Charles and his wife, Mary, Amey and Mrs. J Tillinghast [these were probably some of Pardon's eighty-one grandchildren, or even his great grand-children]. Five black women were also listed—Sarah Gibbs, Mrs. Brown, Nancy Newfield, Violet Cook & Phoebe Sisco.[586] [*The name Sisco makes us wonder if Phoebe was related to the Betsy Sisco, a mulatto girl of 14, mentioned earlier, who, the same year, got caught up in arrests related to "race-mixing." Phoebe's death might explain why she was in this boarding house of questionable reputation.*]

One must reach beyond the 18th century to find the remedy to Providence's need for doctors and for

---

[584] Field, V. 2, pp. 23-24
[585] This and other hospital information from Garland, pp. 2--4.
[586] Field, V. 2, pp. 34-35.

16. Doctors & Epidemics

cleaner streets and environs. In 1856, it established its first permanent sanitary organization. In 1811, Brown University [name changed from Rhode Island College in 1804] opened a medical school (as part of a department) and awarded ninety M.D. degrees before closing the school in 1827. No other doctors received their diplomas in Rhode Island until 1975 when Brown reestablished a medical school, became fully accredited, and again awarded medical degrees—to fifty-eight graduates, thirteen of them women.

17. Travel & Tourists

By 1809, Providence County had nearly 30,000 inhabitants; the town of Providence, 10,000. It was becoming a place that attracted visitors by steamer and by stagecoach.

"As early as 1718 Jonathan Wardwell advertised that he would run a stagecoach to Rhode Island....As early as 1732 some common-carrier lines had wagons which would carry a few passengers."[587] For seven years, beginning in 1736, Alexander Thorp and Isaac Cushno ran a stage between Rhode Island and Massachusetts, but this was only sporadic. It was not until July 1767 that Thomas Sabin advertised a regular run to start "every Tuesday morning from the house of Richard Olney, inn-holder,[588] to carry travelers to Boston, on the most expeditious and cheap rate." It would return on Thursday mornings. There was, probably, an overnight stop en route, still quite common for such a trip. It was also common, on occasion, for "the owner of a stagecoach [to give] a notice a week or ten days before-hand, that on a given day, he would start for Boston, if sufficient encouragement offered, taking care to give notice so that his passengers could settle all their worldly affairs and make their wills, before commencing such an arduous and dangerous journey."[589] [Apparently one that risked life and limb.]

"S. Thurber," an old-timer quoted by Staples, wrote of the time before stagecoaches were available:

> In my youngest days there were but few carriages besides carts, consequently when women wanted to go

---

[587] Earle, *Home Life*, p. 346 & 350
[588] This would have been the Inn run by the father of the Mary Olney who married Moses Brown.
[589] Staples, p. 609

abroad it was very common for them to go on horseback, sitting on a pillion behind a man. Women would often be at market on horseback, with a pair of panniers, selling butter, cheese, eggs, &c.[590]

Staples quotes the old-timer again as he reminisces about the first time he saw a coach. It was owned by Mr. Merritt, an Englishman, "who came and purchased the farm and built the house where the venerable Moses Brown lately died, in his 99th year."[591]

> This coach would once in a while come into the street by way of Olney's lane, then there would be a running of the children, and a looking from the windows, to see the new wonderful thing....May, 1776, I went to Pomfret, thirty-six miles, in a chaise; the road was so stony and rough, that I could not ride out of a slow walk, but very little of the way; I was near two days in going, such was the general state of our road at that time.

After the appearance of almanacs, the stagecoach schedules were regularly listed along with the names of taverns—the depots of the coach lines, called the "forerunner of the automobile inn." An advertisement in the *Providence Gazette* on March 9, 1756 championed the opening of a new tavern by Abigail Williams, suggesting that the numbers venturing forth from home either by horse or carriage was sufficient to make a new tavern profitable, and also establishing that women had gone into the business of operating inns. The ad read:

> For the Convenient Reception and Entertainment of Gentlemen and Ladies, whenever they are disposed to recreate themselves by an Excursion into the Country, whether at Morning or Evening,

---

[590] Staples, p. 605.
[591] *The trip he describes is in 1776, a likely date, but Brown didn't die until 1836. So did Merritt make this trip considerably before purchasing the farm, or does the old-timer have his dates confused?.*

Providence: 1630-1800

> On Monday next will be open'd by
> Abigail Williams,
> At the Sign of the White Horse,
> (the House of Jeremiah Williams, Cranston)
>
> THE RURAL TEA AND COFFEE HOUSE
>
> Very pleasantly situated about three miles from the Town of Providence, on one of the most delightful Roads in New England.
>
> Those who are pleased to favour her with their Company may depend on the best of Entertainment, and the civilest Usage, as it will be her Constant Endeavour to deserve a continuance of their Favour.
>
> N.B. Travellers may be genteely accommodated at the same Place.

"If the performance was at all equal to the promise, Abigail Williams should have done a thriving business. The charms of a leisurely drive for three miles through the country between Providence and Cranston, are among the pleasures which have gone forever, along with the 'Sign of the White Horse.'"[592]

That last bit, however, sounds more like nostalgia than an accurate reflection of what a stagecoach trip might have been like in the early days. A vivid account by one passenger sounds far from pleasing as he encounters the "snapping of whips, rattling, jouncing, swaying, splattering mud in the springtime, bucking drifts in the winter, stuffy inside, wet or freezing outside...creaky, mud-covered old caravans, distiller's vats, ..." He continues:

> Inside—Crammed full of passengers—three fat, fusty old men—a young mother and sick child—a cross old maid—a poll parrot—a bag of red herrings...a snarling lap dog..., [and after an overnight stop] asthmatic old woman

---

[592] Dexter, pp. 14-15

Travel & Tourists

and child with measles—window closed in consequence—unpleasant smell—shoes filled with warm water—look up and find it's the child—obliged to bear it—no appeal—shut your eyes and scold the dog—pretend sleep and pinch the child—pinch dog and get bit—execrate child in return—black looks...[and so he continues]...

Outside-your eye cut by the lash of a clumsy Coachman's whip—hat blown off into a pond by a sudden gust of wind...a drunken fellow half asleep falls off the Coach—and in attempting to save himself drags you along with him into the mud...One leg under cotton...head in hamper of wines—lots of broken bottles versus broken heads...get home—lay down—and laid up.[593]

Perhaps all trips were not that bad, but this account certainly gives you an idea of what you might encounter on a day-long, two-day-long stagecoach trip.

☆☆☆

We previously quoted from the part of Susanna (Susan) Lear's diary about her visit with Avis and Nicholas Brown, shortly after which she married Capt. James Duncan. In her diary entry beginning Saturday, June 17, 1788, she writes of her trip with Avis and other family members on one of the regularly scheduled Packets that carried both passengers and cargo. We may conclude from their choice that boats were still preferred over coaches for long-distance travel, such as between Philadelphia and Providence (or even from New York to Providence). There is little to suggest, however, that travel by boat was either faster or more pleasurable. To quote Susanna:[594]

June 17: Sailed 30 miles...
June 18: "Clouds gathered, wind blew right ahead,

---

[593] Haley, Old Stone Bank, Vol. IV, pp. 115-116
[594] Duncan, Susanna Lear Diary.

waves running high, head swimming, in short, I conceived we were in much danger and wished myself on shore. Cast Anchor, and lay by for the night.

June 20: "Very ill with pain in my breast. Took ten drops of laudanum and went to bed...

June 21: Leaving Point Judith, "sea roaring on one side and breakers on the other...never passed such a night in my life."

June 22: Arrived in Newport at 9 o'clock.

June 23: Left at 11 a.m. for Providence; arrived 6 p.m. "Rain prevented our being on deck."

Susanna has something to say about coach travel, too, when she took the stagecoach from Providence to Boston on June 30, 1788 for a month's visit. The trip took from 7 a.m. that morning until 6 p.m. that evening. However, Susanna's description of her return trip to Providence on July 31st is more colorful. She left at 6 p.m. and had an overnight stay at Dedham, Massachusetts. Among the coach passengers was an "Indian chief", a "Prince," Susanna says, clearly never previously having encountered an Indian.

Susanna writes how an "Indian Chief" frightened her at first, but turned out to be "most agreeable;" he played several tunes on his clarinet at breakfast, and entertained the passengers with a number of anecdotes. Three years earlier the Marquis de la Fayette had paid for him to come to America from France [having previously taken him to France] and was continuing to pay the "expense of giving him a very liberal education."

In the days following, Susanna invited her new Indian friend to dinner at the Brown's where Susanna was staying. He also proved to be a great dancer, though, she comments, the War Dance he did was terrible.

When he had to leave Providence, Susanna quotes him as saying, "He never spent his time so happily."

And, Susanna adds, "Indeed I don't wonder for the ladies of this place are all in love with him and are striving who shall pay him the most attention."

Leaving travel aside for the moment, Susanna also records in her diary some interesting observations about the Providence she encountered on her visit in 1788. She begins on her first day, June 23rd, after a ride through "Towne," stating:

> Am much better pleased with this place than Newport. The houses in general are better, tho built of wood....

Susanna also describes a visit to Mrs. Arnold; "surrounded with splendor and elegance". Later she visits a paper mill, and a large "party" visits Spring Green, Moses Brown's country home outside Providence. There they amused themselves "singing, playing, walking, fishing, etc. When she visited Brown University on June 4th, Susanna had this to say:

> "It is an elegant building, four stories high and contains 56 rooms. We were taken to the library first [and left] to tumble over books till we were tired" Also saw some "philosophical [physics] experiments" and the Museum. "After tea we heard a sermon."

On the 24th, Susanna again visited Brown on a day the towne was rejoicing the fact that New Hampshire had adopted the New Constitution. She then writes:

> We partook of the general joy and have been hugely entertained up at the College by the proof the students gave of their joy. They marched two or three times around the green with drums, flutes and violins, each carrying the different branches of their studies in their hands, some with globes, some with maps and some with large folios. The music was good. In fact, it has been the most interesting procession I have seen in a long time.

After Susannah's return to Providence from her month's stay in Boston, she attended more parties and teas than earlier, but of more interest are her diary entries for the few days prior to her departure for home [in Philadelphia]. They refer to well-known members of the Brown family.

> August 19: Went out a-riding in the morning with James Brown. We were caught in a most violent storm of wind and rain and were obliged to take shelter in a Cottage about two miles from home. Waited nearly an hour for the storm to abate and at last had to turn out in the midst of it. The wind blew so hard we were apprehensive the carriage would blow over. However, we got home at last without meeting any accidents except Mrs. B. being wet to the skin and I having my head blown off....In the evening Moses Brown and his wife came and invited us to their house the next day.
>
> August 20: [The Brown's] live about a mile and a half out of town and are very strict Quakers, but they entertained us with all the kindness and hospitality that was possible. Their house is large and elegant, and the place abounds with all the beauties of nature...

On Saturday, August 23rd, Susanna leaves Providence at 11 a.m. (arriving back in Philadelphia on August 26th). In her last diary entry, she notes:

> I think if we ever forget Providence and the kindness we have received there we shall be the most ungrateful creatures breathing...

☆☆☆

By 1827 there were as many as twenty coaches making regular runs between Boston and Providence. "Passengers from Boston, Worcester, and Springfield would generally come to Providence, hence to proceed by packet to New York. ...Frequently a number of them [from competing lines] would arrive in Providence at once all bound for the same boat and the sight of them thundering down the streets, lurching precariously from side to side crammed with passengers and loaded with baggage, the horse plunging and sweating, the whips snapping and the rival coachmen yelling and blowing blasts on their horns was enough to send townsfolk scurrying for safety in doorways. ...In regard to the time made by such coaches, ...we find the editor of the *Providence Gazette* in 1832 proclaiming in pride":[595]

> We were rattled from Boston to Providence last Monday in *four hours and fifty minutes* including all stops on the road. If any one wants to go faster, he may send to Kentucky and charter a streak of lightning, or wait for a railroad, if he pleases.

This was the hey-day of stagecoach travel when as many as 24,000 passengers were transported by just two lines between Boston and Providence. Dozens of coaches, each with six horses, would be lined up in front of Providence's Manufacturer's Hotel, the staging point for travelers. However, by 1830, railroads were beginning to intrude, and by 1840 it had become difficult for the much slower stagecoaches to compete. Within a surprisingly short time they had become obsolete.

★★★

By 1826 when Mrs. Anne Royal from Virginia visited Providence, it had become a desired stop for travelers. She wrote of her visit:

> Providence is a very romantic town, lying partly on two hills, and partly on a narrow plain, about wide enough for two streets...It contains fourteen houses for public worship, a college, a jail, a theatre, a market-house, eight bands, an alms-house, part of which is a hospital, and 12,800 inhabitants...Providence is mostly built of wood, though there are many fine brick edifices in it...The streets

---

[595] Earle, *Home Life*, p. 346 & 350 and Haley, Old Stone Bank, Vol. IV, p. 117.

are wide and regular, and most of them paved, with handsome sidewalks, planted with trees. It is a very flourishing, beautiful town, and carries on an extensive trade with the East Indies.

The town of Providence owns six cotton factories, two woolen factories, twelve jeweler's shops, where jewelry is manufactured for exportation. The citizens are mostly men of extensive capital...

I made several attempts to see Brown University, but was finally disappointed. I called several times at the house of the President, but never found him in. They [the Brown buildings] are not extraordinary, either for size or architecture...I am told it is well endowed, has a president and ten professors, and averages 150 students.

The citizens of Providence are mild, unassuming, artless, and the very milk of human kindness. They are genteel, but not so refined as the people of Boston. They are stout, fine looking men; the ladies, particularly, are handsome, and many of them highly accomplished. Both sexes...have a very independent carriage. [596]

★★★

Clearly Providence had come a long way since William Blackstone, William Arnold, Roger Williams and the five hearty souls who had accompanied him landed on its shores in 1635.

The brooding forest fell before the axe, giving way to fields and pastures separated by useful groves. The Indian villages vanished, the Indian trails turned into wide, if miry, road. The bay filled with sails. Churches and meeting houses sprang up, some even with steeples to punctuate the skylines of Newport and Providence while the wharves gave pattern to their harbors. Streets were paved and named. The smells of the countryside continued, but the city trades added new ones—distilleries, tanneries, ropewalks and the like. The sounds

---

[596] Kimball, p. 375.

Travel & Tourists

of the commercial bustle added to the variety....The variety of imported dainties for the table—cocoa, tea, spices, tropical fruits, wines, rum—underscored the cosmopolitan quality of the colony. The newly introduced religions brought new thoughts about the relation of the present to the past, of Rhode Island to the rest of the world.[597]

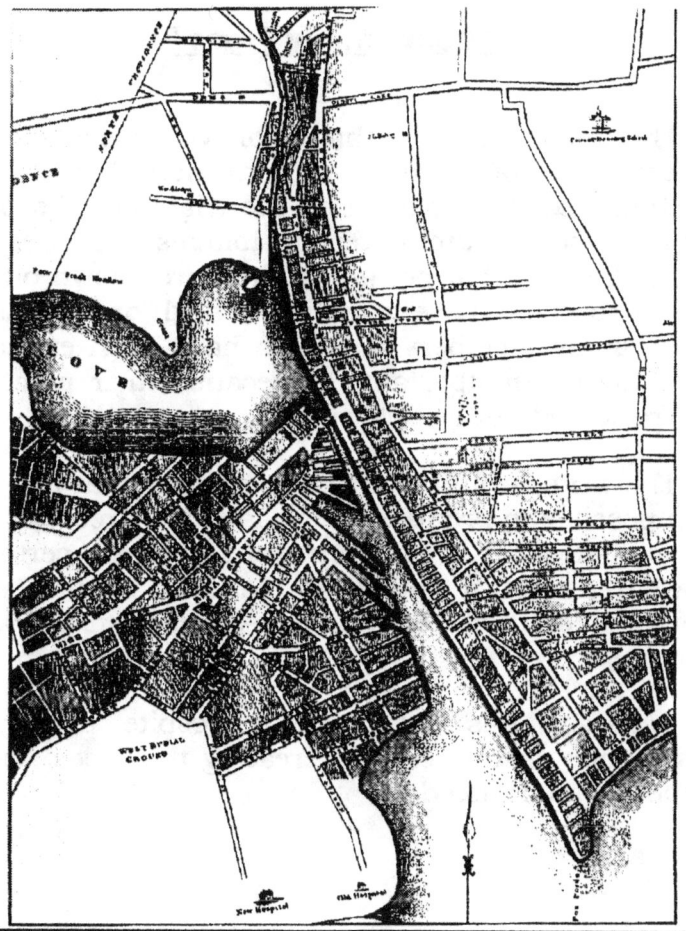

Providence 1823; Not incorporated as a city until 1832

---

[597] James, *History*, p. 230

"About Family Trees"

The few Trees that follow, selected as representative of the early settlers, help demonstrate just how frequent wives faced the trials of child-birth and the time-consuming responsibilities of childcare—despite the fact that not all children are shown on the Trees, especially those who died at birth or in infancy. Other family members may also have been excluded as relatively unimportant, or because their place on the Tree could not be determined.

The writer would also like to suggest that if it had been possible to produce all the families' Trees, or one big football-sized Tree, they would almost certainly show that most, if not *all*, of the early families were related in one way or another—often in more ways than one.

Accuracy has been sought despite the many frustrations encountered in creating the Trees, but it cannot be guaranteed.

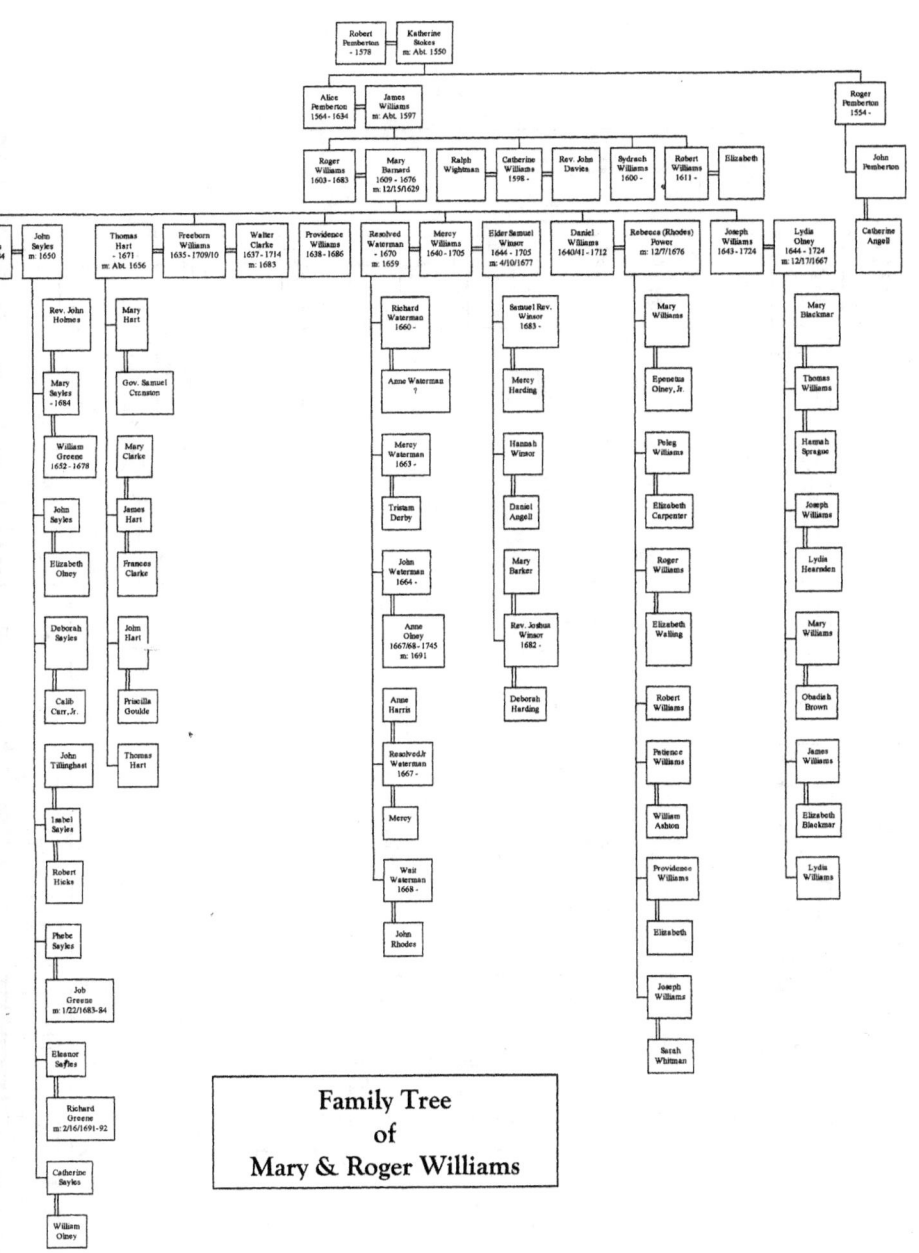

Family Tree of Mary & Roger Williams

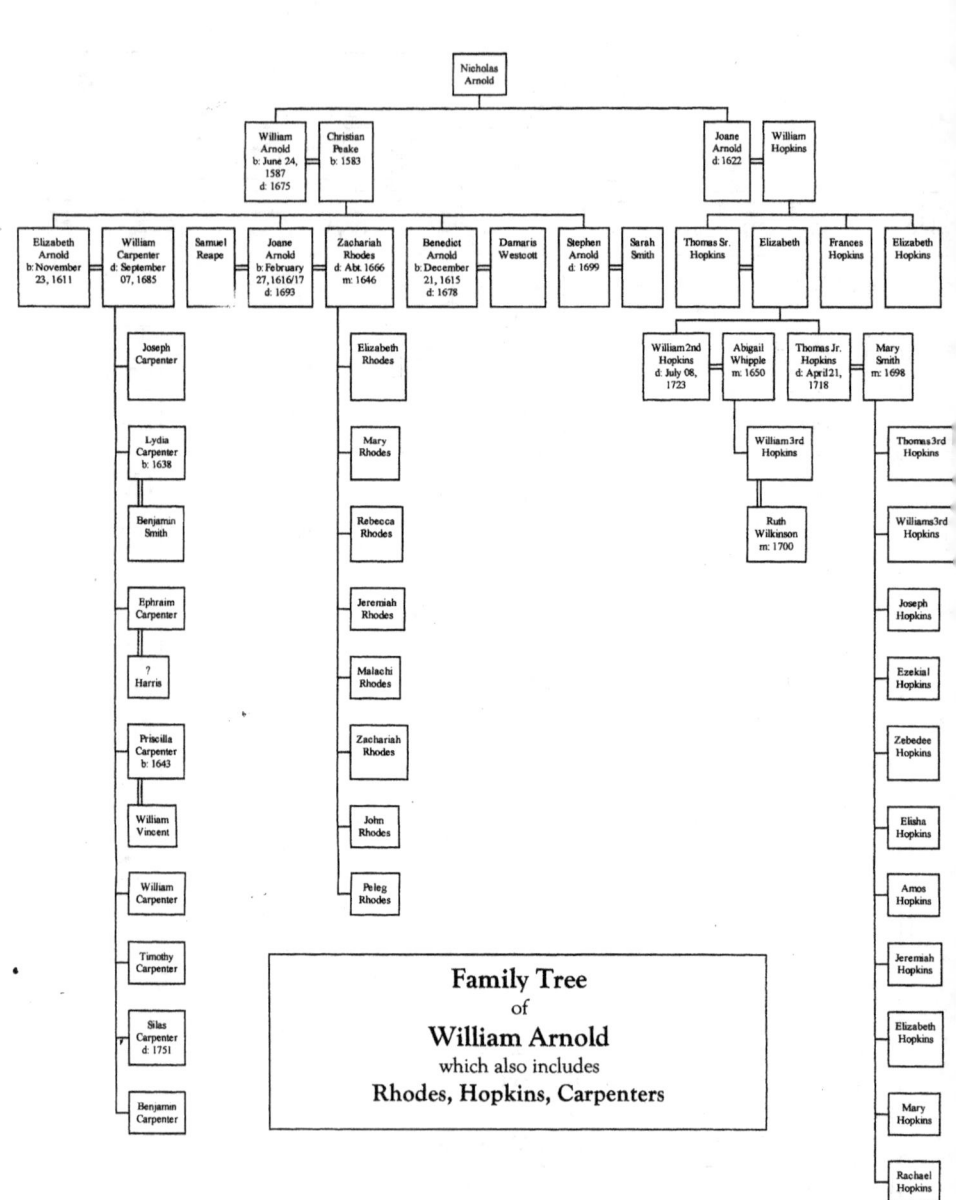

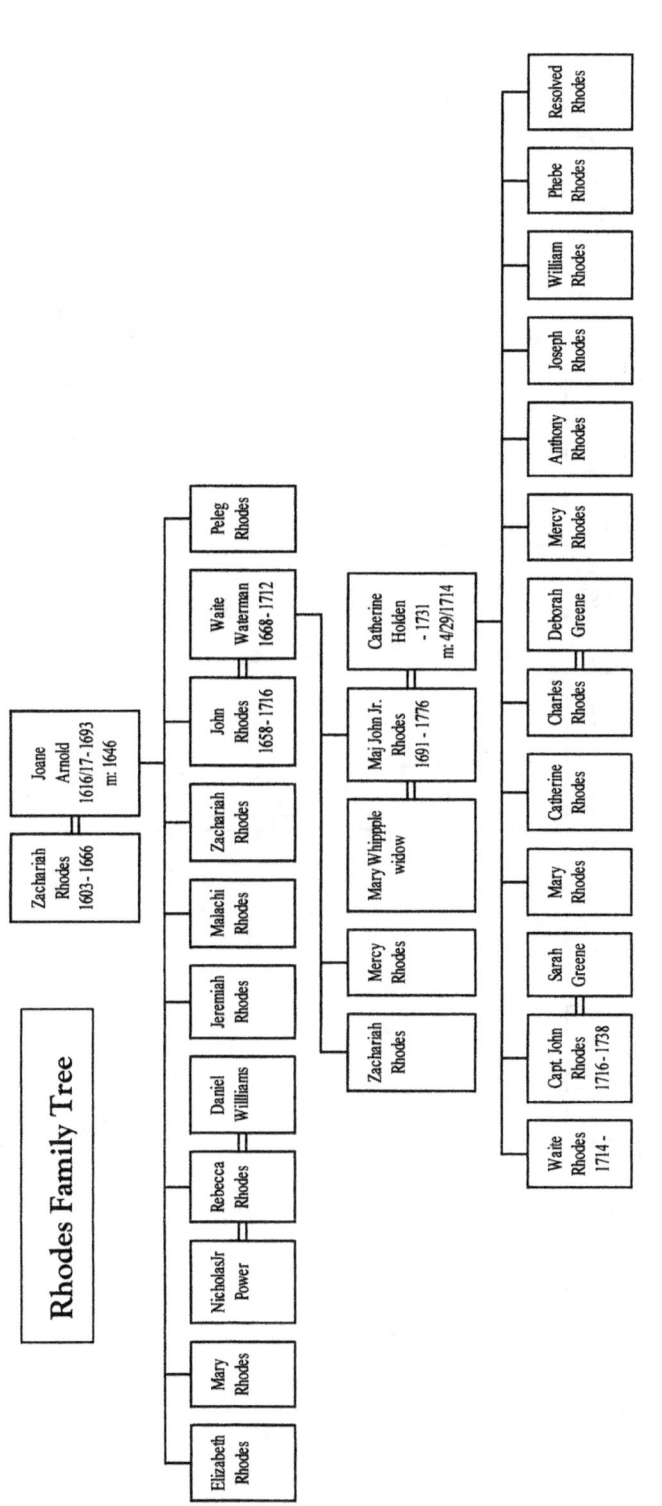

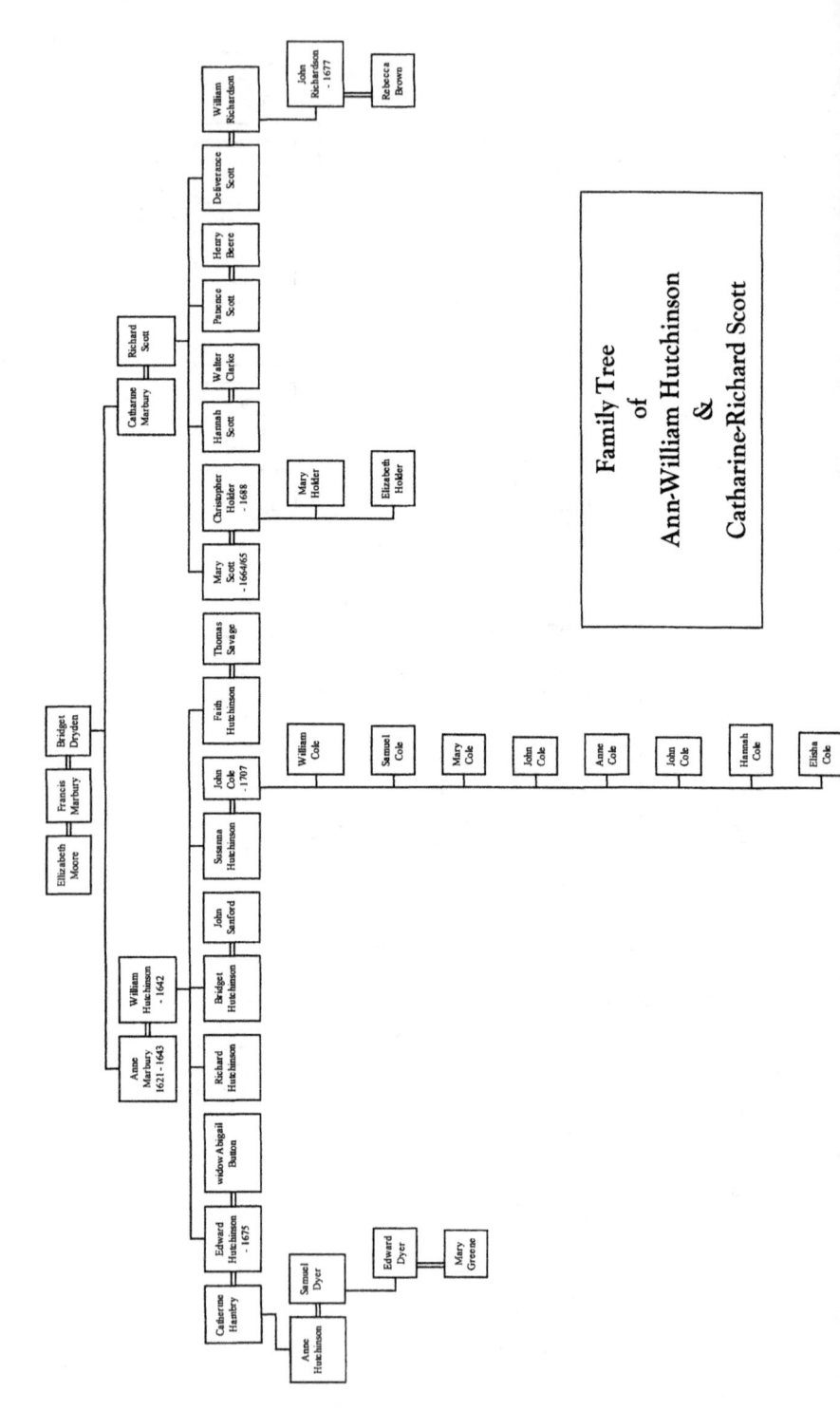

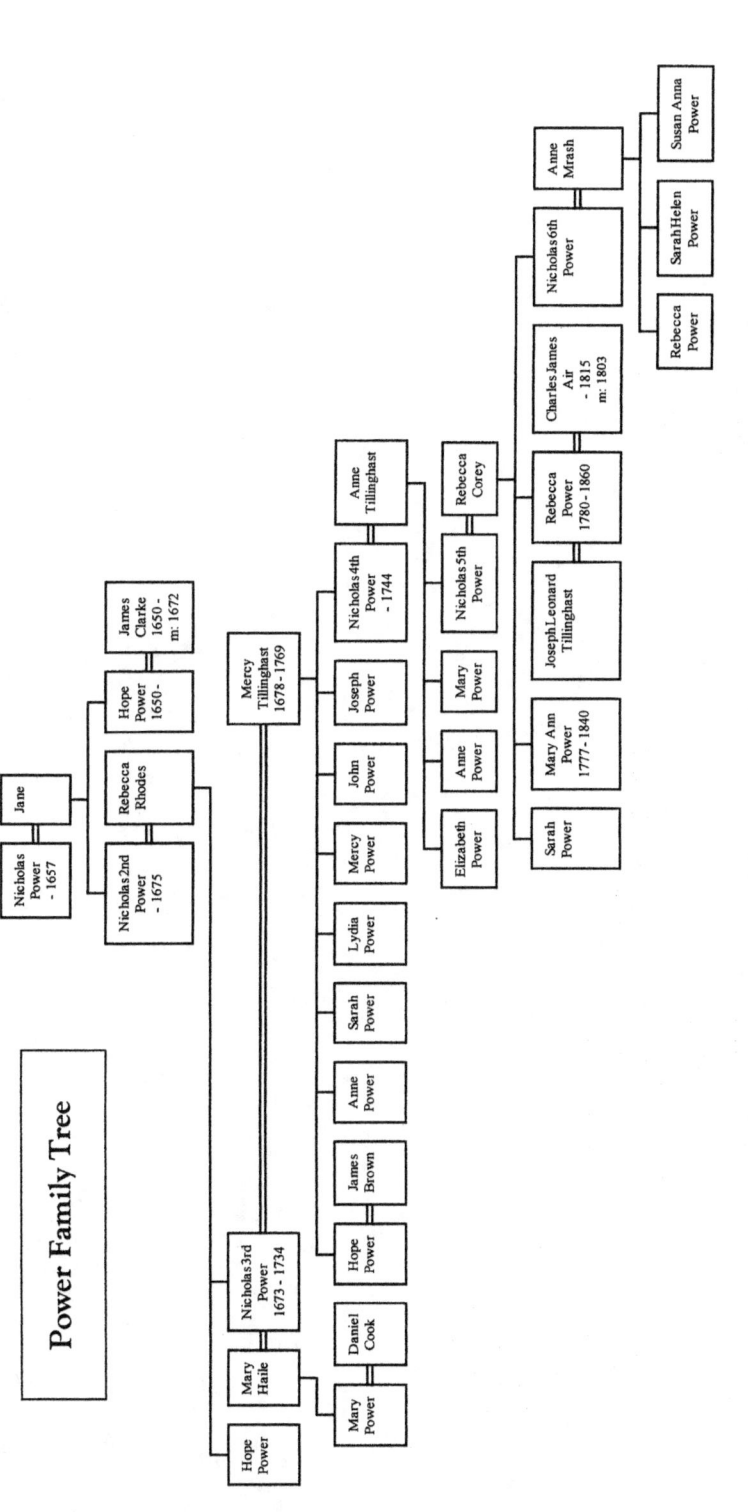

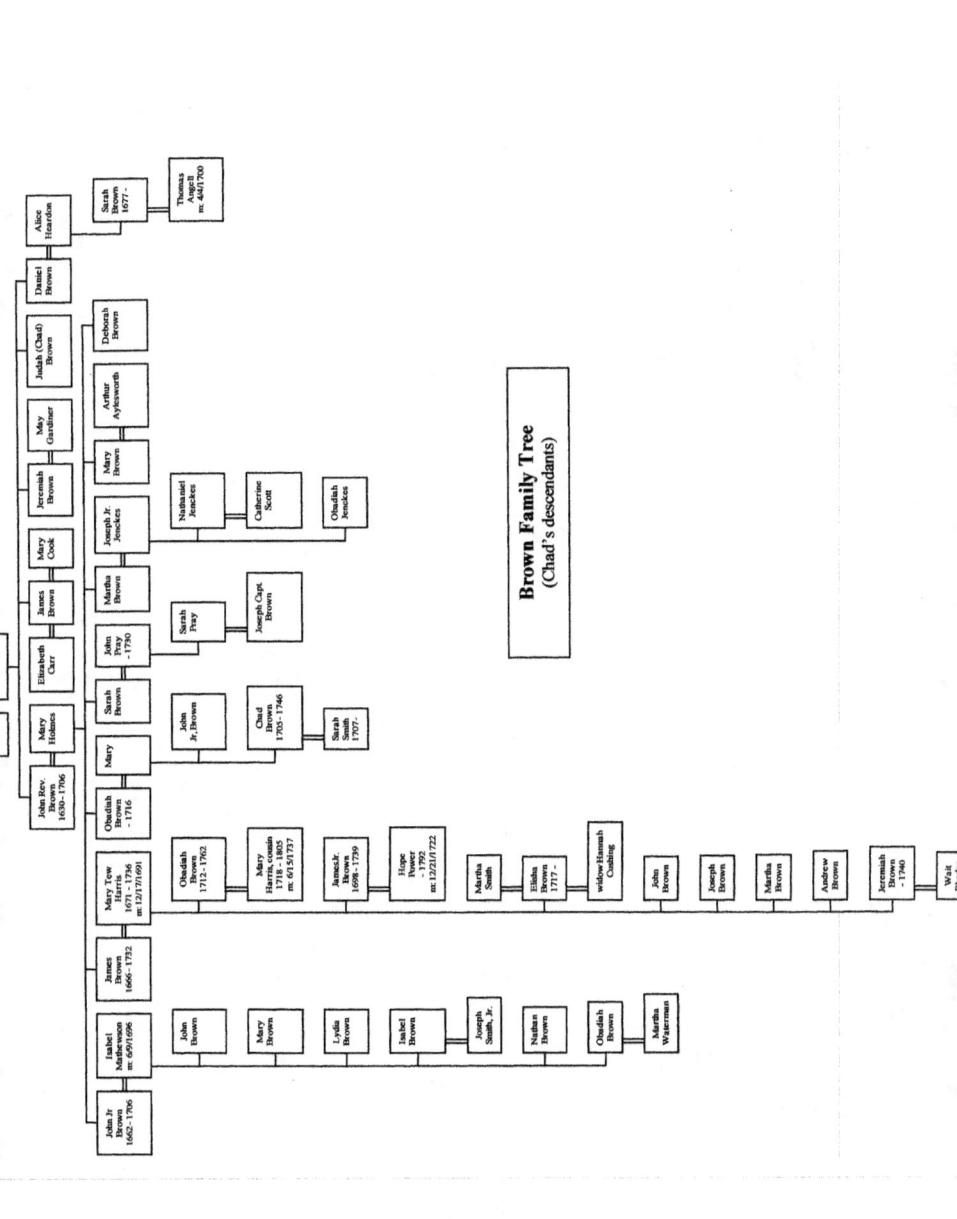

Brown Family Tree
(Chad's descendants)

Resources
(complete citations for quotes in text)

Arnold, Elisha S., *The Arnold Memorial, 1587-1675,* ©1935.

Arnold, Samuel Greene, *History of the State of Rhode Island and Providence Plantations,* Vols. 1 & 2, 1636-1700, Appleton & Co., NY, ©1859.

Bartlett, Irving H., *From Slave to Citizen: The Story of the Negro in Rhode Island,* Urban League of RI, Providence, ©1954.

Bellesilies, Michael, author of article on Arnold, V.1, p. 637, in *American National Biographies,* Oxford Univ. Press, NY, ©1999.

Bicknell, Thomas W., *History of the State of Rhode Island,* V. 1, ©1920.

Biographical: History of State of RI and Providence Plantations, NY American Historical Society, ©1920.

Blockson, Charles L,. *Hippocrene Guide to The Underground Railroad,* Hippocrene Books, New York, ©1994.

Booth, Sally Smith, *Hung, Strung, & Potted: a History of Eating in Colonial America,* Clarkson N. Potter, Inc., ©1971.

Booth, Sally Smith, *The Women of '76,* Hastings House Publishers, ©1973.

Brookhiser, *Founding Father: Rediscovering George Washington,* Simon & Schuster, ©1996.

Carroll, Charles, *Public Education in Rhode Island,* Freeman Co., ©1918.

Chapin, Howard M., *Documentary History of Rhode Island,* Preston & Rounds Co., ©1916.

Chapin, Howard M., *Our Rhode Island Ancestors* (no date or publisher listed).

Christianson, Scott, *With Liberty for Some: 500 years of Imprisonment in America*, Northeastern University Press, ©1998.

Church, Colonel Benjamin, *Diary of King Philip's War 1675-76*, The Pequot Press, ©1975.

Clauson, J. Earl, *These Plantations*, Roger Williams Press, ©1937.

Conley, Patrick T., *An Album of Rhode Island History, 1636-1986*, RI Publications Society, ©1986.

Conley, Patrick T., *First in War, Last in Peace*, RI Publications Society, ©1987.

Conley, Patrick T., *Liberty and Justice: A History of Law and Lawyers in Rhode Island, 1636-1998*, Rhode Island Publications Society ©1998.

Conley, Patrick T., *The State Houses of Rhode Island*, RI Publications Society ©1988.

Coughtry, Jay, *The Notorious Triangle: Rhode Island and the African Slave Trade, 1700-1807*, Temple University Press, ©1981.

Daughters of the American Revolution, *Minority Military Service, RI. 1775-1783*, National Society, 1988 (6 pages)

Davis, Hadassah (translated & edited), *What Cheer, Netop! Selections from A Key into the Language of America by Roger Williams*, Haffenreffer Museum of Anthropology, Brown University, ©1986.

DePauw, Linda Grant & K. Conover Hunt, *"Remember the Ladies": 1750-1815*, ©1976 by The Pilgrim Society. Viking Penguin, a division of Penguin Putnam, Inc.

Dexter, Elizabeth Anthony, *Colonial Women of Affairs: A Study of Women in Business & the Professions Before 1776*, ©1924 by Houghton Mifflin.

Earle, Alice Morse, *Child Life in Colonial Days*, Macmillan, ©1957.

Earle, Alice Morse, *Home Life In Colonial Days*, (NY Macmillan, 1948) ©Scribner, a Division of Simon & Schuster, Inc.

Field, Edward, editor, *State of Rhode Island and Providence Plantations at the End of the Century: a History*, Vols. 1, 2 & 3, Mason Publishing Co., ©1902.

Garland, Joseph, *To Meet These Wants: The Story of Rhode Island Hospital*, RI Hospital, 1963 & 1988.

Gowdy Collection: Vol. 17, "52 Power Street," Research notes available in notebooks, RIHS Library.

Greene, Robert Ewell, *Black Courage, 1775-1783*, National Society of the Daughters of the American Revolution, (especially note Appendix), ©1984.

Greene, Richard A., *Rhode Island Prisons, 1638-1848: A History*, unpublished Masters Thesis, University of Rhode Island, ©1963.

Haley, John William, *"Old Stone Bank" History of Rhode Island*, Providence Institution for Savings, Vols. I-IV, 1929, 1931, 1939, 1944 & Old Stone Bank, "R.I. Portrait in Sound," a script written by Florence Markoff for his radio program, 1975.

Hawes, Alexander Boyd, *Off Soundings: Aspects of the Maritime History of Rhode Island*, Posterity Press, MD, ©1999.

Hedges, James B., *The Browns of Providence Plantations*, Harvard University Press, Cambridge, ©1952.

Higginson, Thomas W., *History of the Public School Systems of Rhode Island: 1636-1876*, Publisher not given (1876).

Holliday, Carl, *Woman's Life in Colonial Days*, Frederick Ungar Publishing Co., ©1922.

Hopkins, Charles Wyman, *The Home Lots of the Early Settlers of the Providence Plantations*, Providence Press Co., ©1886.

Hymowitz, Carol & Weissman, Michaele, *A History of Women in America*, Bantam Books, Inc., ©1978.

James, Sydney V., *John Clarke and His Legacies: Religion and Law in Colonial Rhode Island, 1638-1750*, Pennsylvania State University Press, ©1999.

James, Sydney V., *Colonial Rhode Island: a History*, Charles Scribner's Sons, ©1975.[© held by author's widow]

Kimball, Gertrude Selwyn, *Providence in Colonial Times*, Houghton Mifflin Co., ©1912.

Lancaster, Jane, "An ornament and honor to their sex", ©1994.

Letters of Three Dutiful & Affectionate Children to their Honoured Parents [Browns], Boston, ©1904.

McLoughlin William G., *Rhode Island: A Bicentennial History*, W.W. Norton & Co., Inc, NY, ©1978.

Melish, Joanne Pope, *Disowning Slavery: Gradual Emancipation and "Race" in New England, 1780-1860*, ©1998 by Cornell University. Permission by publisher Cornell University Press.

Miner, George Leland, *Angell's Lane: The History of a Little Street in Providence*, Akerman-Standard Press, ©1948. (An extensive search for publisher, author or heirs has not revealed a copyright holder)

Miner, Lilian Burleigh, *Our State of Rhode Island*, Oxford Press, ©1925.

Miner, Ward L., *William Goddard, Newspaperman*, ©1962, Duke University Press, Durham, NC.

Norton, Mary Beth, *Founding Mothers & Fathers: Gendered Power and the Forming of American Society*, Alfred Knopf, ©1996.

Norton, Mary Beth, *Liberty's Daughters: The Revolutionary Experience of American Women, 1750-1800*, Little, Brown & Co. ©1980.

Palmer, Henrietta R. (ed.), *Rhode Island Tales: Depicting Social Life During the Colonial, Revolutionary and Post-Revolutionary Era*, The Purdy Press, ©1928.

Plimpton, Ruth Talbot, *Mary Dyer: Biography of a Rebel Quaker*, Branden Publishing Co, ©1994.

Printers and Printing in Providence, 1762-1907, published by the Printers' Union, ©1907.

Richman, Irving Berdine, *Rhode Island: A Study in Separatism*, Houghton, Mifflin & Co., ©1905.

Rider, Sidney S., *The Lands of Rhode Island as they were known to Caunounicus and Miantunnomu when Roger Williams came in 1636*, published by the author, 1904. He quotes Williams' book, *Key to Indian Language* and a number of other sources.

R.I. Short Story Club (written by member of), *Revolutionary Portraits: People, Places and Events from RI's Historic Past*, RI Bicentennial Foundation, 1976. (© held by Patrick T. Conley)

Rogers, Horatio, *Mary Dyer of Rhode Island: The Quaker Martyr that was Hanged on Boston Common.*, Preston & Rounds, ©1896.

Savage, James, *History of New England, 1630-1649*, Little, Brown & Co., Boston, ©1853.

Schlesinger, Arthur M., *The Birth of the Nation*, Alfred A. Knopf, Inc., ©1968.

Simister, Florence Parker, *The Fire's Center: RI in the Revolutionary Era, 1763-1790*, RI Bicentennial Foundation ©1979. (© held by Patrick T. Conley)

Simister, Florence Parker, *Streets of the City: An Anecdotal History*, Mowbray Co. Publishers, Prov, © Simister 1968.

Smith, Page, *Daughters of the Promised Land: Women in American History*, Little, Brown & Co., ©1970.

Staples, William R., *Annals of the Town of Providence from its first settlement to the Organization of the City Government in June 1832*, Knowles & Vose, ©1843.

Stewart, Rowena, Lawrence Sykes (designer), *A Heritage Discovered, Blacks in Rhode Island*, R I Black Heritage Society, (no date).

Terhune, Albert Payson, *Stories of the Super-Women*, NY ©1916.

Ulrich, Laurel Thatcher, *Good Wives: Image and Reality in the Lives of Women in Northern New England, 1650-1750*, © 1980,1982 by Laurel Thatcher Ulrich. Used by permission of Alfred A. Knopf, a division of Random House, Inc.

Uroff, Margaret Dickie, Maps by Raymond Houlihan, *Becoming a City: From Fishing Village to Manufacturing Center*, Harcourt, Brace & World, Inc., ©1968.

Weeden, William B., *Early Rhode Island: A Social History of the People*, The Grafton Press, NY, ©1910.

Williams, Roger, Correspondence of, VII, 1654-1682, Brown University Press/ University of New England, 1988.

Wilson, Arthur Edward, *Weybosset Bridge in Providence Plantations*, Pilgrim Press, ©1947.

Women in R.I. History: Making a Difference, first published in observance of Women's History Month, as a series in the *Providence Journal-Bulletin* throughout March 1994.

Woodward, Carl R., *Plantation in Yankeeland*, The Pequot Press, Inc., ©1971. (© held by Cocumscussoc Association, Smith's Castle)

Yeaton, Mary, Project Director, *Underground Railroad in New England*, the American Revolution Bicentennial Administration, Region 1 ©1976.

Rhode Island Historical Society Publications

Brown, Henry A. L. & Richard J. Walton, *John Brown's Tract: Lost Adirondack Empire*, RIHS, ©1988.

Cady, John Hutchins, *Rhode Island History*, a quarterly, RI Historical Society, Vol. VIII, 1/19/1949, #1, "Weybosset Bridge".

Cole, John N., *Rhode Island History*, a quarterly, RI Historical Society, Vol. 57, #2, May 1999, "Henry Marchant's Journal, 1771-1772".

Levin, Linda Lotridge (ed.) *Providence: from Provincial Village to Prosperous Port, 1750-1790*, RI Historical Society, 1978

Diaries/Letters/Miscellaneous (Rhode Island Historical Society/RIHS)

Baker, Betsy Metcalf (1798-1804) Papers. Extracts from Memoir: mss 9001-B and letter dated 1858, in *Miscellaneous Manuscripts Collection.*

"Brown Family Paper Project," first draft," RIHS.

Brown, Henry A.L. Deposit, two letters by Anna and Elisa Bowen to Abigail Goddard, on deposit at RIHS, located in subgroup 6, folder 3. (✻Permission to use granted by Henry A.L. Brown, © owner.)

Brown, James (1698-1739) Papers. Letter to his wife, Hope Brown, August 23, 1737.

Carpenter, Alice, Furniture inventory, March 1796, Rhode Island Manuscripts, Vol. 1, p. 131

Carter Jenckes, Rebecca (Diary, 1794: mss336, Copybook, 1791 & an array of miscellaneous undated notes). Also her sister, Huldah Carter's, Arithmetic Book in the *Carter-Danforth Papers.*

Chace, Henry R. (1859-1916), Several notes/essays he wrote after retirement, on Olney's Tavern, Liberty Tree, Doctors, Peddlers, Dances, Old Providence. In *Chace Papers*, Box 2, Folder 12, MSS 338.

Dexter, Alice, Marriage Agreement to Jos. Jenckes, January 27, 1726/7, *Misc. MSS Collection*, D-523.

Duncan, Susanna Lear, June-August, 1788 (Diary: *Misc. MSS Collection* 9001-L)

Fenner, Arthur Memorial, 2/2/1788, Deed to Howlong 1690, & Accot. of his death, *RIHS Manuscripts*, Vol. XIV, p. 105.

Herreshoff, Sarah (Sally) Brown, Diary April-June, 1796 (: mss487S2) and correspondence with her father and brother, *Herreshoff-Lewis Family Papers*.

Martin, Julia Bowen, Diary, April-July, 1799, *Martin Family Papers*, mss 999) Also see, *A Guide to Women's Diaries* in the Manuscript Collection of the RIHS by Rick Stattler (unpublished typescript)

Olney, Rachel, , Death Inquest, June 1760 in the *Miscellaneous Manuscripts Collection*.

Tillinghast, Lydia, Letters to Capt. Robert Gray, dated 3/18/1807 (v.4, p.226) and an undated letter to her son, Jonathan (v. 4, p. 234), *Tillinghast Papers*.

Whipple, Lydia, Letter from Duncan Miacum (Macomb), 4/18/1700, *RIHS Manuscripts*, v.1, p. 85.

Whipple, Rebecca, Letters to John Whipple, 1692, *RIHS Manuscripts*, v.1, pp. 69-70.

Genealogies

Anthony, Bertha Williams, *Roger Williams of Providence*, V II, 1966.

Austin, John Osborn, *One Hundred and Sixty Allied Families*, Genealogical Publishing Co. Inc., Baltimore, 1977.

Binney, Charles James Fox, *Genealogy of the Binney Family in U.S.*, 1886.

Blackstone, John Wilford, *Lineage & History of William Blackstone*, 1907.

Chad Brown Workbook: Descendents of Chad Brown, 2nd Edition, 1987.

Cafferty, Edward H., *Fenner & Allied Families*, 1988: Supplement, 1990.

Clark, Bertha Winifred, "Christopher Holder" (6 typed pages).

Clark, Bertha W., "Richard and Katherine Scott" (1955, typed carbon).

Cole, Frank T., *The Early Genealogies of the Cole Families in America*, 1887.

Colket, Meredith B. *The Marbury Ancestry*, 1936.

Descendants of Roger Williams, Book 1, The Waterman & Winsor Lines through his daughter Mercy Williams, Gateway Press, Inc. 1991.

Dyer, William Allan (compiled by), *A Dyer Genealogical Record*, 1940.

Genealogies of Rhode Island Families, Genealogical Publishing Co. 1983, Vols. I & II, 1983.

Farnham, Charles William, *John Smith, Miller of Providence, RI*, 1966.

Goddard Book, Vols. I & II, compiled by John W. Harmes, Gateway Press, Inc. Baltimore, 1990.

Green, Gen. George Sears, *Greenes of RI*, N.Y. 1903.

Holman, Winifred L (compiled by), *The Angell Line*, 1944.

Jacobus, Donald L. & Edgar F. Waterman, *Waterman Family, Vol. III, Descendants of Richard Waterman of Providence RI*, 1954.

Newton, Clair, *Capt. John Whipple & Descendents.*

Olney, James H., *The Genealogy of Thomas Olney*, 1889.

Pardon Tillinghast (Elder): His Ancestors and Some of his Descendants, compiled by Charles T. Straight, 1923.

Peckham, Stephen, "Richard Scott & his Wife Catherine Marbury and Some of Their Descendants" (pps. 168–175 extant only, source unstated).

Powers, Franklin E., *A Genealogical Record of the Power Families*, and *"One Line of the Power Family"* by John O. Austin.

Rhodes, Nelson Osgood, *Genealogy of Zachariah Rhodes of RI*.

"Richard Scott of RI & His Pedigree" (carbon, typed).

Roger Williams Family Association, #26, March 1955.

Root, *Genealogy of the Fenner Family*.

Other Primary Sources

Early Records of Town of Providence, Vols. VI, IX, & XV, 1899.

Providence Gazette and Country Journal, miscellaneous editions.

Records of the Colony of Rhode Island in New England, Vol. 1, 1636-1663, compiled by John Russell Bartlett, NY, 1856.

Rhode Island Court Records of the Court of Trials of the Colony of Providence Plantations, V. 1, 1647-1662, & V. 2, 1662-1670, Providence 1920 & 1922.

Credits/Sources of Illustrations

#1, "Indian Broiling Fish," from *What Cheer, Netop!*, pub. by Haffenreffer, 1986; no credit given;

#2, Hopkins, "Plan of First Division of Home Lots, Providence, RI, 1886," Ink on Paper Map BBRI County/Town Maps 33205, courtesy of Rhode Island Historical Society;

#3, "Providence Cove, 1636," from Miner, *Angell's Lane*, 1948; unable to locate pub., author or relatives;

#4, "Blackstone on his Tame Bull" & #27, "Madam 'Betsy' Jumel," from Terhune, *Stories of the Super-Women*, 1916;

#5, "Dexter-Jencks: Pre-Marriage Contract, 1726," #6, "Arthur Fenner Will: About 1703," #7, "Rachel Olney Inquest: 1760," & #12, "Alice Carpenter Inventory, 1796," RIHS manuscripts, courtesy of RIHS;

#8, "Whipping Quakers in Streets," BE031231, ©Bettmann/CORBIS, courtesy of Bettmann/CORBIS;

#9, "Mary Dyer, Quaker, Before the Judges," by Edwin Austin Abbey, courtesy of Social Law Library;

#10, Morden, "New England (Massachusetts, Rhode Island, Connecticut), (United States-North America), 1690," Photostat Map Chamin I xii, RI v. 1 p. 12, courtesy of RIHS;

#11, Strock, "Death of King Philip," courtesy of Haffenreffer Museum of Anthropology;

#13, John Hutchins Cady, "Weybosset Bridge and Vicinity Providence, RI 1711-1940," ink & paper Cady map, 32243, courtesy of RIHS;

#14, "Notorious Triangle" & #18, "Blacks Working at Wharf," from Stewart, *A Heritage Discovered: Blacks in RI*, courtesy of RI Black Heritage Society;

#15, "Slaving Voyagers: Percent by Port" & #16, "Voyages/# of Slaves by Year: 1709-1807" from Coughtry, *The Notorious Triangle*, courtesy of Coughtry;

#17, Historical Society of Pennsylvania (HSP), "Slave Ship," engraving from *The Mirror of Misery*, or *Tyranny Exposed* (LCP Am1811 Mirj. Courtesy of HSP;

#19. "Gaspee Newspaper articles," from June 13, 1772 edition of *Providence Gazette*;

#20, "Fort & Beacon," from Simister, *The Fire's Center*, (©Conley) artist, Edward Field, , by permission of Conley; #21, The "Black Regiment" & #22, "British Rob Women," from Simister, *The Fire's Center*, (©Conley), drawing from calendar issued by Commonwealth Land Title Co, 1926, by permission of Conley;

#23, "Population Table: 1776," prepared by author, Barbara Mills; from figures by Foster and Seamans found in Levin, *Providence: from Provincial Village to Prosperous Port.*

#24, "Brown University: Revolutionary War," from Simister, *The Fire's Center,* (©Conley), sketch by John Groen, private collection of Florence Simister, by permission of Conley;

#25, William Terry, "Mansion House, Providence, RI 1831," engraving, courtesy of RIHS;

#26, Edward Greene Malbone, "Sarah Brown (1773-1846)," 1795 Watercolor on Ivory Painting, Museum Coll. 1972.21.2, courtesy of RIHS;

#28, John Hutchins Cady, "Providence in 1759," Providence, RI 1936. Ink on Paper Map, courtesy of RIHS;

#29, Daniel Anthony "Map of Providence, 1823," Engraving Map, Providence County, Providence RI #54 G33231, courtesy of RIHS.

Acknowledgements

The author wishes to express a special thanks to her daughter, Susan, and to Eileen Mullen from our Women's Book Group for their reading and suggestions of an early draft; to Eleanor Boudreau Goodge and Barbara Bruce Stoddard, classmates at Brown University, for their helpful critiques of a later version; and, finally, to Robin Flynn and Lori Salotto at the Rhode Island Historical Society for critiquing a near-final version. I also want to thank the staffs at the Rhode Island Historical Society Library and the Cranston Public Library for their help in locating needed books and other materials.

INDEX

----, Amelia 259 Betsey 175 Catharine 106 Crazy Cate 340 Esther 174 Job 338 Juliet 314 Nathaniel 218 Philippi 361 Ruth 297-298 Sally 175 Silas 265 Ward 279
ABBOT, Daniel Jr 156
ABBOTT, Daniel 195 Mary 67 195
ABIGAIL, Queen In Africa 191
ABOLITION SOCIETY, Of Providence 185
ADIRONDACK MOUNTAINS, 315
AFRICA, 190
AFRICANS, As Resisting Slavehood 221
ALEXANDER, 121
ALLEN, 190 Samuel 343
ALMANACS, 243 371
ALMEY, Anna 225 Sarah 224-225 William 224
ALMSHOUSE, The First 337
ALTHAM, Joan 6
AMUSEMENTS, Of Young Persons 240
ANGELL, 73 137 Abigail 252-253 Abraham 149 Alice 58-59 Deborah 59 Hope 58-59 James 253-255 Marie 327 Mary 253 Nathan 244 Sarah 173 Thomas 12 14 25 57-59 116 253
ANTHONY, Bertha 143
APPRENTICESHIPS, 153
AQUIDNACK ISLAND, 137
AQUIDNECK, 124
AQUIDNECK ISLAND, 15
ARNOLD, 68 141 Benedict 56-57 Christian 55-57 Damaris 56 Elizabeth 55 170 565 James 367 Joane 169 Joanna 146 167 Jonathan 57 362-363 Joseph 367 Mary 367 Mrs 375 Pink 331 Prime 331

ARNOLD (Cont.)
Richard 327 Samuel 57 Stephen 56 Waite 293 William 25 55-57 70 77 146 169 378
ARTICLES OF CONFEDERATION, 275
ASHTON, Alice 58 James 58 156 Marie 58 72 Mary 72
ASPINWALL, William 87
ASSEMBLY, 276
ATWELL, Sally 365
BAKER, Betsy 156 Obed 156
BALLARD, Rebekah 337
BALLOU, 344 Freelove 343 Reuben 343
BALTIMORE, 250 254
BAPTIST, 62 78
BAPTISTS, 76
BARBADOS, 222 As A Slave Route 181
BARNARD, Dr 363 365-366 Maraschell 8 Mary 5-6 Richard 6
BARRETT, Maria 90 Mary 90
BARRINGTON, Lady 5
BARTLETT, 180 192-193 Charles 367 Dr 363
BATTLE OF RHODE ISLAND, 274
BAY, Colony 322
BEACONS, To Signal Danger 273

BEERE, Henry 107 Patience 107
BEGGERLY, Alice 361 Richard 361
BELLINGHAM, Mr 101
BERNON, Eve 189 Gabriel 189
BERNOON, Emanuel 189 Manna 189 Mary 189
BETS, Black 341
BIBLE, 85 227 359 As The Only Book 32
BICK, James 334
BICKNELL, 13 23 25-26 29 31 55
BILL OF RIGHTS, 120
BINNEY, Avis 200-201 Barnabas 201-202 Mary 201-202
BLACK REGIMENT, 274
BLACKBURNE, John Lynn 259
BLACKSTONE, 48 Catherine 51 John 50-51 John Wilford 49-50 Sarah 49-50 William 47 49-50 338 378
BLACKSTONE'S MEADOW, 50
BONAPARTE, 347
BOONE, Anne 317
BOOTH, 17 38
BORDEN, Dinah 66 Mary 66 71 Thomas 66 71
BORDER DISPUTES, 112
BORDERS, Internal And External Disputes 121

Index

BOSTON TEA PARTY, 270
BOSWORTH, Edward 193
BOUNDARIES, Disputes 119 Establishment 119
BOWEN, Anna 209 Anna H 344 Betsy 341-344 Col 253 Dr 263-264 363 Elisa 209-210 Emma A 344 Ephraim 262 266 362 Ephraim Jr 173 Ephraim Sr 173 George 348 George Washington 343-344 Gov 200 Jabez 213 296 362 John 342-343 Julia 172 174-175 224 Lavinia Ballou 343 Mary Cooke 331 Misses 293 Oliver 331 Phoebe 341-343 Polly 342 Richard 362 Sarah 173 William 213 367
BOWERS, Caleb 258 Mr 215
BOWLER, Margaret 341
BRADFORD, William 238
BRENTON, Eliza C 306
BRETT, Mary 311
BRIGATINE, Seaflower 180
BRIGGS, Isaac 286 Joan 328 Nathaniel 186
BRINLEY, Frances 69
BROWN, 291 369 374 Abigail 204 208-209 211 Alice 175 204 211 Amey 143 Anna 212 218-219 223 Anne 211 Avis 201-202 373 Betsey 174 Chad 143 194-195 203 336 Charles 202 Dorcas 224-225 Elizabeth 194-195 203-204 206 336 Hallelujah 73 Hope 164 168 196-200 202-203 James 194-198 202-206 240 376 James 2nd 195 James 3rd 196 John 143 149 168 194-196 204 207-208 211-212 219 232 266 308 311-312 315 336 John Jr 143 Joseph 149 164 168 196 203-204 206 208 212 223 Mary 143 195-196 198 203 223-224 Miss 258 Moses 137 149 174-175 195-196 198 212-218 220-221 223-225 233 255 258 296 308 371 375-376 Mrs 368 Nancy 218 Nathaniel 159 161 363 Nicholas 149 196 198 200-202 211-212 222-223 373 Nicholas 2nd 164

BROWN (Cont.)
  Nicholas Jr 199
  Nicholas Sr 164 O 210
  Obadiah 143 196-198
  212-213 218 Obadiah
  Moses 219 224-225
  Obediah 195 212
  Phebe 175 219 224
  Rebecca 107 Rhoda
  198-201 Richard 52
  Sally 302 312-313
  Sarah 202 204-208
  211 219 224-225 240
  313 315 Sherburne
  302 Waite 172
BROWN UNIVERSITY,
  195 199 255 294 307
  369
BROWNE, Nathaniel 157
BUCKLIN, Nancy 366
BUISINESSWOMAN, The
  Colony's First 61
BULL, Henry 349
BURDEN, Anne 92-93
BURGLARY, First
  Recorded 326
BURIAL GROUND, North
  136 169 195
BURR, Aaron 344 347
  Betsy 347-348
BUSINESS, Mercantile
  157
BUTLER, Miss 313
BUTTERWORTH, Sarah
  164-165
CABINS, Settlers' First 22
CAMBRIDGE, 279

CANDLE-MAKING, 206
  Description And
  History Of 203
CAPITAL, On Potomac
  Not New York Or
  Philadelphia 276
CARDER, Susanna 63
CARIBBEAN ISLANDS,
  176
CARPENTER, 57 Alice
  151 Benedict 55
  Elizabeth 55-56
  Ephraim 71 Joane 55-
  56 Stephen 55
  Susanna 71 William
  25 55-56 70 125
  William Jr 125
CARPINTOR, Comfort
  197
CARROLL, 316
CARTER, 254 Amey 158
  256 Ann 257 Huldah
  256 John 158 245 248
  253 255-256 Rebecca
  257-259
CATHOLIC, 7
CAZNEAU, Miss 217 Mr
  215
CELEBRATIONS, 295
CEMETERY, Trinity
  Church 348
CHACE, 213 216 A 259
  Dr 366 Henry 212
CHAMPLAIN, Margaret
  296
CHAMPLIN, Margaret
  292 Mary 292

Index

CHARLES I, 7 King 91
CHARLES II, 119 King 105 117
CHARLES X, King Of France 347
CHARTER, 1638 119 1644 112 1663 119 121 Second 112
CHAUNCY, Walter 45
CHECKLEY, John 195
CHEESE, Cheshire 108
CHILDREN, Died In Infancy 59 Died Young 59 Illegitimate And Policy Toward 337-339 Illegitimate And Policy Toward 342-343
CHINA, 212
CHORES, Household 40-41
CHRISTMAS, 16
CHURCH, And State Separation 76 80 And Wives Membership 79 Anglican 7 237 Baptist 42 67 73 164 194 199 Baptist Description Of 163 Benjamin 131 Bethel A M E 220 Capt 130 Christian 91 Congregational 229 237 294 First Baptist 63 King's 27 237 310 Of England 8 10 Presbyterian 237 Providence Baptist 142 Puritan 7

CHURCH (Cont.) Saint Johns 27 Salem 10 27 Sally 293 St Peter's 346 St. John's 259
CLARKE, 88 120 Content 138 Elizabeth 113 117 358-359 Freeborn 140 Hannah 107 138 360 Hope 167 James 167 Jane 359 Jeremiah 362 John 87 113-114 117 167 325 357-359 Jonathan 343 Mary 362 Mercy 360 Phoebe 343 Sarah 140 359-360 Sarah Davis 360 Simon 360 Thomas 360 Walter 107 138-140 362
CLIFTON, Hope 100 106
COAST, African 197 Windward 197
CODDINGTON, 88 112 114 William 87
COKE, Edward 4
COLE, John 89 Robert 25 Samuel 89 Susanna 89
COLLEGE, Baptist 308
COLLWELL, Margrett 330 Robert 330
COLMAN, Dr 172
COLONIAL ASSEMBLY, 116
COLONY HOUSE, 310

COMMERCE, Providence 158
CONANICUT ISLAND, 15
CONCORD, Battle Of 272
CONGRESS, 188 223 275 283 U S 212
CONLEY, Patrick 298
CONNECTICUT, 303 Border Disputes With 304
CONSTITUTION, Federal 300
CONTINENTAL ARMY, 273
CONTINENTAL CONGRESS, 251 272 297
CONTINENTAL CONVENTIONS, 232
CONTINENTAL LOAN CERTIFICATES, Paid To Slave-Masters 275
COOK, Violet 368
COOKING, 35-39 Utensils 32
COREY, Rebecca 169
CORLIS, 213
CORNWALLIS, 282
CORY, Rebecca 169
COTTON, John 84
COUGHTRY, Jay 178
COURT, U S Circuit 348 U S Supreme 348
COURT HOUSE, 195
COVE, The Great Salt 22
COWDALL, Joan 333 John 333

CRANSTON, Gov 161 John 157 362 Mary 139 362 Samuel 138-139 362
CRAWFORD, 190 Amey 158 256 Freelove 157 256 259 Gideon 156-157 256 Huldah 307 James 157 John 158 John Jr 158 Mr 172 Susannah 307 William 149 157
CROESE, Gerald 90
CROIX, 345 Peter 344
CROMWELL, Oliver 5 117
CUMBERLAND ISLAND, 285
CURTICE, Abigail 337
CUSHNO, Isaac 370
DANCES, Popular At Time 293
DANIELS, Alice 27 361
DAUGHTERS OF LIBERTY, 262 Actions Of 263-264 270 298
DAUGHTERS OF THE AMERICAN REVOLUTION, 348
DAVICE, Abigail 327
DAVIES, Simon 172
DAVIS, Nicholas 359 Sarah 359
DEBROGLIE, Prince 292
DECLARATION OF BREDA, 119

Index

DECLARATION OF INDEPENDENCE, 251 272 300
DEED, Dated March 24 1638 20
DELAFAYETTE, Marquis 374
DELAWARE BAY, 218
DEPONCEAU, 280
DEWOLFE, Capt 185 James 184 John 232 Mark Anthony 193
DEXTER, 126 A 257-258 Abby 259 Abigail 170 172 Alice 53 Edward 149 Gregory 73 172 John 322 Knight 244 Stephen 170 172
DICKENS, Joane 27 Nathaniel 27
DIEHL, Pat 13
DISTILLERS, 176
DIVORCE, 331 333 359 And The General Assembly 332
DOCTORS, 361-369
DORR, 136
DOUGLASS, Frederick 234
DOWAGER, Queen Of Denmark 266
DRYDEN, Bridget 82 Erasmus 82 John 82
DUDINGSTON, William 266
DUGGLASS, Joanna 153
DUNCAN, Susan 373

DUNCAN (Cont.) Susanna 373-376
DURBY, Francis 333
DUTCH, Colony 21
DYER, 88 114 Anne 90 93 Catharine 84 Charles 91 93 Elizabeth 106 Henry 93 Maher 93 Maria 90 Mary 82 84-86 88-90 90-94 100-102 104- 106 113 357 Samuel 90 93 105 W 101 Will 93 102 Will Jr 101 William 86 90 93 105- 106 113 William Allan 91
EDDY, Capt 177 Martha 308
EDWARD, Sir 7
ELECTIONS, Annual 119
ELIZABETH, Queen 10
ELLERY, Misses 292
ELTON, Ann 328-329
ENDICOTT, Gov 93 102 104 John 49 99
ENGLAND, King Of 44
ENGLISH, William 182
ENGLISH SLAVER, Brookes 181
ENGS, Avis 201
EPIDEMICS, 363-368
ESCAPES, Of Prisoners 354
EXPORTING TRADE, 157
FAIRCHILD, Margaret 341

FALL, River 220
FANSHER, Sylvanus 365
FENNER, 213 Alice 66
  Arthur 63-67 74 140
  156-157 365 Arthur Jr
  65 Dinah 66-67
  Eleazar 67 Freelove 67
  157 256 Gov 301
  Howlong 64-65 67
  John 67 219-220
  Joseph 67 Mary 65 67
  74 Mehitabel 63 67
  365 Phebe 219 Polly
  65 Richard 67 Sarah
  67 Thomas 66-67 74
  William 66
FERRY, The Old South
  110
FEVER, Malignant 367
  Pestilential 367 Putrid
  367 Yellow 367-368
FFENER, Arthur 65
  Dinah 66
FFENNER, Thomas 65
FIELD, 71 105 316 320
  Thomas 63 William 56
  Zachariah 156
FIGHT, Great Swamp
  123-124
FINES, And Imprisonment
  95 99-100
FIREHOUSE, 237
FISKE, Dr 362
FLAGG, M 217
FLETCHER, Jane 359
FOSTER, Mrs 366 Sally
  313 Theodore 289 365

FOX, 92 George 91 105
  359
FRANCIS, Abby 210
  Abigail 209 211 Anne
  211 John 209 211
  John Jr 211
FRANKLIN, Ann 245-246
  Ben 246 265
  Benjamin 238 245 254
  262 James 245-246
FRENCH ALLIANCE,
  Signing Of 280
FRENCH OCCUPATION,
  293
FRIENDS MEETING
  HOUSE, 256
FROG POND, 101
FRY, Eleanor 264
FURNACE, Pig Iron 212
GALLOWAY, Joseph 248
GAOL, 342 Towne Street
  310
GAOLS, Inadequate 353
GARDINER, Hannah 231
GARRATT, William 334
GARRISH, Mr 258
GAY, Lucy 154
GENEALOGIES, 144
GENERAL ASSEMBLY,
  232-233 239 272 274
  289 308 And Divorce
  332 And The Code Of
  Law 325 Code Of Laws
  Based On Laws Of
  England 322 Rhode
  Island 180
GEORGE III, King 272

Index

GEORGIA, 283
GERMANY, 314
GIBBS, Dr 362 James 164 Rebecca 337 Sarah 368
GOAT ISLAND, 43 108
GODDARD, 262 313 Abbie Angell 255 Abigail 209 252-255 Ann Elizabeth 255 Giles 238 Mary Angell 255 Mary Katherine 238 244 248 250-254 Sarah 237-238 244-245 247-249 Sarah Updike 255 William 237-238 240-241 243-245 248-256
GODFREY, Cleb 177 John 196
GOLDEN BALL INN, 301 344
GOODWIN, Adam 336 Margaret 336
GORTON, Samuel 46 325
GOULD, John 140 Sarah 140
GRAHAM, John 283
GRAY, Robert 166
GREAT AWAKENING, 226
GREAT SALT RIVER, 22
GREEN, Alice 27 Eleazer 335 John Sr 27
GREENE, 137 276 Alice 361 Catherine 278-280 282-285

GREENE (Cont.) Christopher 274 Cornelia Lott 281 Gen 286 George Washington 279 285 Jacob 279 Joan 361 John Sr 25 361 Katy 278 280-281 284 Louisa Catherine 282 Martha Washington 286 Mr 77 Nathanael 279 281 283-284 Nathanael Ray 282 Nathaniel 278 Polly 218 294 Thomas 218 294 William 278
GREENMAN, Content 138
GUINEA, Coast 221
HADWEN, Dorcas 224-225 Mary 225 Ruth 225
HAILE, Mary 166 168
HAIRSTYLES, Women's 293
HAITI, 346
HALL, Samuel 246
HALSEY, Nicholas 204 Thomas 204
HAMBY, Catherine 93
HAMILTON, Alexander 344
HAMMET, Thomas 353
HAMMOND, Polypus 177
HANNIBAL, 230
HARGES, Elizabeth 358
HARRIS, 141

HARRIS (Cont.)
  Andrew 71-72 Anne 141 Howlong 64 67 70-72 Mary 66 72 Susan 69 Susanna 68-69 71-72 Susannah 67 69 72 Thomas 68 156 338 Toleration 72 126 William 13 25 56 66-72 112 121 124-125 157 189
HARRISON, Ann 221
  Peggy 221
HART, Mary 139 Thomas 138
HAVENS, Patience 368
HAWES, 196
HAYMAN, Hannah 338
HAZARD, Robert 188 190 Sarah 192 Tom 312
HAZZARD, 231
HERINGTON, Sarah 333
HERRESCHOFF, Charles 207 314-315 Lewis 316 Sarah 207-208 314-316
HEWES, Joseph 362
HIGGINSON, 317
HISTORICAL SOCIETY, 259
HOAR, John 130
HOLDEN, Hope 106 Randall 88
HOLDER, 95-99
  Christopher 84 94 100 106-107 Elizabeth 106 Mary 97 100 106-107

HOLLIDAY, 2 35
HOLMES, Martha 165 168
HOLT, 244 John 238
HOLZMAN, Ezekiel 25
HOOKE, Jane 5 William 5
HOPE FURNACE, 164 212
HOPKINS, 222-223
  Abigail 170 Elizabeth 55 170 Esek 221 Frances 55 Joane 55 169 John 266 Mary 170 Mr 343 S 298 Samuel 230 233 Santealger 367 Stephen 204 233 296-297 317 Thomas 55 156 169-170 Thomas Jr 170 Thomas Sr 169 William 55 169 William 2nd 170 William Jr 170
HOUSE OF COMMONS, 178
HOUSE OF REPRESENTATIVES, 188
HOUSES, Descriptions Of 148-152
HOUSING, Improvements 33-34
HOWELL, Sarah 174
HOWLAND, John 204
HOYLE, John 362-363
HUBBARD, Samuel 135

Index

HUDSON, Sally 199
HUNTER, Nancy 292 William 357
HURLEY, Mrs 306 Rev Mr 306
HUTCHINSON, Anne 82-90 92-93 357 Capt 98 Catherine 93 Edward 90 93 97 Susanna 89 Susannah 90 William 84 87
IMMIGRANTS, 320-321
IMPORTING TRADE, 157
INDIAN, Canonicus 124 Chief Canonchet 123 Chief Canonicus 20-21 42-43 88 Chief Massasoit 13 Chief Prince 374 Mascus 124 Massasoit 121 128 Mexanno 124 Miantanomi 124 Miantinomi 20-21 88 Nanhiggan 326 Quanopen 130 Queen Quaiapen 124 Quinnapin 127-128 Squaw Queen 43 Wamsutta 128 Weetamo 128-131 Wesountup 326
INDIANS, And Slaves Creating Mixed Ancestry 180 Attack 89 Children 19 Men Teach White Men 15

INDIANS (Cont.) Women Teach White Women 17
INNS, 371-372
INSLEE, Samuel 244
IVES, Hope 164 Thomas 164
JACKSON, Anne 317 Sally 317 Stephen 317
JAIL, Description Of 351 Providence County 354
JAMAICA, 222
JAMES I, 7 Of England 4
JAMES, King 178
JAMES, Thomas 25
JEFFERSON, 302 Thomas 301
JENCKS, 137 Alice 53 Amos Jr 259 Amos Throop 259 Daniel 198 Francis Carter 259 Freelove 259 Jonna 198 Joseph 53 337 Rebecca 259 Rhoda 198 200
JENNER, Edward 365
JOHNNY CAKES, 16
JOHNSTON, 311
JONES, George 331 John 362-363 Sarah 331
JOSEPHINE, Empress 346
JOSLIN, Hannah 153 Thomas 153
JOURNALISM HALL OF FAME, 246

JUG, Joan 6
JUMEL, 348 Betsy 345-347 Stephen 345
KEEN, Ester Barbut 353
KEENE, Mary 340
KIMBALL, 136 149-150
L'OUVERTURE, Toussaint 346
LAFAYETTE, 285
LARNED, Mr 257
LASALLE, Mrs 305
LAUD, Archbishop 7
LAW-BREAKERS, Penalties For 324
Penalties For 321-323
LAWTON, Polly 292-293
LEAR, Susan 201-202 207 373 Susanna 201 373
LECUESTA, John L 166
LEE, Gen 298
LESBIANISM, 86
LEXINGTON, Battle Of 272
LIBRARY, 237 Town 156
LICENSE, First Medical 362
LIDDEASON, Job 339
LITTLEFIELD, Catherine 278-279 Katy 278
LOCKWOOD, Phebe 175 224
LOOMIS, Emma A 344
LOPEZ, Aaron 182 Jacob 182
LOTS, Building 23

LOVEMAKING, Premarital 52-53
LYNDON, Caesar 230 Sarah 230
LYNDSAY, Sarah 333 Thomas 333
MACAULAY, Catharine 269
MACSPARRAN, Hannah 231 James 230 Rev 231
MANNING, 308 James 233 307
MANTON, Elizabeth 61 Shadrach 61
MARBURY, Anne 82-83 Bridget 82 Catharine 76 82-83 89 Elizabeth 82 Francis 82 Mr 99
MARCHANT, 269-270 Henry 266
MARKET HOUSE, 237 295
MARKET SQUARE, 322
MARRIAGE, And Intermarriage 52 Indian And White Woman 19
MARTIN, John 175 Julia 172 175
MASHAM, 5 Lady 6 William 4
MASON, Abby 211 Alice 211 James 211
MASSACHUSETTS, 322 334 374 Border Disputes With 304

Index 405

MASSACHUSETTS BAY, 55 265
MAWNEY, Dr 362 John 266 Mary 253
MEETING HOUSE, First Baptist 163
MEMORIAL, Roger Williams 137
MENTAL ILLNESS, 335 337
MERRITT, John 149 Mr 371
METCALF, Betsy 154-156 277 Joel 154-155 Lucy 154
MIDWIVES, 357
MILITIA, Raising And Governing 119
MILL, Paper At Elk-Ridge Landing 251 Slater 194
MILLER, Catherine 285-287 Phineas 284-286
MILTON, John 113
MINER, 59 133
MOORE, Elizabeth 82
MOREAU, Gen 347
MORGAN, Lydia 341
MORRIS, Capt 330
MOSHASSUC RIVER, 13 60
MOSHASSUCK RIVER, 21-23 32 55
MOWSHAUSUCK RIVER, 20
MUMFORD, Mr 199

MURDER, And Punishment 340
MUSIC, Sheet 316
NAMES, Women's Passing On Of 62
NAPOLEON, 346 Louis 348
NARRAGANSETT BAY, 14 46 59
NARRAGANSETT RIVER, 55
NAVY, U S 221
NEGRO, Prince 169
NEW ENGLAND, United Colonies Of 122
NEW JERSEY, Middlebrook 281
NEW YORK, 297 314
NEWFIELD, Nancy 368
NEWPORT, British Capture Of 273 Occupation 291
NEWPORT ASYLUM, 337
NEWSPAPER, Boston Gazette 201 Gazette 243 247 252-253 296 302 Maryland Journal 250 New York Gazette 249 Newport 238 Newport Mercury 241 311 Pennsylvania Chronicle 248 Providence Gazette 209 218-219 231 234 245-246 248 256 263 266 271 343 377

NEWSPAPER (Cont.)
  Providence Gazette
  And Country Journal
  241 Rhode Island
  American 255 Rhode
  Island Gazette 246
  The Chronicle 250 The
  Journal 251 The
  Newport Mercury 246
NICOLS, Martha 153
NIGHTINGALE, Col 210
  Martha Washington
  286 Phineas Miller
  286
NOTAQUONUCKANET
  HILLS, 20
NOYES, Robert 312
OLNEY, 60 137 Col 274
  Epenetus 72
  Hallelujah 73 James
  73 Jo 216 Joseph 73
  214 Lydia 73 143
  Marie 58 72 Mary 72-
  73 171 223 Mary
  Small 143 Mr 172
  Nebadiah 73 Polly
  213-218 293-294
  Rachel 74 Richard 223
  370 Sally 317 Stephen
  73 297 Susanna 332
  Thomas 58 156 332
  Thomas Jr 72 143 156
  Thomas Sr 25 72 143
  Tilly Merrick 317
  William 368
OLNEY'S TAVERN, 265
OLNEY INN, 74 213-214

OLNEY TAVERN, 73 214
  216
OSBORN, Sarah Haggar
  229-230
OSGOOD, Samuel 252
OSWALD, Eleazer 251
OWNERSHIP, Of Slaves
  189
PAGE, Benjamin 266
PAGET, 213 Henry 195
  Miss 216
PAINE, Nathaniel 50
PALFREY, 214-218
  William 214 294
PAPER, Shipped From
  England 245
PAPER MILL, 245 375
PARKER, 244 James 238
PATIENCE ISLAND, 106
PAUTUCKETT RIVER, 20
PAWTUCKETT RIVER, 21
PAWTUXET FALLS, 68
PAWTUXET PURCHASE,
  134
PAWTUXET RIVER, 25
  55-56 68
PAWTUXETT RIVER, 21
PEAKE, Christian 55
PECK, Mrs 314
PEEK, Justice 338
PELHAM BAY, 88
PEMBERTON, Alice 3
  Katherine 3 Katherine
  Stokes 4 Robert 3
PEMBROKE COLLEGE, 4
PHILADELPHIA, 245-246
  249-250 297

Index

PHILIP, King 121-123 127 130-131 133
PIRATES, Barbary 68
PLACE, Peter 156
POCASSET VALLEY, 68
POCHASSET RIVER, 67
POCOCKE, Howlong 64 Mr 64
POLITICAL PARTY, Loyalist 288 Tories 288
POOR, Treatment Of The 334
POPP, Stephan 290
POPULATION, Count 365
POPULATION GROWTH, Causing More Crime 349
PORTER, John 332
PORTSMOUTH COMPACT, 87 120
POSTMASTER GENERAL, 252
POSTMISTRESS, Of Baltimore 252
POTTER, William 228
POWEL, Mrs S 314
POWER, Anne 168-169 203 Elizabeth 203 Hope 167-168 196 202 Jane 167 Mary 166 168 Mercy 166 168 196 Nicholas 27 150 167 189 326 Nicholas 2nd 146 167-168 Nicholas 3rd 166-168 196

POWER (Cont.) Nicholas 4th 168 203 Nicholas 5th 169 Nicholas 6th 169 Nichols Jr 57 Rebecca 57 146 167-169 Sarah Helen 169 Susan Anna 169
POWERS, Molly 199
PRAY, Ephraim 156
PRIOR, Mary 140 Matthew 140 Sarah 140
PRISON, 350
PRISON EXPERIENCE, 353
PROVIDENCE, Manufacturing And Commerce 262
PROVIDENCE'S TEA PARTY, 272
PROVIDENCE RIVER, 211 368
PUBLISHERS, 238
PURCHASE, Pawtuxet 25 69 The Grand Of Providence 25
PURITANS, 8 10-11 52-53 76 Theocracy 9
QUAKER MEETING HOUSE, 175
QUAKERS, 62 219
QUINNAPIN, Queen 127
RABBIT ISLAND, 43
RACE, Mixing 340
RALPH, Alicc 66 Mary 66 Thomas 66

RANDALL, Stephen 136
RAWONS, Mr 97
REAL ESTATE, 145
REAPE, Joane 57 Joanne 57 Samuel 57
REBAPTISM, 76
REDWOOD, Mehetable 292
REEVE, Widow 27
RELIGION, Baptist 155 163-164 237 Jews 106 Jews And Discrimination Of 308 Puritan 92 242 Quaker 80-83 86 92 94-95 97-99 101 105 107 224 232-233 237 242 257 359 Quaker Opposing Slavery 226
RELIGIOUS LIBERTY, 120
RHOADES, Elizabeth 305 Mary 305 Rebecca 305 Zachary 305
RHODE ISLAND ALMANAC, 246
RHODE ISLAND COLLEGE, 195 307-308 369
RHODES, 141 Joane 56 Joanna 146 167 John 57 Rebecca 146 167 Zachariah 56 146 167
RI HISTORICAL SOCIETY, 214
RICE, Thomas 351

RICHARDSON, Deliverance 107 John 107 Rebecca 107 William 107
RICHMAN, 90 216 292-293
RICHMOND, Edward 327 Sally 154
ROBERTS, Susanna 71 Thomas 71
ROBINSON, 111-112 231 Anstis 110 Hannah 109-110 191 Mary 110 Rowland 109 190-191 William 100 110
ROCHAMBEAU, 292 295 297
ROGERS, William 308
ROOLENBURG, Mary 339
ROWLAND, Mr 264
ROWLANDSON, Joseph 127 Mary 126 Mrs 127-130
ROYAL, Anne 377
RUSSELL, Mary 139
SABBEER, Deborah 59
SABIN, Thomas 370
SABIN TAVERN, 266
SANITARY ORGANIZATION, First 369
SANTO DOMINGO, 346
SARATOGA, 274
SAVANNAH RIVER, 285
SAYER, Jane 27
SAYLES, John 137 339

Index

SAYLES (Cont.)
  Mary 137
SAYRE, Widow 326
SCHOOL, And
  Separation Of Church And State 318 At Home 304 Charterhouse 4 Dame Taught By Widows Or Spinsters 305 Discipline 312 For Blacks Only 311 For Young Ladies 306 Formal Public System 304 George Taylor's 311 Instructed By A Preacher 304 Latin 307 Male Explained Arithmetic 306 Male Explained English 306 Male Explained French 306 Male Explained Geography 306 Male Explained Grammar 306 Male Explained History 306 Male Explained Reading 306 Male Explained Writing 306 Mr Larned 257 Normal 319 Separate Sessions For Girls And Boys 307 Teachers Paid By Religious Society In England 304 Textbooks From London 308

SCHOOL (Cont.)
  Towne Street 310 Women Taught Drawing 306 Women Taught Embroidery 306 Women Taught Music 306 Women Taught Painting 306
SCHOOLS, Public For Blacks 319 Public For Whites 319
SCHOONER, Gaspee 266
SCOTT, Catharine 76 80 82-83 92 94 97-100 106-107 Catherine 104 Deliverance 107 Hannah 107 138 Joanna 198 Mary 97 100 106-107 Patience 98 107 Rebecca 171 Richard 27 76 97
SEAMANS, Martin 289
SEARINGS, Sarah 230
SEARS, Jane 27
SEEKONK RIVER, 13 211
SENATE, 189
SERVANTS, Household 153
SEWALL, Samuel 150 152
SEWING, 306
SHARPUROWE, Elizabeth 194
SHEARMAN, Amy 153
SHELTER ISLAND, 104
SHEPARD, Thomas 86

SHERMAN, Phillip 86
SHIP, Eliza 346 Griffin 84 Martin 194 Planter 72 Sally 221-222 Speedwell 94 The Lyon 68 The President 302 The Sally 212 Wheel Of Fortune 197
SHIPS, 373
SHIPYARDS, 157
SHOEMAKER, Jacob 233
SICKNESS, And Death 355
SIMMONS, Amelia 37
SIMONS, Hannah 109-112 Peter 109-112
SISCO, Betsy 341 Phoebe 368
SKIRMISHES, Between Indians And White Settlers 121
SLATER, Samuel 224 306
SLAVE, Abigail 191 Amey 189 Ann 147 187 Betsey 187 Elizabeth 187 Fanny 187 Freelove 187 Genne 147 Hope 147 187 Jack 147 Lucy 187 Mamie 196 Manny 189 Mary 187 Marygold 187 Nancy 187 Polly 187 Prince 110 191 Sally 187 Sukey 187 Three Sisters 187

SLAVE (Cont.) Yockwhy 219
SLAVE TRADE, As Profitable Enterprise 176
SLAVE TRADERS, As Successful Businessmen 188
SLAVERY, 134 234 As Part Of Rhode Island's Past History 193 Death By Transport Biggest Threat To Profit 185 Federal Legislation Making Slaver Pirates Subject To Death 235 Milder In Narragansett Country 190 Of Africans 178 Of Indians 133 Transport Conditions Determine Profit 184 Voyages To Africa 181
SLAVES, 147 And Sexual Assaults 186 As Taxable Property 179 Average Price Of 188 Death Of Aboard Ship 223 Emancipation Of 189 From The Gold Coast Of Africa 182 Held In Low Esteem 231 Offered Freedom For Enlisting In Washington's Army 274

Index

SLAVES (Cont.)
  Perils Of Transport 177 Restrictions Of 192 Rights 235-236 Rights In Court 324 Sale Of 187
SLOCUM, Sarah 288
SLOOP, Mary 196
SMALL POX, 70 364-366
SMITH, 52-53 57 109
  Alice 61 Daniel 50 204 Dorcas 204 Elizabeth 61 170 Joan 108 John 13 60 170 172 John 3rd 61 John Jr 61 John The Miller 61 Mary 65 170 Misses 305 Mr 205 Phoebe 335 Richard 108 237 Sarah 61 204 Sophia 174 Turpin 266
SOUCHONG, Madam 271
SOUTH CAROLINA, 283
  Charleston 282
SPARROWS, Mary 312
SPRAGUE, Jonathan 334
SQUATTERS, 44
STAGECOACHES, 370-374 376-377
STAMP ACT, 244 262 264 Repeal Of 244 265
STANTON, Betsy 340
STAPLES, 233 271 371
  Freelove 241 Jonathan 241 Judge 133
STARKWEATHER, Mehitabel 67

STARLING, Belinda 252
STATE HOUSE, Old 294
STATEN ISLAND, 348
STEAMERS, 370
STELLE, Benjamin 307
  Huldah 307
STEPHENSON, James 49
  John 49 Ouesimus 49 Sarah 49
STERLING, Dr 362
STERRY, Capt 186
STEVENSON, John 49 51 Marmaduke 100
STILES, Dr 286 Ezra 230
STILLMAN, Miss 199 210
STOCKES, Mary 329-330
STOKES, Katherine 3
STRAW BONNETS,
  Braiding Of 154
  Business Of 155
  Industry Of 156
SUCKLIN, Elizabeth 125
  Thomas 125
SUGARS, Jerusha 153
SUPREME COURT, 325
  Ruling 319
SWEETE, Mary 27
SWEETING, Henry 362-363
SYNAGOGUE, Touro The First In The New World 117
TABER, Lydia 164
TALLMAN, Ann 327-328
  Esther 328 Joan 328 Peter 327
TATTERSALL, Joan 361

TAVERN-KEEPERS, 213
  Description Of 170-
  171
TAYLER, Benjamin 166
TAYLOR, George 310-311
  George Jr 317 Thomas
  333
TEMBERLAKE, Will 329
TEW, Mary 195
THANKSGIVING, 16
THAYER, David 331
  Rebecca 331
THEATER, Construction
  Of A Permanent 240
  Productions 313-314
  Raising Money For A
  239
THEATRE, 238
THEOLOGICAL
  DISCUSSION, 30
THORNTON, John 135
THORP, Alexander 370
THROCKMORTON, John
  25
THROOP, Amos 362
THURBER, S 370
TILAR, Joane 27
TILER, Joane 27
TILLINGHAST, 167 Amey
  368 Anne 168 203
  Benjamin 165-166
  168 Charles 368 Col
  366 Henry 367 John
  165 367-368 Joseph
  165 Lidia 166 Lydia
  164-166 Martha 165
  168

TILLINGHAST (Cont.)
  Mary 52 367-368
  Mercy 166 168 196
  Pardon 156 163-166
  168 253 Pardon Jr
  165 Philip 165 168
  Sarah 164-165
  William 367
TIMMINS, John 218 Polly
  218
TOLLMAN, 329 Ann 327
  Peter 327-328
TOWN COUNCIL, 239
  335
TOWNSEND ACT, Repeal
  Of 270 Taxing Imports
  265
TRADE, Shipping 165
  With West Indies 162
TRAVEL, 370-376
TREBY, Bridget 299
TREE, Apple 136
TREE OF LIBERTY, 265
TURNER, Freelove 56
TURPIN, 309 William
  308
TURPIN'S INN, 309
ULRICH, 18 72 129 307
UNDERHILL, John 87
UNIVERSITY, Grammar
  Schools 316
UNIVERSITY GRAMMAR
  SCHOOL, 308
UNIVERSITY HALL, 294
  302
UNIVERSITY OF RHODE
  ISLAND, 246

Index

UNMARRIED WOMEN, Cultural Status Of 305
UPDIKE, Abigail 109-110 191 Esther 238 John 307 Lodowick 237 Ludovick 109 Sarah 237 Susannah 307
VALLEY FORGE, 280
VANDERLIGHT, John 203 Mary 203
VANE, Harry 117
VERIN, 79 Joseph 25 Joshua 13 76-77 333 Mary 76-77 Philip 78
VERNON, William 292
VIRGINIA, 222
VONSTEUBEN, Baron 280
WALTON, John 362
WANASQUUATUCKUT RIVER, 20
WAR, 130 298 343 American Revolution 178 180 For Independence 272 French Revolution 285 King Philip's 50 56 63 66 68 71 90 131 135 140 143 145 170-171 King Philip's War 146 Of Independence 232 351 Revolutionary 202 212-213 218 231 250-251 276 288 348 365 Revolutionary In Copenhagen 266 Seven Years' 197 241

WARD, Henry 233
WARDWELL, Jonathan 370
WARNER, Ann 332 John 332 Susanna 332
WASHINGTON, 296-297 302 Cornelia 281 Gen 281 295 George 173 218 252 274 278 285 298 300-301 344 348 Martha 281 285 Mrs 279-280 282
WATER-WORKS, Providence City 142
WATERHOUSE, Benjamin 364
WATERMAN, 73 Ann 147 Anne 141 Bethia 63 Mary 144 Mehitabel 63 365 Mercy 125 141 Nathaniel 63 Phebe 224 Resolved 125 141 Resolved 3rd 141 Resolved Jr 141 Richard 13 25 62-63 141 147 Susanna 63
WEALTH, And Belongings Of Slave Owners 192-193
WEEDON, 51 188 305
WEEKS, Francis 13
WELDE, Thomas 89
WEST, Benjamin 243
WEST INDIES, 176-177 181 196-197
WESTCOTT, Anna H 344 Damaris 56

WESTCOTT (Cont.)
　Freelove 56 67 Presilla
　56 Stukeley 25 56
WESTON, Francis 25 Mrs
　336
WEYBOSSET BRIDGE,
　159-160
WEYBOSSET MARSHES,
　15
WHALLEY, Jane 5-6
WHARTON, 248
WHEELRIGHT, Nathaniel
　214
WHEELWRIGHT, John
　85-87
WHIPPLE, 50 137 Abigail
　170 172 Abraham 266
　Alice 59 Capt 317
　Daughters 157 David
　51 338 Eleazer 59
　John 69 170-172 362
　John Jr 73 156 171
　338 Liddea 338 Lydia
　338-339 Mary 73 171
　Rebecca 171-172
　Rebeka 171 Rebekah
　172 Robert 172
　Samuel 156 266 322
　Sarah 61 170-173
WHITE, First Killing Of
　122 Mary 126 Woman
　Debby 341
WHITMAN, Mr 253
　Valentin 27
WHITNEY, 285 Eli 284
WICKES, Francis 13 25
　R 51

WICKFORD HARBOR,
　42-43
WILBUR, Smith 344
WILCOX, Edward 108
WILKINSON, A B 200
　Jemima 226-228 Mrs
　199-200
WILLAMS, Mary 114
WILLIAMS, 15 40 58 60
　81 88 122 134 Abigail
　371-372 Alice 3-4 45
　Bertha 143 Betsy 144
　Catherine 4 Daniel 27
　46 57 135 145-147
　168 189 Freeborn 11
　14 31 138 James 144-
　145 Jeremiah 372
　Joane 55 Joseph 19
　46 73 142-143 145
　147 Joseph Sr 144
　Liddea 143 Lydia 73
　143-145 Mary 6-12 14
　16 19-20 29 31-32 44-
　46 49 68 73 78 113
　115-116 134-137 140
　142-145 335 Mary
　Barnard 3 Mercy 31
　46 125 140-142 Mrs
　71 Nathaniel 144
　Patience 147 Peleg 147
　Providence 140 147
　156 Rebecca 57 135
　146 168 Rebekah 147
　Robert 125 Roger 3-14
　16-22 25-27 29-32 42-
　48 55 57 62 68 71-73
　76-78 80 87 105 108

Index

WILLIAMS (Cont.)
112-116 120 124-125
133 135-137 140 142-
146 159 172 189 230
237 253 320 325 335
356 361 378 Ruth 225
Sydrach 4 45 Thomas
144
WILSON, John 86 102
105
WINDSOR, Thomas 180
WINSOR, 73 Joshua
141-142 Mary 142
Mercy 141-142
Samuel 141-142 156
Samuel Jr 142 Sarah
142 Susanna 142
WINTHROP, 97 Gov 13
76-77 85 115 John 84
142 230 John Jr 83
WODELL, William 333
WOMEN, And Property
Settlements 328-329
As Auxiliary To Male
Units 287

WOMEN (Cont.)
As Caregivers 355 As
Enablers To Men 1
Death In Childbirth
357 No Right To Vote
299 Penalties For
Adultery 330-331
Penalties For Adultery
Or Fornication 327-
328 Rhode Island
Pioneer White 2 Rights
29 77 Roles In
Revolutionary War
277-278 White Pioneer
18 Working In Former
Men's Positions 299
WOODROW, Mary 201-
202
WOODWARD, 136
WREN, Christopher 164
WYATT, 343
YALE UNIVERSITY, 284

About the Author

Born in Daytona Beach, Florida, childhood in small mountain town of Jackson, Kentucky. Graduate of Cranston High School and Brown University in Rhode Island; Masters from University of Birmingham, England and from Rutgers University, New Jersey. Now retired and living in Cranston after an absence of about 45 years. Two children, both attorneys, and two grandchildren.

www.ingramcontent.com/pod-product-compliance
Lightning Source LLC
Chambersburg PA
CBHW050426240426
43661CB00055B/2287